Publisher's Note

The book descriptions we ask booksellers to display prominently warn that the book may have numerous typos, missing text, images and indexes.

We scanned this book using character recognition software that includes an automated spell check. Our software is 99 percent accurate if the book is in good condition. However, we do understand that even one percent can be a very annoying number of typos! And sometimes all or part of a page is missing from our copy of a book. Or the paper may be so discolored from age that you can no longer read the type. Please accept our sincere apologies.

After we re-typeset and design a book, the page numbers change so the old index and table of contents no longer work. Therefore, we often remove them.

We would like to manually proof read and fix the typos and indexes, manually scan and add any illustrations, and track down another copy of the book to add any missing text. But our books sell so few copies, you would have to pay up to a thousand dollars for the book as a result.

Therefore, whenever possible, we let our customers download a free copy of the original typo-free scanned book. Simply enter the barcode number from the back cover of the paperback in the Free Book form at www.general-books. net. You may also qualify for a free trial membership in our book club to download up to four books for free. Simply enter the barcode number from the back cover onto the membership form on the same page. The book club entitles you to select from more than a million books at no additional charge. Simply enter the title or subject onto the search form to find the books.

If you have any questions, could you please be so kind as to consult our Frequently Asked Questions page at www. general-books.net/faqs.cfm? You are also welcome to contact us there.

General Books LLC®, 2012. ISBN: 9780217401746.

❄❄ ❄❄ ❄❄ ❄❄ ❄❄ ❄❄ ❄❄

BY THEODORE ROOSEVELT

Essays on Practical Politics. (Being No. 49 in the " Questions of the Day" series.) 8vo, cloth 75 cents

The Winning of the West and Southwest, from the AUeghanies to the Mississippi, 1769-1783. Two vols, octavo, cloth.. f 5 00

"Written in a free and flowing style, always graceful, but never turgid, that makes the narrative delightful reading from the first page to the end."—*Chicago Times.*

Hunting Trips of a Ranchman. Sketches of Sport on the Northern Cattle Plains. With 27 full-page wood engravings and 8 smaller engravings, from designs by A. B. Frost, R. Swain Gifford, J. C. Beard, Fannie E. Gifford, and Henry Sandham. Octavo, cloth, bevelled boards.. $3 00

"The seven heads of large game figured in this book are faithfully copied from the originals, shot by myself, and now in my possession; the proportions have been verified by the camera."

The Naval War of 1812; or, The History of the United States Navy during the Last War with Great Britain; to which is appended an account of the Battle of New Orleans.

Third edition. Octavo, cloth %i 50

"A model book of reference."—*Boston Advertiser.*

"The volume is an excellent one in every respect, and shows in so young an author the best promise for a good historian—fearlessness of statement, caution, endeavor to be impartial, and a brisk and interesting way of telling events.—.A. *Y. Times.*

The Wilderness Hunter; with an Account of the Big Game of the United States, and its Chase, with Horse, Hound, and Rifle.

With full-page illustrations by Frederic Remington, A. B. Frost, J. C Beard, IIenry Sandham, and C. Harry Eaton.

IS, Publishers
NEW "They saw the silences
Move by and beckon; saw the forms,
The very beards, of burly storms,
And heard them talk like sounding seas.
..
They saw the snowy mountains rolled
And heaved along the nameless lands
Like mighty billows; saw the gold
Of awful sunsets; saw the blush
Of sudden dawn, and felt the hush
Of heaven when the day sat down
And hid his face in dusky hands."
yoaquin Miller.

"In vain the speeding or shyness;
In vain the elk takes to the inner passes of the woods...
... where geese nip their food with short jerks, Where sundown shadows lengthen over the limitless prairie, Where herds of buffalo make a crawling spread of the square miles, far and near,
Where winter wolves bark amid wastes of snow and ice-clad trees...
The moose, large as an ox, cornered by hunters, plunging with his forefeet, the hoofs as sharp as knives...
The blazing fire at night, the sweet taste of supper, the talk, the bed of hemlock boughs, and the bear-skin." *Walt Whitman.* FULL-PAGE ILLUSTRATIONS.
PAGS

FOR a number of years much of my life was spent either in the wilderness or on the borders of the settled country—if, indeed, "settled" is a term that can rightly be applied to the vast, scantily peopled regions where cattle-ranching is the only regular industry. During this time I hunted much, among the mountains and on the plains, both as a pastime and to procure hides, meat, and robes for use on the ranch; and it was my good luck to kill all the various kinds of large game that can properly be considered to belong to temperate North America.

In hunting, the finding and killing of the game is after all but a part of the whole. The free, self-reliant, adventurous life, with its rugged and stalwart democracy; the wild surroundings, the grand beauty of the scenery, the chance to study the ways and habits of the woodland creatures—all these unite to give to the career of the wilderness hunter its peculiar charm. The chase is among the best of all national pastimes; it cultivates that vigorous manliness for the lack of which in a nation, as in an individual, the possession of no other qualities can possibly atone.

No one, but he who has partaken thereof, can understand the keen delight of hunting in lonely lands. For him is the joy of the horse well ridden and the rifle well held; for him the long days of toil and hardship, resolutely endured, and crowned at the end with triumph. In after years there shall come forever to his mind the memory of endless prairies shimmering in the bright sun; of vast snow-clad wastes lying desolate under gray skies; of the melancholy marshes; of the rush of mighty rivers; of the breath of the evergreen forest in summer; of the crooning of ice-armored pines at the touch of the winds of winter; of cataracts roaring between hoary mountain masses; of all the innumerable sights and sounds of the wilderness; of its immensity and mystery; and of the silences that brood in its still depths.

Theodore Roosevelt.

Sagamore Hill,

June, 1893.

The Wilderness Hunter. CHAPTER I.

THE AMERICAN WILDERNESS; WILDERNESS HUNTERS AND WILDERNESS GAME. MANIFOLD are the shapes taken by the American wilderness. In the east, from the Atlantic coast to the Mississippi valley, lies a land of magnificent hardwood forest. In endless variety and beauty, the trees cover the ground, save only where they have been cleared away by man, or where towards the west the expanse of the forest is broken by fertile prairies. Towards the north, this region of hardwood trees merges insensibly into the southern extension of the great subarctic forest; here the silver stems of birches gleam against the sombre background of coniferous evergreens. In the southeast again, by the hot, oozy coasts of the South Atlantic and the Gulf, the forest becomes semitropical; palms wave their feathery fronds, and the tepid swamps teem with reptile life.

Some distance beyond the Mississippi, stretching from Texas to North Dakota, and westward to the Rocky Mountains, lies the plains country. This is a region of light rainfall, where the ground is clad with short grass, while cottonwood trees fringe the courses of the winding plains streams; streams that are alternately turbid torrents and mere dwindling threads of water. The great stretches of natural pasture are broken by gray sage-brush plains, and tracts of strangely shaped and colored Bad Lands; sun-scorched wastes in summer, and in winter arctic in their iron desolation. Beyond the plains rise the Rocky Mountains, their flanks covered with coniferous woods; but the trees are small, and do not ordinarily grow very closely together. Towards the north the forest becomes denser, and the peaks higher; and glaciers creep down towards the valleys from the fields of everlasting snow. The brooks are brawling, trout-filled torrents; the swift rivers foam over rapid and cataract, on their way to one or the other of the two great oceans.

Southwest of the Rockies evil and terrible deserts stretch for leagues and leagues, mere waterless wastes of sandy plain and barren mountain, broken here and there by narrow strips of fertile ground. Rain rarely falls, and there are no clouds to dim the brazen sun. The rivers run in deep canyons, or are swallowed by the burning sand; the smaller watercourses are dry throughout the greater part of the year.

Beyond this desert region rise the sunny Sierras of California, with their flower-clad slopes and groves of giant trees; and north of them, along the coast, the rain shrouded mountain chains of Oregon and Washington, matted with the towering growth of the mighty evergreen forest.

The white hunters, who from time to time first penetrated the different parts of this wilderness, found themselves in such hunting grounds as those wherein, long ages before, their Old-World forefathers had dwelt; and the game they chased was much the same as that their lusty barbarian ancestors followed, with weapons of bronze and of iron, in the dim years before history dawned. As late as the end of the seventeenth century the turbulent village nobles of Lithuania and Livonia hunted the bear, the bison, the elk, the wolf, and the stag, and hung the spoils in their smoky wooden palaces; and so, two hundred years later, the free hunters of Montana, in the interludes between hazardous mining quests and-bloody Indian campaigns, hunted game almost or quite the same in kind, through the cold mountain forests surrounding the Yellowstone and Flathead lakes, and decked their log cabins and ranch houses with the hides and horns of the slaughtered beasts.

Zoologically speaking, the north temperate zones of the Old and New Worlds are very similar, differing from one another much less than they do from the various regions south of them, or than these regions differ among themselves. The untrodden American wilderness resembles both in game and physical character the forests, the mountains, and the steppes of the Old World as it was at the beginning of our era. Great woods of pine and fir, birch and beech, oak and chestnut; streams where the chief game fish are spotted trout and silvery salmon; grouse of various kinds as the most common game birds; all these the hunter finds as characteristic of the New World as of the Old. So it is with most of the beasts of the chase, and so also with the fur-bearing animals that furnish to the trapper alike his life work and his means of livelihood. The bear, wolf, bison, moose, caribou, wapiti, deer, and bighorn, the lynx, fox, wolverine, sable, mink, ermine, beaver, badger, and otter of both worlds are either identical or more or less closely kin to one another. Sometimes of the two forms, that found in the Old World is the largest. Perhaps more often the reverse is true, the American beast being superior in size. This is markedly the case with the wapiti, which is merely a giant brother of the European stag, exactly as the fisher is merely a very large cousin of the European sable or marten. The extraordinary prong-buck, the only hollowhorned ruminant which sheds its horns annually, is a distant representative of the Old-World antelopes of the steppes; the queer white antelope-goat has for its nearest kinsfolk certain Himalayan species. Of the animals commonly known to our hunters and trappers, only a few, such as the cougar, peccary, raccoon, possum (and among birds the wild turkey), find their nearest representatives and type forms in tropical America.

Of course this general resemblance does not mean identity. The differences in plant life and animal life, no less than in the physical features of the land, are sufficiently marked to give the American wilderness a character distinctly its own. Some of the most characteristic of the woodland animals, some of those

which have most vividly impressed themselves on the imagination of the hunters and pioneer settlers, are the very ones which have no Old-World representatives. The wild turkey is in every way the king of American game birds. Among the small beasts the coon and the possum are those which have left the deepest traces in the humbler lore of the frontier; exactly as the cougar— usually under the name of panther or mountain lion—is a favorite figure in the wilder hunting tales. Nowhere else is there anything to match the wealth of the eastern hardwood forests, in number, variety, and beauty of trees; nowhere else is it possible to find conifers approaching in size the giant redwoods and sequoias of the Pacific slope. Nature here is generally on a larger scale than in the Old-World home of our race. The lakes are like inland seas, the rivers like arms of the sea. Among stupendous mountain chains there are valleys and canyons of fathomless depth and incredible beauty and majesty. There are tropical swamps, and sad, frozen marshes; deserts and Death Valleys, weird and evil, and the strange wonderland of the Wyoming geyser region. The waterfalls are rivers rushing over precipices; the prairies seem without limit, and the forest never ending.

At the time when we first became a nation, nine tenths of the territory now included within the limits of the United States was wilderness. It was during the stirring and troubled years immediately preceding the outbreak of the Revolution that the most adventurous hunters, the vanguard of the hardy army of pioneer settlers, first crossed the Alleghanies, and roamed far and wide through the lonely, danger-haunted forests which filled the Noman's-land lying between the Tennessee and the Ohio. They waged ferocious warfare with Shawnee and Wyandott and wrought huge havoc among the herds of game with which the forests teemed. While the first Continental Congress was still sitting, Daniel Boone, the archetype of the American hunter, was leading his bands of tall backwoods riflemen to settle in the beautiful country of Ken-

tucky, where the red and the white warriors strove with such obstinate rage that both races alike grew to know it as "the dark and bloody ground."

Boone and his fellow-hunters were the heralds of the oncoming civilization, the pioneers in that conquest of the wilderness which has at last been practically achieved in our own day. Where they pitched their camps and built their log huts or stockaded hamlets, towns grew up, and men who were tillers of the soil, not mere wilderness wanderers, thronged in to take and hold the land. Then, ill-at-ease among the settlements for which they had themselves made ready the way, and fretted even by the slight restraints of the rude and uncouth semi-civilization of the border, the restless hunters moved onward into the yet unbroken wilds where the game dwelt and the red tribes marched forever to war and hunting. Their untamable souls ever found something congenial and beyond measure attractive in the lawless freedom of the lives of the very savages against whom they warred so bitterly.

Step by step, often leap by leap, the frontier of settlement was pushed westward; and ever from before its advance fled the warrior tribes of the red men and the scarcely less intractable array of white Indian fighters and game hunters. When the Revolutionary war was at its height, George Rogers Clarke, himself a mighty hunter of the old backwoods type, led his handful of huntersoldiers to the conquest of the French towns of the Illinois. This was but one of the many notable feats of arms performed by the wild soldiery of the backwoods. Clad in their fringed and tasselled hunting shirts of buckskin or homespun; with coonskin caps and deer-hide leggings and moccasins, with tomahawk and scalping knife thrust into their bead-worked belts, and long rifles in hand, they fought battle after battle of the most bloody character, both against the Indians, as at the Great Kanawha, at the Fallen Timbers, and at Tippecanoe, and against more civilized foes, as at King's Mountain, New Orleans, and the River Thames.

Soon after the beginning of the present century Louisiana fell into our hands, and the most daring hunters and explorers pushed through the forests of the Mississippi valley to the great plains, steered across these vast seas of grass to the Rocky Mountains, and then through their rugged defiles onwards to the Pacific Ocean. In every work of exploration, and in all the earlier battles with the original lords of the western and southwestern lands, whether Indian or Mexican, the adventurous hunters played the leading part; while close behind came the swarm of hard, dogged, border-farmers,—a masterful race, good fighters and good breeders, as all masterful races must be.

Very characteristic in its way was the career of quaint, honest, fearless Davy Crockett, the Tennessee rifleman and Whig Congressman, perhaps the best shot in all our country, whose skill in the use of his favorite weapon passed into a proverb, and who ended his days by a hero's death in the ruins of the Alamo. An even more notable man was another mighty hunter, Houston, who when a boy ran away to the Indians; who while still a lad returned to his own people to serve under Andrew Jackson in the campaigns which that greatest of all the backwoods leaders waged against the Creeks, the Spaniards, and the British. He was wounded at the storming of one of the strongholds of Red Eagle's doomed warriors, and returned to his Tennessee home to rise to high civil honor, and become the foremost man of his State. Then, while Governor of Tennessee, in a sudden fit of moody anger, and of mad longing for the unfettered life of the wilderness, he abandoned his office, his people, and his race, and fled to the Cherokees beyond the Mississippi. For years he lived as one of their chiefs; until one day, as he lay in ignoble ease and sloth, a rider from the south, from the rolling plains of the San Antonio and Brazos, brought word that the Texans were up, and in doubtful struggle striving to wrest their freedom from the lancers and carbineers of Santa Anna. Then his dark soul flamed again into burning life; riding by night and day he joined the risen Tex-

ans, was hailed by them as a heavensent leader, and at the San Jacinto led them on to the overthrow of the Mexican host. Thus the stark hunter, who had been alternately Indian fighter and Indian chief, became the President of the new Republic, and, after its admission into the United States, a Senator at Washington; and, to his high honor, he remained to the end of his days staunchly loyal to the flag of the Union.

By the time that Crockett fell, and Houston became the darling leader of the Texans, the typical hunter and Indian fighter had ceased to be a backwoodsman; he had become a plainsman, or mountain-man; for the frontier, east of which he never willingly went, had been pushed beyond the Mississippi. Restless, reckless, and hardy, he spent years of his life in lonely wanderings through the Rockies as a trapper; he guarded the slowmoving caravans, which for purposes of trade journeyed over the dangerous Santa Fe trail; he guided the large parties of frontier settlers who, driving before them their cattle, with all their household goods in their whitetopped wagons, spent perilous months and seasons on their weary way to Oregon or California. Joining in bands, the stalwart, skin-clad riflemen waged ferocious war on the Indians scarcely more savage than themselves, or made long raids for plunder and horses against the outlying Mexican settlements. The best, the bravest, the most modest of them all was the renowned Kit Carson. He was not only a mighty hunter, a daring fighter, a finder of trails, and maker of roads through the unknown, untrodden wilderness, but also a real leader of men. Again and again he crossed and re-crossed the continent, from the Mississippi to the Pacific; he guided many of the earliest military and exploring expeditions of the United States Government; he himself led the troops in victorious campaigns against Apache and Navahoe; and in the Civil War he was made a colonel of the Federal army.

After him came many other hunters. Most were pure-blooded Americans, but many were Creole Frenchmen,

Mexicans, or even members of the so-called civilized Indian tribes, notably the Delawares. Wide were their wanderings, many their strange adventures in the chase, bitter their unending warfare with the red lords of the land. Hither and thither they roamed, from the desolate, burning deserts of the Colorado to the grassy plains of the Upper Missouri; from the rolling Texas prairies, bright beneath their sunny skies, to the high snow peaks of the northern Rockies, or the giant pine forests, and soft rainy weather, of the coasts of Puget Sound. Their main business was trapping, furs being the only articles yielded by the wilderness, as they knew it, which were both valuable and portable. These early hunters were all trappers likewise, and, indeed, used their rifles only to procure meat or repel attacks. The chief of the fur-bearing animals they followed was the beaver, which abounded in the streams of the plains and mountains; in the far north they also trapped otter, mink, sable, and fisher. They married squaws from among the Indian tribes with which they happened for the moment to be at peace; they acted as scouts for the United States troops in their campaigns against the tribes with which they happened to be at war.

Soon after the Civil War the life of these hunters, taken as a class, entered on its final stage. The Pacific coast was already fairly well settled, and there Were a few mining camps in the Rockies; but most of this Rocky Mountains region, and the entire stretch of plains country proper, the vast belt of level or rolling grass land lying between the Rio Grande and the Saskatchewan, still remained primeval wilderness, inhabited only by roving hunters and formidable tribes of Indian nomads, and by the huge herds of game on which they preyed. Beaver swarmed in the streams and yielded a rich harvest to the trapper; but trapping was no longer the mainstay of the adventurous plainsmen. Foremost among the beasts of the chase, on account of its numbers, its size, and its economic importance, was the bison or American buffalo: its innumerable multitudes darkened the limitless prairies.

As the transcontinental railroads were pushed towards completion, and the tide of settlement rolled onwards with ever increasing rapidity, buffalo robes became of great value. The hunters forthwith turned their attention mainly to the chase of the great clumsy beasts, slaughtering them by hundreds of thousands for their hides; sometimes killing them on horseback, but more often on foot, by still-hunting, with the heavy long-range Sharp's rifle. Throughout the fifteen years during which this slaughter lasted, a succession of desperate wars was waged with the banded tribes of the Horse Indians. All the time, in unending succession, long trains of big white-topped wagons crept slowly westward across the prairies, marking the steady oncoming of the frontier settlers-.

By the close of 1883 the last buffalo herd was destroyed. The beaver were trapped out of all the streams, or their numbers so thinned that it no longer paid to follow them. The last formidable Indian war had been brought to a successful close. The flood of the incoming whites had risen over the land; tongues of settlement reached from the Mississippi to the Rocky Mountains, and from the Rocky Mountains to the Pacific. The frontier had come to an end; it had vanished. With it vanished also the old race of wilderness hunters, the men who spent all their days in the lonely wilds, and who killed game as their sole means of livelihood. Great stretches of wilderness still remain in the Rocky Mountains, and here and there in the plains country, exactly as much smaller tracts of wild land are to be found in the Alleghanies and northern New York and New England; and on these tracts occasional hunters and trappers still linger; but as a distinctive class, with a peculiar and important position in American life, they no longer exist.

There were other men beside the professional hunters, who lived on the borders of the wilderness, and followed hunting, not only as a pastime, but also as yielding an important portion of their subsistence. The frontier farmers were all hunters. In the eastern backwoods, and in certain places in the west, as in Oregon, these adventurous tillers of the soil were the pioneers among the actual settlers; in the Rockies their places were taken by the miners, and on the great plains by the ranchmen and cowboys, the men who lived in the saddle, guarding their branded herds of horses and horned stock. Almost all of the miners and cowboys were obliged on occasions-to turn hunters.

Moreover, the regular army which played so important a part in all the later stages of the winning of the west produced its full share of mighty hunters. The later Indian wars were fought principally by the regulars. The West Point officer and his little company of trained soldiers appeared abreast of the first hardy cattlemen and miners. The ordinary settlers rarely made their appearance until in campaign after campaign, always inconceivably wearing and harassing, and often very bloody in character, the scarred and tattered troops had broken and overthrown the most formidable among the Indian tribes. Faithful, uncomplaining, unflinching, the soldiers wearing the national uniform lived for many weary years at their lonely little posts, facing unending toil and danger with quiet endurance, surrounded by the desolation of vast solitudes, and menaced by the most merciless of foes. Hunting was followed not only as a sport, but also as the only means of keeping the posts and the expeditionary trains in meat. Many of the officers became equally proficient as marksmen and hunters. The three most famous Indian fighters since the Civil War, Generals Custer, Miles, and Crook, were all keen and successful followers of the chase.

Of American big game the bison, almost always known as the buffalo, was the largest and most important to man. When the first white settlers landed in Virginia the bison ranged east of the Alleghanies almost to the sea-coast, westward to the dry deserts lying beyond the Rocky Mountains, northward to the Great Slave Lake and southward to Chihuahua. It was a beast of the forests and mountains, in the Alleghanies no less than in the Rockies; but its true home was on the prairies, and the high plains. Across these it roamed, hither and thither, in herds of enormous, of incredible magnitude; herds so large that they covered the waving grass land for hundreds of square leagues, and when on the march occupied days and days in passing a given point. But the seething myriads of shaggy-maned wild cattle vanished with remarkable and melancholy rapidity before the inroads of the white hunters, and the steady march of the oncoming settlers. Now they are on the point of extinction. Two or three hundred are left in that great national game preserve, the Yellowstone Park; and it is said that others still remain in the wintry desolation of Athabasca. Elsewhere only a few individuals exist—probably considerably less than half a hundred all told—scattered in small parties in the wildest and most remote and inaccessible portions of the Rocky Mountains. A bison bull is the largest American animal. His huge bulk, his short, curved black horns, the shaggy mane clothing his great neck and shoulders, give him a look of ferocity which his conduct belies. Yet he is truly a grand and noble beast, and his loss from our prairies and forest is as keenly regretted by the lover of nature and of wild life as by the hunter.

Next to the bison in size, and much superior in height to it and to all other American game—for it is taller than the tallest horse—comes the moose, or broad-horned elk. It is a strange, uncouth-looking beast, with very long legs, short thick neck, a big, ungainly head, a swollen nose, and huge shovel horns. Its home is in the cold, wet pine and spruce forests, which stretch from the sub-arctic region of Canada southward in certain places across our frontier. Two centuries ago it was found as far south as Massachusetts. It has now been exterminated from its former haunts in northern New York and Vermont, and is on the point of vanishing from northern Michigan. It is still found in northern Maine and northeastern Minnesota and in portions of northern Idaho and Washington; while along the

Rockies it extends its range southward through western Montana to northwestern Wyoming, south of the Tetons. In 1884 I fresh hide of one that was killed in the Bighorn Mountains.

The wapiti, or round-horned elk, like the bison, and unlike the moose, had its centre of abundance in the United States, though extending northward into Canada. Originally its range reached from ocean to ocean and it went in herds of thousands of individuals; but it has suffered more from the persecution of hunters than any other game except the bison. By the beginning of this century it had been exterminated in most localities east of the Mississippi; but a few lingered on for many years in the Alleghanies. Col. Cecil Clay informs me that an Indian whom he knew killed one in Pennsylvania in 1869. A very few still exist here and there in northern Michigan and Minnesota, and in one or two spots on the western boundary of Nebraska and the Dakotas; but it is now properly a beast of the wooded western mountains. It is still plentiful in western Colorado, Wyoming, and Montana, and in parts of Idaho, Washington, and Oregon. Though not as large as the moose it is the most beautiful and stately of all animals of the deer kind, and its antlers are marvels of symmetrical grandeur.

The woodland caribou is inferior to the wapiti both in size and symmetry. The tips of the many branches of its long, irregular antlers are slightly palmated. Its range is the same as that of the moose, save that it does not go so far southward. Its hoofs are long and round; even larger than the long, oval hoofs of the moose, and much larger than those of the wapiti. The tracks of all three can be told apart at a glance, and cannot be mistaken for the footprints of other game. Wapiti tracks, however, look much like those of yearling and two-year-old cattle, unless the ground is steep or muddy, in which case the marks of the false hoofs appear, the joints of wapiti being more flexible than those of domestic stock.

The whitetail deer is now, as it always has been, the best known and most abundant of American big game, and though its numbers have been greatly thinned it is still found in almost every State of the Union. The common blacktail or mule deer, which has likewise been sadly thinned in numbers, though once extraordinarily abundant, extends from the great plains to the Pacific; but is supplanted on the Puget Sound coast by the Columbian blacktail. The delicate, heart-shaped footprints of all three are nearly indistinguishable; when the animal is running the hoof points are of course separated. The track of the antelope is more oval, growing squarer with age. Mountain sheep leave footmarks of a squarer shape, the points of the hoof making little indentations in the soil, well apart, even when the animal is only walking; and a yearling's track is not unlike that made by a big prongbuck when striding rapidly with the toes well apart. White-goat tracks are also square, and as large as those of the sheep; but there is less indentation of the hoof points, which come nearer together.

The antelope, or prong-buck, was once found in abundance from the eastern edge of the great plains to the Pacific, but it has everywhere diminished in numbers, and has been exterminated along the eastern and western borders of its former range. The bighorn, or mountain sheep, is found in the Rocky Mountains from northern Mexico to Alaska; and in the United States from the Coast and Cascade ranges to the Bad Lands of the western edges of the Dakotas, wherever there are mountain chains or tracts of rugged hills. It was never very abundant, and, though it has become less so, it has held its own better than most game. The white goat, however, alone among our game animals, has positively increased in numbers since the advent of settlers; because white hunters rarely follow it, and the Indians who once sought its skin for robes now use blankets instead. Its true home is in Alaska and Canada, but it crosses our borders along the lines of the Rockies and Cascades, and a few small isolated colonies are found here and there southward to California and New Mexico.

The cougar and wolf, once common throughout the United States, have now completely disappeared from all save the wildest regions. The black bear holds its own better; it was never found on the great plains. The huge grisly ranges from the great plains to the Pacific. The little peccary or Mexican wild hog merely crosses our southern border.

The finest hunting ground in America was, and indeed is, the mountainous region of western Montana and northwestern Wyoming. In this high, cold land, of lofty mountains, deep forests, and open prairies, with its beautiful lakes and rapid rivers, all the species of big game mentioned above, except the peccary and Columbian blacktail, are to be found. Until 1880 they were very abundant, and they are still, with the exception of the bison, fairly plentiful. On most of the long hunting expeditions which I made away from my ranch, I went into this region.

The bulk of my hunting has been done in the cattle country, near my ranch on the Little Missouri, and in the adjoining lands round the lower Powder and Yellowstone. Until 1881 the valley of the Little Missouri was fairly thronged with game, and was absolutely unchanged in any respect from its original condition of primeval wildness. With the incoming of the stockmen all this changed, and the game was wofully slaughtered; but plenty of deer and antelope, a few sheep and bear, and an occasional elk are still left.

Since the professional hunters have vanished, with the vast herds of game on which they preyed, the life of the ranchman is that which yields most chance of hunting. Life on a cattle ranch, on the great plains or among the foothills of the high mountains, has a peculiar attraction for those hardy, adventurous spirits who take most kindly to a vigorous out-of-doors existence, and who are therefore most apt to care passionately for the chase of big game. The free ranchman lives in a wild, lonely country, and exactly as he breaks and tames his own horses, and guards and tends his own branded herds, so he takes the keenest enjoyment in the chase, which is to him not merely the pleasantest of sports but also a means of adding materially to his comforts, and often his only method of providing himself with fresh meat.

Hunting in the wilderness is of all pastimes the most attractive, and it is doubly so when not carried on merely as a pastime. Shooting over a private game preserve is of course in no way to be compared to it. The wilderness hunter must not only show skill in the use of the rifle and address in finding and approaching game, but he must also show the qualities of hardihood, self-reliance, and resolution needed for effectively grappling with his wild surroundings. The fact that the hunter needs the game, both for its meat and for its hide, undoubtedly adds a zest to the pursuit. Among the hunts which I have most enjoyed were those made when I was engaged in getting in the winter's stock of meat for the ranch, or was keeping some party of cowboys supplied with game from day to day.

CHAPTER II. HUNTING FROM THE RANCH; THE BLACKTAIL DEER. NO life can be pleasanter than life during the months of fall on a ranch in the northern cattle country. The weather is cool; in the evenings and on the rare rainy days we are glad to sit by the great fireplace, with its roaring cottonwood logs. But on most days not a cloud dims the serene splendor of the sky; and the fresh pure air is clear with the wonderful clearness of the high plains. We are in the saddle from morning to night.

The long, low, roomy ranch house, of clean hewed logs, is as comfortable as it is bare and plain. We fare simply but well; for the wife of my foreman makes excellent bread and cake, and there are plenty of potatoes, grown in the forlorn little garden-patch on the bottom. We also have jellies and jams, made from wild plums and buffalo berries; and all the milk we can drink. For meat we depend on our rifles; and, with an occasional interlude of ducks or prairie chickens, the mainstay of each meal is venison, roasted, broiled, or fried.

Sometimes we shoot the deer when we happen on them while about our ordinary business,—indeed throughout the time that I have lived on the ranch, very many of the deer and antelope I killed were thus obtained. Of course while doing the actual round-up work it is impossible to attend to anything else; but we generally carry rifles while riding after the saddle band in the early morning, while visiting the line camps, or while in the saddle among the cattle on the range; and get many a shot in this fashion.

In the fall of 1890 some friends came to my ranch; and one day we took them to see a round-up. The OX, a Texan steer-outfit, had sent a couple of wagons to work down the river, after beef cattle, and one of my men had gone along to gather any of my own scattered steers that were ready for shipping, and to brand the late calves. There were perhaps a dozen riders with the wagons; and they were camped for the day on a big bottom where Blacktail and Whitetail creeks open into the river, several miles below my ranch.

At dawn one of the men rode off to bring in the saddle band. The rest of us were up by sunrise; and as we stood on the verandah under the shimmering cottonwood trees, revelling in the blue of the cloudless sky, and drinking in the cool air before going to breakfast, we saw the motley-colored string of ponies file down from the opposite bank of the river, and splash across the broad, shallow ford in front of the ranch house. Cantering and trotting the band swept towards the high, round horse-corral, in the open glade to the rear of the house. Guided by the jutting wing which stuck out at right angles, they entered the open gate, which was promptly closed by the cowboy who had driven them in.

After breakfast we strolled over to the corral, with our lariats, and, standing by the snubbing-post in the middle, roped the horses we wished for the party— some that were gentle, and others that were not. Then every man saddled his horse; and at the moment of mounting for the start there was, as always, a thrill of mild excitement, each rider hoping that his own horse would not buck, and that his neighbor's would. I had no young horses on the ranch at the time;

but a number of the older ones still possessed some of the least amiable traits of their youth.

Once in the saddle we rode off down river, along the bottoms, crossing the stream again and again. We went in Indian file, as is necessary among the trees and in broken ground, following the cattle-trails—which themselves had replaced or broadened the game paths that alone crossed the plateaus and bottoms when my ranch house was first built. Now we crossed open reaches of coarse grass, thinly sprinkled with large, brittle cottonwood trees, their branches torn and splintered; now we wound our way through a dense jungle where the gray, thorny buffalo bushes, spangled with brilliant red berry clusters, choked the spaces between the thick-growing boxalders; and again the sure-footed ponies scrambled down one cut bank and up another, through seemingly impossible rifts, or with gingerly footsteps trod a path which cut the side of a butte or overhung a bluff. Sometimes we racked, or shacked along at the fox trot which is the cow-pony's ordinary gait; and sometimes we loped or galloped and ran.

At last we came to the ford beyond which the riders of the round-up had made their camp. In the bygone days of the elk and buffalo, when our branded cattle were first driven thus far north, this ford had been dangerous from quicksand; but the cattle, ever crossing and re-crossing, had trodden down and settled the sand, and had found out the firm places; so that it was now easy to get over.

Close beyond the trees on the farther bank stood the two round-up wagons; near by was the cook's fire, in a trench, so that it might not spread; the bedding' of the riders and horse-wranglers lay scattered about, each roll of blankets wrapped and corded in a stout canvas sheet. The cook was busy about the fire; the night-wrangler was snatching an hour or two's sleep under one of the wagons. Half a mile away, on the plain of sage brush and long grass, the day-wrangler was guarding the grazing or resting horse herd, of over a hundred head. Still farther distant, at the mouth of a ravine, was the day-herd of cattle, two or three cowboys watching it as they lolled drowsily in their saddles. The other riders were off on circles to bring in cattle to the round-up; they were expected every moment.

With the ready hospitality always shown in a cow-camp we were pressed to alight and take dinner, or at least a lunch; and accordingly we jumped off our horses and sat down. Our tin plates were soon heaped with fresh beef, bread, tomatoes, rice, and potatoes, all very good; for the tall, bearded, scrawny cook knew his work, and the OX outfit always fed its men well,—and saw that they worked well too.

Before noon the circle riders began to appear on the plain, coming out of the ravines, and scrambling down the steep hills, singly or in twos and threes. They herded before them bunches of cattle, of varying size; these were driven together and left in charge of a couple of cowpunchers. The other men rode to the wagon to get a hasty dinner—lithe, sinewy fellows, with weather-roughened faces and fearless eyes; their broad felt hats flapped as they galloped, and their spurs and bridle chains jingled. They rode well, with long stirrups, sitting straight in the deep stock saddles, and their wiry, ponies showed no signs of fatigue from the long morning's ride.

The horse-wrangler soon drove the saddle band to the wagons, where it was caught in a quickly improvised ropecorral. The men roped fresh horses, fitted for the cuttingwork round the herd, with its attendant furious galloping and flash-like turning and twisting. In a few minutes all were in the saddle again and riding towards the cattle.

Then began that scene of excitement and turmoil, and seeming confusion, but real method and orderliness, so familiar to all who have engaged in stock-growing on the great plains. The riders gathered in a wide ring round the herd of uneasy cattle, and a couple of men rode into their midst to cut out the beef steers and the cows that were followed by unbranded calves. As soon as the animal was picked out the cowboy began to dri-

ve it slowly towards the outside of the herd, and when it was near the edge he suddenly raced it into the open. The beast would then start at full speed and try to double back among its fellows; while the trained cow-pony followed like a shadow, heading it off at every turn. The riders round that part of the herd opened out and the chosen animal was speedily hurried off to some spot a few hundred yards distant, where it was left under charge of another cowboy. The latter at first had his hands full in preventing his charge from rejoining the herd; for cattle dread nothing so much as being separated from their comrades. However, as soon as two or three others were driven out, enough to form a little bunch, it became a much easier matter to hold the "cut" as it is called. The cows and calves were put in one place, the beeves in another; the latter were afterwards run into the day-herd.

Meanwhile from time to time some clean-limbed young steer or heifer, able to run like an antelope and double like a jack-rabbit, tried to break out of the herd that was being worked, when the nearest cowboy hurried in pursuit at top speed and brought it back, after a headlong, break-neck race, in which no heed was paid to brush, fallen timber, prairie-dog holes, or cut banks. The dust rose in little whirling clouds, and through it dashed bolting cattle and galloping cowboys, hither and thither, while the air was filled with the shouts and laughter of the men, and the bellowing of the herd.

As soon as the herd was worked it was turned loose, while the cows and calves were driven over to a large corral, where the branding was done. A fire was speedily kindled, and in it were laid the branding irons of the different outfits represented on the round-up. Then two of the best ropers rode into the corral and began to rope the calves, round the hind legs by preference, but sometimes round the head. The other men dismounted to "wrestle" and brand them. Once roped, the calf, bawling and struggling, was swiftly dragged near the fire, where one or two of the calf-

wrestlers grappled with and threw the kicking, plunging little beast, and held it while it was branded. If the calf was large the wrestlers had hard work; and one or two young maverick bulls—that is, unbranded yearling bulls, which had been passed by in the round-ups of the preceding year—fought viciously, bellowing and charging, and driving some of the men up the sides of the corral, to the boisterous delight of the others.

After watching the work for a little while we left and rode homewards. Instead of going along the river bottoms we struck back over the buttes. From time to time we came out on some sharp bluff overlooking the river. From these points of vantage we could see for several mues up and down the valley of the Little Missouri. The level bottoms were walled in by rows of sheer cliffs, and steep, grassy slopes. These bluff lines were from a quarter of a mile to a mile apart; they did not run straight, but in a succession of curves, so as to look like the halves of many amphitheatres. Between them the river swept in great bends from side to side; the wide bed, brimful during the time of freshets, now held but a thin stream of water. Some of the bottoms were covered only with grass and sage brush; others with a dense jungle of trees; while yet others looked like parks, the cottonwoods growing in curved lines or in clumps scattered here and there.

On our way we came across a bunch of cattle, among which the sharp eyes of my foreman detected a maverick two-year-old heifer. He and one of the cowboys at once got down their ropes and rode after her; the rest of us first rounding up the bunch so as to give a fair start. After a sharp run one of the men, swinging his lariat round his head, got close up; in a second or two the noose settled round the heifer's neck, and as it became taut she was brought to with a jerk; immediately afterwards the other man made his throw and cleverly heeled her. In a trice the red heifer was stretched helpless on the ground, the two fierce little ponies, a pinto and a buckskin, keeping her down on their own account, tossing their heads and backing so that the ropes which led from the saddle-horns to her head and hind feet never slackened. Then we kindled a fire; one of the cinch rings was taken off to serve as a branding iron, and the heifer speedily became our property—for she was on our range.

When we reached the ranch it was still early, and after finishing dinner it lacked over an hour of sundown. Accordingly we went for another ride; and I carried my rifle. We started up a winding coulie which opened back of the ranch house; and after half an hour's canter clambered up the steep head-ravines, and emerged on a high ridge which went westward, straight as an arrow, to the main divide between the Little Missouri and the Big Beaver. Along this narrow, grassy crest we loped and galloped; we were so high that we could look far and wide over all the country round about. To the southward, across a dozen leagues of rolling and broken prairie, loomed Sentinel Butte, the chief landmark of all that region. Behind us, beyond the river, rose the weird chaos of Bad Lands which at this point lie for many miles east of the Little Missouri. Their fantastic outlines were marked against the sky as sharply as if cut with a knife; their grim and forbidding desolation warmed into wonderful beauty by the light of the dying sun. On our right, as we loped onwards, the land sunk away in smooth green-clad slopes and valleys; on our left it fell in sheer walls. Ahead of us the sun was sinking behind a mass of blood-red clouds; and on either hand the flushed skies were changing their tint to a hundred hues of opal and amethyst. Our tireless little horses sprang under us, thrilling with life; we were riding through a fairy world of beauty and color and limitless space and freedom.

Suddenly a short hundred yards in front three blacktail leaped out of a little glen and crossed our path, with the peculiar bounding gait of their kind. At once I sprang from my horse and, kneeling, fired at the last and largest of the three. My bullet sped too far back, but struck near the hip, and the crippled deer went slowly down a ravine. Run-

ning over a hillock to cut it off, I found it in some brush a few hundred yards beyond and finished it with a second ball. Quickly dressing it, I packed it on my horse, and trotted back leading him; an hour afterwards we saw through the waning light the quaint, home-like outlines of the ranch house.

After all, however, blacktail can only at times be picked up by chance in this way. More often it is needful to kill them by fair still-hunting, among the hills or wooded mountains where they delight to dwell. If hunted they speedily become wary. By choice they live in such broken country that it is difficult to pursue them with hounds; and they are by no means such water-loving animals as whitetail. On the other hand, the land in which they dwell is very favorable to the still-hunter who does not rely merely on stealth, but who can walk and shoot well. They do not go on the open prairie, and, if possible, they avoid deep forests, while, being good climbers, they like hills. In the mountains, therefore, they keep to what is called park country, where glades alternate with open groves. On the great plains they avoid both the heavily timbered river bottoms and the vast treeless stretches of level or rolling grass land; their chosen abode being the broken and hilly region, scantily wooded, which skirts almost every plains river and forms a belt, sometimes very narrow, sometimes many miles in breadth, between the alluvial bottom land and the prairies beyond. In these Bad Lands dwarfed pines and cedars grow in the canyon-like ravines and among the high steep hills; there are also basins and winding coulies, filled with brush and shrubbery and small elm or ash. In all such places the blacktail loves to make its home.

I have not often hunted blacktail in the mountains, because while there I was generally after larger game; but round my ranch I have killed more of them than of any other game, and for me their chase has always possessed a peculiar charm. We hunt them in the loveliest season of the year, the fall and early winter, when it is keen pleasure

merely to live out-of-doors. Sometimes we make a regular trip, of several days' duration, taking the ranch wagon, with or without a tent, to some rugged and little disturbed spot where the deer are plenty; perhaps returning with eight or ten carcasses, or even more —enough to last a long while in cold weather. We often make such trips while laying in our winter supply of meat.

At other times we hunt directly from the ranch house. We catch our horses overnight, and are in the saddle for an all-day's hunt long before the first streak of dawn, possibly not returning until some hours after nightfall. The early morning and late evening are the best time for hunting game, except in regions where it is hardly ever molested, and where in consequence it moves about more or less throughout the day.

During the rut, which begins in September, the deer are in constant motion, and are often found in bands. The necks of the bucks swell and their sides grow gaunt; they chase the does all night, and their flesh becomes strong and stringy—far inferior to that of the barren does and yearlings. The old bucks then wage desperate conflicts with one another, and bully their smaller brethren unmercifully. Unlike the elk, the blacktail, like the whitetail, are generally silent in the rutting season. They occasionally grunt when fighting; and once, on a fall evening, I heard two young bucks barking in a ravine back of my ranch house, and crept up and shot them; but this was a wholly exceptional instance.

At this time I hunt on foot, only using the horse to carry me to and from the hunting ground; for while rutting, the deer, being restless, do not try to escape observation by lying still, and on the other hand are apt to wander about and so are easily seen from a distance. When I have reached a favorable place I picket my horse and go from vantage point to vantage point, carefully scanning the hillsides, ravines, and brush coulies from every spot that affords a wide outlook. The quarry once seen it may be a matter of hours, or only of minutes, to approach it, accordingly as the wind and cover are or are not favorable. The walks for many miles over the hills, the exercise of constant watchfulness, the excitement of the actual stalk, and the still greater excitement of the shot, combine to make still-hunting the blacktail, in the sharp fall weather, one of the most attractive of hardy outdoor sports. Then after the long, stumbling walk homewards, through the cool gloom of the late evening, comes the meal of smoking venison and milk and bread, and the sleepy rest, lying on the bear-skins, or sitting in the rocking chair before the roaring fire, while the icy wind moans outside.

Earlier in the season, while the does are still nursing the fawns, and until the bucks have cleaned the last vestiges of velvet from their antlers, the deer lie very close, and wander round as little as may be. In the spring and early summer, in the ranch country, we hunt big game very little, and then only antelope; because in hunting antelope there is no danger of killing aught but bucks. About the first of August we begin to hunt blacktail, but do not kill does until a month later—and then only when short of meat. In the early weeks of the deer season we frequently do even the actual hunting on horseback instead of on foot; because the deer at this time rarely appear in view, so as to afford chance for a stalk, and yet are reluctant to break cover until very closely approached. In consequence we keep on our horses, and so get over much more ground than on foot, beating through or beside all likely-looking cover, with the object of jumping the deer close by. Under such circumstances bucks sometimes lie until almost trodden on.

One afternoon in mid-August, when the ranch was entirely out of meat, I started with one of my cow-hands, Merrifield, to kill a deer. We were on a couple of stout, quiet ponies, accustomed to firing and to packing game. After riding a mile or two down the bottoms we left the river and struck off up a winding valley, which led back among the hills. In a short while we were in a blacktail country, and began to keep a sharp lookout for game, riding parallel to, but some little distance from, one another. The sun, beating down through the clear air, was very hot; the brown slopes of short grass, and still more the white clay walls of the Bad Lands, threw the heat rays in our faces. We skirted closely all likely-looking spots, such as the heavy brush-patches in the bottoms of the winding valleys, and the groves of ash and elm in the basins and pockets flanking the high plateaus; sometimes we followed a cattle trail which ran down the middle of a big washout, and again we rode along the brink of a deep cedar canyon. After a while we came to a coulie with a small muddy pool at its mouth; and round this pool there was much fresh deer sign. The coulie was but half a mile long, heading into and flanked by the spurs of some steep, bare hills. Its bottom, which was fifty yards or so across, was choked by a dense growth of brush, chiefly thorny bullberries, while the sides were formed by cut banks twelve or fifteen feet high. My companion rode up the middle, while I scrambled up one of the banks, and, dismounting, led my horse along its edge, that I might have a clear shot at whatever we roused. We went nearly to the head, and then the cowboy reined up and shouted to me that he "guessed there were no deer in the coulie." Instantly there was a smashing in the young trees midway between us, and I caught a glimpse of a blacktail buck speeding round a shoulder of the cut bank; and though I took a hurried shot I missed. However, another buck promptly jumped up from the same place; evidently the two had lain secure in their day-beds, shielded by the dense cover, while the cowboy rode by them, and had only risen when he halted and began to call to me across them. This second buck, a fine fellow with big antlers not yet clear of velvet, luckily ran up the opposite bank and I got a fair shot at him as he galloped broadside to me along the open hillside. When I fired he rolled over with a broken back. As we came up he bleated loudly, an unusual thing for a buck to do.

Now these two bucks must have heard us coming, but reckoned on our passing them by without seeing them; which we would have done had they not been startled when the cowboy halted and spoke. Later in the season they would probably not have let us approach them, but would have run as soon as they knew of our presence. Of course, however, even later in the season, a man may by chance stumble across a deer close by. I remember one occasion when my ranch partner, Robert Munro Ferguson, and I almost corralled an unlucky deer in a small washout.

It was October, and our meat supply unexpectedly gave out; on our ranch, as on most ranches, an occasional meat famine of three or four days intervenes between the periods of plenty. So Ferguson and I started together, to get venison; and at the end of two days' hard work, leaving the ranch by sunrise, riding to the hunting grounds and tramping steadily until dark, we succeeded. The weather was stormy and there were continual gusts of wind and of cold rain, sleet, or snow. We hunted through a large tract of rough and broken country, six or eight miles from the ranch. As often happens in such wild weather the deer were wild too; they were watchful and were on the move all the time. We saw a number, but either they ran off before we could get a shot, or if we did fire it was at such a distance or under such unfavorable circumstances that we missed. At last, as we were plodding drearily up a bare valley, the sodden mud caking round our shoes, we roused three deer from the mouth of a short washout but a few paces from us. Two bounded off; the third by mistake rushed into the washout, where he found himself in a regular trap and was promptly shot by my companion. We slung the carcass on a pole and carried it down to where we had left the horses; and then we loped homewards, bending to the cold slanting rain.

Although in places where it is much persecuted the blacktail is a shy and wary beast, the successful pursuit of which taxes to the uttermost the skill and energy of the hunter, yet, like the elk, if little molested it often shows astonishing tameness and even stupidity. In the Rockies I have sometimes come on blacktail within a very short distance, which would merely stare at me, then trot off a few yards, turn and stare again, and wait for several minutes before really taking alarm. What is much more extraordinary I have had the same thing happen to me in certain little hunted localities in the neighborhood of my ranch, even of recent years. In the fall of 1890 I was riding down a canyon-coulie with my foreman, Sylvane Ferris, and a young friend from Boston, when we almost rode over a barren blacktail doe. She only ran some fifty yards, round a corner of the coulie, and then turned and stood until we ran forward and killed her—for we were in need of fresh meat. One October, a couple of years before this, my cousin, West Roosevelt, and I took a trip with the wagon to a very wild and rugged country, some twenty miles from the ranch. We found that the deer had evidently been but little disturbed. One day while scrambling down a steep, brushy hill, leading my horse, I came close on a doe and fawn; they merely looked at me with curiosity for some time, and then sauntered slowly off, remaining within shot for at least five minutes. Fortunately we had plenty of meat at the time, and there was no necessity to harm the graceful creatures. A few days later we came on two bucks sunning themselves in the bottom of a valley. My companion killed one. The other was lying but a dozen rods off; yet it never moved, until several shots had been fired at the first. It was directly under me and in my anxiety to avoid overshooting, to my horror I committed the opposite fault, and away went the buck.

Every now and then any one will make most unaccountable misses. A few days after thus losing the buck I spent nearly twenty cartridges in butchering an unfortunate yearling, and only killed it at all because it became so bewildered by the firing that it hardly tried to escape. I never could tell why I used so many cartridges to such little purpose. During the next fortnight I killed seven deer without making a single miss, though some of the shots were

rather difficult.

THE WHITETAIL DEER; AND THE BLACK-TAIL OF THE COLUMBIA.

THE whitetail deer is much the commonest game animal of the United States, being still found,, though generally in greatly diminished numbers throughout most of the Union. It is a shrewd, wary, knowing beast; but it owes its prolonged stay in the land chiefly to the fact that it is an inveterate skulker, and fond of the thickest cover. Accordingly it usually has to be killed by stealth and stratagem, and not by fair, manly hunting; being quite easily slain in any one of half a dozen unsportsmanlike ways. In consequence I care less for its chase than for the chase of any other kind of American big game. Yet in the few places where it dwells in open, hilly forests and can be killed by still-hunting as if it were a blacktail; or better still, where the nature of the ground is such that it can be run down in fair chase on horseback, either with greyhounds, or with a pack of trackhounds, it yields splendid sport.

Killing a deer from a boat while the poor animal is swimming in the water, or on snow-shoes as it flounders helplessly in the deep drifts, can only be justified on the plea of hunger. This is also true of lying in wait at a lick. Whoever indulges in any of these methods save from necessity, is a butcher, pure and simple, and has no business in the company of true sportsmen.

Fire hunting may be placed in the same category; yet it is possibly allowable under exceptional circumstances to indulge in a fire hunt, if only for the sake of seeing the wilderness by torchlight. My first attempt at big-game shooting, when a boy, was "jacking " for deer in the Adirondacks, on a pond or small lake surrounded by the grand northern forests of birch and beech, pine, spruce, and fir. I killed a spike buck; and while I have never been willing to kill another in this manner, I cannot say that I regret having once had the experience. The ride over the glassy, black water, the witchcraft of such silent progress through the mystery of the night, cannot but impress one. There

is pleasure in the mere buoyant gliding of the birch-bark canoe, with its curved bow and stern; nothing else that floats possesses such grace, such frail and delicate beauty, as this true craft of the wilderness, which is as much a creature of the wild woods as the deer and bear themselves. The light streaming from the bark lantern in the bow cuts a glaring lane through the gloom; in it all objects stand out like magic, shining for a moment white and ghastly and then vanishing into the impenetrable darkness; while all the time the paddler in the stern makes not so much as a ripple, and there is never a sound but the occasional splash of a muskrat, or the moaning *uloo-oo—uloo-uloo* of an owl from the deep forests; and at last perchance the excitement of a shot at a buck, standing at gaze, with luminous eyeballs.

The most common method of killing the whitetail is by hounding; that is, by driving it with hounds past runways where hunters are stationed—for all wild animals when on the move prefer to follow certain definite routes. This is a legitimate, but inferior, kind of sport.

However, even killing driven deer may be good fun at certain times. Most of the whitetail we kill round the ranch are obtained in this fashion. On the Little Missouri —as throughout the plains country generally—these deer cling to the big wooded river bottoms, while the blacktail are found in the broken country back from the river. The tangled mass of cottonwoods, box-alders, and thorny bullberry bushes which cover the bottoms afford the deer a nearly secure shelter from the still-hunter; and it is only by the aid of hounds that they can be driven from their wooded fastnesses. They hold their own better than any other game. The great herds of buffalo, and the bands of elk, have vanished completely; the swarms of antelope and blacktail have been wofully thinned; but the whitetail, which were never found in such throngs as either buffalo or elk, blacktail or antelope, have suffered far less from the advent of the white hunters, ranchmen, and settlers. They are of course not as plentiful as formerly; but some are still to be found in almost all their old haunts. Where the river, winding between rows of high buttes, passes my ranch house, there is a long succession of heavily wooded bottoms; and on all of these, even on the one whereon the house itself stands, there are a good many whitetail yet left.

When we take a day's regular hunt we usually wander afar, either to the hills after blacktail or to the open prairie after antelope. But if we are short of meat, and yet have no time for a regular hunt, being perhaps able to spare only a couple of hours after the day's work is over, then all hands turn out to drive a bottom forwhitetail. We usually have one or two trackhounds at the ranch; true southern deer-hounds, black and tan, with lop ears and hanging lips, their wrinkled faces stamped with an expression of almost ludicrous melancholy. They are not fast, and have none of the alert look of the pied and spotted modern foxhound; but their noses are very keen, their voices deep and mellow, and they are wonderfully staunch on a trail.

All is bustle and laughter as we start on such a hunt. The baying hounds bound about, as the rifles are taken down; the wiry ponies are roped out of the corral, and each broad-hatted hunter swings joyfully into the saddle. If the pony bucks or "acts mean " the rider finds that his rifle adds a new element of interest to the performance, which is of course hailed with loud delight by all the men on quiet horses. Then we splash off over the river, scramble across the faces of the bluffs, or canter along the winding cattle paths, through the woods, until we come to the bottom we intend to hunt. Here a hunter is stationed at each runway along which it is deemed likely that the deer will pass; and one man, who has remained on horseback, starts into the cover with the hounds; occasionally this horseman himself, skilled, as most cowboys are, in the use of the revolver, gets a chance to kill a deer. The deep baying of the hounds speedily gives warning that the game is afoot; and the watching hunters, who have already hid their horses carefully, look to their rifles. Sometimes the

deer comes far ahead of the dogs, running very swiftly with neck stretched straight out; and if the cover is thick such an animal is hard to hit. At other times, especially if the quarry is a young buck, it plays along not very far ahead of its baying pursuers, bounding and strutting with head up and white flag flaunting. If struck hard, down goes the flag at once, and the deer plunges into a staggering run, while the hounds yell with eager ferocity as they follow the bloody trail. Usually we do not have to drive more than one or two bottoms before getting a deer, which is forthwith packed behind one of the riders, as the distance is not great, and home we come in triumph. Sometimes, however, we fail to find game, or the deer take unguarded passes, or the shot is missed. Occasionally I have killed deer on these hunts; generally I have merely sat still a long while, listened to the hounds, and at last heard somebody else shoot. In fact such hunting, though good enough fun if only tried rarely, would speedily pall if followed at all regularly.

Personally the chief excitement I have had in connection therewith has a-isen from some antic of my horse; a halfbroken bronco is apt to become unnerved when a man with a gun tries to climb on him in a hurry. On one hunt in 1890 I rode a wild animal named Whitefoot. He had been a confirmed and very bad bucker three years before, when I had him in my string on the round-up; but had grown quieter with years. Nevertheless I found he had some fire left; for a hasty vault into the saddle on my part, was followed on his by some very resolute pitching. I lost my rifle and hat, and my revolver and knife were bucked out of my belt; but I kept my seat all right, and finally got his head up and mastered him without letting him throw himself over backwards, a trick he sometimes practised. Nevertheless, in the first jump when I was taken unawares, I strained myself across the loins, and did not get entirely over it for six months.

To shoot running game with the rifle it is always necessary to be a good and quick marksman; for it is never easy to

kill an animal, when in rapid motion, with a single bullet. If on a runway a man who is a fairly skilful rifleman, has plenty of time for a clear shot, on open ground, at comparatively short distance, say under eighty yards, and if the deer is cantering, he ought to hit; at least I generally do under such circumstances, by remembering to hold well forward, in fact just in front of the deer's chest. But I do not always kill by any means; quite often when I thought I held far enough ahead, my bullet has gone into the buck's hips or loins. However, one great feature in the use of dogs is that they enable one almost always to recover wounded game.

If the animal is running at full speed a long distance off, the difficulty of hitting is of course very much increased; and if the country is open the value of a repeating rifle is then felt. If the game is bounding over logs or dodging through underbrush, the difficulty is again increased. Moreover, the natural gait of the different kinds of game must be taken into account. Of course the larger kinds, such as elk and moose, are the easiest to hit; then comes the antelope, in spite of its swiftness, and the sheep, because of the evenness of their running; then the whitetail, with its rolling gallop; and last and hardest of all, the blacktail, because of its extraordinary stifflegged bounds.

Sometimes on a runway the difficulty is not that the game is too far, but that it is too close; for a deer may actually almost jump on the hunter, surprising him out of all accuracy of aim. Once something of the sort happened to me.

Winter was just beginning. I had been off with the ranch wagon on a last round-up of the beef steers; and had suffered a good deal, as one always does on these cold weather round-ups, sleeping out in the snow, wrapped up in blankets and tarpaulin, with no tent and generally no fire. Moreover, I became so wear' of the interminable length of the nights, that I almost ceased to mind the freezing misery of standing night guard round the restless cattle; while roping, saddling, and mastering the rough horses each morning, with numbed and stiffened limbs, though warming to the blood was harrowing to the temper.

On my return to the ranch I found a strange hunter staying there; a clean, square-built, honest-looking little fellow, but evidently not a native American. As a rule, nobody displays much curiosity about any one's else antecedents in the Far West; but I happened to ask my foreman who the new-comer was,—chiefly because the said new-comer, evidently appreciating the warmth and comfort of the clean, roomy, ranch house, with its roaring fires, books, and good fare, seemed inclined to make a permanent stay, according to the custom of the country. My foreman, who had a large way of looking at questions of foreign ethnology and geography, responded with indifference: "Oh, he's a kind of a Dutchman; but he hates the other Dutch, mortal. He's from an island Germany took from France in the last war!" This seemed puzzling; but it turned out that the " island " in question was Alsace. Native Americans predominate among the dwellers in and on the borders of the wilderness, and in the wild country over which the great herds of the cattlemen roam; and they take the lead in every way. The sons of the Germans, Irish, and other European new-comers are usually quick to claim to be " straight United States," and to disavow all kinship with the fellowcountrymen of their fathers. Once, while with a hunter bearing a German name, we came by chance on a German hunting party from one of the eastern cities. One of them remarked to my companion that he must be part German himself, to which he cheerfully answered: "Well, my father was a Dutchman, but my mother was a white woman! I'm pretty white myself!" whereat the Germans glowered at him gloomily.

As we were out of meat the Alsatian and one of the cowboys and I started down the river with a wagon. The first day in camp it rained hard, so that we could not hunt. Towards evening we grew tired of doing nothing, and as the rain had become a mere fine drizzle, we sallied out to 1 drive one of the bottoms

for whitetail. The cowboy and our one trackhound plunged into the young cottonwood, which grew thickly over the sandy bottom; while the little hunter and I took our stands on a cut bank, twenty feet high and half a mile long, which hedged in the trees from behind. Three or four game trails led up through steep, narrow clefts in this bank; and we tried to watch these. Soon I saw a deer in an opening below, headed towards one end of the bank, round which another game trail led; and I ran hard towards this end, where it turned into a knife-like ridge of clay. About fifty yards from the point there must have been some slight irregularities in the face of the bank, enough to give the deer a foothold; for as I ran along the animal suddenly bounced over the crest, so close that I could have hit it with my right hand. As I tried to pull up short and swing round, my feet slipped from under me in the wet clay, and down I went; while the deer literally turned a terrified somersault backwards. I flung myself to the edge and missed a hurried shot as it raced back on its tracks. Then, wheeling, I saw the little hunter running towards me along the top of the cut bank, his face on a broad grin. He leaped over one of the narrow clefts, up which a game trail led; and hardly was he across before the frightened deer bolted up it, not three yards from his back. He did not turn, in spite of my shouting and handwaving, and the frightened deer, in the last stage of panic at finding itself again almost touching one of its foes, sped off across the grassy slopes like a quarter horse. When at last the hunter did turn, it was too late; and our long-range fusillade proved harmless. During the next two days I redeemed myself, killing four deer.

Coming back our wagon broke down, no unusual incident in ranch-land, where there is often no road, while the strain is great in hauling through quicksands, and up or across steep broken hills; it rarely makes much difference beyond the temporary delay, for plainsmen and mountain-men are very handy and self-helpful. Besides, a mere breakdown sinks into nothing compared to

having the team play out; which is, of course, most apt to happen at the times when it insures hardship and suffering, as in the middle of a snowstorm, or when crossing a region with no water. However, the reinsmen of the plains must needs face many such accidents, not to speak of runaways, or having the wagon pitchpole over on to the team in dropping down too steep a hillside. Once after a three days' rainstorm some of us tried to get the ranch wagon along a trail which led over the ridge of a gumbo or clay butte. The sticky stuff clogged our shoes, the horses' hoofs, and the wheels; and it was even more slippery than it was sticky. Finally we struck a sloping shoulder; with great struggling, pulling, pushing, and shouting, we reached the middle of it, and then, as one of my men remarked, "the whole darned outfit slid into the coulie. "

These hunting trips after deer or antelope with the wagon usually take four or five days. I always ride some tried hunting horse; and the wagon itself when on such a hunt is apt to lead a chequered career, as half the time there is not the vestige of a trail to follow. Moreover we often make a hunt when the good horses are on the round-up, or otherwise employed, and we have to get together a scrub team of cripples or else of outlaws—vicious devils, only used from dire need. The best teamster for such a hunt that we ever had on the ranch was a weatherbeaten old fellow known as " Old Man Tompkins." In the course of a long career as lumberman, plains teamster, buffalo hunter, and Indian fighter, he had passed several years as a Rocky Mountain stage driver; and a stage driver of the Rockies is of necessity a man of such skill and nerve that he fears no team and no country. No matter how wild the unbroken horses, Old Tompkins never asked help; and he hated to drive less than a four-in-hand. When he once had a grip on the reins, he let no one hold the horses' heads. All he wished was an open plain for the rush at the beginning. The first plunge might take the wheelers' fore-feet over the cross-bars of the leaders, but he never stopped for that; on went the team, running, bounding, rearing, tumbling, while the wagon leaped behind, until gradually things straightened out of their own accord. I soon found, however, that I could not allow him to carry a rifle; for he was an inveterate game butcher. In the presence of game the old fellow became fairly wild with excitement, and forgot the years and rheumatism which had crippled him. Once, after a long and tiresome day's hunt, we were walking home together; he was carrying his boots in his hands, bemoaning the fact that his feet hurt him. Suddenly a whitetail jumped up; down dropped Old Tompkins' boots, and away he went like a college sprinter, entirely heedless of stones and cactus. By some indiscriminate firing at long range we dropped the deer; and as Old Tompkins cooled down he realized that his bare feet had paid full penalty for his dash.

One of these wagon trips I remember because I missed a fair running shot which I much desired to hit; and afterwards hit a very much more difficult shot about which I cared very little. Ferguson and I, with Sylvane and one or two others, had gone a day's journey down the river for a hunt. We went along the bottoms, crossing the stream every mile or so, with an occasional struggle through mud or quicksand, or up the steep, rotten banks. An old buffalo hunter drove the wagon, with a couple of shaggy, bandy-legged ponies; the rest of us jogged along in front on horseback, picking out a trail through the bottoms and choosing the best crossing places. Some of the bottoms were grassy pastures; on others great, gnarled cottonwoods, with shivered branches, stood in clumps; yet others were choked with a true forest growth. Late in the afternoon we went into camp, choosing a spot where the cottonwoods were young; their glossy leaves trembled and rustled unceasingly. We speedily picketed the horses—changing them about as they ate off the grass,—drew water, and hauled great logs in front of where we had pitched the tent, while the wagon stood nearby. Each man laid out his bed; the food and kitchen kit were taken from the wagon; supper was cooked and eaten; and we then lay round the campfire, gazing into it. or up at the brilliant stars, and listening to the wild, mournful wailing of the coyotes. They were very plentiful round this camp; before sunrise and after sundown they called unceasingly.

Next day I took a long tramp and climb after mountain sheep and missed a running shot at a fine ram, about a hundred yards off; or rather I hit him and followed his bloody trail a couple of miles, but failed to find him; whereat I returned to camp much cast down.

Early the following morning Sylvane and I started for another hunt, this time on horseback. The air was crisp and pleasant; the beams of the just-risen sun struck sharply on the umber-colored hills and white cliff walls guarding the river, bringing into high relief their strangely carved and channelled fronts. Below camp the river was little but a succession of shallow pools strung along the broad sandy bed which in spring-time was filled from bank to bank with foaming muddy water. Two mallards sat in one of these pools; and I hit one with the rifle, so nearly missing that the ball scarcely ruffled a feather; yet in some way the shock told, for the bird after flying thirty yards dropped on the sand.

Then we left the river and our active ponies scrambled up a small canyon-like break in the bluffs. All day we rode among the hills; sometimes across rounded slopes, matted with short buffalo grass; sometimes over barren buttes of red or white clay, where only sage brush and cactus grew; or beside deep ravines, black with stunted cedar; or along beautiful winding coulies, where the grass grew rankly, and the thickets of ash and wild plum made brilliant splashes of red and yellow and tender green. Yet we saw nothing.

As evening drew on we rode riverwards; we slid down the steep bluff walls, and loped across a great bottom of sage brush and tall grass, our horses now and then leaping like cats over the trunks of dead cottonwoods. As we came to the brink of the cut bank which forms the hither boundary of the river in freshet time, we suddenly saw two deer, a doe and a well grown fawn—of course long out of the spotted coat. They were walking with heads down along the edge of a sand-bar, near a pool, on the farther side of the stream bed, over two hundred yards distant. They saw us at once, and turning, galloped away, with flags aloft, the pictures of springing, vigorous beauty. I jumped off my horse in an instant, knelt, and covered the fawn. It was going straight away from me, running very evenly, and I drew a coarse sight at the tip of the white flag. As I pulled trigger down went the deer, the ball having gone into the back of its head. The distance was a good three hundred yards; and while of course there was much more chance than skill in the shot I felt well pleased with it—though I could not help a regret that while making such a difficult shot at a mere whitetail I should have missed a much easier shot at a noble bighorn. Not only I, but all the camp, had a practical interest in my success; for we had no fresh meat, and a fat whitetail fawn, killed in October, yields the best of venison. So after dressing the deer I slung the carcass behind my saddle, and we rode swiftly back to camp through the dark; and that evening we feasted on the juicy roasted ribs.

The degree of tameness and unsuspiciousness shown by whitetail deer depends, of course, upon the amount of molestation to which they are exposed. Their times for sleeping, feeding, and coming to water vary from the same cause. Where they are little persecuted they feed long after sunrise and before sunset, and drink when the sun is high in the heavens, sometimes even at midday; they then show but little fear of man, and speedily become indifferent to the presence of deserted dwellings.

In the cattle country the ranch houses are often shut during the months of warm weather, when the round-ups succeed one another without intermission, as thecalvesmust be branded, the beeves gathered and shipped, long trips made to collect strayed animals, and the trail stock driven from the breeding to the fattening grounds. At that time all the men-folk may have to be away in the white-topped wagons, working among the horned herds, whether plodding along the trail, or wandering to and fro on the range. Late one summer, when my own house had been thus closed for many months, I rode thither with a friend to pass a week. The place already wore the look of having slipped away from the domain of man. The wild forces, barely thrust back beyond the threshold of our habitation, were prompt to spring across it to renewed possession the moment we withdrew. The rank grass grew tall in the yard, and on the sodded roofs of the stable and sheds; the weather-beaten log walls of the house itself were one in tint with the trunks of the gnarled cottonwoods by which it was shaded. Evidently the woodland creatures had come to regard the silent, deserted buildings as mere outgrowths of the wilderness, no more to be feared than the trees around them 'or the gray, strangely shaped buttes behind.

Lines of delicate, heart-shaped footprints in the muddy reaches of the half-dry river-bed showed where the deer came to water; and in the dusty cattle-trails among the ravines many round tracks betrayed the passing and repassing of timber wolves,—once or twice in the late evening we listened to their savage and melancholy howling. Cotton-tail rabbits burrowed under the verandah. Within doors the bushy-tailed pack-rats had possession, and at night they held a perfect witches' sabbath in the garret and kitchen; while a little white-footed mouse, having dragged half the stuffing out of a mattress, had made thereof a big fluffy nest, entirely filling the oven.

Yet, in spite of the abundant sign of game, we at first suffered under one of those spells of ill-luck which at times befall all hunters, and for several days we could kill nothing, though we tried hard, being in need of fresh meat. The moon was full—each evening, sitting on the ranch verandah, or walking homeward, we watched it rise over the line of bluffs beyond the river—and the deer were feeding at night; moreover in such hot weather they lie very close, move as little as possible, and are most difficult to find. Twice we lay out from dusk until dawn, in spite of the mosquitoes, but saw nothing; and the chances we did get we failed to profit by.

One morning, instead of trudging out to hunt I stayed at home, and sat in a rocking-chair on the verandah read ing, rocking, or just sitting still listening to the low rustling of the cottonvvood branches overhead, and gazing across the river. Through the still, clear, hot air, the faces of the bluffs shone dazzling white; no shadow fell from the cloudless sky on the grassy slopes, or on the groves of timber; only the faraway cooing of a mourning dove broke the silence. Suddenly my attention was arrested by a slight splashing in the water; glancing up from my book I saw three deer, which had come out of the thick fringe of bushes and young trees across the river, and were strolling along the sand-bars directly opposite me. Slipping stealthily into the house I picked up my rifle, and slipped back again. One of the deer was standing motionless, broadside to me; it was a long shot, two hundred and fifty yards, but I had a rest against a pillar of the verandah. I held true, and as the smoke cleared away the deer lay struggling on the sands.

As the whitetail is the most common and widely distributed of American game, so the Columbian blacktail has the most sharply limited geographical range; for it is confined to the northwest coast, where it is by far the most abundant deer. In antlers it is indistinguishable from the common blacktail of the Rockies and the great plains, and it has the regular blacktail gait, a succession of stiff-legged bounds on all four feet at once; but its tail is more like a whitetail's in shape, though black above. As regards methods of hunting, and the amount of sport yielded, it stands midway between its two brethren. It lives in a land of magnificent timber, where the trees tower far into the sky, the giants of their kind; and there are few more attractive sports than still-hunting on the mountains, among these forests of marvellous beauty and grandeur. There are many lakes among the mountains where it dwells, and as it cares more for water than the ordinary blacktail, it is comparatively easy for hounds to drive it into some pond where it can be killed at leisure. It is thus often killed by hounding.

The only one I ever killed was a fine young buck. We had camped near a little pond, and as evening fell I strolled off towards it and sat down. Just after sunset the buck came out of the woods. For some moments he hesitated and then walked forward and stood by the edge of the water, about sixty yards from me. We were out of meat, so I held right behind his shoulder, and though he went off, his bounds were short and weak, and he fell before he reached the wood.

ON THE CATTLE RANGES; THE PRONGHORN ANTELOPE. EARLY one June just after the close of the regular spring round-up, a couple of wagons, with a score of riders between them, were sent to work some hitherto untouched country, between the little Missouri and the Yellowstone. I was to go as the representative of our own and of one or two neighboring brands; but as the round-up had halted near my ranch I determined to spend a day there, and then to join the wagons;—the appointed meeting-place being a cluster of red scoria buttes, some forty miles distant, where there was a spring of good water.

Most of my day at the ranch was spent in slumber; for I had been several weeks on the round-up, where nobody ever gets quite enough sleep. This is the only drawback to the work; otherwise it is pleasant and exciting, with just that slight touch of danger necessary to give it zest, and without the wearing fatigue of such labor as lumbering or mining. But there is never enough sleep, at least on the spring and mid-summer round-ups. The men are in the saddle from dawn until dusk, at the time when the days are longest on these great northern plains; and in addition there is the regular night guarding and now and then a furious storm or a stampede, when for twenty-four hours at a stretch the riders only dismount to change horses or snatch a mouthful of food.

I started in the bright sunrise, riding one horse and driving loose before me eight others, one carrying my bedding. They travelled strung out in single file. I kept them trotting and loping, for loose horses are easiest to handle when driven at some speed, and moreover the way was long. My rifle was slung under my thigh; the lariat was looped on the saddle-horn.

At first our trail led through winding coulies, and sharp grassy defiles; the air was wonderfully clear, the flowers were in bloom, the breath of the wind in my face was odorous and sweet. The patter and beat of the unshod hoofs, rising in half-rhythmic measure, frightened the scudding deer; but the yellow-breasted meadow larks, perched on the budding tops of the bushes, sang their rich full songs without heeding us as we went by.

When the sun was well on high and the heat of the day had begun we came to a dreary and barren plain, broken by rows of low clay buttes. The ground in places was whitened by alkali; elsewhere it was dull gray. Here there grew nothing save sparse tufts of coarse grass, and cactus, and sprawling sage brush. In the hot air all things seen afar danced and wavered. As I rode and gazed at the shimmering haze the vast desolation of the landscape bore on me; it seemed as if the unseen and unknown powers of the wastes were moving by and marshalling their silent forces. No man save the wilderness dweller knows the strong melancholy fascination of these long rides through lonely lands.

At noon, that the horses might graze and drink, I halted where some box-alders grew by a pool in the bed of a half-dry creek; and shifted my saddle to a fresh beast. When we started again we came out on the rolling prairie, where the green sea of wind-rippled grass stretched limitless as far as the eye could reach. Little striped gophers scuttled away, or stood perfectly straight at the mouths of their burrows, looking like picket pins. Curlews clamored mournfully as they circled overhead. Prairie fowl swept off, clucking and calling, or strutted about with their sharp tails erect. Antelope were very plentiful, running like race-horses across the level, or uttering their queer, barking grunt as they stood at gaze, the white hairs on their rumps all on end, their neck bands of broken brown and white vivid in the sunlight. They were found singly or in small straggling parties; the master bucks had not yet begun to drive out the younger and weaker ones as later in the season, when each would gather into a herd as many does as his jealous strength could guard from rivals. The nursing does whose kids had come early were often found with the bands; the others kept apart. The kids were very conspicuous figures on the prairies, across which they scudded like jack rabbits, showing nearly as much speed and alertness as their parents; only the very young sought safety by lying flat to escape notice.

The horses cantered and trotted steadily over the mat of buffalo grass, steering for the group of low scoria mounds which was my goal. In mid-afternoon I reached it. The two wagons were drawn up near the spring; under them lay the night-wranglers, asleep; nearby the teamster-cooks were busy about the evening meal. A little way off the two day-wranglers were watching the horse-herd; into which I speedily turned my own animals. The riders had already driven in the bunches of cattle; and were engaged in branding the calves, and turning loose the animals that were not needed, while the remainder were kept, forming the nucleus of the herd which was to accompany the wagon.

As soon as the work was over the men rode to the wagons; sinewy fellows, with tattered broad-brimmed hats and clanking spurs, some wearing leather shaps or leggings, others having their trousers tucked into their high-heeled top-boots, all with their flannel shirts and loose neckerchiefs dusty and sweaty. A few were indulging in rough, good-natured horse play, to an accompaniment of yelling mirth; most were grave and taciturn, greeting me with a silent nod or a " How! friend." A very talkative man, unless the acknowledged wit of the party, according to the somewhat florid frontier notion of wit, is always looked on with disfavor in a cow-camp. After supper, eaten in silent haste, we gathered round the embers of the small fires, and the conversation glanced fitfully over the threadbare subjects common to all such camps; the antics of some particularly vicious bucking bronco, how the different brands of cattle were showing up, the smallness of the calf drop, the respective merits of rawhide lariats and grass ropes, and bits of rather startling and violent news concerning the fates of certain neighbors. Then one by one we began to turn in under our blankets.

Our wagon was to furnish the night guards for the cattle; and each of us had his gentlest horse tied ready to hand. The night guards went on duty two at a time for two-hour watches. By good luck my watch came last. My comrade was a happy-go-lucky young Texan who for some inscrutable reason was known as "Latigo Strap"; he had just come from the south with a big drove of trail cattle.

A few minutes before two one of the guards who had gone on duty at midnight rode into camp and wakened us by shaking our shoulders. Fumbling in the dark I speedily saddled my horse; Latigo had left his saddled, and he started ahead of me. One of the annoyances of night guarding, at least in thick weather, is the occasional difficulty of finding the herd after leaving camp, or in returning to camp after the watch is over; there are few things more exasperating than to be helplessly wandering about in the dark under such circumstances. However, on this occasion there was no such trouble; for it was a brilliant starlight night and the herd had been bedded down by a sugar-loaf butte which made a good landmark. As we reached the spot we could make out the loom of the cattle lying close together on the level plain; and then the dim figure of a horseman rose vaguely from the darkness and moved by in silence; it was the other of the two midnight guards, on his way back to his broken slumber.

At once we began to ride slowly round the cattle in opposite directions. We were silent, for the night was clear, and the herd quiet; in wild weather, when the cattle are restless, the cowboys never cease calling and singing as they circle them, for the sounds seem to quiet the beasts.

For over an hour we steadily paced the endless round, saying nothing, with our great-coats buttoned, for the air is chill towards morning on the northern plains, even in summer. Then faint streaks of gray appeared in the east. Latigo Strap began to call merrily to the cattle. A coyote came sneaking over the butte nearby, and halted to yell and wail; afterwards he crossed the coulie and from the hillside opposite again shrieked in dismal crescendo. The dawn brightened rapidly; the little skylarks of the plains began to sing, soaring far overhead, while it was still much too dark to see them. Their song is not powerful, but it is so clear and fresh and long-continued that it always appeals to one very strongly; especially because it is most often heard in the rose-tinted air of the glorious mornings, while the listener sits in the saddle, looking across the endless sweep of the prairies.

As it grew lighter the cattle became restless, rising and stretching themselves, while we continued to ride round them.

"Then the bronc' began to pitch
And I began to ride;
He bucked me off a cut bank,
Hell! 1 nearly died!"
sang Latigo from the other side of the herd. A yell from the wagons told that the cook was summoning the sleeping cow-punchers to breakfast; we were soon able to distinguish their figures as they rolled out of their bedding, wrapped and corded it into bundles, and huddled sullenly round the little fires. The horse wranglers were driving in the saddle bands. All the cattle got on their feet and started feeding. In a few minutes the hasty breakfast at the wagons

had evidently been despatched for we could see the men forming rope corrals into which the ponies were driven; then each man saddled, bridled, and mounted his horse, two or three of the half-broken beasts bucking, rearing, and plunging frantically in the vain effort to unseat their riders.

The two men who were first in the saddle relieved Latigo and myself and we immediately galloped to camp, shifted our saddles to fresh animals, gulped down a cup or two of hot coffee, and some pork, beans, and bread, and rode to the spot where the others were gathered, lolling loosely in their saddles, and waiting for the round-up boss to assign them their tasks. We were the last, and as soon as we arrived the boss divided all into two parties for the morning work, or "circle riding," whereby the cattle were to be gathered for the round-up proper. Then, as the others started, he turned to me and remarked: " We 've got enough hands to drive this open country without you; but we 're out of meat, and I don't want to kill a beef for such a small outfit; can't you shoot some antelope this morning? We 'll pitch camp by the big blasted cottonwood at the foot of the ash coulies, over yonder, below the breaks of Dry Creek. "

Of course I gladly assented, and was speedily riding alone across the grassy slopes. There was no lack of the game I was after, for from every rise of ground I cor.ld see antelope scattered across the prairie, singly, in couples, or in bands. But their very numbers, joined to the lack of cover on such an open, flattish country, proved a bar to success; while I was stalking one band another was sure to see me and begin running, whereat the first would likewise start; I missed one or two very long shots, and noon found me still without game.

However, I was then lucky enough to see a band of a dozen feeding to windward of a small butte, and by galloping in a long circle I got within a quarter of a mile of them before having to dismount. The stalk itself was almost too easy; for I simply walked to the butte, climbed carefully up a slope where the

soil was firm and peered over the top to see the herd, a little one, a hundred yards off. They saw me at once and ran, but I held well ahead of a fine young prong-buck, and rolled him over like a rabbit, with both shoulders broken. In a few minutes I was riding onwards once more with the buck lashed behind my saddle.

The next one I got, a. couple of hours later, offered a much more puzzling stalk. He was a big fellow in company with four does or small bucks. All five were lying in the middle of a slight basin, at the head of a gentle valley. At first sight it seemed impossible to get near them, for there was not so much cover as a sage brush, and the smooth, shallow basin in which they lay was over a thousand yards across, while they were looking directly down the valley. However, it is curious how hard it is to tell, even from nearby, whether a stalk can or cannot be made; the difficulty being to estimate the exact amount of shelter yielded by little inequalities of ground. In this instance a small shallow watercourse, entirely dry, ran along the valley, and after much study I decided to try to crawl up it, although the big bulging telescopic eyes of the prong-buck—which have much keener sight than deer or any other game—would in such case be pointed directly my way.

Having made up my mind I backed cautiously down from the coign of vantage whence I had first seen the game, and ran about a mile to the mouth of a washout which formed the continuation of the watercourse in question. Protected by the high clay banks of this washout I was able to walk upright until within half a mile of the prong-bucks; then my progress became very tedious and toilsome, as I had to work my way up the watercourse flat on my stomach, dragging the rifle beside me. At last I reached a spot beyond which not even a snake could crawl unnoticed. In front was a low bank, a couple of feet high, crested with tufts of coarse grass. Raising my head very cautiously I peered through these and saw the prong-horn about a hundred and fifty yards distant. At the same time I found that I had crawled to the edge of a village of prairie dogs, which had already made me aware of their presence by their shrill yelping. They saw me at once; and all those away from their homes scuttled towards them, and dived down the burrows, or sat on the mounds at the entrances, scolding convulsively and jerking their fat little bodies and short tails. This commotion at once attracted the attention of the antelope. They rose forthwith, and immediately caught a glimpse of the black muzzle of the rifle which I was gently pushing through the grass tufts. The fatal curiosity which so often in this species offsets wariness and sharp sight, proved my friend; evidently the antelope could not quite make me out and wished to know what I was. They moved nervously to and fro, striking the earth with their fore hoofs, and now and then uttering a sudden bleat. At last the big buck stood still broadside to me, and I fired. He went off with the others, but lagged behind as they passed over the hill crest, and when I reached it I saw him standing, not very far off, with his head down. Then he walked backwards a few steps, fell over on his side, and died.

As he was a big buck I slung him across the saddle, and started for camp afoot, leading the horse. However my hunt was not over, for while still a mile from the wagons, going down a coulie of Dry Creek, a yearling prong-buck walked over the divide to my right and stood still until I sent a bullet into its chest; so that I made my appearance in camp with three antelope.

I spoke above of the sweet singing of the western meadow lark and plains skylark; neither of them kin to the true skylark, by the way, one being a cousin of the grakles and hang-birds, and the other a kind of pipit. To me both of these birds are among the most attractive singers to which I have ever listened; but with all birdmusic much must be allowed for the surroundings, and much for the mood, and the keenness of sense, of the listener. The lilt of the little plains skylark is neither very powerful nor very melodious; but it is sweet, pure, long-sustained, with a ring of

courage befitting a song uttered in highest air.

The meadow lark is a singer of a higher order, deserving to rank with the best. Its song has length, variety, power and rich melody; and there is in it sometimes a cadence of wild sadness, inexpressibly touching. Yet I cannot say that either song would appeal to others as it appeals to me; for to me it comes forever laden with a hundred memories and associations; with the sight of dim hills reddening in the dawn, with the breath of cool morning winds blowing across lonely plains, with the scent of flowers on the sunlit prairie, with the motion of fiery horses, with all the strong thrill of eager and buoyant life. I doubt if any man can judge dispassionately the bird songs of his own country; he cannot disassociate them from the sights and sounds of the land that is so dear to him.

This is not a feeling to regret, but it must be taken into account in accepting any estimate of bird music— even in considering the reputation of the European skylark and nightingale. To both of these birds I have often listened in their own homes; always with pleasure and admiration, but always with a growing belief that relatively to some other birds they were ranked too high. They are pre-eminently birds with literary associations; most people take their opinions of them at second-hand, from the poets.

No one can help liking the lark; it is such a brave, honest, cheery bird, and moreover its song is uttered in the air, and is very long-sustained. But it is by no means s a musician of the first rank. The nightingale is a performer of a very different and far higher order; yet though it is indeed a notable and admirable singer, it is an exaggeration to call it unequalled. In melody, and above all in that finer, higher melody where the chords vibrate with the touch of eternal sorrow, it cannot rank with such singers as the wood thrush and hermit thrush. The serene, ethereal beauty of the hermit's song, rising and falling through the still evening, under the archways of hoary mountain forests that

have endured from time everlasting; the golden, leisurely chiming of the wood thrush, sounding on June afternoons, stanza by stanza, through sun-flecked groves of tall hickories, oaks, and chestnuts; with these there is nothing in the nightingale's song to compare. But in volume and continuity, in tuneful, voluble, rapid outpouring and ardor, above all in skilful and intricate variation of theme, its song far surpasses that of either of the thrushes. In all these respects it is more just to compare it with the mocking-bird's, which, as a rule, likewise falls short precisely on those points where the songs of the two thrushes excel.

The mocking-bird is a singer that has suffered much in reputation from its powers of mimicry. On ordinary occasions, and especially in the daytime, it insists on playing the harlequin. But when free in its own favorite haunts at night in the love season it has a song, or rather songs, which are not only purely original, but are also more beautiful than any other bird music whatsoever. Once I listened to a mocking-bird singing the livelong spring night, under the full moon, in a magnolia tree; and I do not think I shall ever forget its song.

It was on the plantation of Major Campbell Brown, near Nashville, in the beautiful, fertile mid-Tennessee country. The mocking-birds were prime favorites on the place; and were given full scope for the development, not only of their bold friendliness towards mankind, but also of that marked individuality and originality of character in which they so far surpass every other bird as to become the most interesting of all feathered folk. One of the mockers, which lived in the hedge bordering the garden, was constantly engaged in an amusing feud with an honest old setter dog, the point of attack being the tip of the dog's tail. For some reason the bird seemed to regard any hoisting of the setter's tail as a challenge and insult. It would flutter near the dog as he walked; the old setter would become interested in something and raise his tail. The bird would promptly fly at it and peck the tip; whereupon down went the tail until in a couple of minutes the old fellow would forget himself, and the scene would be repeated. The dog usually bore the assaults with comic resignation; and the mocker easily avoided any momentary outburst of clumsy resentment.

On the evening in question the moon was full. My host kindly assigned me a room of which the windows opened on a great magnolia tree, where, I was told, a mocking-bird sang every night and all night long. I went to my room about ten. The moonlight was shining in through the open window, and the mocking-bird was already in the magnolia. The great tree was bathed in a flood of shining silver; I could see each twig, and mark every action of the singer, who was pouring forth such a rapture of ringing melody as I have never listened to before or since. Sometimes he would perch motionless for many minutes, his body quivering and thrilling with the outpour of music. Then he would drop softly from twig to twig, until the lowest limb was reached, when he would rise, fluttering and leaping through the branches, his song never ceasing for an instant, until he reached the summit of the tree and launched into the warm, scent-laden air, floating in spirals, with outspread wings, until, as if spent, he sank gently back into the tree and down through the branches, while his song rose into an ecstasy of ardor and passion. His voice rang like a clarionet, in rich, full tones, and his execution covered the widest possible compass; theme followed theme, a torrent of music, a swelling tide of harmony, in which scarcely any two bars were alike. I stayed till midnight listening to him; he was singing when I went to sleep; he was still singing when I woke a couple of hours later; he sang through the live-long night.

There are many singers beside the meadow lark and little skylark in the plains country; that brown and desolate land, once the home of the thronging buffalo, still haunted by the bands of the prong-buck, and roamed over in ever increasing numbers by the branded herds of the ranchman. In the brush of the riv-

er bottoms there are the thrasher and song sparrow; on the grassy uplands the lark finch, vesper sparrow, and lark bunting; and in the rough canyons the rock wren, with its ringing melody.

Yet in certain moods a man cares less for even the loveliest bird songs than for the wilder, harsher, stronger sounds of the wilderness; the guttural booming and clucking of the prairie fowl and the great sage fowl in spring; the honking of gangs of wild geese, as they fly in rapid wedges; the bark of an eagle, wheeling in the shadow of stormscarred cliffs; or the far-off clanging of many sand-hill cranes, soaring high overhead in circles which cross and recross at an incredible altitude. Wilder yet, and stranger, are the cries of the great four-footed beasts; the rhythmic pealing of a bull-elk's challenge; and that most sinister and mournful sound, ever fraught with foreboding of murder and rapine, the long-drawn baying of the gray wolf.

Indeed, save to the trained ear most mere bird songs are not very noticeable. The ordinary wilderness dweller, whether hunter or cowboy, scarcely heeds them; and in fact knows but little of the smaller birds. If a bird has some conspicuous peculiarity of look or habit he will notice its existence; but not otherwise. He knows a good deal about magpies, whiskey jacks, or water ousels; but nothing whatever concerning the thrushes, finches, and warblers.

It is the same with mammals. The prairie-dogs he cannot help noticing. With the big pack-rats also he is well acquainted; for they are handsome, with soft gray fur, large eyes, and bushy tails; and, moreover, no one can avoid remarking their extraordinary habit of carrying to their burrows everything bright, useless, and portable, from an empty cartridge case to a skinning knife. But he knows nothing of mice, shrews, pocket gophers, or weasels; and but little even of some larger mammals with very marked characteristics. Thus I have met but one or two plainsmen who knew anything of the curious plains ferret, that rather rare weasel-like animal, which plays the same part on the plains that the mink does by the edges of all

our streams and brooks, and the tree-loving sable in the cold northern forests. The ferret makes its home in burrows, and by preference goes abroad at dawn and dusk, but sometimes even at midday. It is as blood-thirsty as the mink itself, and its life is one long ramble for prey, gophers, prairie-dogs, sage rabbits, jack-rabbits, snakes, and every kind of ground bird furnishing its food. I have known one to fairly depopulate a prairie-dog town, it being the arch foe of these little rodents, because of its insatiable blood lust and its capacity to follow them into their burrows. Once I found the bloody body and broken eggs of a poor prairie-hen which a ferret had evidently surprised on her nest. Another time one of my men was eye-witness to a more remarkable instance of the little animal's blood-thirsty ferocity. He was riding the range, and being attracted by a slight commotion in a clump of grass, he turned his horse thither to look, and to his astonishment found an antelope fawn at the last gasp, but still feebly struggling, in the grasp of a ferret, which had throttled it and was sucking its blood with hideous greediness. He avenged the murdered innocent by a dexterous blow with the knotted end of his lariat.

That mighty bird of rapine, the war eagle, which on the great plains and among the Rockies supplants the bald-headed eagle of better-watered regions, is another dangerous foe of the young antelope. It is even said that under exceptional circumstances eagles will assail a full grown prong-horn; and a neighboring ranchman informs me that he was once an eye-witness to such an attack. It was a bleak day in the late winter, and he was riding home across a wide dreary plateau, when he saw two eagles worrying and pouncing on a prong-buck—seemingly a yearling. It made a gallant fight. The eagles hovered over it with spread wings, now and then swooping down, their talons outthrust, to strike at the head, or to try to settle on the loins. The antelope reared and struck with hoofs and horns like a goat; but its strength was failing rapidly, and doubtless it would have succumbed in the end had not the approach of the ranchman driven off. the marauders.

I have likewise heard stories of eagles attacking badgers, foxes, bob-cats, and coyotes; but I am inclined to think all such cases exceptional. I have never myself seen an eagle assail anything bigger than a fawn, lamb, kid, or jack-rabbit. It also swoops at geese, sage fowl, and prairie fowl. On one occasion while riding over the range I witnessed an attack on a jack-rabbit. The eagle was soaring overhead, and espied the jack while the latter was crouched motionless. Instantly the great bird rushed down through the humming air, with closed wings; checked itself when some forty yards above the jack, hovered for a moment, and again fell like a bolt. Away went long-ears, running as only a frightened jack can; and after him the eagle, not with the arrowy rush of its descent from high air, but with eager, hurried flapping. In a short time it had nearly overtaken the fugitive, when the latter dodged sharply to one side, and the eagle overshot it precisely as a grayhound would have done, stopping itself by a powerful, setting motion of the great pinions. Twice this manoeuvre was repeated; then the eagle made a quick rush, caught and overthrew the quarry before it could turn, and in another moment was sitting triumphant on the quivering body, the crooked talons driven deep into the soft, furry sides.

Once while hunting mountain sheep in the Bad Lands I killed an eagle on the wing with the rifle. I was walking beneath a cliff of gray clay, when the eagle sailed into view over the crest. As soon as he saw me he threw his wings aback, and for a moment before wheeling poised motionless, offering a nearly stationary target; so that my bullet grazed his shoulder, and down he came through the air, tumbling over and over. As he struck the ground he threw himself on his back, and fought against his death with the undaunted courage proper to his brave and cruel nature.

Indians greatly prize the feathers of this eagle. With them they make their striking and beautiful war bonnets, and bedeck the manes and tails of their spir-

ited war ponies. Every year the Grosventres and Mandans from the Big Missouri come to the neighborhood of my ranch to hunt. Though not good marksmen they kill many whitetail deer, driving the bottoms for them in bands, on horseback; and they catch many eagles. Sometimes they take these alive by exposing a bait near which a hole is dug, where one of them lies hidden for days, with Indian patience, until an eagle lights on the bait and is noosed.

Even eagles are far less dangerous enemies to antelope than are wolves and coyotes. These beasts are always prowling round the bands, to snap up the sick or unwary; and in spring they revel in carnage of the kids and fawns. They are not swift enough to overtake the grown animals by sheer speed; but they are superior in endurance, and especially in winter, often run them down in fair chase. A prong-buck is a plucky little beast, and when cornered it often makes a gallant, though not a very effectual, fight.

CHAPTER V. HUNTING THE PRONG-BUCK; FROST, FIRE, AND THIRST. better than the bigger game; on the whole even better than the blacktail; but their numbers have been wofully thinned, and in many places they have been completely exterminated. The most exciting method of chasing them is on horseback with grayhounds; but they are usually killed with the rifle. Owing to the open nature of the ground they frequent the shots must generally be taken at long range; hence this kind of hunting is preeminently that needing judgment of distance and skill in the use of the long-range rifle at stationary objects. On the other hand the antelope are easily seen, making no effort to escape observation, as deer do, and are so curious that in very wild districts to this day they can sometimes be tolled within rifle shot by the judicious waving of a red flag. In consequence, a good many very long, but tempting, shots can be obtained. More cartridges are used, relatively to the amount of game killed, on antelope, than in any other hunting. with all other American game man is a worse foe to the prong-horns than all their brute en-

emies combined. They hold their own much

Often I have killed prong-bucks while riding between the outlying line camps, which are usually stationed a dozen miles or so back from the river, where the Bad Lands melt into the prairie. In continually trying long shots, of course one occasionally makes a remarkable hit. Once I remember while riding down a broad, shallow coulie with two of my cow-hands—Seawell and Dow, both keen hunters and among the staunchest friends I have ever had,—rousing a band of antelope which stood irresolute at about a hundred yards until I killed one. Then they dashed off, and I missed one shot, but with my next, to my own utter astonishment, killed the last of the band, a big buck, just as he topped a rise four hundred yards away. To offset such shots I have occasionally made an unaccountable miss. Once I was hunting with the same two men, on a rainy day, when we came on a bunch of antelope some seventy yards off, lying down on the side of a coulie, to escape the storm. They huddled together a moment to gaze, and, with stiffened fingers I took a shot, my yellow oilskin slicker flapping around me in the wind and rain. Down went one buck, and away went the others. One of my men walked up to the fallen beast, bent over it, and then asked, " Where did you aim?" Not reassured by the question, I answered doubtfully, "Behind the shoulder"; whereat he remarked drily, " Well, you hit it in the eye!" I never did know whether I killed the antelope I aimed at or another. Yet that same day I killed three more bucks at decidedly long shots; at the time we lacked meat at the ranch, and were out to make a good killing.

Besides their brute and human foes, the prong-horn must also fear the elements, and especially the snows of winter. On the northern plains the cold weather is of polar severity, and turns the green, grassy prairies of midsummer into ironbound wastes. The blizzards whirl and sweep across them with a shrieking fury which few living things may face. The snow is like fine ice dust, and the white waves glide across the grass with a stealthy, crawling motion which has in it something sinister and cruel. Accordingly, as the bright fall weather passes, and the dreary winter draws nigh, when the days shorten, and the nights seem interminable, and gray storms lower above the gray horizon, the antelope gather in bands and seek sheltered places, where they may abide through the winter-time of famine and cold and deep snow. Some of these bands travel for many hundred miles, going and returning over the same routes, swimming rivers, crossing prairies, and threading their way through steep defiles. Such bands make their winter home in places like the Black Hills, or similar mountainous regions, where the shelter and feed are good, and where in consequence antelope have wintered in countless thousands for untold generations. Other bands do not travel for any very great distance, but seek some sheltered grassy table-land in the Bad Lands, or some well-shielded valley, where their instinct and experience teach them that the snow does not lie deep in winter. Once having chosen such a place they stand much persecution before leaving it.

One December, an old hunter whom I knew told me that such a band was wintering a few miles from a camp where two line-riders of the W Bar brand were stationed; and I made up my mind to ride thither and kill a couple. The line camp was twenty miles from my ranch; the shack in which the old hunter lived was midway between, and I had to stop there to find out the exact lay of the land.

At dawn, before our early breakfast, I saddled a tough, shaggy sorrel horse; hastening in-doors as soon as the job was over, to warm my numbed fingers. After breakfast I started, muffled in my wolf-skin coat, with beaver-fur cap, gloves, and shaps, and great felt over-shoes. The windless air was bitter cold, the thermometer showing well below zero. Snow lay on the ground, leaving bare patches here and there, but drifted deep in the hollows. Under the steel-

blue heavens the atmosphere had a peculiar glint as if filled with myriads of tiny crystals. As I crossed the frozen river, immediately in front of the ranch house, the strangely carved tops of the bluffs were reddening palely in the winter sunrise. Prairie fowl were perched in the bare cottonwoods along the river brink, showing large in the leafless branches; they called and clucked to one another.

Where the ground was level and the snow not too deep I loped, and before noon I reached the sheltered coulie where, with long poles and bark, the hunter had built his tepee—wigwam, as eastern woodsmen would have called it. It stood in a loose grove of elms and box-alders; from the branches of the nearest trees hung saddles of frozen venison. The smoke rising from the funnel-shaped top of the tepee showed that there was more fire than usual within; it is easy to keep a good tepee warm, though it is so smoky that no one therein can stand upright. As I drew rein the skin door was pushed aside, and the hard old face and dried, battered body of the hunter appeared. He greeted me with a surly nod. and a brief request to "light and hev somethin' to eat"—the invariable proffer of hospitality on the plains. He wore a greasy buckskin shirt or tunic, and an odd cap of badger skin, from beneath which strayed his tangled hair; age, rheumatism, and the many accidents and incredible fatigue, hardship, and exposure of his past life had crippled him, yet he still possessed great power of endurance, and in his seamed weather-scarred face his eyes burned fierce and piercing as a hawk's. Ever since early manhood he had wandered over the plains, hunting and trapping; he had waged savage private war against half the Indian tribes of the north; and he had wedded wives in each of the tribes of the other half. A few years before this time the great buffalo herds had vanished, and the once swarming beaver had shared the same fate; the innumerable horses and horned stock of the cattlemen, and the daring rough riders of the ranches, had supplanted alike the game and the red and white wander-

ers who had followed it with such fierce rivalry. When the change took place the old fellow, with failing bodily powers, found his life-work over. He had little taste for the career of the desperado, horse-thief, highwayman, and man-killer, which not a few of the old buffalo hunters adopted when their legitimate occupation was gone; he scorned still more the life of vicious and idle semi-criminality led by others of his former companions who were of weaker mould. Yet he could not do regular work. His existence had been one of excitement, adventure, and restless roaming, when it was not passed in lazy ease; his times of toil and peril varied by fits of brutal revelry. He had no kin, no ties of any kind. He would accept no help, for his wants were very few, and he was utterly self-reliant. He got meat, clothing, and bedding from the antelope and deer he killed; the spare hides and venison he bartered for what little else he needed. So he built him his tepee in one of the most secluded parts of the Bad. Lands, where he led the life of a solitary hunter, awaiting in grim loneliness the death which he knew to be near at hand.

I unsaddled and picketed my horse, and followed the old hunter into his smoky tepee; sat down on the pile of worn buffalo robes which formed his bedding, and waited in silence while he fried some deer meat, and boiled some coffee—he was out of flour. As I ate, he gradually unbent and talked quite freely, and before I left he told me exactly where to find the band, which he assured me was located for the winter, and would not leave unless much harried.

After a couple of hours' rest I again started, and pushed out to the end of the Bad Lands. Here, as there had been no wind, I knew I should find in the snow the tracks of one of the riders from the line camp, whose beat lay along the edge of the prairie for some eight miles, until it met the beat of a rider from the line camp next above. As nightfall came on it grew even colder; long icicles hung from the lips of my horse; and I shivered slightly in my fur coat. I had reckoned the distance ill, and it was dusk when I struck the trail; but my horse at once turned along it of his own accord and began to lope. Half an hour later I saw through the dark what looked like a spark on the side of a hill. Toward this my horse turned; and in another moment a whinneying from in front showed I was near the camp. The light was shining through a small window, the camp itself being a dugout with a log roof and front—a kind of frontier building always warm in winter. After turning my horse into the rough log stable with the horses of the two cowboys, I joined the latter at supper inside the dugout; being received of course with hearty cordiality. After the intense cold outside the warmth within was almost oppressive, for the fire was roaring in the big stone fireplace. The bunks were broad; my two friends turned into one, and I was given the other, with plenty of bedding; so that my sleep was sound.

We had breakfasted and saddled our horses and were off by dawn next morning. My companions, muffled in furs, started in opposite directions to ride their lonely beats, while I steered for my hunting-ground. It was a lowering and gloomy day; at sunrise pale, lurid sundogs hung in the glimmering mist; gusts of wind moaned through the ravines.

At last I reached a row of bleak hills, and from a ridge looked cautiously down on the chain of plateaus, where I had been told I should see the antelope. Sure enough, there they were, to the number of several hundred, scattered over the level snow-streaked surface of the nearest and largest plateau, greedily cropping the thick, short grass. Leaving my horse tied in a hollow I speedily stalked up a coulie to within a hundred yards of the nearest band and killed a good buck. Instantly all the antelope in sight ran together into a thick mass and raced away from me, until they went over the opposite edge of the plateau; but almost as soon as they did so they were stopped by deep drifts of powdered snow, and came back to the summit of the table-land. They then circled round the edge at a gallop, and finally broke madly by me, jostling one another in their frantic haste and crossed

by a small ridge into the next plateau beyond; as they went by I shot a yearling.

I now had all the venison I wished, and would shoot no more, but I was curious to see how the antelope would act, and so walked after them. They ran about half a mile, and then the whole herd, of several hundred individuals, wheeled into line fronting me, like so many cavalry, and stood motionless, the white and brown bands on their necks looking like the facings on a uniform. As I walked near they again broke and rushed to the end of the valley. Evidently they feared to leave the flats for the broken country beyond, where the rugged hills were riven by gorges, in some of which snow lay deep even thus early in the season. Accordingly, after galloping a couple of times round the valley, they once more broke by me, at short range, and tore back along the plateaus to that on which I had first found them. Their evident and extreme reluctance to venture into the broken country round about made me readily understand the tales I had heard of game butchers killing over a hundred individuals at a time out of a herd so situated.

I walked back to my game, dressed it, and lashed the saddles and hams behind me on my horse; I had chosen old Sorrel Joe for the trip because he was strong, tough, and quiet. Then I started for the ranch, keeping to the prairie as long as I could, because there the going was easier; sometimes I rode, sometimes I ran on foot leading Sorrel Joe.

Late in the afternoon, as I rode over a roll in the prairie I saw ahead of me a sight very unusual at that season; a small emigrant train going westward. There were three white-topped prairie schooners, containing the household goods, the tow-headed children, and the hardfaced, bony women; the tired horses were straining wearily in the traces; the bearded, moody men walked alongside. They had been belated by sickness, and the others of their company had gone ahead to take up claims along the Yellowstone; now they themselves were pushing forward in order to reach the holdings of their friends before the

first deep snows stopped all travel. They had no time to halt; for there were still two or three miles to go that evening before they could find a sheltered resting-place with fuel, grass, and water. A little while after passing them I turned in the saddle and looked back. The lonely little train stood out sharply on the sky-line, the wagons looming black against the cold red west as they toiled steadily onward across the snowy plain.

Night soon fell; but I cared little, for I was on ground I knew. The old horse threaded his way at a lope along the familiar game trails and cattle paths; in a couple of hours I caught the gleam from the firelit windows of the ranch house. No man who, for his good-fortune, has at times in his life endured toil and hardship, ever fails to appreciate the strong elemental pleasures of rest after labor, food after hunger, warmth and shelter after bitter cold.

So much for the winter hunting. But in the fall, when the grass is dry as tinder, the antelope hunter, like other plainsmen, must sometimes face fire instead of frost. Fire is one of the most dreaded enemies of the ranchmen on the cattle ranges; and fighting a big prairie fire is a work of extraordinary labor, and sometimes of danger. The line of flame, especially when seen at night, undulating like a serpent, is very beautiful; though it lacks the terror and grandeur of the great forest fires.

One October, Ferguson and I, with one of the cowhands, and a friend from the East, took the wagon for an antelope hunt in the broken country between the Little Missouri and the Beaver. The cowboy drove the wagon to a small spring, near some buttes which are well distinguished by a number of fossil tree-stumps; while the rest of us, who were mounted on good horses, made a circle after antelope. We found none, and rode on to camp, reaching it about the middle of the afternoon. We had noticed several columns of smoke in the southeast, showing that prairie fires were under way; but we thought that they were too far off to endanger our camp, and accordingly unsaddled our horses and sat down to a dinner of bread, beans, and coffee. Before we were through the smoke began to pour over a ridge a mile distant in such quantities that we ran thither with our slickers, hoping to find some stretch of broken ground where the grass was sparse, and where we could fight the fire with effect. Our hopes were vain. Before we reached the ridge the fire came over its crest, and ran down in a long tongue between two scoria buttes. Here the grass was quite short and thin, and we did our best to beat out the flames; but they gradually gained on us, and as they reached the thicker grass lower down the slope, they began to roar and dart forward in a way that bade us pay heed to our own safety. Finally they reached a winding line of brushwood in the bottom of the coulie; and as this burst into a leaping blaze we saw it was high time to look to the safety of our camp, and ran back to it at top speed. Ferguson, who had been foremost in fighting the fire, was already scorched and blackened.

We were camped on the wagon trail which leads along the divide almost due south to Sentinel Butte. The line of fire was fanned by a southeasterly breeze, and was therefore advancing diagonally to the divide. If we could drive the wagon southward on the trail in time to get it past the fire before the latter reached the divide, we would be to windward of the flames, and therefore in safety. Accordingly, while the others were hastily harnessing the team, and tossing the bedding and provisions into the wagon, I threw the saddle on my horse, and galloped down the trail, to see if there was yet time to adopt this expedient. I soon found that there was not. Half a mile from camp the trail dipped into a deep coulie, where fair-sized trees and dense undergrowth made a long winding row of brush and timber. The trail led right under. the trees at the upper end of this coulie. As I galloped by I saw that the fire had struck the trees a quarter of a mile below me; in the dried timber it instantly sprang aloft like a giant, and roared in a thunderous monotone as it swept up the coulie. I galloped to the hill ridge ahead, saw that the fire line had already reached the divide, and

turned my horse sharp on his haunches. As I again passed under the trees, the fire, running like a racehorse in the brush, had reached the road; its breath was hot in my face; tongues of quivering flame leaped over my head and kindled the grass on the hillside fifty yards away.

When I got back to camp Ferguson had taken measures for the safety of the wagon. He had moved it across the coulie, which at this point had a wet bottom, making a bar to the progress of the flames until they had time to work across lower down. Meanwhile we fought to keep the fire from entering a well-grassed space on the hither side of the coulie, between it and a row of scoria buttes. Favored by a streak of clay ground, where the grass was sparse, we succeeded in beating out the flame as it reached this clay streak, and again beating it out when it ran round the buttes and began to back up towards us against the wind. Then we recrossed the coulie with the wagon, before the fire swept up the farther side; and so, when the flames passed by, they left us camped on a green oasis in the midst of a charred, smoking desert. We thus saved some good grazing for our horses.

But our fight with the fire had only begun. No stockman will see a fire waste the range and destroy the winter feed of the stock without spending every ounce of his strength in the effort to put a stop to its ravages—even when, as in our case, the force of men and horses at hand is so small as to offer only the very slenderest hope of success.

We set about the task in the way customary in the cattle country. It is impossible for any but a very large force to make head against a prairie fire while there is any wind; but the wind usually fails after nightfall, and accordingly the main fight is generally waged during the hours of darkness.

Before dark we drove to camp and shot a stray steer, and then split its carcass in two lengthwise with an axe. After sundown the wind lulled; and we started towards the line of fire, which was working across a row of broken grassy hills, three quarters of a mile dis-

tant. Two of us were on horseback, dragging a half carcass, bloody side down, by means of ropes leading from our saddle-horns to the fore and hind legs; the other two followed on foot with slickers and wet saddle blankets. There was a reddish glow in the night air, and the waving, bending lines of flame showed in great bright curves against the hillsides ahead of us.

When we reached them, we found the fire burning in a long, continuous line. It was not making rapid headway, for the air was still, and the flames stood upright, two or three feet high. Lengthening the ropes, one of us spurred his horse across the fire line and then, wheeling, we dragged the carcass along it; one horseman being on the burnt ground, and one on the unburnt grass, while the body of the steer lay lengthwise across the line. The weight and the blood smothered the fire as we twitched the carcass over the burning grass; and the two men following behind with their blankets and slickers readily beating out any isolated tufts of flame.

The fire made the horses wild, and it was not always easy to manage both them and the ropes, so as to keep the carcass true on the line. Sometimes there would be a slight puff of wind, and then the man on the grass side of the line ran the risk of a scorching. We were blackened with smoke, and the taut ropes hurt our thighs; while at times the plunging horses tried to buck or bolt. It was worse when we came to some deep gully or ravine, breaking the line of fire. Into this we of course had to plunge, so as to get across to the fire on the other side. After the glare of the flame the blackness of the ravine was Stygian; we could see nothing, and simply spurred our horses into it anywhere, taking our chances. Down we would go, stumbling, sliding, and pitching, over cut banks and into holes and bushes, while the carcass bounded behind, now catching on a stump, and now fetching loose with a "pluck" that brought it full on the horses' haunches, driving them nearly crazy with fright. The pull up the opposite bank was, if anything, worse.

By midnight the half carcass was

worn through; but we had stifled the fire in the comparatively level country to the eastwards. Back we went to camp, drank huge draughts of muddy water, devoured roast ox-ribs, and dragged out the other half carcass to fight the fire on the west. But after hours of wearing labor we found ourselves altogether baffled by the exceeding roughness of the ground. There was some little risk to us who were on horseback, dragging the carcass; we had to feel our way along knife-like ridges in the dark, one ahead and the other behind, while the steer dangled over the precipice on one side; and in going down the buttes and into the canyons only by extreme care could we avoid getting tangled in the ropes and rolling down in a heap. Moreover the fire was in such rough places that the carcass could not be twitched fairly over it, and so we could not put it out. Before dawn we were obliged to abandon our fruitless efforts and seek camp, stiffened and weary. From a hill we looked back through the pitchy night at the fire we had failed to conquer. It had been broken into many lines by the roughness of the chasm-strewn and hilly country. Of these lines of flame some were in advance, some behind, some rushing forward in full blast and fury, some standing still; here and there one wheeling towards a flank, or burning in a semicircle, round an isolated hill. Some of the lines were flickering out; gaps were showing in others. In the darkness it looked like the rush of a mighty army, bearing triumphantly onwards, in spite of a resistance so stubborn as to break its formation into many fragments and cause each one of them to wage its own battle for victory or defeat.

On the wide plains where the prong-buck dwells the hunter must sometimes face thirst, as well as fire and frost. The only time I ever really suffered from thirst was while hunting prong-buck.

It was late in the summer. I was with the ranch wagon on the way to join a round-up, and as we were out of meat I started for a day's hunt. Before leaving in the morning I helped to haul the wagon across the river. It was fortunate I stayed, as it turned out. There was no regular ford where we made the crossing; we anticipated no trouble, as the water was very low, the season being dry. However, we struck a quicksand, in which the wagon settled, while the frightened horses floundered helplessly. All the riders at once got their ropes on the wagon, and hauling from the saddle, finally pulled it through. This took time; and it was ten o'clock when I rode away from the river, at which my horse and I had just drunk—our last drink for over twenty-four hours as it turned out.

After two or three hours' ride, up winding coulies, and through the scorched desolation of patches of Bad Lands, I reached the rolling prairie. The heat and drought had long burned the short grass dull brown; the bottoms of what had been pools were covered with hard, dry, cracked earth. The day was cloudless, and the heat oppressive. There were many antelope, but I got only one shot, breaking a buck's leg; and though I followed it for a couple of hours I could not overtake it. By this time it was late in the afternoon, and I was far away from the river; so I pushed for a creek, in the bed of which I had always found pools of water, especially towards the head, as is usual with plains watercourses. To my chagrin, however, they all proved to be dry; and though I rode up the creek bed toward the head, carefully searching for any sign of water, night closed on me before I found any. For two or three hours I stumbled on, leading my horse, in my fruitless search; then a tumble over a cut bank in the dark warned me that I might as well stay where I was for the rest of the warm night. Accordingly I unsaddled the horse, and tied him to a sage brush; after awhile he began to feed on the dewy grass. At first I was too thirsty to sleep. Finally I fell into slumber, and when I awoke at dawn I felt no thirst. For an hour or two more I continued my search for water in the creek bed; then abandoned it and rode straight for the river. By the time we reached it my thirst had come back with redoubled force, my mouth was parched, and the horse was in quite as bad a plight; we rushed down to the brink, and it seemed as if we could neither of us ever drink our fill of the tepid, rather muddy water. Of course this experience was merely unpleasant; thirst is not a source of real danger in the plains country proper, whereas in the hideous deserts that extend from southern Idaho through Utah and Nevada to Arizona, it ever menaces with death the hunter and explorer.

In the plains the weather is apt to be in extremes; the heat is tropical, the cold arctic, and the droughts are relieved by furious floods. These are generally most severe and lasting in the spring, after the melting of the snow; and fierce local freshets follow the occasional cloudbursts. The large rivers then become wholly impassable, and even the smaller are formidable obstacles. It is not easy to get cattle across a swollen stream, where the current runs like a turbid mill-race over the bed of shifting quicksand. Once five of us took a thousand head of trail steers across the Little Missouri when the river was up, and it was no light task. The muddy current was boiling past the banks, covered with driftwood and foul yellow froth, and the frightened cattle shrank from entering it. At last, by hard riding, with much loud shouting and swinging of ropes, we got the leaders in, and the whole herd followed. After them we went in our turn, the horses swimming at one moment, and the next staggering and floundering through the quicksand. I was riding my pet cutting horse, Muley, which has the provoking habit of making great bounds where the water is just not deep enough for swimming; once he almost unseated me. Some of the cattle were caught by the currents and rolled over and over; most of these we were able, with the help of our ropes, to put on their feet again; only one was drowned, or rather choked in a quicksand. Many swam down stream, and in consequence struck a difficult landing, where the river ran under a cut bank; these we had to haul out with our ropes. Both men and horses were well tired by the time the whole herd was across.

Although I have often had a horse

down in quicksand, or in crossing a swollen river, and have had to work hard to save him, I have never myself lost one under such circumstances. Yet once I saw the horse of one of my men drown under him directly in front of the ranch house, while he was trying to cross the river. This was in early spring, soon after the ice had broken.

When making long wagon trips over the great plains, antelope often offer the only source of meat supply, save for occasional water fowl, sage fowl, and prairie fowl— the sharp-tailed prairie fowl, be it understood. This is the characteristic grouse of the cattle country; the true prairie fowl is a bird of the farming land farther east.

Towards the end of the summer of '92 I found it necessary to travel from my ranch to the Black Hills, some two hundred miles south. The ranch wagon went with me, driven by an all-round plainsman, a man of iron nerves and varied past, the sheriff of our county. He was an old friend of mine; at one time I had served as deputy-sheriff for the northern end of the county. In the wagon we carried our food and camp kit, and our three rolls of bedding, each wrapped in a thick, nearly waterproof canvas sheet; we had a tent, but we never needed it. The load being light, the wagon was drawn by but a span of horses, a pair of wild runaways, tough, and good travellers. My foreman and I rode beside the wagon on our wiry, unkempt, unshod cattle-ponies. They carried us all day at a rack, pace, single-foot or slow lope, varied by rapid galloping when we made long circles after game; the trot, the favorite gait with eastern park-riders, is disliked by all peoples who have to do much of their life-work in the saddle.

The first day's ride was not attractive. The heat was intense and the dust stifling, as we had to drive some loose horses for the first few miles, and afterwards to ride up and down the sandy river bed, where the cattle had gathered, to look over some young steers we had put on the range the preceding spring. When we did camp it was by a pool of stagnant water, in a creek bottom, and

the mosquitoes were a torment. Nevertheless, as evening fell, it was pleasant to climb a little knoll nearby and gaze at the rows of strangely colored buttes, grass-clad, or of bare earth and scoria, their soft reds and purples showing as through a haze, and their irregular outlines gradually losing their sharpness in the fading twilight.

Next morning the weather changed, growing cooler, and we left the tangle of ravines and Bad Lands, striking out across the vast sea-like prairies. Hour after hour, under the bright sun, the wagon drew slowly ahead, over the immense rolling stretches of short grass, dipping down each long slope until it reached the dry, imperfectly outlined creek bed at the bottom,—wholly devoid of water and without so much as a shrub of wood,—and then ascending the gentle rise on the other side until at last it topped the broad divide, or watershed, beyond which lay the shallow winding coulies of another creek system. From each rise of ground we looked far and wide over the sunlit prairie, with its interminable undulations. The sicklebill curlews which rn spring, while breeding, hover above the travelling horseman with ceaseless clamor, had for the most part gone southward. We saw only one small party of half a dozen birds; they paid little heed to us, but piped to one another, making short flights, and on alighting stood erect, first spreading and then folding and setting their wings with a slow, graceful motion. Little horned larks continually ran along the ruts of the faint wagon track, just ahead of the team, and twittered plaintively as they rose, while flocks of longspurs swept hither and thither, in fitful, irregular flight.

My foreman and I usually rode far off to one side of the wagon, looking out for antelope. Of these we at first saw few, but they grew more plentiful as we journeyed onward, approaching a big scantily wooded creek, where I had found the prong-horn abundant in previous seasons. They were very wary and watchful whether going singly or in small parties, and the lay of the land made it exceedingly difficult to get within range.

The last time I had hunted in this neighborhood was in the fall, at the height of the rutting season. Prong-bucks, even more than other game, seem fairly maddened by erotic excitement. At the time of my former hunt they were in ceaseless motion; each master buck being incessantly occupied in herding his harem, and fighting would-be rivals, while single bucks chased single does as greyhounds chase hares, or else, if no does were in sight, from sheer excitement ran to and fro as if crazy, racing at full speed in one direction, then halting, wheeling, and tearing back again just as hard as they could go.

At this time, however, the rut was still some weeks off, and all the bucks had to do was to feed and keep a lookout for enemies. Try my best, I could not get within less than four or five hundred yards, and though I took a number of shots at these, or at even longer, distances, I missed. If a man is out merely for a day's hunt, and has all the time he wishes, he will not scare the game and waste cartridges by shooting at such long ranges, preferring to spend half a day or more in patient waiting and careful stalking; but if he is travelling, and is therefore cramped for time, he must take his chances, even at the cost of burning a good deal of powder.

I was finally helped to success by a characteristic freak of the game I was following. No other animals are as keen-sighted, or are normally as wary as prong-horns; but no others are so whimsical and odd in their behavior at times, or so subject to fits of the most stupid curiosity and panic. Late in the afternoon, on topping a rise I saw two good bucks racing off about three hundred yards to one side; I sprang to the ground, and fired three shots at them in vain, as they ran like quarter-horses until they disappeared over a slight swell. In a minute, however, back they came, suddenly appearing over the crest of the same swell, immediately in front of me, and, as I afterwards found by pacing, some three hundred and thirty yards away. They stood side by side facing me, and remained motionless, unheeding the crack of the Winchester, I aimed at the right-hand one, but a front shot of the kind, at such a distance, is rather difficult, and it was not until I fired for the fourth time that he sank back out of sight. I could not tell whether I had killed him, and took two shots at his mate, as the latter went off, but without effect. Running forward, I found the first one dead, the bullet having gone through him lengthwise; the other did not seem satisfied even yet, and kept hanging round in the distance for some minutes, looking at us.

I had thus bagged one prong-buck, as the net outcome of the expenditure of fourteen cartridges. This was certainly not good shooting; but neither was it as bad as it would seem to the man inexperienced in antelope hunting. When fresh meat is urgently needed, and when time is too short, the hunter who is after antelope in an open flattish country must risk many long shots. In no other kind of hunting is there so much long-distance shooting, or so many shots fired for every head of game bagged.

Throwing the buck into the wagon we continued our journey across the prairie, no longer following any road, and before sunset jolted down towards the big creek for which we had been heading. There were many water-holes therein, and timber of considerable size; box alder and ash grew here and there in clumps and fringes, beside the serpentine curves of the nearly dry torrent bed, the growth being thickest under the shelter of the occasional low bluffs. We drove down to a heavily grassed bottom, near a deep, narrow pool, with, at one end, that rarest of luxuries in the plains country, a bubbling spring of pure, cold water. With plenty of wood, delicious water, ample feed for the horses, and fresh meat we had every comfort and luxury incident to camp life in good weather. The bedding was tossed out on a smooth spot beside the wagon; the horses were watered and tethered to picket pins where the feed was best; water was fetched from the spring; a deep hole was dug for the fire, and the grass roundabout carefully burned off; and in a few moments the bread was baking in the Dutch oven, the potatoes were boil-

ing, antelope steaks were sizzling in the frying-pan, and the kettle was ready for the tea. After supper, eaten with the relish known well to every hard-working and successful hunter, we sat for half an hour or so round the fire, and then turned in under the blankets, pulled the tarpaulins over us, and listened drowsily to the wailing of the coyotes until we fell sound asleep.

We determined to stay in this camp all day, so as to try and kill another prong-buck, as we would soon be past the good hunting grounds. I did not have to go far for my game next morning, for soon after breakfast, while sitting on my canvas bag cleaning my rifle, the sheriff suddenly called to me that a bunch of antelope were coming towards us. Sure enough there they were, four in number, rather over half a mile off, on the first bench of the prairie, two or three hundred yards back from the creek, leisurely feeding in our direction. In a minute or two they were out of sight, and I instantly ran along the creek towards them for a quarter of a mile, and then crawled up a short shallow coulie, close to the head of which they seemed likely to pass. When nearly at the end I cautiously raised my hatless head, peered through some straggling weeds, and at once saw the horns of the buck. He was a big fellow, about a hundred and twenty yards off; the others, a doe and two kids, were in front. As I lifted myself on my elbows he halted and turned his raised head towards me; the sunlight shone bright on his supple, vigorous body with its markings of sharply contrasted brown and white. I pulled trigger, and away he went; but I could see that his race was nearly run, and he fell after going a few hundred yards.

Soon after this a wind storm blew up so violent that we could hardly face it. In the late afternoon it died away, and I again walked out to hunt, but saw only does and kids, at which I would not shoot. As the sun set, leaving bars of amber and pale red in the western sky, the air became absolutely calm. In the waning evening the low, far-off ridges were touched with a violet light; then

the hues grew sombre, and still darkness fell on the lonely prairie.

Next morning we drove to the river, and kept near it for several days, most of the time following the traoks made by the heavy wagons accompanying the trail herds —this being one of the regular routes followed by the great throng of slow-moving cattle yearly driven from the south. At other times we made our own road. Twice or thrice we passed ranch houses; the men being absent on the round-up they were shut, save one which was inhabited by two or three lean Texan cow-punchers, with sun-burned faces and reckless eyes, who had come up with a trail herd from the Cherokee strip. Once, near the old Sioux crossing, where the Dakota war bands used to ford the river on their forays against the Crows and the settlers along the Yellowstone, we met a large horse herd. The tough, shabby, tired-looking animals, one or two of which were loaded with bedding and a scanty supply of food, were driven by three travel-worn, hardfaced men, with broad hats, shaps, and long pistols in their belts. They had brought the herd over plain and mountain pass all the way from far distant Oregon.

It was a wild, rough country, bare of trees save for a fringe of cottonwoods along the river, and occasional clumps of cedar on the jagged, brown buttes; as we went farther the hills turned the color of chalk, and were covered with a growth of pine. We came upon acres of sunflowers as we journeyed southward; they are not as tall as they are in the rich bottom lands of Kansas, where the splendid blossoms, on their strong stalks, stand as high as the head of a man on horseback.

Though there were many cattle here, big game was scarce. However, I killed plenty of prairie chickens and sage hens for the pot; and as the sage hens were still feeding largely on crickets and grasshoppers, and not exclusively on sage, they were just as good eating as the prairie chickens. I used the rifle, cutting off their heads or necks, and, as they had to be shot on the ground, and often while in motion, or else while some distance away, it was more difficult than shooting off the heads of grouse in the mountains, where the birds sit motionless in trees. The head is a small mark, while to hit the body is usually to spoil the bird; so I found that I averaged three or four cartridges for every head neatly taken off, the remaining shots representing spoiled birds and misses.

For the last sixty or seventy miles of our trip we left the river and struck off across a great, desolate gumbo prairie. There was no game, no wood for fuel, and the rare water-holes were far apart, so that we were glad when, as we toiled across the monotonous succession of long, swelling ridges, the dim, cloud-like mass, looming vague and purple on the rim of the horizon ahead of us, gradually darkened and hardened into the bold outline of the Black Hills.

AMONG THE HIGH HILLS J THE BIGHORN OR MOUNTAINSHEEP. DURING the summer of 1886 I hunted chiefly to keep the ranch in meat. It was a very pleasant summer; although it was followed by the worst winter we ever witnessed on the plains. I was much at the ranch, where I had a good deal of writing to do; but every week or two I left, to ride among the line camps, or spend a few days on any round-up which happened to be in the neighborhood.

These days of vigorous work among the cattle were themselves full of pleasure. At dawn we were in the saddle, the morning air cool in our faces; the red sunrise saw us loping across the grassy reaches of prairie land, or climbing in single file among the rugged buttes. All the forenoon we spent riding the long circle with the cowpunchers of the round-up; in the afternoon we worked the herd, cutting the cattle, with much breakneck galloping and dextrous halting and wheeling. Then came the excitement and hard labor of roping, throwing, and branding the wild and vigorous range calves; in a corral, if one was handy, otherwise in a ring of horse-men. Soon after nightfall we lay down, in a log hut or tent, if at a line camp; under the open sky, if with the round-up wagon.

After ten days or so of such work, in which every man had to do his full share—for laggards and idlers, no matter who, get no mercy in the real and healthy democracy of the round-up—I would go back to the ranch to turn to my books with added zest for a fortnight. Yet even during these weeks at the ranch there was some out-door work; for I was breaking two or three colts. I took my time, breaking them gradually and gently, not, after the usual cowboy fashion, in a hurry, by sheer main strength and rough riding, with the attendant danger to the limbs of the man and very probable ruin to the manners of the horse. We rose early; each morning I stood on the low-roofed verandah, looking out under the line of murmuring, glossy-leaved cottonwoods, across the shallow river, to see the sun flame above the line of bluffs opposite. In the evening I strolled off for an hour or two's walk, rifle in hand. The roomy, homelike ranch house, with its log walls, shingled roof, and big chimneys and fireplaces, stands in a glade, in the midst of the thick forest, which covers half the bottom; behind rises, bare and steep, the wall of peaks, ridges, and table-lands.

During the summer in question, I once or twice shot a whitetail buck right on this large bottom; once or twice I killed a blacktail in the hills behind, not a mile from the ranch house. Several times I killed and brought in prong-bucks, rising before dawn, and riding off on a good horse for an all day's hunt in the rolling prairie country twelve or fifteen miles away. Occasionally I took the wagon and one of the men, driving to some good hunting ground and spending a night or two; usually returning with two or three prong-bucks, and once with an elk—but this was later in the fall. Not infrequently I went away by myself on horseback for a couple of days, when all the men were on the round-up, and when I wished to hunt thoroughly some country quite a distance from the ranch. I made one such hunt in late August, because I happened to hear that a small bunch of mountain sheep were haunting a tract of very bro-

ken ground, with high hills, about fifteen miles away.

I left the ranch early in the morning, riding my favorite hunting horse, old Manitou. The blanket and oilskin slicker were rolled and strapped behind the saddle; for provisions I carried salt, a small bag of hard tack, and a little tea and sugar, with a metal cup in which to boil my water. The rifle and a score of cartridges in my woven belt completed my outfit. On my journey I shot two prairie chickens from a covey in the bottom of a brush coulie.

I rode more than six hours before reaching a good spot to camp. At first my route lay across grassy plateaus, and along smooth, wooded coulies; but after a few miles the ground became very rugged and difficult. At last I got into the heart of the Bad Lands proper, where the hard, wrinkled earth was torn into shapes as sullen and grotesque as those of dreamland. The hills rose high, their barren flanks carved and channelled, their tops mere needles and knife crests. Bands of black, red, and purple varied the gray and yellow-brown of their sides; the tufts of scanty vegetation were dull green. Sometimes I rode my horse at the bottom of narrow washouts, between straight walls of clay, but a few feet apart; sometimes I had to lead him as he scrambled up, down, and across the sheer faces of the buttes. The glare from the bare clay walls dazzled the eye; the air was burning under the hot August sun. I saw nothing living except the rattlesnakes, of which there were very many.

At last, in the midst of this devil's wilderness, I came on a lovely valley. A spring trickled out of a cedar canyon, and below this spring the narrow, deep ravine was green with luscious grass and was smooth for some hundred of yards. Here I unsaddled, and turned old Manitou loose to drink and feed at his leisure. At the edge of the dark cedar wood I cleared a spot for my bed, and drew a few dead sticks for the fire. Then I lay down and watched drowsily until the afternoon shadows filled the wild and beautiful gorge in which I was camped. This happened early, for the valley was very narrow and the hills on either hand were steep and high.

Springing to my feet, I climbed the nearest ridge, and then made my way, by hard clambering, from peak to peak and from crest to crest, sometimes crossing and sometimes skirting the deep washouts and canyons. When possible I avoided appearing on the sky line, and I moved with the utmost caution, walking in a wide sweep so as to hunt across and up wind. There was much sheep sign, some of it fresh, though I saw none of the animals themselves; the square slots, with the indented marks of the toe points wide apart, contrasting strongly with the heart-shaped and delicate footprints of deer. The animals had, according to their habit, beaten trails along the summits of the higher crests; little side trails leading to any spur, peak, or other vantage-point from which there was a wide outlook over the country roundabout.

The bighorns of the Bad Lands, unlike those of the mountains, shift their range but little, winter or summer. Save in the breeding season, when each master ram gets together his own herd, the ewes, lambs, and yearlings are apt to go in bands by themselves, while the males wander in small parties; now and then a very morose old fellow lives by himself, in some precipitous, out-of-the way retreat. The rut begins with them much later than with deer; the exact time varies with the locality, but it is always after the bitter winter weather has set in. Then the old rams fight fiercely together, and on rare occasions utter a long grunting bleat or call. They are marvellous climbers, and dwell by choice always among cliffs and jagged, broken ground, whether wooded or not. An old bighorn ram is heavier than the largest buck; his huge, curved horns, massive yet supple build, and proud bearing mark him as one of the noblest beasts of the chase. He is wary; great skill and caution must be shown in approaching him; and no one but a good climber, with a steady head, sound lungs, and trained muscles, can successfully hunt him in his own rugged fastnesses. The chase of no other kind of American big game ranks higher, or more thoroughly tests the manliest qualities of the hunter.

I walked back to camp in the gloaming, taking care to reach it before it grew really dark; for in the Bad Lands it is entirely impossible to travel, or to find any given locality, after nightfall. Old Manitou had eaten his fill, and looked up at me with pricked ears, and wise, friendly face as I climbed down the side of the cedar canyon; then he came slowly towards me to see if I had not something for him. I rubbed his soft nose and gave him a cracker; then I picketed him to a solitary cedar, where the feed was good. Afterwards I kindled a small fire, roasted both prairie fowl, ate one, and put the other by for breakfast; and soon rolled myself in my blanket, with the saddle for a pillow, and the oilskin beneath. Manitou was munching the grass nearby. I lay just outside the line of stiff black cedars; the night air was soft in my face; I gazed at the shining and brilliant multitude of stars until my eyelids closed.

The chill breath which comes before dawn awakened me. It was still and dark. Through the gloom I could indistinctly make out the loom of the old horse, lying down. I was speedily ready, and groped and stumbled slowly up the hill, and then along its crest to a peak. Here I sat down and waited a quarter of an hour or so, until gray appeared in the east, and the dim light-streaks enabled me to walk farther. Before sunrise I was two miles from camp; then I crawled cautiously to a high ridge and crouching behind it scanned all the landscape eagerly. In a few minutes a movement about a third of a mile to the right, midway down a hill, caught my eye. Another glance showed me three white specks moving along the hillside. They were the white rumps of three fine mountain sheep, on their way to drink at a little alkaline pool in the bottom of a deep, narrow valley. In a moment they went out of sight round a bend of the valley; and I rose and trotted briskly towards them, along the ridge. There were two or three deep gullies to cross, and a high shoulder over which to clamber; so I was out of breath when I reached the bend beyond which they had disappeared. Taking advantage of a scrawny sage brush as cover I peeped over the edge, and at once saw the sheep, three big young rams. They had finished drinking and were standing beside the little mirey pool, about three hundred yards distant. Slipping back I dropped down into the bottom of the valley, where a narrow washout zigzagged from side to side, between straight walls of clay. The pool was in the upper end of this washout, under a cut bank.

An indistinct game trail, evidently sometimes used by both bighorn and blacktail, ran up this washout; the bottom was of clay so that I walked noiselessly; and the crookedness of the washout's course afforded ample security against discovery by the sharp eyes of the quarry. In a couple of minutes I stalked stealthily round the last bend, my rifle cocked and at the ready, expecting to see the rams by the pool. However, they had gone, and the muddy water was settling in their deep hoof marks. Running on I looked over the edge of the cut bank and saw them slowly quartering up the hillside, cropping the sparse tufts of coarse grass. I whistled, and as they stood at gaze I put a bullet into the biggest, a little too far aft of the shoulder, but ranging forward. He raced after the others, but soon fell behind, and turned off on his own line, at a walk, with drooping head. As he bled freely I followed his tracks, found him, very sick, in a washout a quarter of a mile beyond, and finished him with another shot. After dressing him, and cutting off the saddle and hams, as well as the head, I walked back to camp, breakfasted, and rode Manitou to where the sheep lay. Packing it securely behind the saddle, and shifting the blanket roll to in front of the saddle-horn, I led the horse until we were clear of the Bad Lands; then mounted him, and was back at the ranch soon after midday. The mutton of a fat young mountain ram, at this season of the year, is delicious.

Such quick success is rare in hunting sheep. Generally each head has cost me several days of hard, faithful work; and more than once I have hunted over a week without any reward whatsoever. But the quarry is so noble that the ultimate triumph—sure to come, if the hunter will but persevere long enough—atones for all previous toil and failure.

Once a lucky stalk and shot at a bighorn was almost all that redeemed a hunt in the Rockies from failure. I was high among the mountains at the time, but was dogged by ill luck; I had seen but little, and I had not shot very well. One morning I rose early, and hunted steadily until midday without seeing anything. A mountain hunter was with me. At noon we sat down to rest, and look over the country, from behind a shield of dwarf evergreens, on the brink of a mighty chasm. The rocks fell downwards in huge cliffs, stern and barren; from far below rose the strangled roaring of the torrent, as the foaming masses of green and white water churned round the boulders in the stream bed. Except this humming of the wild water, and the soughing of the pines, there was no sound. We were sitting on a kind of jutting promontory of rock so that we could scan the cliffs far and near. First I took the glasses and scrutinized the ground almost rod by rod, for nearly half an hour; then my companion took them in turn. It is very hard to make out game, especially when lying down, and still; and it is curious to notice how, after fruitlessly scanning a country through the glasses for a considerable period, a herd of animals will suddenly appear in the field of vision as if by magic. In this case, while my companion held the glasses for the second time, a slight motion caught his eye; and looking attentively he made out, five or six hundred yards distant, a mountain ram lying among some loose rocks and small bushes at the head of a little grassy cove or nook, in a shallow break between two walls of the cliff. So well did the bluish gray of its body harmonize in tint with the rocks and shrubbery that it was some time before I could see it, even when pointed out to me.

The wind was favorable, and we at once drew back and began a cautious stalk. It was impossible, owing to the nature of the cliffs above and below the bighorn's restingplace, to get a shot save by creeping along nearly on a level with him. Accordingly we worked our way down through a big cleft in the rocks, being forced to go very slowly and carefully lest we should start a loose stone; and at last reached a narrow terrace of rock and grass along which we walked comparatively at our ease. Soon it dwindled away, and we then had to do our only difficult piece of climbing—a clamber for fifty or sixty feet across a steep cliff shoulder. Some little niches and cracks in the rock and a few projections and diminutive ledges on its surface, barely enabled us to swarm across, with painstaking care—not merely to avoid alarming the game this time, but also to avoid a slip which would have proved fatal. Once across we came on a long, grassy shelf, leading round a shoulder into the cleft where the ram lay. As I neared the end I crept forward on hands and knees, and then crawled flat, shoving the rifle ahead of me, until I rounded the shoulder and peered into the rift. As my eyes fell on the ram he sprang to his feet, with a clatter of loose stones, and stood facing me, some sixty yards off, his dark face and white muzzle brought out finely by the battered, curved horns. I shot into his chest, hitting him in the sticking place; and after a few mad bounds he tumbled headlong, and fell a very great distance, unfortunately injuring one horn.

When much hunted, bighorn become the wariest of all American game, and their chase is then peculiarly laborious and exciting. But where they have known nothing of men, not having been molested by hunters, they are exceedingly tame. Professor John Bache McMaster informs me that in 1877 he penetrated to the Uintah Mountains of Wyoming, which were then almost unknown to hunters; he found all the game very bold, and the wild sheep in particular so unsuspicious that he could walk up to within short rifle range of them in the open.

On the high mountains bighorn occasionally get killed by a snow-slide. My old friend, the hunter Woody, once saw a band which started such an avalanche by running along a steep sloping snow field, it being in the spring; for several hundred yards it thundered at their heels, but by desperate racing they just managed to get clear. Woody was also once an eye-witness to the ravages the cougar commits among these wild sheep. He was stalking a band in the snow when he saw them suddenly scatter at a run in every direction. Coming up he found the traces of a struggle, and the track of a body being dragged through the snow, together with the round footmarks of the cougar; a little farther on lay a dead ewe, the blood flowing from the fang wounds in her throat.

MOUNTAIN GAME; THE WHITE GOAT. LATE one August I started on a trip to the Big Hole Basin, in Western Montana, to hunt white goats. With me went a friend of many hunts, John Willis, a tried mountain man.

We left the railroad at the squalid little hamlet of Divide, where we hired a team and wagon from a "busted" granger, suspected of being a Mormon, who had failed, even with the help of irrigation, in raising a crop. The wagon was in fairly good order; the harness was rotten, and needed patching with ropes; while the team consisted of two spoiled horses, overworked and thin, but full of the devil the minute they began to pick up condition. However, on the frontier one soon grows to accept little facts of this kind with bland indifference; and Willis was not only an expert teamster, but possessed that inexhaustible fertility of resource and unfailing readiness in an emergency so characteristic of the veteran of the border. Through hard experience he had become master of plainscraft and woodcraft, skilled in all frontier lore.

For a couple of days we jogged up the valley of the Big Hole River, along the mail road. At night we camped under our wagon. At the mouth of the stream the valley was a mere gorge, but it broadened steadily the farther up we went, till the rapid river wound through a wide expanse of hilly, treeless prairie.

On each side the mountains rose, their lower flanks and the foot-hills covered with the evergreen forest. We got milk and bread at the scattered log-houses of the few settlers; and for meat we shot sage fowl, which abounded. They were feeding on grasshoppers at this time, and the flesh, especially of the young birds, was as tender and well tasting as possible; whereas, when we again passed through the valley in September, we found the birds almost uneatable, being fairly bitter with sage. Like all grouse they are far tamer earlier in the season than later, being very wild in winter; and, of course, they are boldest where they are least hunted; but for some unexplained reason they are always tamer than the sharp-tail prairie fowl which are to be found in the same locality.

Finally we reached the neighborhood of the Battle Ground, where a rude stone monument commemorates the bloody drawn fight between General Gibbons' soldiers and the Nez Perces warriors of Chief Joseph. Here, on the third day of our journey, we left the beaten road and turned towards the mountains, following an indistinct trail made by wood-choppers. We met with our full share of the usual mishaps incident to prairie travel; and towards evening our team got mired in crossing a slough. We attempted the crossing with some misgivings, which were warranted by the result; for the second plunge of the horses brought them up to their bellies in the morass, where they stuck. It was freezing cold, with a bitter wind blowing, and the bog holes were skimmed with ice; so that we passed a thoroughly wretched two hours while freeing the horses and unloading the wagon. However, we eventually got across; my companion preserving an absolutely unruffled temper throughout, perseveringly whistling the "Arkansas Traveller." At one period, when we were up to our waists in the icy mud, it began to sleet and hail, and I muttered that I would " rather it did n't storm "; whereat he stopped whistling for a moment to make the laconic rejoinder, "We 're not having our rathers this trip."

At nightfall we camped among the willow bushes by a little brook. For firewood we had only dead willow sticks; they made a hot blaze which soon died out; and as the cold grew intense, we rolled up in our blankets as soon as we had eaten our supper. The climate of the Big Hole Basin is alpine; that night, though it was the 20th of August, the thermometer sank to 1o F.

Early next morning we struck camp, shivering with cold as we threw the stiff, frozen harness on the horses. We soon got among the foot-hills, where the forest was open and broken by large glades, forming what is called a park country. The higher we went the smaller grew the glades and the denser the woodland; and it began to be very difficult to get the wagon forward. In many places one man had to go ahead to pick out the way, and if necessary do a little chopping and lopping with the axe, while the other followed driving the team. At last we were brought to a standstill, and pitched camp beside a rapid, alder-choked brook in the uppermost of a series of rolling glades, hemmed in by mountains and the dense coniferous forest. Our tent stood under a grove of pines, close to the brook; at night we built in front of it a big fire of crackling, resinous logs. Our goods were sheltered by the wagon, or covered with a tarpaulin; we threw down sprays of odorous evergreens to make a resting-place for our bedding; we built small scaffolds on which to dry the flesh of elk and deer. In an hour or two we had round us all the many real comforts of such a little wilderness home.

Whoever has long roamed and hunted in the wilderness always cherishes with wistful pleasure the memory of some among the countless camps he has made. The camp by the margin of the clear, mountain-hemmed lake; the camp in the dark and melancholy forest, where the gusty wind booms through the tall pine tops; the camp under gnarled cottonwoods, on the bank of a shrunken river, in the midst of endless grassy prairies,—of these, and many like them, each has had its own charm. Of course in hunting one must expect much hardship and repeated disappointment; and in many a camp, bad weather, lack of shelter, hunger, thirst, or ill success with game, renders the days and nights irksome and trying. Yet the hunter worthy of the name always willingly takes the bitter if by so doing he can get the sweet, and gladly balances failure and success, spurning the poorer souls who know neither.

We turned our horses loose, hobbling one; and as we did not look after them for several days, nothing but my companion's skill as a tracker enabled us to find them again. There was a spell of warm weather which brought out a few of the big bull-dog flies, which drive a horse— or indeed a man—nearly frantic; we were in the haunts of these dreaded and terrible scourges, which up to the beginning of August render it impossible to keep stock of any description unprotected where they abound, but which are never formidable after the first frost. In many parts of the wilderness these pests, or else the incredible swarms of mosquitoes, blackflies, and buffalo gnats, render life not worth living during the last weeks of spring and the early months of summer.

There were elk and deer in the neighborhood; also ruffed, blue, and spruce grouse; so that our camp was soon stocked with meat. Early one morning while Willis was washing in the brook, a little black bear thrust its sharp nose through the alders a few feet from him, and then hastily withdrew and was seen no more. The smaller wild-folk were more familiar. As usual in the northern mountains, the gray moose-birds and voluble, nervous little chipmunks made themselves at home in the camp. Parties of chickadees visited us occasionally. A family of flying squirrels lived overhead in the grove; and at nightfall they swept noiselessly from tree to tree, in long graceful curves. There were sparrows of several kinds moping about in the alders; and now and then one of them would sing a few sweet, rather mournful bars.

After several days' preliminary exploration we started on foot for white goat. We took no packs with us, each carrying merely his jacket, with a loaf of bread and a paper of salt thrust into the pockets. Our aim was to get well to one side of a cluster of high, bare peaks, and then to cross them and come back to camp; we reckoned that the trip would take three days.

All the first day we tramped through dense woods and across and around steep mountain spurs. We caught glimpses of two or three deer and a couple of elk, all does or fawns, however, which we made no effort to molest. Late in the afternoon we stumbled across a family of spruce grouse, which furnished us material for both supper and breakfast. The mountain men call this bird the fool-hen; and most certainly it deserves the name. The members of this particular flock, consisting of a hen and her three-parts grown chickens, acted with a stupidity unwonted even for their kind. They were feeding on the ground among some young spruce, and on our approach flew up and perched in the branches four or five feet above our heads. There they stayed, uttering a low, complaining whistle, and showed not the slightest suspicion when we came underneath them with long sticks and knocked four off their perches—for we did not wish to alarm any large game that might be in the neighborhood by firing. One particular bird was partially saved from my first blow by the intervening twigs; however, it merely flew a few yards, and then sat with its bill open,—having evidently been a little hurt,—until I came up and knocked it over with a better directed stroke.

Spruce grouse are plentiful in the mountain forests of the northern Rockies, and, owing to the ease with which they are killed, they have furnished me my usual provender when off on trips of this kind, where I carried no pack. They are marvellously tame and stupid. The young birds are the only ones I have ever killed in this manner with a stick; but even a full plumaged old cock in September is easily slain with a stone by any one who is at all a good thrower. A man who has played much base-ball need never use a gun when after spruce grouse. They are the smallest of the

grouse kind; the cock is very handsome, with red eyebrows and dark, glossy plumage. Moreover, he is as brave as he is stupid and good-looking, and in the love season becomes fairly crazy: at such time he will occasionally make a feint of attacking a man, strutting, fluttering, and ruffling his feathers. The flesh of the spruce grouse is not so good as that of his ruffed and blue kinsfolk; and in winter, when he feeds on spruce buds, it is ill tasting. I have never been able to understand why closely allied species, under apparently the same surroundings, should differ so radically in such important traits as wariness and capacity to escape from foes. Yet the spruce grouse in this respect shows the most marked contrast to the blue grouse and the ruffed grouse. Of course all three kinds vary greatly in their behavior accordingly as they do or do not live in localities where they have been free from man's persecutions. The ruffed grouse, a very wary game bird in all old-settled regions, is often absurdly tame in the wilderness; and under persecution, even the spruce grouse gains some little wisdom; but the latter never becomes as wary as the former, and under no circumstances is it possible to outwit the ruffed grouse by such clumsy means as serve for his simple-minded brother. There is a similar difference between the sage fowl and prairie fowl, in favor of the latter. It is odd that the largest and the smallest kinds of grouse found in the United States should be the tamest; and also the least savory.

After tramping all day through the forest, at nightfall we camped in its upper edge, just at the foot of the steep rock walls of the mountain. We chose a sheltered spot, where the small spruce grew thick, and there was much dead timber; and as the logs, though long, were of little girth, we speedily dragged together a number sufficient to keep the fire blazing all night. Having drunk our full at a brook we cut two forked willow sticks, and then each plucked a grouse, split it, thrust the willow-fork into it, and roasted it before the fire. Besides this we had salt, and bread; moreover we were hungry and healthily tired; so

the supper seemed, and was, delicious. Then we turned up the collars of our jackets, and lay down, to pass the night in broken slumber; each time the fire died down the chill waked us, and we rose to feed it with fresh logs.

At dawn we rose, and cooked and ate the two remaining grouse. Then we turned our faces upwards, and passed a day of severe toil in climbing over, the crags. Mountaineering is very hard work; and when we got high among the peaks, where snow filled the rifts, the thinness of the air forced me to stop for breath every few hundred yards of the ascent. We found much sign of white goats, but in spite of steady work and incessant careful scanning of the rocks, we did not see our quarry until early in the afternoon.

We had clambered up one side of a steep saddle of naked rock, some of the scarped ledges being difficult, and indeed dangerous, of ascent. From the top of the saddle a careful scrutiny of the neighboring peaks failed to reveal any game, and we began to go down the other side. The mountain fell away in a succession of low cliffs, and we had to move with the utmost caution. In letting ourselves down from ledge to ledge one would hold the guns until the other got safe footing, and then pass them down to him. In many places we had to work our way along the cracks in the faces of the frost-riven rocks. At last, just as we reached a little smooth shoulder, my companion said, pointing down beneath us, "Look at the white goat!"

A moment or two passed before I got my eyes on it. We were looking down into a basin-like valley, surrounded by high mountain chains. At one end of the basin was a low pass, where the ridge was cut up with the zigzag trails made by the countless herds of game which had travelled it for many generations. At the other end was a dark gorge, through which a stream foamed. The floor of the basin was bright emerald green, dotted with darker bands where belts of fir trees grew; and in its middle lay a little lake.

At last I caught sight of the goat, feeding on a terrace rather over a hundred and twenty-five yards below me. I promptly fired, but overshot. The goat merely gave a few jumps and stopped. My second bullet went through its lungs; but fearful lest it might escape to some inaccessible cleft or ledge I fired again, missing; and yet again, breaking its back. Down it went, and the next moment began to roll over and over, from ledge to ledge. I greatly feared it would break its horns; an annoying and oft-recurring incident of white-goat shooting, where the nature of the ground is such that the dead quarry often falls hundreds of feet, its body being torn to ribbons by the sharp crags. However in this case the goat speedily lodged unharmed in a little dwarf evergreen.

Hardly had I fired my fourth shot when my companion again exclaimed, " Look at the white goats! look at the white goats!" Glancing in the direction in which he pointed I speedily made out four more goats standing in a bunch rather less than a hundred yards off, to one side of my former line of fire. They were all looking up at me. They stood on a slab of white rock, with which the color of their fleece harmonized well; and their black horns, muzzles, eyes, and hoofs looked like dark dots on a light-colored surface, so that it took me more than one glance to determine what they were. White goat invariably run up hill when alarmed, their one idea seeming to be to escape danger by getting above it; for their brute foes are able to overmatch them on anything like level ground, but are helpless against them among the crags. Almost as soon as I saw them these four started up the mountain, nearly in my direction, while I clambered down and across to meet them. They halted at the foot of a cliff, and I at the top, being unable to see them; but in another moment they came bounding and cantering up the sheer rocks, not moving quickly, but traversing the most seemingly impossible places by main strength and sure-footedness. As they broke by me, some thirty yards off, I fired two shots at the rearmost, an old buck, somewhat smaller than the one I had just killed; and he rolled down the mountain dead. Two of

the others, a yearling and a kid, showed more alarm than their elders, and ran off at a brisk pace. The remaining one, an old she, went off a hundred yards, and then deliberately stopped and turned round to gaze at us for a couple of minutes! Verily the white goat is the fool-hen among beasts of the chase.

Having skinned and cut off the heads we walked rapidly onwards, slanting down the mountain side, and then over and down the pass of the game trails; for it was growing late and we wished to get well down among the timber before nightfall. On the way an eagle came soaring over head, and I shot at it twice without success. Having once killed an eagle on the wing with a rifle, I always have a lurking hope that sometime I may be able to repeat the feat. I revenged myself for the miss by knocking a large blue goshawk out of the top of a blasted spruce, where it was sitting in lazy confidence, its crop stuffed with rabbit and grouse.

A couple of hours' hard walking brought us down to timber; just before dusk we reached a favorable camping spot in the forest, beside a brook, with plenty of dead trees for the night-fire. Moreover, the spot fortunately yielded us our supper too, in the shape of a flock of young spruce grouse, of which we shot off the heads of a couple. Immediately afterwards I ought to have procured our breakfast, for a cock of the same kind suddenly flew down nearby; but it was getting dark, I missed with the first shot, and with the second must have merely creased the neck, for though the tough old bird dropped, it fluttered and ran off among the underbrush and escaped.

We broiled our two grouse before our fire, dragged plenty of logs into a heap beside it, and then lay down to sleep fitfully, an hour or so at a time, throughout the night. We were continually wakened by the cold, when we had to rise and feed the flames. In the early morning we again started, walking for some time along the fresh trail made by a large band of elk, cows and calves. We thought we knew exactly the trend and outlet of the valley in which we were,

and that therefore we could tell where the camp was; but, as so often happens in the wilderness, we had not reckoned aright, having passed over one mountain spur too many, and entered the ravines of an entirely different water-course-system. In consequence we became entangled in a network of hills and valleys, making circle after circle to find our bearings; and we only reached camp after twelve hours' tiresome tramp without food.

On another occasion I shot a white goat while it was in a very curious and characteristic attitude. I was hunting, again with an old mountain man as my sole companion, among the high mountains of the Kootenai country, near the border of Montana and British Columbia. We had left our main camp, pitched by the brink of the river, and were struggling wearily on foot through the tangled forest and over the precipitous mountains, carrying on our backs light packs, consisting of a little food and two or three indispensable utensils, wrapped in our blankets. One day we came to the foot of a great chain of bare rocks, and climbed laboriously to its crest, up cliff after cliff, some of which were almost perpendicular. Swarming round certain of the rock shoulders, crossing an occasional sheer chasm, and in many places clinging to steep, smooth walls by but slight holds, we reached the top. The climbing at such a height was excessively fatiguing; moreover, it was in places difficult and even dangerous. Of course it was not to be compared to the ascent of towering, glacier-bearing peaks, such as those of the Selkirks and Alaska, where climbers must be roped to one another and carry ice axes.

Once at the top we walked very cautiously, being careful not to show ourselves against the sky line, and scanning the mountain sides through our glasses. At last we made out three goats, grazing unconcernedly on a narrow grassy terrace, which sloped abruptly to the brink of a high precipice. They were not very far off, and there was a little rock spur above them which offered good cover for a stalk; but we had to crawl so slowly, partly to avoid falling, and partly to avoid detaching loose rocks, that it was nearly an hour before we got in a favorable position above them, and some seventy yards off. The frost-disintegrated mountains in which they live are always sending down showers of detached stones, so that the goats are not very sensitive to this noise; still, they sometimes pay instantaneous heed to it, especially if the sound is repeated.

When I peeped over the little ridge of rock, shoving my rifle carefully ahead of me, I found that the goats had finished feeding and were preparing to leave the slope. The old billy saw me at once, but evidently could not quite make me out. Thereupon, gazing intently at me, he rose gravely on his haunches, sitting up almost in the attitude of a dog when begging. I know no other horned animal that ever takes this position.

As I fired he rolled backwards, slipped down the grassy slope, and tumbled over the brink of the cliff, while the other two, a she and a kid, after a moment's panic-struck pause, and a bewildered rush in the wrong direction, made off up a little rocky gully, and were out of sight in a moment. To my chagrin when I finally reached the carcass, after a tedious and circuitous climb to the foot of the cliff, I found both horns broken off.

It was late in the afternoon, and we clambered down to the border of a little marshy alpine lake, which we reached in an hour or so. Here we made our camp about sunset, in a grove of stunted spruces, which furnished plenty of dead timber for the fire. There were many white-goat trails leading to this lake, and from the slide rock roundabout we heard the shrill whistling of hoary rock-woodchucks, and the querulous notes of the little conies—two of the sounds most familiar to the white-goat hunter. These conies had gathered heaps of dried plants, and had stowed them carefully away for winter use in the cracks between the rocks.

While descending the mountain we came on a little pack of snow grouse or mountain ptarmigan, birds which, save in winter, are always found above tim-

ber line. They were tame and fearless, though hard to make out as they ran among the rocks, cackling noisily, with their tails cocked aloft; and we had no difficulty in killing four, which gave us a good breakfast and supper. Old white goats are intolerably musky in flavor, there being a very large musk-pod between the horn and ear. The kids are eatable, but of course are rarely killed; the shot being usually taken at the animal with best horns—and the shes and young of any game should only be killed when there is a real necessity.

These two hunts may be taken as samples of most expeditions after white goat. There are places where the goats live in mountains close to bodies of water, either ocean fiords or large lakes; and in such places canoes can be used, to the greatly increased comfort and lessened labor of the hunters. In other places, where the mountains are low and the goats spend all the year in the timber, a pack-train can be taken right up to the hunting grounds. But generally one must go on foot, carrying everything on one's back, and at night lying out in the open or under a brush lean-to; meanwhile living on spruce grouse and ptarmigan, with an occasional meal of trout, and in times of scarcity squirrels, or anything else. Such a trip entails severe fatigue and not a little hardship. The actual hunting, also, implies difficult and laborious climbing, for the goats live by choice among the highest and most inaccessible mountains; though where they are found, as they sometimes are, in comparatively low forest-clad ranges, I have occasionally killed them with little trouble by lying in wait beside the well-trodden game trails they make in the timber.

In any event the hard work is to get up to the grounds where the game is found. Once the animals are spied there is but little call for the craft of the still-hunter in approaching them. Of all American game the white goat is the least wary and most stupid. In places where it is much hunted it of course gradually grows wilder and becomes difficult to approach and kill; and much of its silly tameness is doubtless due

to the inaccessible nature of its haunts, which renders it ordinarily free from molestation; but aside from this it certainly seems as if it was naturally less wary than either deer or mountain sheep. The great point is to get above it. All its foes live in the valleys, and while it is in the mountains, if they strive to approach it at all, they must do so from below. It is in consequence always on the watch for danger from beneath; but it is easily approached from above, and then, as it generally tries to escape by running up hill, the hunter is very apt to get a shot.

Its chase is thus laborious rather than exciting; and to my mind it is less attractive than is the pursuit of most of our other game. Yet it has an attraction of its own after all; while the grandeur of the scenery amid which it must be carried on, the freedom and hardihood of the life and the pleasure of watching the queer habits of the game, all combine to add to the hunter's enjoyment.

White goats are self-confident, pugnacious beings. An old billy, if he discovers the presence of a foe without being quite sure what it is, often refuses to take flight, but walks around, stamping, and shaking his head. The needle-pointed black horns are alike in both sexes, save that the males' are a trifle thicker; and they are most effective weapons when wielded by the muscular neck of a resolute and wicked old goat. They wound like stilettos and their bearer is in consequence a much more formidable foe in a hand-to-hand struggle than either a branchingantlered deer or a mountain ram, with his great battering head. The goat does not butt; he thrusts. If he can cover his back by a tree trunk or boulder he can stand off most carnivorous animals, no larger than he is.

Though awkward in movement, and lacking all semblance of lightness or agility, goats are excellent climbers. One of their queer traits is their way of getting their forehoofs on a slight ledge, and then drawing or lifting their bodies up by simple muscular exertion, stretching out their elbows, much as a man would. They do a good deal of their climbing by strength and command over their muscles; although they are also capable of making astonishing bounds. If a cliff surface has the least slope, and shows any inequalities or roughness whatever, goats can go up and down it with ease. With their short, stout legs, and large, sharp-edged hoofs they clamber well over ice, passing and repassing the mountains at a time when no man would so much as crawl over them. They bear extreme cold with indifference, but are intolerant of much heat; even when the weather is cool they are apt to take their noontide rest in caves; I have seen them solemnly retiring, for this purpose, to great rents in the rocks, at a time when my own teeth chattered because of the icy wind.

They go in small flocks; sometimes in pairs or little family parties. After the rut the bucks often herd by themselves, or go off alone, while the young and the shes keep together throughout the winter and the spring. The young are generally brought forth above timber line, or at its uppermost edge, save of course in those places where the goats live among mountains wooded to the top. Throughout the summer they graze on the short mountain plants which in many places form regular mats above timber line; the deep winter snows drive them low down in the wooded valleys, and force them to subsist by browsing. They are so strong that they plough their way readily through deep drifts; and a flock of goats at this season, when their white coat is very long and thick, if seen waddling off through the snow, have a comical likeness to so many diminutive polar bears. Of course they could easily be run down in the snow by a man on snowshoes, in the plain; but on a mountain side there are always bare rocks and cliff shoulders, glassy with winter ice, which give either goats or sheep an advantage over their snowshoe-bearing foes that deer and elk lack. Whenever the goats pass the winter in woodland they leave plenty of sign in the shape of patches of wool clinging to all the sharp twigs and branches against which they have brushed. In the spring they often form the habit of drinking at certain low pools, to which they beat deep paths; and at this season, and to a less extent in the summer and fall, they are very fond of frequenting mineral licks. At any such lick the ground is tramped bare of vegetation, and is filled with pits and hollows, actually dug by the tongues of innumerable generations of animals; while the game paths lead from them in a dozen directions.

In spite of the white goat's pugnacity, its clumsiness renders it no very difficult prey when taken unawares by either wolf or cougar, its two chief enemies. They cannot often catch it when it is above timber line; but it is always in sore peril from them when it ventures into the forest. Bears, also, prey upon it in the early spring; and one midwinter my friend Willis found a wolverine eating a goat which it had killed in a snowdrift at the foot of a cliff. The savage little beast growled and showed fight when he came near the body. Eagles are great enemies of the young kids, as they are of the young lambs of the bighorn.

The white goat is the only game beast of America which has not decreased in numbers since the arrival of the white man. Although in certain localities it is now decreasing, yet, taken as a whole, it is probably quite as plentiful now as it was fifty years back; for in the early part of the present century there were Indian tribes who hunted it perseveringly to make the skins into robes, whereas now they get blankets from the traders and no longer persecute the goats. The early trappers and mountain-men knew but little of the animal. Whether they were after beaver, or were hunting big game, or were merely exploring, they kept to the valleys; there was no inducement for them to climb to the tops of the mountains; so it resulted that there was no animal with which the old hunters were so unfamiliar as with the white goat. The professional hunters of to-day likewise bother it but little; they do not care to undergo severe toil for an animal with worthless flesh and a hide of little value—for it is only in the late fall and winter that the long hair and fine wool give the robe any beauty.

So the quaint, sturdy, musky beasts, with their queer and awkward ways, their boldness and their stupidity, with their white coats and big black hoofs, black muzzles, and sharp, gently-curved span-long black horns, have held their own well among the high mountains that they love. In the Rockies and the Coast ranges they abound from Alaska south to Montana, Idaho, and Washington; and here and there isolated colonies are found among the high mountains to the southward, in Wyoming, Colorado, even in New Mexico, and, strangest of all, in one or two spots among the barren coast mountains of southern California. Long after the elk has followed the buffalo to the happy hunting grounds the white goat will flourish among the towering and glacier-riven peaks, and, grown wary with succeeding generations, will furnish splendid sport to those hunters who are both good riflemen and hardy cragsmen.

HUNTING IN THE SELKIRKS; THE CARIBOU. IN September, 1888, I was camped on the shores of Kootenai Lake, having with me as companions, John Willis and an impassive-looking Indian named Ammal. Coming across through the dense coniferous forests of northern Idaho we had struck the Kootenai River. Then we went down with the current as it wound in half circles through a long alluvial valley of mixed marsh and woodland, hemmed in by lofty mountains. The lake itself, when we reached it, stretched straight away like a great fiord, a hundred miles long and about three in breadth. The frowning and rugged Selkirks came down sheer to the water's edge. So straight were the rock walls that it was difficult for us to land with our batteau, save at the places where the rapid mountain torrents entered the lake. As these streams of swift water broke from their narrow gorges they made little deltas of level ground, with beaches of fine white sand; and the streambanks were edged with cottonwood and poplar, their shimmering foliage relieving the sombre coloring of the evergreen forest.

Close to such a brook, from which we drew strings of large silver trout, our tent was pitched, just within the forest. From between the trunks of two gnarled, windbeaten trees, a pine and a cottonwood, we looked out across the lake. The little bay in our front, in which we bathed and swam, was sometimes glassily calm; and again heavy wind squalls arose, and the surf beat strongly on the beach where our boat was drawn up. Now and then great checker-back loons drifted buoyantly by, stopping with bold curiosity to peer at the white tent gleaming between the tree-trunks, and at the smoke curling above their tops; and they called to one another, both at dawn and in the daytime, with shrieks of unearthly laughter. Troops of noisy, parti-colored Clark's crows circled over the tree-tops or hung from among the pine cones; jays and chickadees came round camp, and woodpeckers hammered lustily in the dead timber. Two or three times parties of Indians passed down the lake, in strangely shaped bark canoes, with peaked, projecting prows and sterns; craft utterly unlike the graceful, feather-floating birches so beloved by both the red and the white woodsmen of the northeast. Once a couple of white men, in a dugout or pirogue made out of a cottonwood log, stopped to get lunch. They were mining prospectors, French Canadians by birth, but beaten into the usual frontier-mining stamp; doomed to wander their lives long, ever hoping, in the quest for metal wealth.

With these exceptions there was nothing to break the silent loneliness of the great lake. Shrouded as we were in the dense forest, and at the foot of the first steep hills, we could see nothing of the country on the side where we were camped; but across the water the immense mountain masses stretched away from our vision, range upon range, until they turned to a glittering throng of ice peaks and snow fields, the feeding beds of glaciers. Between the lake and the snow range were chains of gray rock peaks, and the mountain sides and valleys were covered by the primeval forest. The woods were on fire across the lake from our camp, burning steadily. At night the scene was very grand, as the fire worked slowly across the mountain sides in immense zigzags of quivering red; while at times isolated pines of unusual size kindled, and flamed for hours, like the torches of a giant. Finally the smoke grew so thick as to screen from our views the grand landscape opposite.

We had come down from a week's fruitless hunting in the mountains; a week of excessive toil, in a country where we saw no game—for in our ignorance we had wasted time, not going straight back to the high ranges, from which the game had not yet descended. After three or four days of rest, and of feasting on trout—a welcome relief to the monotony of frying-pan bread and coarse salt pork—we were ready for another trial; and early one morning we made the start. Having to pack everything for a fortnight's use on our backs, through an excessively rough country, we of course travelled as light as possible, leaving almost all we had with the tent and boat. Each took his own blanket; and among us we carried a frying-pan, a teapot, flour, pork, salt, tea, and matches. I also took a jacket, a spare pair of socks, some handkerchiefs, and my washing kit. Fifty cartridges in my belt completed my outfit.

We walked in single file, as is necessary in thick woods. The white hunter led and I followed, each with rifle on shoulder and pack on back. Ammal, the Indian, pigeon-toed along behind, carrying his pack, not as we did ours, but by help of a forehead-band, which he sometimes shifted across his breast. The travelling through the tangled, brush-choked forest, and along the boulder-strewn and precipitous mountain sides, was inconceivably rough and difficult. In places we followed the valley, and when this became impossible we struck across the spurs. Every step was severe toil. Now we walked through deep moss and rotting mould, every few feet clambering over huge trunks; again we pushed through a stiff jungle of bushes and tall, prickly plants—called "devil's clubs,"—which stung our hands and faces. Up the almost perpendicular hillsides we in many places went practically on all fours, forcing our way over the rocks and through the dense thickets of laurels or young spruce. Where there were windfalls or great stretches of burnt forest, black and barren wastes, we balanced and leaped from log to log, sometimes twenty or thirty feet above the ground; and when such a stretch was on a steep hill-side, and especially if the logs were enveloped in a thick second growth of small evergreens, the footing was very insecure, and the danger from a fall considerable. Our packs added greatly to our labor, catching on the snags and stubs; and where a grove of thick-growing young spruces or balsams had been burned, the stiff and brittle twigs pricked like so much coral. Most difficult of all were the dry watercourses, choked with alders, where the intertwined tangle of tough stems formed an almost literally impenetrable barrier to our progress. Nearly every movement—leaping, climbing, swinging one's self up with one's hands, bursting through stiff bushes, plunging into and out of bogs—was one of strain and exertion; the fatigue was tremendous, and steadily continued, so that in an hour every particle of clothing I had on was wringing wet with sweat.

At noon we halted beside a little brook for a bite of lunch—a chunk of cold frying-pan bread, which was all we had.

While at lunch I made a capture. I was sitting on a great stone by the edge of the brook, idly gazing at a water-wren which had come up from a short flight—I can call it nothing else—underneath the water, and was singing sweetly from a spray-splashed log. Suddenly a small animal swam across the little pool at my feet. It was less in size than a mouse, and as it paddled rapidly underneath the water its body seemed flattened like a disc and was spangled with tiny bubbles, like specks of silver. It was a water-shrew, a rare little beast. I sat motionless and watched both the shrew and the waterwren—water-ousel, as it should rightly be named. The latter, emboldened by my quiet, presently flew by me to a little rapids close at hand, lighting on a round stone, and then slipping unconcernedly into the swift water. Anon he emerged, stood on another stone, and trilled a few bars, though it was late in the season for singing; and then dove again into the stream. I gazed at him eagerly; for this strange, pretty water-thrush is to me one of the most attractive and interesting birds to be found in the gorges of the great Rockies. Its haunts are romantically beautiful, for it always dwells beside and in the swift-flowing mountain brooks; it has a singularly sweet song; and its ways render it a marked bird at once, for though looking much like a sober-colored, ordinary woodland thrush, it spends half its time under the water, walking along the bottom, swimming and diving, and flitting through as well as over the cataracts.

In a minute or two the shrew caught my eye again. It got into a little shallow eddy and caught a minute fish, which it carried to a half-sunken stone and greedily devoured, tugging voraciously at it as it held it down with its paws. Then its evil genius drove it into a small puddle alongside the brook, where I instantly pounced on and slew it; for I knew a friend in the Smithsonian at Washington who would have coveted it greatly. It was a soft, pretty creature, dark above, snow-white below, with a very long tail. I turned the skin inside out and put a bent twig in, that it might dry; while Ammal, who had been intensely interested in the chase and capture, meditatively shook his head and said "wagh," unable to fathom the white man's medicine. However, my labor came to nought, for that evening I laid the skin out on a log, Ammal threw the log into the fire, and that was the end of the shrew.

When this interlude was over we resumed our march, toiling silently onwards through the wild and rugged country. Towards evening the valley widened a little, and we were able to walk in the bottoms, which much lightened our labor. The hunter, for greater ease, had tied the thongs of his heavy pack across his breast, so that he could not use his rifle; but my pack was lighter, and I carried it in a manner that would not interfere with my shooting, lest we should come unawares on game.

It was well that I did so. An hour or two before sunset we were travelling, as usual, in Indian file, beside the stream, through an open wood of great hemlock trees. There was no breeze, and we made no sound as we marched, for our feet sunk noiselessly into the deep sponge of moss, while the incessant dashing of the torrent, churning among the stones, would have drowned a far louder advance.

Suddenly the hunter, who was leading, dropped down in his tracks, pointing forward; and some fifty feet beyond I saw the head and shoulders of a bear as he rose to make a sweep at some berries. He was in a hollow where a tall, rank, prickly plant, with broad leaves, grew luxuriantly; and he was gathering its red berries, rising on his hind legs and sweeping them down into his mouth with his paw, and was much too intent on his work to notice us, for his head was pointed the other way. The moment he rose again I fired, meaning to shoot through the shoulders, but instead, in the hurry, taking him in the neck. Down he went, but whether hurt or not we could not see, for the second he was on all fours he was no longer visible. Rather to my surprise he uttered no sound—for bear when hit or when charging often make a great noise—so I raced forward to the edge of the hollow, the hunter close behind me, while Ammal danced about in the rear, very much excited, as Indians always are in the presence of big game. The instant we reached the hollow and looked down into it from the low bank on which we stood we saw by the swaying of the tall plants that the bear was coming our way. The hunter was standing some ten feet distant, a hemlock trunk being between us; and the next moment the bear sprang clean up the bank the other side of the hemlock, and almost within arm's length of my companion. I do not think he had intended to charge; he was probably confused by the bullet through his neck, and had by chance blundered out of the hollow in our direction; but when he saw the hunter so close he turned for him, his hair bristling and his teeth showing. The man had no cartridge in his weapon, and with his pack on could

not have used it anyhow; and for a moment it looked as if he stood a fair chance of being hurt, though it is not likely that the bear would have done more than knock him down with his powerful forepaw, or perchance give him a single bite in passing. However, as the beast sprang out of the hollow he poised for a second on the edge of the bank to recover his balance, giving me a beautiful shot, as he stood sideways to me; the bullet struck between the eye and ear, and he fell as if hit with a pole axe.

Immediately the Indian began jumping about the body, uttering wild yells, his usually impassive face lit up with excitement, while the hunter and I stood at rest, leaning on our rifles and laughing. It was a strange scene, the dead bear lying in the shade of the giant hemlocks, while the fantastic-looking savage danced round him with shrill whoops, and the tall frontiersman looked quietly on.

Our prize was a large black bear, with two curious brown streaks down his back, one on each side the spine. We skinned him and camped by the carcass, as it was growing late. To take the chill off the evening air we built a huge fire, the logs roaring and crackling. To one side of it we made our beds—of balsam and hemlock boughs; we did not build a brush lean-to, because the night seemed likely to be clear. Then we supped on sugarless tea, frying-pan bread, and quantities of bear meat, fried or roasted—and how very good it tasted only those know who have gone through much hardship and some little hunger, and have worked violently for several days without flesh food. After eating our fill we stretched ourselves around the fire; the leaping sheets of flame lit the tree-trunks round about, causing them to start out against the cavernous blackness beyond, and reddened the interlacing branches that formed a canopy overhead. The Indian sat on his haunches, gazing steadily and silently into the pile of blazing logs, while the white hunter and I talked together.

The morning after killing Bruin, we again took up our march, heading up stream, that we might go to its sources amidst the mountains, where the snow fields fed its springs. It was two full days' journey thither, but we took much longer to make it, as we kept halting to hunt the adjoining mountains. On such occasions Ammal was left as camp guard, while the white hunter and I would start by daybreak and return at dark utterly worn out by the excessive fatigue. We knew nothing of caribou, nor where to hunt for them; and we had been told that thus early in the season they were above tree limit on the mountain sides. Accordingly we would climb up to the limits of the forests, but never found a caribou trail; and once or twice we went on to the summits of the crag-peaks, and across the deep snow fields in the passes. There were plenty of white goats, however, their trails being broad paths, especially at one spot where they led down to a lick in the valley; round the lick, for a space of man)-yards, the ground was trampled as if in a sheepfold.

The mountains were very steep, and the climbing was in places dangerous, when we were above the timber and had to make our way along the jagged knife-crests and across the faces of the cliffs; while our hearts beat as if about to burst in the high, thin air. In walking over rough but not dangerous ground—across slides or in thick timber—my companion was far more skilful than I was; but rather to my surprise I proved to be nearly as good as he when we came to the really dangerous places, where we had to go slowly, and let one another down from ledge to ledge, or crawl by narrow cracks across the rock walls.

The view from the summits was magnificent, and I never tired of gazing at it. Sometimes the sky was a dome of blue crystal, and mountain, lake, and valley lay spread in startling clearness at our very feet; and again snow-peak and rock-peak were thrust up like islands through a sea of billowy clouds. At the feet of the topmost peaks, just above the edge of the forest, were marshy alpine valleys, the boggy ground soaked with water, and small bushes or stunted trees fringing the icy lakes. In the stony mountain sides surrounding these lakes there were hoary woodchucks, and conies. The former resembled in their habits the alpine marmot, rather than our own common eastern woodchuck. They lived alone or in couples among the rocks, their gray color often making them difficult to see as they crouched at the mouths of their burrows, or sat bolt upright; and as an alarm note they uttered a loud piercing whistle, a strong contrast to the querulous, plaintive "p-a-a-y" of the timid conies. These likewise loved to dwell where the stones and slabs of rock were heaped on one another; though so timid, they were not nearly as wary as the woodchucks. If we stood quite still the little brown creatures would venture away from their holes and hop softly over the rocks as if we were not present.

The white goats were too musky to eat, and we saw nothing else to shoot; so we speedily became reduced to tea, and to bread baked in the frying-pan, save every now and then for a feast on the luscious mountain blueberries. This rather meagre diet, coupled with incessant fatigue and exertion, made us fairly long for meat food; and we fell off in flesh, though of course in so short a time we did not suffer in either health or strength. Fortunately the nights were too cool for mosquitoes; but once or twice in the afternoons, while descending the lower slopes of the mountains, we were much bothered by swarms of gnats; they worried us greatly, usually attacking us at a time when we had to go fast in order to reach camp before dark, while the roughness of the ground forced us to use both hands in climbing, and thus forbade us to shield our faces from our tiny tormentors. Our chief luxury was, at the end of the day, when footsore and weary, to cast aside our sweat-drenched clothes and plunge into the icy mountain torrent for a moment's bath that freshened us as if by magic. The nights were generally pleasant, and we slept soundly on our beds of balsam boughs, but once or twice there were sharp frosts, and it was so cold that the hunter and I huddled together for warmth and kept the fires going till morning. One day, when we were on the march, it rained heavily, and we were soaked through, and stiff and chilly when we pitched camp; but we speedily built a great brush lean-to, made a roaring fire in front, and grew once more to warmth and comfort as we sat under our steaming shelter. The only discomfort we really minded was an occasional night in wet blankets.

In the evening the Indian and the white hunter played interminable games of seven-up with a greasy pack of cards. In the course of his varied life the hunter had been a professional gambler; and he could have easily won all the Indian's money, the more speedily inasmuch as the untutored red man was always attempting to cheat, and was thus giving his far more skilful opponent a certain right to try some similar deviltry in return. However, it was distinctly understood that there should be no gambling, for I did not wish Ammal to lose all his wages while in my employ; and the white man stood loyally by his agreement. Animal's people, just before I engaged him, had been visited by their brethren, the Upper Kootenais, and in a series of gambling matches had lost about all their belongings.

Ammal himself was one of the Lower Kootenais; I had hired him for the trip, as the Indians west of the Rockies, unlike their kinsman of the plains, often prove hard and willing workers. His knowledge of English was almost nil; and our very scanty conversation was carried on in the Chinook jargon, universally employed between the mountains and the Pacific. Apparently he had three names: for he assured us that his " Boston" *(t. e.,* American) name was Ammal; his " Siwash" (/. ?., Indian) name was Appak; and that the priest called him Abel—for the Lower Kootenais are nominally Catholics. Whatever his name he was a good Indian, as Indians go. I often tried to talk with him about game and hunting, but we understood each other too little to exchange more than the most rudimentary ideas. His face brightened one night when I happened to tell him of my baby boys at home; he must have been an affectionate father in his way, this dark Ammal, for he at once proceeded to tell me about his own papoose, who had also seen one snow, and to describe how the little fellow was old enough to take one step and then fall down. But he never displayed so much vivacity as on one occasion when the white hunter happened to relate to him a rather gruesome feat of one of their mutual acquaintances, an Upper Kootenai Indian named Three Coyotes. The latter was a quarrelsome, adventurous Indian, with whom the hunter had once had a difficulty—" I had to beat the cuss over the head with my gun a little," he remarked parenthetically. His last feat had been done in connection with a number of Chinamen who had been working among some placer mines, where the Indians came to visit them. Now the astute Chinese are as fond of gambling as any of the borderers, white or red, and are very successful, generally fleecing the Indians unmercifully. Three Coyotes lost all he possessed to one of the pigtailed gentry; but he apparently took his losses philosophically, and pleasantly followed the victor round, until the latter had won all the cash and goods of several other Indians. Then he suddenly fell on the exile from the Celestial Empire, slew him and took all his plunder, retiring unmolested, as it did not seem any one's business to avenge a mere Chinaman. Ammal was immensely interested in the tale, and kept recurring to it again and again, taking two little sticks and making the hunter act out the whole story. The Kootenais were then only just beginning to consider the Chinese as human. They knew they must not kill white people, and they had their own code of morality among themselves; but when the Chinese first appeared they evidently thought that there could not be any especial objection to killing them, if any reason arose for doing so. I think the hunter himself sympathized somewhat with this view.

Ammal objected strongly to leaving the neighborhood of the lake. He went the first day's journey willingly enough, but after that it was increasingly difficult to get him along, and he gradually grew sulky. For some time we could not find out the reason; but finally he gave us to understand that he was afraid because up in the high mountains there were "little bad Indians" who would kill him if they caught him alone, especially at night. At first we thought he was speaking of stray warriors of the Blackfeet tribe; but it turned out that he was not thinking of human beings at all, but of hobgoblins.

Indeed the night sounds of these great stretches of mountain woodland were very weird and strange. Though I have often and for long periods dwelt and hunted in the wilderness, yet I never before so well understood why the people who live in lonely forest regions are prone to believe in elves, wood spirits, and other beings of an unseen-world. Our last camp, whereat we spent several days, was pitched in a deep valley nearly at the head of the stream. Our brush shelter stood among the tall coniferous trees that covered the valley bottom; but the altitude was so great that the forest extended only a very short distance up the steep mountain slopes. Beyond, on either hand, rose walls of gray rock, with snow beds in their rifts, and, high above, toward the snow peaks, the great white fields dazzled the eyes. The torrent foamed swiftly by but a short distance below the mossy level space on which we had built our slight weather-shield of pine boughs; other streams poured into it, from ravines through which they leaped down the mountain sides.

After nightfall, round the camp fire, or if I awakened after sleeping a little while, I would often lie silently for many minutes together, listening to the noises of the wilderness. At times the wind moaned harshly through the tops of the tall pines and hemlocks; at times the branches were still; but the splashing murmur of the torrent never ceased, and through it came other sounds —the clatter of huge rocks falling down the cliffs, the dashing of cataracts in far-off ravines, the hooting of owls. Again, the breeze would shift, and bring to my ears the ringing of other brooks and cataracts and wind-stirred forests, and perhaps at long intervals the cry of some wild beast, the crash of a falling tree, or the faint rumble of a snow avalanche. If I listened long enough, it would almost seem that I heard thunderous voices laughing and calling to one another, and as if at any moment some shape might stalk out of the darkness into the dim light of the embers.

Until within a couple of days of turning our faces back towards the lake we did not come across any caribou, and saw but a few old signs; and we began to be fearful lest we should have to return without getting any, for our shoes had been cut to ribbons by the sharp rocks, we were almost out of flour, and therefore had but little to eat. However, our perseverance was destined to be rewarded.

The first day after reaching our final camp, we hunted across a set of spurs and hollows but saw nothing living; yet we came across several bear tracks, and in a deep, mossy quagmire, by a spring, found where a huge silvertip had wallowed only the night before.

Next day we started early, determined to take a long walk and follow the main stream up to its head, or at least above timber line. The hunter struck so brisk a pace, plunging through thickets and leaping from log to log in the slashes of fallen timber, and from boulder to boulder in crossing the rockslides, that I could hardly keep up to him, struggle as I would, and we each of us got several ugly tumbles, saving our rifles at the expense of scraped hands and bruised bodies. We went up one side of the stream, intending to come down the other; for the forest belt was narrow enough to hunt thoroughly. For two or three hours we toiled through dense growth, varied by rock-slides, and once or twice by marshy tracts, where water oozed and soaked through the mossy hillsides, studded rather sparsely with evergreens. In one of these places we caught a glimpse of an animal which the track showed to be a wolverine.

Then we came to a spur of open hemlock forest; and no sooner had we entered it than the hunter stopped and pointed exultingly to a well-marked game trail, in which it was easy at a glance to discern the great round footprints of our quarry. We hunted carefully over the spur and found several trails, generally leading down along the ridge; we also found a number of beds, some old and some recent, usually placed where the animal could keep a lookout for any foe coming up from the valley. They were merely slight hollows or indentations in the pineneedles; and, like the game trails, were placed in localities similar to those that would be chosen by blacktail deer. The caribou droppings were also very plentiful; and there were signs of where they had browsed on the blueberry bushes, cropping off the berries, and also apparently of where they had here and there plucked a mouthful of a peculiar kind of moss, or cropped off some little mushrooms. But the beasts themselves had evidently left the hemlock ridge, and we went on.

We were much pleased at finding the sign in open timber, where the ground was excellent for still-hunting; for in such thick forest as we had passed through, it would have been by mere luck only that we could have approached game.

After a little while the valley became so high that the large timber ceased, and there were only occasional groves of spindling evergreens. Beyond the edge of the big timber was a large boggy tract, studded with little pools; and here again we found plenty of caribou tracks. A caribou has an enormous foot, bigger than a cow's, and admirably adapted for travelling over snow or bogs; hence they can pass through places where the long slender hoofs of moose or deer, or the rounded hoofs of elk, would let their owners sink at once; and they are very difficult to kill by following on snowshoes—a method much in vogue among the brutal game butchers for slaughtering the more helpless animals. Spreading out his great hoofs, and bending his legs till he walks almost on the joints, a caribou will travel swiftly over a crust through which a moose breaks at every stride, or through deep snow in which

a deer cannot flounder fifty yards. Usually he trots; but when pressed he will spring awkwardly along, leaving tracks in the snow almost exactly like magnified imprints of those of a great rabbit, the long marks of the two hind legs forming an angle with each other, while the forefeet make a large point almost between.

The caribou had wandered all over the bogs and through the shallow pools, but evidently only at night or in the dusk, when feeding or in coming to drink; and we again went on. Soon the timber disappeared almost entirely, and thick brushwood took its place; we were in a high, bare alpine valley, the snow lying in drifts along the sides. In places there had been enormous rock-slides, entirely filling up the bottom, so that for a quarter of a mile at a stretch the stream ran underground. In the rock masses of this alpine valley we, as usual, saw many conies and hoary woodchucks.

The caribou trails had ceased, and it was evident that the beasts were not ahead of us in the barren, treeless recesses between the mountains of rock and snow; and we turned back down the valley, crossing over to the opposite or south side of the stream. We had already eaten our scanty lunch, for it was afternoon. For several miles of hard walking, through thicket, marsh, and rockslide, we saw no traces of the game. Then we reached the forest, which soon widened out, and crept up the mountain sides; and we came to where another stream entered the one we were following. A high, steep shoulder between the two valleys was covered with an open growth of great hemlock timber, and in this we again found the trails and beds plentiful. There was no breeze, and after beating through the forest nearly to its upper edge, we began to go down the ridge, or point of the shoulder. The comparative freedom from brushwood made it easy to walk without noise, and we descended the steep incline with the utmost care, scanning every object, and using every caution not to slip on the hemlock needles, nor to strike a stone or break a stick with our feet. The sign was very fresh, and when still half a mile or

so from the bottom we at last came on three bull caribou.

Instantly the hunter crouched down, while I ran noiselessly forward behind the shelter of a big hemlock trunk until within fifty yards of the grazing and unconscious quarry. They were feeding with their heads up-hill, but so greedily that they had not seen us; and they were rather difficult to see themselves, for their bodies harmonized well in color with the brown tree-trunks and lichen-covered boulders. The largest, a big bull with a good but by no means extraordinary head, was nearest. As he stood fronting me with his head down I fired into his neck, breaking the bone, and he turned a tremendous back somersault. The other two halted a second in stunned terror; then one, a yearling, rushed past us up the valley down which we had come, while the other, a large bull with small antlers, crossed right in front of me, at a canter, his neck thrust out, and his head—so coarse-looking compared to the delicate outlines of an elk's—turned towards me. His movements seemed clumsy and awkward, utterly unlike those of a deer; but he handled his great hoofs cleverly enough, and broke into a headlong, rattling gallop as he went down the hillside, crashing through the saplings and leaping over the fallen logs. There was a spur a little beyond, and up this he went at a swinging trot, halting when he reached the top, and turning to look at me once more. He was only a hundred yards away; and though I had not intended to shoot him (for his head was not good), the temptation was sore; and I was glad when, in another second, the stupid beast turned again and went off up the valley at a slashing run.

Then we hurried down to examine with pride and pleasure the dead bull—his massive form, sleek coat, and fine antlers. It was one of those moments that repay the hunter for days of toil and hardship; that is if he needs repayment, and does not find life in the wilderness pleasule enough in itself.

It was getting late, and if we expected to reach camp that night it behooved us not to delay; so we merely halted long enough to dress the caribou, and take a steak with us—which we did not need, by the way, for almost immediately we came on a band of spruce grouse and knocked off the heads of five with our rifles. The caribou's stomach was filled with blueberries, and with their leaves, and with a few small mushrooms also, and some mouthfuls of moss. We went home very fast, too much elated to heed scratches and tumbles; and just as it was growing so dark that further travelling was impossible we came opposite our camp, crossed the river on a fallen hemlock, and walked up to the moody Indian, as he sat crouched by the fire.

He lost his sullenness when he heard what we had done; and next day we all went up and skinned and butchered the caribou, returning to camp and making ready to start back to the lake the following morning; and that night we feasted royally.

We were off by dawn, the Indian joyfully leading. Coming up into the mountains he had always been the rear man of the file; but now he went first and struck a pace that, continued all day long, gave me a little trouble to follow. Each of us carried his pack; to the Indians' share fell the caribou skull and antlers, which he bore on his head. At the end of the day he confessed to me that it had made his head "heap sick "—as well it might. We had made four short days', or parts of days', march coming up; for we had stopped to hunt, and moreover we knew nothing of the country, being probably the first white men in it, while none of the Indians had ever ventured a long distance from the lake. Returning we knew how to take the shortest route, we were going down hill, and we walked or trotted very fast; and so we made the whole distance in twelve hours' travel. At sunset we came out on the last range of steep foot-hills, overlooking the cove where we had pitched our permanent camp; and from a bare cliff shoulder we saw our boat on the beach, and our white tent among the trees, just as we had left them, while the glassy mirror of the lake reflected the outlines of the mountains opposite.

Though this was the first caribou I had ever killed, it was by no means the first I had ever hunted. Among my earliest hunting experiences, when a lad, were two fruitless and toilsome expeditions after caribou in the Maine woods. One I made in the fall, going to the head of the Munsungin River in a pirogue, with one companion. The water was low, and all the way up we had to drag the pirogue, wet to our middles, our ankles sore from slipping on the round stones under the rushing water, and our muscles aching with fatigue. When we reached the headwaters we found no caribou sign, and came back without slaying anything larger than an infrequent duck or grouse.

The following February I made a trip on snow-shoes after the same game, and with the same result. However, I enjoyed the trip, for the northland woods are very beautiful and strange in winter, as indeed they are at all other times—and it was my first experience on snow-shoes. I used the ordinary webbed racquets, and as the snow, though very deep, was only imperfectly crusted, I found that for a beginner the exercise was laborious in the extreme, speedily discovering that, no matter how cold it was, while walking through the windless woods I stood in no need of warm clothing. But at night, especially when lying out, the cold was bitter. Our plan was to drive in a sleigh to some logging camp, where we were always received with hearty hospitality, and thence make hunting trips, in very light marching order, through the heart of the surrounding forest. The woods, wrapped in their heavy white mantle, were still and lifeless. There were a few chickadees and woodpeckers; now and then we saw flocks of red-polls, pine linnets, and large, rosy grossbeaks; and once or twice I came across a grouse or white rabbit, and killed it for supper; but this was nearly all. Yet, though bird life was scarce, and though we saw few beasts beyond an occasional porcupine or squirrel, every morning the snow was dotted with a network of trails made during the hours of darkness; the fine tracery of the footprints of the little red wood-mouse, the marks which showed

the loping progress of the sable, the V and dot of the rabbit, the round pads of the lucivee, and many others. The snow reveals, as nothing else does, the presence in the forest of the many shy woodland creatures which lead their lives abroad only after nightfall. Once we saw a coon, out early after its winter nap, and following I shot it in a hollow tree. Another time we came on a deer and the frightened beast left its " yard," a tangle of beaten paths, or deep furrows. The poor animal made but slow headway through the powdery snow; after going thirty or forty rods it sank exhausted in a deep drift, and lay there in helpless panic as we walked close by. Very different were the actions of the only caribou we saw—a fine beast which had shed its antlers. I merely caught a glimpse of it as it leaped over a breastwork of down timbers; and we never saw it again. Alternately trotting and making a succession of long jumps, it speedily left us far behind; with its great splayhoofs it could snow-shoe better than we could. It is among deer the true denizen of the regions of heavy snowfall; far more so than the moose. Only under exceptional conditions of crust-formation is it in any danger from a man on snow-shoes.

In other ways it is no better able to take care of itself than moose and deer; in fact I doubt whether its senses are quite as acute, or at least whether it is as wary and knowing, for under like conditions it is rather easier to still-hunt. In the fall caribou wander long distances, and are fond of frequenting the wet barrens which break the expanse of the northern forest in tracts of ever increasing size as the subarctic regions are neared. At this time they go in bands, each under the control of a master bull, which wages repeated and furious battles for his harem; and in their ways of life they resemble the wapiti more than they do the moose or deer. They sometimes display a curious boldness, the bulls especially showing both stupidity and pugnacity when in districts to which men rarely penetrate.

On our way out of the woods, after this hunt, there was a slight warm spell, followed by rain and then by freezing weather, so as to bring about what is known as a silver thaw. Every twig was sheathed in glittering ice, and in the moonlight the forest gleamed as if carved out of frosted silver.

THE WAPITI OR ROUND-HORNED ELK. ONCE, while on another hunt with John Willis, I spent a week in a vain effort to kill moose among the outlying mountains at the southern end of the Bitter Root range. Then, as we had no meat, weetermined to try for elk, of which we had seen much sign.

We were camped with a wagon, as high among the foot-hills as wheels could go, but several hours' walk from the range of the game; for it was still early in the season, and they had not yet come down from the upper slopes. Accordingly we made a practice of leaving the wagon for two or three days at a time to hunt; returning to get a night's rest in the tent, preparatory to a fresh start. On these trips we carried neither blankets nor packs, as the walking was diffícult and we had much ground to cover. Each merely put on his jacket with a loaf of frying-pan bread and a paper of salt stuffed into the pockets. We were cumbered with nothing save our rifles and cartridges.

On the morning in question we left camp at sunrise. For two or three hours we walked up-hill through a rather open growth of small pines and spruces, the travelling being easy. Then we came to the edge of a deep valley, a couple of miles across. Into this we scrambled, down a steep slide, where the forest had grown up among the immense boulder masses. The going here was difficult to a degree; the great rocks, dead timber, slippery pine needles, and loose gravel entailing caution at every step, while we had to guard our rifles carefully from the consequences of a slip. It was not much better at the bottom, which was covered by a tangled mass of swampy forest. Through this we hunted carefully, but with no success, in spite of our toil; for the only tracks we saw that were at all fresh were those of a cow and calf moose. Finally, in the afternoon, we left the valley and began to

climb a steep gorge, down which a mountain torrent roared and foamed in a succession of cataracts.

Three hours' hard climbing brought us to another valley, but of an entirely different character. It was several miles long, but less than a mile broad. Save at the mouth, it was walled in completely by chains of high rockpeaks, their summits snow-capped; the forest extended a short distance up their sides. The bottom of the valley was in places covered by open woodland, elsewhere by marshy meadows, dotted with dense groves of spruce.

Hardly had we entered this valley before we caught a glimpse of a yearling elk walking rapidly along a game path some distance ahead. We followed as quickly as we could without making a noise, but after the first glimpse never saw it again; for it is astonishing how fast an elk travels, with its ground-covering walk. We went up the valley until we were well past its middle, and saw abundance of fresh elk sign. Evidently two or three bands had made the neighborhood their headquarters. Among them were some large bulls, which had been trying their horns not only on the quaking-asp and willow saplings, but also on one another, though the rut had barely begun. By one pool they had scooped out a kind of wallow or bare spot in the grass, and had torn and tramped the ground with their hoofs. The place smelt strongly of their urine.

By the time the sun set we were sure the elk were towards the head of the valley. We utilized the short twilight in arranging our sleeping place for the night, choosing a thick grove of spruce beside a small mountain tarn, at the foot of a great cliff. We were chiefly influenced in our choice by the abundance of dead timber of a size easy to handle; the fuel question being all-important on such a trip, where one has to lie out without bedding, and to keep up a fire, with no axe to cut wood.

Having selected a smooth spot, where some low-growing firs made a wind break, we dragged up enough logs to feed the fire throughout the night. Then we drank our fill at the icy pool, and ate

a few mouthfuls of bread. While it was still light we heard the querulous bleat of the conies, from among the slide rocks at the foot of the mountain; and the chipmunks and chickarees scolded at us. As dark came on, and we sat silently gazing into the flickering blaze, the owls began muttering and hooting.

Clearing the ground of stones and sticks, we lay down beside the fire, pulled our soft felt hats over our ears, buttoned our jackets, and went to sleep. Of course our slumbers were fitful and broken, for every hour or two the fire got low and had to be replenished. We wakened shivering out of each spell of restless sleep to find the logs smouldering; we were alternately scorched and frozen.

As the first faint streak of dawn appeared in the dark sky my companion touched me lightly on the arm. The fire was nearly out; we felt numbed by the chill air. At once we sprang up, stretched our arms, shook ourselves, examined our rifles, swallowed a mouthful or two of bread, and walked off through the gloomy forest.

At first we could scarcely see our way, but it grew rapidly lighter. The gray mist rose and wavered over the pools and wet places; the morning voices of the wilderness began to break the death-like stillness. After we had walked a couple of miles the mountain tops on our right hand reddened in the sun-rays.

Then, as we trod noiselessly over the dense moss, and on the pine needles under the scattered trees, we heard a sharp clang and clatter up the valley ahead of us. We knew this meant game of some sort; and stealing lightly and cautiously forward we soon saw before us the cause of the noise.

In a little glade, a hundred and twenty-five yards from us, two bull elk were engaged in deadly combat, while two others were looking on. It was a splendid sight. The great beasts faced each other with lowered horns, the manes that covered their thick necks, and the hair on their shoulders, bristling and erect. Then they charged furiously, the crash of the meeting antlers resounding through the valley. The shock threw them both on their haunches; with locked horns and glaring eyes they strove against each other, getting their hind legs well under them, straining every muscle in their huge bodies, and squealing savagely. They were evenly matched in weight, strength, and courage; and push as they might, neither got the upper hand, first one yielding a few inches, then the other, while they swayed to and fro in their struggles, smashing the bushes and ploughing up the soil.

Finally they separated and stood some little distance apart, under the great pines; their sides heaving, and columns of steam rising from their nostrils through the frosty air of the brightening morning. Again they rushed together with a crash, and each strove mightily to overthrow the other, or get past his guard; but the branching antlers caught every vicious lunge and thrust. This set-to was stopped rather curiously. One of the onlooking elk was a yearling; the other, though scarcely as heavy-bodied as either of the fighters, had a finer head. He was evidently much excited by the battle, and he now began to walk towards the two combatants, nodding his head and uttering a queer, whistling noise. They dared not leave their flanks uncovered to his assault; and as he approached they promptly separated, and walked off side by side a few yards apart. In a moment, however, one spun round and jumped at his old adversary, seeking to stab him in his unprotected flank; but the latter was just as quick, and as before caught the rush on his horns. They closed as furiously as ever; but the utmost either could do was to inflict one or two punches on the neck and shoulders of his foe, where the thick hide served as a shield. Again the peace-maker approached, nodding his head, whistling, and threatening; and again they separated.

This was repeated once or twice; and I began to be afraid lest the breeze which was very light and puffy should shift and give them my wind. So, resting my rifle on my knee I fired twice, putting one bullet behind the shoulder of the peace-maker, and the other behind the shoulder of one of the combatants. Both were deadly shots, but, as so often with wapiti, neither of the wounded animals at the moment showed any signs of being hit. The yearling ran off unscathed. The other three crowded together and trotted behind some spruce on the left, while we ran forward for another shot. In a moment one fell; whereupon the remaining two turned and came back across the glade, trotting to the right. As we opened fire they broke into a lumbering gallop, but were both downed before they got out of sight in the timber.

As soon as the three bulls were down we busied ourselves taking off their heads and hides, and cutting off the best portions of the meat—from the saddles and hams—to take back to camp, where we smoked it. But first we had breakfast. We kindled a fire beside a little spring of clear water and raked out the coals. Then we cut two willow twigs as spits, ran on each a number of small pieces of elk loin, and roasted them over the fire. We had salt; we were very hungry; and I never ate anything that tasted better.

The wapiti is, next to the moose, the most quarrelsome and pugnacious of American deer. It cannot be said that it is ordinarily a dangerous beast to hunt; yet there are instances in which wounded wapiti, incautiously approached to within striking distance, have severely misused their assailants, both with their antlers and their forefeet. I myself knew one man who had been badly mauled in this fashion. When tamed the bulls are dangerous to human life in the rutting season. In a grapple they are of course infinitely more to be dreaded than ordinary deer, because of their great strength.

However, the fiercest wapiti bull, when in a wild state, flees the neighborhood of man with the same panic terror shown by the cows; and he makes no stand against a grisly, though when his horns are grown he has little fear of either wolf or cougar if on his guard and attacked fairly. The chief battles of the bulls are of course waged with one another. Before the beginning of the rut they keep by themselves: singly, while the sprouting horns are still very young, at which time they lie in secluded spots and move about as little as possible; in large bands, later in the season. At the beginning of the fall these bands join with one another and with the bands of cows and calves, which have likewise been keeping to themselves during the late winter, the spring, and the summer. Vast herds are thus sometimes formed, containing, in the old days when wapiti were plenty, thousands of head. The bulls now begin to fight furiously with one another, and the great herd becomes split into smaller ones. Each of these has one master bull, who has won his position by savage battle, and keeps it by overcoming every rival, whether a solitary bull, or the lord of another harem, who challenges him.

When not fighting or love-making he is kept on the run, chasing away the young bulls who venture to pay court to the cows. He has hardly time to eat or sleep, and soon becomes gaunt and worn to a degree. At the close of the rut many of the bulls become so emaciated that they retire to some secluded spot to recuperate. They are so weak that they readily succumb to the elements, or to their brute foes; many die from sheer exhaustion.

The battles between the bulls rarely result fatally. After a longer or shorter period of charging, pushing, and struggling the heavier or more enduring of the two begins to shove his weaker antagonist back and round; and the latter then watches his chance and bolts, hotly, but as a rule harmlessly, pursued for a few hundred yards. The massive branching antlers serve as effective guards against the most wicked thrusts. While the antagonists are head on, the worst that can happen is a punch on the shoulder which will not break the thick hide, though it may bruise the flesh underneath. It is only when a beast is caught while turning that there is a chance to deliver a possibly deadly stab in the flank, with the brow prongs, the "dogkillers" as they are called in bucks.

Sometimes, but rarely, fighting wapiti get their antlers interlocked and perish miserably; my own ranch, the Elkhorn, was named from finding on the spot where the ranch house now stands two splendid pairs of elk antlers thus interlocked.

Wapiti keep their antlers until the spring, whereas deer and moose lose theirs by midwinter. The bull's behavior in relation to the cow is merely that of a vicious and brutal coward. He bullies her continually, and in times of danger his one thought is for sneaking off to secure his own safety. For all his noble looks he is a very unamiable beast, who behaves with brutal ferocity to the weak, and shows abject terror of the strong. According to his powers, he is guilty of rape, robbery, and even murder. I never felt the least compunction at shooting a bull, but I hate to shoot a cow, even when forced by necessity. Maternity must always appeal to any one. A cow has more courage than a bull. She will fight valiantly for her young calf, striking such blows with her forefeet that most beasts of prey at once slink away from the combat. Cougars and wolves commit great ravages among the bands; but they often secure their quarry only at the cost of sharp preliminary tussles—and in tussles of this kind they do not always prove victors or escape scathless.

During the rut the bulls are very noisy; and their notes of amorous challenge are called "whistling " by the frontiersmen,—very inappropriately. They begin to whistle about ten days before they begin to run; and they have in addition an odd kind of bark, which is only heard occasionally. The whistling is a most curious, and to me a most attractive sound, when heard in the great lonely mountains. As with so many other things, much depends upon the surroundings. When listened to nearby and under unfavorable circumstances, the sound resembles a succession of hoarse whistling roars, ending with two or three gasping grunts.

But heard at a little distance, and in its proper place, the call of the wapiti is one of the grandest and most beautiful sounds in nature. Especially is this the case when several rivals are answering one another, on some frosty moonlight night in the mountains. The wild melody rings from chasm to chasm under the giant pines, sustained and modulated, through bar after bar, filled with challenge and proud anger. It thrills the soul of the listening hunter.

Once, while in the mountains, I listened to a peculiarly grand chorus of this kind. We were travelling with pack ponies at the time, and our tent was pitched in a grove of yellow pine, by a brook in the bottom of a valley. On either hand rose the mountains, covered with spruce forest. It was in September, and the first snow had just fallen.

The day before we had walked long and hard; and during the night I slept the heavy sleep of the weary. Early in the morning, just as the east began to grow gray, I waked; and as I did so, the sounds that smote on my ear, caused me to sit up and throw off the warm blankets. Bull elk were challenging among the mountains on both sides of the valley, a little way from us, their notes echoing like the calling of silver bugles. Groping about in the dark, I drew on my trousers, an extra pair of thick socks, and my moccasins, donned a warm jacket, found my fur cap and gloves, and stole out of the tent with my rifle.

The air was very cold; the stars were beginning to pale in the dawn; on the ground the snow glimmered white, and lay in feathery masses on the branches of the balsams and young pines. The air rang with the challenges of many wapiti; their incessant calling came pealing down through the still, snow-laden woods. First one bull challenged; then another answered; then another and another. Two herds were approaching one another from opposite sides of the valley, a short distance above our camp; and the master bulls were roaring defiance as they mustered their harems.

I walked stealthily up the valley, until I felt that I was nearly between the two herds; and then stood motionless under a tall pine. The ground was quite open at this point, the pines, though large, being scattered; the little brook ran with a strangled murmur between its rows of willows and alders, for the ice along its edges nearly skimmed its breadth. The stars paled rapidly, the gray dawn brightened, and in the sky overhead faint rose-colored streaks were turning blood-red. What little wind there was breathed in my face and kept me from discovery.

I made up my mind, from the sound of the challenging, now very near me, that one bull on my right was advancing towards a rival on my left, who was answering every call. Soon the former approached so near that I could hear him crack the branches, and beat the bushes with his horns; and I slipped quietly from tree to tree, so as to meet him when he came out into the more open woodland. Day broke, and crimson gleams played across the snow-clad mountains beyond.

At last, just as the sun flamed red above the hill-tops, I heard the roar of the wapiti's challenge not fifty yards away; and I cocked and half raised my rifle, and stood motionless. In a moment more, the belt of spruces in front of me swayed and opened, and the lordly bull stepped out. He bore his massive antlers aloft; the snow lay thick on his mane; he snuffed the air and stamped on the ground as he walked. As I drew a bead, the motion caught his eye; and instantly his bearing of haughty and warlike self-confidence changed to one of alarm. My bullet smote through his shoulder-blades, and he plunged wildly forward, and fell full length on the blood-stained snow.

Nothing can be finer than a wapiti bull's carriage when excited or alarmed; he then seems the embodiment of strength and stately grace. But at ordinary times his looks are less attractive, as he walks with his neck level with his body and his head outstretched, his horns lying almost on his shoulders. The favorite gait of the wapiti is the trot, which is very fast, and which they can keep up for countless miles; when suddenly and greatly alarmed, they break into an awkward gallop, which is faster, but which speedily tires them.

I have occasionally killed elk in the

neighborhood of my ranch on the Little Missouri. They were very plentiful along this river until 1881, but the last of the big bands were slaughtered or scattered about that time. Smaller bunches were found for two or three years longer; and to this day, scattered individuals, singly or in parties of two or three, linger here and there in the most remote and inaccessible parts of the broken country. In the old times they were often found on the open prairie, and were fond of sunning themselves on the sand bars by the river, even at midday, while they often fed by daylight (as they do still in remote mountain fastnesses). Nowadays the few survivors dwell in the timber of the roughest ravines, and only venture abroad at dusk or even after nightfall. Thanks to their wariness and seclusiveness, their presence is often not even suspected by the cowboys or others who occasionally ride through their haunts; and so the hunters only know vaguely of their existence. It thus happens that the last individuals of a species may linger in a locality for many years after the rest of their kind have vanished; on the Little Missouri to-day every elk (as in the Rockies every buffalo) killed is at once set down as "the last of its race." For several years in succession I myself kept killing one or two such "last survivors."

A yearling bull which I thus obtained was killed while in company with my staunch friend Will Dow, on one of the first trips which I took with that prince of drivers, old man Tompkins. We were laying in our stock of winter meat; and had taken the wagon to go to a knot of high and very rugged hills where we knew there were deer, and thought there might be elk. Old Tompkins drove the wagon with unmoved composure up, down, and across frightful-looking hills, and when they became wholly impassable, steered the team over a cut bank and up a kind of winding ravine or wooded washout, until it became too rough and narrow for farther progress. There was good grass for the horses on a hill off to one side of us; and stunted cottonwood trees grew between the straight white walls of clay and sandstone which hemmed in the washout. We pitched our tent by a little trickling spring and kindled a great fire, the fitful glare lighting the bare cliffs and the queer, sprawling tops of the cottonwoods; and after a dinner of fried prairie-chicken went to bed. At dawn we were off, and hunted till nearly noon; when Dow, who had been walking to one side, beckoned to me and remarked," There's something mighty big in the timber down under the cliff; I guess it's an elk" (he had never seen one before); and the next moment, as old Tompkins expressed it, "the elk came bilin' out of thecoulie." Old Tompkins had a rifle on this occasion and the sight of game always drove him crazy; as I aimed I heard Dow telling him " to let the boss do the shooting"; and I killed the elk to a savage interjectional accompaniment of threats delivered at old man Tompkins between the shots.

Elk are sooner killed off than any other game save buffalo, but this is due to their size and the nature of the ground they frequent rather than to their lack of shyness. They like open woodland, or mountainous park country, or hills riven by timber coulies; and such ground is the most favorable to the hunter, and the most attractive in which to hunt. On the other hand moose, for instance, live in such dense cover that it is very difficult to get at them; when elk are driven by incessant persecution to take refuge in similar fastnesses they become almost as hard to kill. In fact, in this respect the elk stands to the moose much as the blacktail stands to the whitetail. The moose and whitetail are somewhat warier than the elk and blacktail; but it is the nature of the ground which they inhabit that tells most in their favor. On the other hand, as compared to the blacktail, it is only the elk's size which puts it at a disadvantage in the struggle for life when the riflebearing hunter appears on the scene. It is quite as shy and difficult to approach as the deer; but its bulk renders it much more eagerly hunted, more readily seen, and more easily hit. Occasionally elk suffer from fits of stupid tameness or equally stupid pan-

ic; but the same is true of blacktail. In two or three instances, I have seen elk showsilly ignorance of danger; but half a dozen times I have known blacktail behave with an even greater degree of stupid familiarity.

There is another point in which the wapiti and blacktail agree in contrast to the moose and whitetail. Both the latter delight in water-lilies, entering the ponds to find them, and feeding on them greedily. The wapiti is very fond of wallowing in the mud, and of bathing in pools and lakes; but as a rule it shows as little fondness as the blacktail for feeding on water-lilies or other aquatic plants.

In reading of the European red deer, which is nothing but a diminutive wapiti, we often see a "stag of ten" alluded to as if a full-grown monarch. A full-grown wapiti bull, however, always has twelve, and may have fourteen, regular normal points on his antlers, besides irregular additional prongs; and he occasionally has ten points when a two-year-old, as I have myself seen with calves captured young and tamed. The calf has no horns. The yearling carries two foot-long spikes, sometimes bifurcated, so as to make four points. The two-year-old often has six or eight points on his antlers; but sometimes ten, although they are always small. The three-year-old has eight or ten points, while his body may be nearly as large as that of a full-grown animal. The four-year-old is normally a ten or twelve pointer, but as yet with much smaller antlers than those so proudly borne by the old bulls.

Frontiersmen only occasionally distinguish the prongs by name. The brow and bay points are called dog-killers or war-tines; the tray is known simply as the third point; and the most characteristic prong, the long and massive fourth, is now and then called the dagger-point; the others being known as the fifth and sixth.

In the high mountain forest into which the wapiti has been driven, the large, heavily furred northern lynx, the lucivee, takes the place of the smaller, thinner-haired lynx of the plains and of the more southern districts, the bobcat or wildcat. On the Little Missouri the latter is the common form; yet I have seen a lucivee which was killed there. On Clarke's Fork of the Columbia both occur, the lucivee being the most common. They feed chiefly on hares, squirrels, grouse, fawns, etc.; and the lucivee, at least, also occasionally kills foxes and cocns, and has in its turn to dread the pounce of the big timber wolf. Both kinds of lynx can most easily be killed with dogs, as they tree quite readily when thus pursued. The wildcat is often followed on horseback, with a pack of hounds, when the country is favorable; and when chased in this fashion yields excellent sport. The skin of both these lynxes is tender. They often maul an inexperienced pack quite badly, inflicting severe scratches and bites on any hound which has just resolution enough to come to close quarters, but not to rush in furiously; but a big fighting dog will readily kill either. At Thompson's Falls two of Willis' hounds killed a lucivee unaided, though one got torn. Archibald Rogers' dog Sly, a cross between a greyhound and a bull mastiff, killed a bobcat singlehanded. He bayed the cat and then began to threaten it, leaping from side to side; suddenly he broke the motion, and rushing in got his foe by the small of the back and killed it without receiving a scratch.

The porcupine is sure to attract the notice of any one going through the mountains. It is also found in the timber belts fringing the streams of the great plains, where it lives for a week at a time in a single tree or clump of trees, peeling the bark from the limbs. But it is the easiest of all animals to exterminate, and is now abundant only in deep mountain forests. It is very tame and stupid; it goes on the ground, but its fastest pace is a clumsy waddle, and on trees, but is the poorest of treeclimbers,—grasping the trunk like a small, slow bear. It can neither escape nor hide. It trusts to its quills for protection, as the skunk does to its odor; but it is far less astute and more helpless than the skunk. It is readily made into a very unsuspicious and familiar, but un-

interesting, pet. I have known it come into camp in the daytime, and forage round the fire by which I was sitting. Its coat protects it against most foes. Bears sometimes eat it when very hungry, as they will eat anything; and I think that elk occasionally destroy it in sheer wantonness. One of its most resolute foes is the fisher, that big sable —almost a wolverine—which preys on everything, from a coon to a fawn, or even a small fox.

The noisy, active little chickarees and chipmunks, however, are by far the most numerous and lively denizens of these deep forests. They are very abundant and very noisy; scolding the travellers exactly as they do the bears when the latter dig up the caches of ants. The chipmunks soon grow tame and visit camp to pick up the crusts. The chickarees often ascend to the highest pine tops, where they cut off the cones, dropping them to the ground with a noise which often for a moment puzzles the still-hunter.

Two of the most striking and characteristic birds to be seen by him who hunts and camps among the pine-clad and spruce-clad slopes of the northern Rockies are a small crow and a rather large woodpecker. The former is called Clarke's crow, and the latter Lewis' woodpecker. Their names commemorate their discoverers, the explorers Lewis and Clarke, the first white men who crossed the United States to the Pacific, the pioneers of that great army of adventurers who since then have roamed and hunted over the Great Plains and among the Rocky Mountains.

These birds are nearly of a size, being about as large as a flicker. The Clarke's crow, an ash-colored bird with black wings and white tail and forehead, is as common as it is characteristic, and is sure to attract attention. It is as knowing as the rest of its race, and very noisy and active. It flies sometimes in a straight line, with regular wing-beats, sometimes in a succession of loops like a woodpecker, and often lights on rough bark or a dead stump in an attitude like the latter; and it is very fond of scram-

bling and clinging, often head downwards, among the outermost cones on the top of a pine, chattering loudly all the while. One of the noticeable features of its flight is the hollow, beating sound of the wings. It is restless and fond of company, going by preference in small parties. These little parties often indulge in regular plays, assembling in some tall tree-top and sailing round and round it, in noisy pursuit of one another, lighting continually among the branches.

The Lewis' woodpecker, a handsome, dark-green bird, with white breast and red belly, is much rarer, quite as shy, and generally less noisy and conspicuous. Its flight is usually strong and steady, like a jay's, and it perches upright among the twigs, or takes short flights after passing insects, as often as it scrambles over the twigs in the ordinary woodpecker fashion. Like its companion, the Clarke's crow, it is ordinarily a bird of the high tree-tops, and around these it indulges in curious aerial games, again like those of the little crow. It is fond of going in troops, and such a troop frequently choose some tall pine and soar round and above it in irregular spirals.

The remarkable and almost amphibious little water wren, with its sweet song, its familiarity, and its very curious habit of running on the bottom of the stream, several feet beneath the surface of the race of rapid water, is the most noticeable of the small birds of the Rocky Mountains. It sometimes sings loudly while floating with half-spread wings on the surface of a little pool. Taken as a whole, small birds are far less numerous and noticeable in the wilderness, especially in the deep forests, than in the groves and farmland of the settled country. The hunter and trapper are less familiar with small-bird music than with the screaming of the eagle and the large hawks, the croaking bark of the raven, the loon's cry, the crane's guttural clangor, and the unearthly yelling and hooting of the big owls.

No bird is so common around camp, so familiar, so amusing on some occasions, and so annoying on others, as that drab-colored imp of iniquity, the whisky jack—also known as the moose bird and camp robber. The familiarity of these birds is astonishing, and the variety of their cries, —generally harsh, but rarely musical—extraordinary. They snatch scraps of food from the entrances of the tents, and from beside the camp fire; and they shred the venison hung in the trees unless closely watched. I have seen an irate cook of accurate aim knock one off an elk-haunch, with a club seized at random; and I have known another to be killed with a switch, and yet another to be caught alive in the hand. When game is killed they are the first birds to come to the carcass. Following them come the big jays, of a uniform dark-blue color, who bully them, and are bullied in turn by the next arrivals, the magpies; while when the big ravens come, they keep all the others in the background, with the exception of an occasional wide-awake magpie.

For a steady diet no meat tastes better or is more nourishing than elk venison; moreover the different kinds of grouse give variety to the fare, and delicious trout swarm throughout the haunts of the elk in the Rockies. I have never seen them more numerous than in the wonderful and beautiful Yellowstone Canyon, a couple of miles below where the river pitches over the Great Falls, in windswayed cataracts of snowy foam. At this point it runs like a mill-race, in its narrow winding bed, between immense walls of queerly carved and colored rock which tower aloft in almost perpendicular cliffs. Late one afternoon in the fall of '90 Ferguson and I clambered down into the canyon, with a couple of rods, and in an hour caught all the fish we could carry. It then lacked much less than an hour of nightfall, and we had a hard climb to get out of the canyon before darkness overtook us; as there was not a vestige of a path, and as the climbing was exceedingly laborious and at one or two points not entirely without danger, the rocks being practicable in very few places, we could hardly have made much progress after it became too dark to see. Each of us carried the bag of trout in turn, and I personally was nearly done out when we reached the top; and then had to trot three miles to the horses.

AN ELK-HUNT AT TWO-OCEAN PASS. IN September, 1891, with my ranch-partner, Ferguson, I made an elk-hunt in northwestern Wyoming among the Shoshone Mountains, where they join the Hoodoo and Absoraka ranges. There is no more beautiful gamecountry in the United States. It is a park land, where glades, meadows, and high mountain pastures break the evergreen forest; a forest which is open compared to the tangled density of the woodland farther north. It is a high, cold region of many lakes and clear rushing streams. The steep mountains are generally of the rounded form so often seen in the ranges of the Cordilleras of the United States; but the Hoodoos, or Goblins, are carved in fantastic and extraordinary shapes; while the Tetons, a group of isolated rock-peaks, show a striking boldness in their lofty outlines.

This was one of the pleasantest hunts I ever made. As always in the mountains, save where the country is so rough and so densely wooded that one must go a-foot, we had a pack-train; and we took a more complete outfit than we had ever before taken on such a hunt, and so travelled in much comfort. Usually when in the mountains I have merely had one companion, or at most a couple, and two or three pack-ponies; each of us doing his share of the packing, cooking, fetching water, and pitching the small square of canvas which served as tent. In itself packing is both an art and a mystery, and a skilful professional packer, versed in the intricacies of the "diamond hitch," packs with a speed which no non-professional can hope to rival, and fixes the side packs and top packs with such scientific nicety, and adjusts the doubles and turns of the lash-rope so accurately, that everything stays in place under any but the most adverse conditions. Of course, like most hunters, I can myself in case of need throw the diamond hitch after a fashion, and pack on either the off or near side. Indeed, unless a man can pack it is not possible to make a really hard hunt in the mountains, if alone, or with only a single companion. The mere fair-weather hunter, who trusts entirely to the exertions of others, and does nothing more than ride or walk about under favorable circumstances, and shoot at what somebody else shows him, is a hunter in name only. Whoever would really deserve the title must be able at a pinch to shift for himself, to grapple with the difficulties and hardships of wilderness life unaided, and not only to hunt, but at times to travel for days, whether on foot or on horseback, alone. However, after one has passed one's novitiate, it is pleasant to be comfortable when the comfort does not interfere with the sport; and although a man sometimes likes to hunt alone, yet often it is well to be with some old mountain hunter, a master of woodcraft, who is a first-rate hand at finding game, creeping upon it, and tracking it when wounded. With such a companion one gets much more game, and learns many things by observation instead of by painful experience.

On this trip we had with us two hunters, Tazewell Woody and Elwood Hofer, a packer who acted as cook, and a boy to herd the horses. Of the latter, there were twenty; six saddle-animals and fourteen for the packs—two or three being spare horses, to be used later in carrying the elk-antlers, sheep-horns, and other trophies. Like most hunters' pack-animals, they were either half broken, or else broken down; tough, unkempt, jaded-looking beasts of every color—sorrel, buckskin, pinto, white, bay, roan. After the day's work was over, they were turned loose to shift for themselves; and about once a week they strayed, and all hands had to spend the better part of the day hunting for them. The worst ones for straying, curiously enough, were three broken-down old "bear-baits," which went by themselves, as is generally the case with the castoff horses of a herd. There were two sleeping-tents, another for the provisions,—in which we ate during bad weather,—and a canvas tepee, which was put up with lodge-poles, Indian fashion, like a wigwam. A tepee is more difficult to put up than an ordinary tent; but it is very convenient when there is rain or snow. A small fire kindled in the middle keeps it warm, the smoke escaping through the open top—that is, when it escapes at all; strings are passed from one pole to another, on which to hang wet clothes and shoes, and the beds are made around the edges. As an offset to the warmth and shelter, the smoke often renders it impossible even to sit upright. We had a very good camp-kit, including plenty of cooking-and eating-utensils; and among our provisions were some canned goods and sweetmeats, to give a relish to our meals of meat and bread. We had fur coats and warm clothes,—which are chiefly needed at night,—and plenty of bedding, including water-proof canvas sheeting and a couple of caribouhide sleeping-bags, procured from the survivors of a party of arctic explorers. Except on rainy days I used my buckskin hunting-shirt or tunic; in dry weather I deem it, because of its color, texture, and durability, the best possible garb for the still-hunter, especially in the woods.

Starting a day's journey south of Heart Lake, we travelled and hunted on the eastern edge of the great basin, wooded and mountainous, wherein rise the head-waters of the mighty Snake River. There was not so much as a spotted line—that series of blazes made with the axe, man's first highway through the hoary forest,—but this we did not mind, as for most of the distance we followed well-worn elk-trails. The train travelled in Indian file. At the head, to pick the path, rode tall, silent old Woody, a true type of the fast-vanishing race of game hunters and Indian fighters, a man who had been one of the California fortyniners, and who ever since had lived the restless, reckless life of the wilderness. Then came Ferguson and myself; then the pack-animals, strung out in line; while from the rear rose the varied oaths of our three companions, whose miserable duty it was to urge forward the beasts of burden.

It is heart-breaking work to drive a pack-train through thick timber and over mountains, where there is either a dim trail or none. The animals have a perverse faculty for choosing the wrong turn at critical moments; and they are continually scraping under branches and squeezing between tree-trunks, to the jeopardy or destruction of their burdens. After having been laboriously driven up a very steep incline, at the cost of severe exertion both to them and to the men, the foolish creatures turn and run down to the bottom, so that all the work has to be done over again. Some travel too slow; others travel too fast. Yet one cannot but admire the toughness of the animals, and the surefootedness with which they pick their way along the sheer mountain sides, or among boulders and over fallen logs.

As our way was so rough, we found that we had to halt at least once ever)' hour to fix the packs. Moreover, we at the head of the column were continually being appealed to for help by the unfortunates in the rear. First it would be " that white-eyed cayuse; one side of its pack's down!" then we would be notified that the saddle-blanket of the "lop-eared Indian buckskin" had slipped back; then a shout " Look out for the pinto!" would be followed by that pleasing beast's appearance, bucking and squealing, smashing dead timber, and scattering its load to the four winds. It was no easy task to get the horses across some of the boggy places without miring; or to force them through the denser portions of the forest, where there was much down timber. Riding with a pack-train, day in and day out, becomes both monotonous and irritating, unless one is upheld by the hope of a game-country ahead, or by the delight of exploration of the unknown. Yet when buoyed by such a hope, there is pleasure in taking a train across so beautiful and wild a country as that which lay on the threshold of our hunting grounds in the Shoshones. We went over mountain passes, with ranges of scalped peaks on either hand; we skirted the edges of lovely lakes, and of streams with boulder-strewn beds; we plunged into depths of sombre woodland, broken by wet prairies. It was a picturesque sight to see the loaded pack-train stringing across one of these high mountain meadows, the motley colored line of ponies winding round the marshy spots through the bright green grass, while beyond rose the dark line of frowning forest, with lofty peaks towering in the background. Some of the meadows were beautiful with many flowers—goldenrod, purple aster, bluebells, white immortelles, and here and there masses of blood-red Indian pinks. In the park-country, on the edges of the evergreen forest, were groves of delicate quaking-aspen, the trees often growing to quite a height; their tremulous leaves were already changing to bright green and yellow, occasionally with a reddish blush. In the Rocky Mountains the aspens are almost the only deciduous trees, their foliage offering a pleasant relief to the eye after the monotony of the unending pine and spruce woods, which afford so striking a contrast to the hardwood forest east of the Mississippi.

For two days our journey was uneventful, save that we came on the camp of a squawman—one Beaver Dick, an old mountain hunter, living in a skin tepee, where dwelt his comely Indian wife and half-breed children. He had quite a herd of horses, many of them mares and colts; they had evidently been well treated, and came up to us fearlessly.

The morning of the third day of our journey was gray and lowering. Gusts of rain blew in my face as I rode at the head of the train. It still lacked an hour of noon, as we were plodding up a valley beside a rapid brook running through narrow willow-flats, the dark forest crowding down on either hand from the low foot-hills of the mountains. Suddenly the call of a bull elk came echoing down through the wet woodland on our right, beyond the brook, seemingly less than half a mile off; and was answered by a faint, far-off call from a rival on the mountain beyond. Instantly halting the train, Woody and I slipped off our horses, crossed the brook, and started to still-hunt the first bull.

In this place the forest was composed

of the western tamarack; the large, tall trees stood well apart, and there was much down timber, but the ground was covered with deep wet moss, over which we trod silently. The elk was travelling up-wind, but slowly, stopping continually to paw the ground and thresh the bushes with his antlers. He was very noisy, challenging every minute or two, being doubtless much excited by the neighborhood of his rival on the mountain. We followed, Woody leading, guided by the incessant calling.

It was very exciting as we crept toward the great bull, and the challenge sounded nearer and nearer. While we were still at some distance the pealing notes were like those of a bugle, delivered in two bars, first rising, then abruptly falling; as we drew nearer they took on a harsh squealing sound. Each call made our veins thrill; it sounded like the cry of some huge beast of prey. At last we heard the roar of the challenge not eighty yards off. Stealing forward three or four yards, I saw the tips of the horns through a mass of dead timber and young growth, and I slipped to one side to get a clean shot. Seeing us, but not making out what we were, and full of fierce and insolent excitement, the wapiti bull stepped boldly toward us with a stately swinging gait. Then he stood motionless, facing us, barely fifty yards away, his handsome twelve-tined antlers tossed aloft, as he held his head with the lordly grace of his kind. I fired into his chest, and as he turned I raced forward and shot him in the flank; but the second bullet was not needed, for the first wound was mortal, and he fell before going fifty yards.

The dead elk lay among the young evergreens. The huge, shapely body was set on legs that were as strong as steel rods, and yet slender, clean, and smooth; they were in color a beautiful dark brown, contrasting well with the yellowish of the body. The neck and throat were garnished with a mane of long hair; the symmetry of the great horns set off the fine, delicate lines of the noble head. He had been wallowing, as elk are fond of doing, and the dried mud clung in patches to his flank; a stab in the haunch showed that he had been overcome in battle by some master bull who had turned him out of the herd.

We cut off the head, and bore it down to the train. The horses crowded together, snorting, with their ears pricked forward, as they smelt the blood. We also took the loins with us, as we were out of meat, though bull elk in the rutting season is not very good. The rain had changed to a steady downpour when we again got under way. Two or three miles farther we pitched camp, in a clump of pines on a hillock in the bottom of the valley, starting hot fires of pitchy stumps before the tents, to dry our wet things.

Next day opened with fog and cold rain. The drenched pack-animals, when driven into camp, stood mopingly, with drooping heads and arched backs; they groaned and grunted as the loads were placed on their backs and the cinches tightened, the packers bracing one foot against the pack to get a purchase as they hauled in on the lash-rope. A stormy morning is a trial to temper; the packs are wet and heavy, and the cold makes the work even more than usually hard on the hands. By ten we broke camp. It needs between two and three hours to break camp and get such a train properly packed; once started, our day's journey was six to eight hours, making no halt. We started up a steep, pine-clad mountain side, broken by cliffs. My hunting-shoes, though comfortable, were old and thin, and let the water through like a sieve. On the top of the first plateau, where black spruce groves were strewn across the grassy surface, we saw a band of elk, cows and calves, trotting off through the rain. Then we plunged down into a deep valley, and, crossing it, a hard climb took us to the top of a great bare table-land, bleak and wind-swept. We passed little alpine lakes, fringed with scattering dwarf evergreens. Snow lay in drifts on the north sides of the gullies; a cutting wind blew the icy rain in our faces. For two or three hours we travelled toward the farther edge of the table-land. In one place a spike bull elk stood half a mile off, in the open; he travelled to and fro, watching us.

As we neared the edge the storm lulled, and pale, watery sunshine gleamed through the rifts in the lows-cudding clouds. At last our horses stood on the brink of a bold cliff. Deep down beneath our feet lay the wild and lonely valley of Two-Ocean Pass, walled in on either hand by rugged mountain chains, their flanks scarred and gashed by precipice and chasm. Beyond, in a wilderness of jagged and barren peaks, stretched the Shoshones. At the middle point of the pass, two streams welled down from either side. At first each flowed in but one bed, but soon divided into two; each of the twin branches then joined the like branch of the brook opposite, and swept one to the east and one to the west, on their long journey to the two great oceans. They ran as rapid brooks, through wet meadows and willow-flats, the eastern to the Yellowstone, the western to the Snake. The dark pine forests swept down from the flanks and lower ridges of the mountains to the edges of the marshy valley. Above them jutted gray rock peaks,snow-drifts lying in the rents that seamed their northern faces. Far below us, from a great basin at the foot of the cliff, filled with the pine forest, rose the musical challenge of a bull elk; and we saw a band of cows and calves looking like mice as they ran among the trees.

It was getting late, and after some search we failed to find any trail leading down; so at last we plunged over the brink at a venture. It was very rough scrambling, dropping from bench to bench, and in places it was not only difficult but dangerous for the loaded pack-animals. Here and there we were helped by well-beaten elk-trails, which we could follow for several hundred yards at a time. On one narrow pine-clad ledge, we met a spike bull face to face; and in scrambling down a very steep, bare, rockstrewn shoulder the loose stones started by the horses' hoofs, bounding in great leaps to the forest below, dislodged two cows.

As evening fell, we reached the bottom, and pitched camp in a beautiful point of open pine forest, thrust out into the meadow. There was good shelter, and plenty of wood, water, and grass; we built a huge fire and put up our tents, scattering them in likely places among the pines, which grew far apart and without undergrowth. We dried our steaming clothes, and ate a hearty supper of elk-meat; then we turned into our beds, warm and dry, and slept soundly under the canvas, while all night long the storm roared without. Next morning it still stormed fitfully; the high peaks and ridges round about were all capped with snow. Woody and I started on foot for an all-day tramp; the amount of game seen the day before showed that we were in a good elk-country, where the elk had been so little disturbed that they were travelling, feeding, and whistling in daylight. For three hours we walked across the forest-clad spurs of the foot-hills. We roused a small band of elk in thick timber; but they rushed off before we saw them, with much smashing of dead branches. Then we climbed to the summit of the range. The wind was light and baffling; it blew from all points, veering every few minutes. There were occasional rain-squalls; our feet and legs were well soaked; and we became chilled through whenever we sat down to listen. We caught a glimpse of a big bull feeding up-hill, and followed him; it needed smart running to overtake him, for an elk, even while feeding, has a ground-covering gait. Finally we got within a hundred and twenty-five yards, but in very thick timber, and all I could see plainly was the hip and the after-part of the flank. I waited for a chance at the shoulder, but the bull got my wind and was off before I could pull trigger. It was just one of those occasions when there are two courses to pursue, neither very good, and when one is apt to regret whichever decision is made.

At noon we came to the edge of a deep and wide gorge, and sat down shivering to await what might turn up, our fingers numb, and our wet feet icy. Suddenly the love-challenge of an elk came pealing across the gorge, through the fine, cold rain, from the heart of the forest opposite. An hour's stiff climb, down and up, brought us nearly to him; but the wind forced us to advance from below through a series of open glades. He was lying on a point of the cliff-shoulder, surrounded by his cows; and he saw us and made off. An hour afterward, as we were trudging up a steep hill-side dotted with groves of fir and spruce, a young bull of ten points, roused from his daybed by our approach, galloped across us some sixty yards off. We were in need of better venison than can be furnished by an old rutting bull; so I instantly took a shot at the fat and tender young ten-pointer. I aimed well ahead and pulled trigger just as he came to a small gully; and he fell into it in a heap with a resounding crash. This was on the birthday of my eldest small son; so I took him home the horns, "for his very own." On the way back that afternoon I shot off the heads of two blue grouse, as they perched in the pines.

That evening the storm broke, and the weather became clear and very cold, so that the snow made the frosty mountains gleam like silver. The moon was full, and in the flood of light the wild scenery round our camp was very beautiful. As always where we camped for several days, we had fixed long tables and settles, and were most comfortable; and when we came in at nightfall, or sometimes long afterward, cold, tired, and hungry, it was sheer physical delight to get warm before the roaring fire of pitchy stumps, and then to feast ravenously on bread and beans, on stewed or roasted elk venison, on grouse and sometimes trout, and flapjacks with maple syrup.

Next morning dawned clear and cold, the sky a glorious blue. Woody and I started to hunt over the great table-land, and led our stout horses up the mountain-side, by elk-trails so bad that they had to climb like goats. All these elk-trails have one striking peculiarity. They lead through thick timber, but every now and then send off short, well-worn branches to some cliff-edge or jutting crag, commanding a view far and wide over the country beneath. Elk love to stand on these lookout points, and scan the valleys and mountains round about.

Blue grouse rose from beside our path; Clarke's crows flew past us, with a hollow, flapping sound, or lit in the pine-tops, calling and flirting their tails; the gray-clad whisky-jacks, with multitudinous cries, hopped and fluttered near us. Snow-shoe rabbits scuttled away, the big furry feet which give them their name already turning white. At last we came out on the great plateau, seamed with deep, narrow ravines. Reaches of pasture alternated with groves and open forests of varying size. Almost immediately we heard the bugle of a bull elk, and saw a big band of cows and calves on the other side of a valley. There were three bulls with them, one very large, and we tried to creep up on them; but the wind was baffling and spoiled our stalk. So we returned to our horses, mounted them, and rode a mile farther, toward a large open wood on a hill-side. When within two hundred yards we heard directly ahead the bugle of a bull, and pulled up short. In a moment I saw him walking through an open glade; he had not seen us. The slight breeze brought us down his scent. Elk have a strong characteristic smell; it is usually sweet, like that of a herd of Alderney cows; but in old bulls, while rutting, it is rank, pungent, and lasting. We stood motionless till the bull was out of sight, then stole to the wood, tied our horses, and trotted after him. He was travelling fast, occasionally calling; whereupon others in the neighborhood would answer. Evidently he had been driven out of some herd by the master bull.

He went faster than we did, and while we were vainly trying to overtake him we heard another very loud and sonorous challenge to our left. It came from a ridgecrest at the edge of the woods, among some scattered clumps of the northern nut-pine or pinyon—a queer conifer, growing very high on the mountains, its multiforked trunk and wide-spreading branches giving it the rounded top, and, at a distance, the general look of an oak rather than a pine. We at once walked toward the ridge, upwind. In a minute or two, to our chagrin, we stumbled on an outlying spike bull, evidently kept on the outskirts of the herd by the master bull. I thought he would alarm all the rest; but, as we stood motionless, he could not see clearly what we were. He stood, ran, stood again, gazed at us, and trotted slowly off. We hurried forward as fast as we dared, and with too little care; for we suddenly came in view of two cows. As they raised their heads to look, Woody squatted down where he was, to keep their attention fixed, while I cautiously tried to slip off to one side unobserved. Favored by the neutral tint of my buckskin hunting-shirt, with which my shoes, leggins, and soft hat matched, I succeeded. As soon as I was out of sight I ran hard and came up to a hillock crested with pinyons, behind which I judged I should find the herd. As I approached the crest, their strong, sweet smell smote my nostrils. In another moment I saw the tips of a pair of mighty antlers, and I peered over the crest with my rifle at the ready. Thirty yards off, behind a clump of pinyons, stood a huge bull, his head thrown back as he rubbed his shoulders with his horns. There were several cows around him, and one saw me immediately, and took alarm. I fired into the bull's shoulder, inflicting a mortal wound; but he went off, and I raced after him at top speed, firing twice into his flank; then he stopped, very sick, and I broke his neck with a fourth bullet. An elk often hesitates in the first moments of surprise and fright, and does not get really under way for two or three hundred yards; but, when once fairly started, he may go several miles, even though mortally wounded; therefore, the hunter, after his first shot, should run forward as fast as he can, and shoot again and again until the quarry drops. In this way many animals that would otherwise be lost are obtained, especially by the man who has a repeating-rifle. Nevertheless the hunter should beware of being led astray by the ease with which he can fire half a dozen shots from his repeater; and he should aim as carefully with each shot as if it were his last. No possible rapidity of fire can atone for habitual carelessness of aim with the first shot.

The elk I thus slew was a giant. His body was the size of a steer's, and his antlers, though not unusually long, were very massive and heavy. He lay in a glade, on the edge of a great cliff. Standing on its brink we overlooked a most beautiful country, the home of all homes for the elk: a wilderness of mountains, the immense evergreen forest broken by park and glade, by meadow and pasture, by bare hill-side and barren table-land. Some five miles off lay the sheet of water known to the old hunters as Spotted Lake; two or three shallow, sedgy places, and spots of geyser formation, made pale green blotches on its wind-rippled surface. Far to the southwest, in daring beauty and majesty, the grand domes and lofty spires of the Tetons shot into the blue sky. Too sheer for the snow to rest on their sides, it yet filled the rents in their rough flanks, and lay deep between the towering pinnacles of dark rock. That night, as on more than one night afterward, a bull elk came down whistling to within two or three hundred yards of the tents, and tried to join the horse herd. The moon had set, so I could not go after it. Elk are very restless and active throughout the night in the rutting season; but where undisturbed they feed freely in the daytime, resting for two or three hours about noon.

Next day, which was rainy, we spent in getting in the antlers and meat of the two dead elk; and I shot off the heads of two or three blue grouse on the way home. The following day I killed another bull elk, following him by the strong, not unpleasing, smell, and hitting him twice as he ran, at about eighty yards. So far I had had good luck, killing everything I had shot at; but now the luck changed, through no fault of mine, as far as I could see, and Ferguson had his innings. The day after I killed this bull he shot two fine mountain rams; and during the remainder of our hunt he killed five elk,—one cow, for meat, and four good bulls. The two rams were with three others, all old and with fine horns; Ferguson peeped over a lofty precipice and saw them coming up it only fifty yards below him. His two first and finest bulls were obtained by hard running and good shooting; the herds were on the move at the time, and only his speed of foot and soundness of wind enabled him to get near enough for a shot. One herd started before he got close, and he killed the master bull by a shot right through the heart, as it trotted past, a hundred and fifty yards distant.

As for me, during the next ten days. I killed nothing save one cow for meat; and this though I hunted hard every day from morning till night, no matter what the weather. It was stormy, with hail and snow almost every day; and after working hard from dawn until nightfall, laboriously climbing the slippery mountain-sides, walking through the wet woods, and struggling across the bare plateaus and cliff-shoulders, while the violent blasts of wind drove the frozen rain in our faces, we would come in after dusk wet through and chilled to the marrow. Even when it rained in the valleys it snowed on the mountain-tops, and there was no use trying to keep our feet dry. I got three shots at bull elk, two being very hurried snap-shots at animals running in thick timber, the other a running-shot in the open, at over two hundred yards; and I missed all three. On most days I saw no bull worth shooting; the two or three I did see or hear we failed to stalk, the light, shifty wind baffling us, or else an outlying cow which we had not seen giving the alarm. There were many blue and a few ruffed grouse in the woods, and I occasionally shot off the heads of a couple on my way homeward in the evening. In racing after one elk, I leaped across a gully and so bruised and twisted my heel on a rock that, for the remainder of my stay in the mountains, I had to walk on the fore part of that foot. This did not interfere much with my walking, however, except in going down-hill.

Our ill success was in part due to sheer bad luck; but the chief element therein was the presence of a great hunting-party of Shoshone Indians. Split into bands of eight or ten each, they scoured the whole country on their tough, sure-footed ponies. They always hunted on horseback, and followed the elk at full speed wherever they went. Their method of hunting was to organize great drives, the riders strung in lines far apart; they signalled to one another by means of willow whistles, with which they also imitated the calling of the bull elk, thus tolling the animals to them, or making them betray their whereabouts. As they slew whatever they could, but by preference cows and calves, and as they were very persevering, but also very excitable and generally poor shots, so that they wasted much powder, they not only wrought havoc among the elk, but also scared the survivors out of all the country over which they hunted.

Day in and day out we plodded on. In a huntingtrip the days of long monotony in getting to the ground, and the days of unrequited toil after it has been reached, always far outnumber the red-letter days of success. But it is just these times of failure that really test the hunter. In the long run, common-sense and dogged perseverance avail him more than any other qualities. The man who does not give up, but hunts steadily and resolutely through the spells of bad luck until the luck turns, is the man who wins success in the end.

After a week at Two-Ocean Pass, we gathered our pack-animals one frosty morning, and again set off across the mountains. A two-days' jaunt took us to the summit of Wolverine Pass, near Pinyon Peak, beside a little mountain tarn; each morning we found its surface skimmed with black ice, for the nights were cold. After three or four days, we shifted camp to the mouth of Wolverine Creek, to get off the hunting grounds of the Indians. We had used up our last elk-meat that morning, and when we were within a couple of hours' journey of our intended halting-place, Woody and I struck off on foot for a hunt. Just before sunset we came on three or four elk; a spike bull stood for a moment behind some thick evergreens a hundred yards off. Guessing at his shoulder, I fired, and he fell dead after running a few rods. I had broken the luck, after ten days of ill success.

Next morning Woody and I, with the packer, rode to where this elk lay. We loaded the meat on a pack-horse, and let the packer take both the loaded animal and our own saddle-horses back to camp, while we made a hunt on foot. We went up the steep, forest-clad mountain-side, and before we had walked an hour heard two elk whistling ahead of us. The woods were open, and quite free from undergrowth, and we were able to advance noiselessly; there was no wind, for the weather was still, clear, and cold. Both of the elk were evidently very much excited, answering each other continually; they had probably been master bulls, but had become so exhausted that their rivals had driven them from the herds, forcing them to remain in seclusion until they regained their lost strength. As we crept stealthily forward, the calling grew louder and louder, until we could hear the grunting sounds with which the challenge of the nearest ended. He was in a large wallow, which was also a lick. When we were still sixty yards off, he heard us, and rushed out, but wheeled and stood a moment to gaze, puzzled by my buckskin suit. I fired into his throat, breaking his neck, and down he went in a heap. Rushing in and turning, I called to Woody, "He'sa twelve-pointer, but the horns are small!" As I spoke I heard the roar of the challenge of the other bull not two hundred yards ahead, as if in defiant answer to my shot.

Running quietly forward, I speedily caught a glimpse of his body. He was behind some fir-trees about seventy yards off, and I could not see which way he was standing, and so fired into the patch of flank which was visible, aiming high, to break the back. My aim was true, and the huge beast crashed downhill through the evergreens, pulling himself on his fore legs for fifteen or twenty rods, his hind quarters trailing. Racing forward, I broke his neck. His antlers were the finest I ever got. A couple of whiskyjacks appeared at the first crack of the rifle with their customary astonishing familiarity and heedlessness of the hunter; they followed the wounded bull as he dragged his great carcass down the hill, and pounced with ghoulish bloodthirstiness on the gouts of blood that were sprinkled over the green herbage.

These two bulls lay only a couple of hundred yards apart, on a broad game-trail, which was as well beaten as a good bridle-path. We began to skin out the heads; and as we were finishing we heard another bull challenging far up the mountain. He came nearer and nearer, and as soon as we had ended our work we grasped our rifles and trotted toward him along the game-trail. He was very noisy, uttering his loud, singing challenge every minute or two. The trail was so broad and firm that we walked in perfect silence. After going only five or six hundred yards, we got very close indeed, and stole forward on tiptoe, listening to the roaring music. The sound came from a steep, narrow ravine, to one side of the trail, and I walked toward it with my rifle at the ready. A slight puff gave the elk my wind, and he dashed out of the ravine like a deer; but he was only thirty yards off, and my bullet went into his shoulder as he passed behind a clump of young spruce. I plunged into the ravine, scrambled out of it, and raced after him. In a minute I saw him standing with drooping head, and two more shots finished him. He also bore fine antlers. It was a great piece of luck to get three such fine bulls at the cost of half a day's light work; but we had fairly earned them, having worked hard for ten days, through rain, cold, hunger, and fatigue, to no purpose. That evening my homecoming to camp, with three elk-tongues and a brace of ruffed grouse hung at my belt, was most happy.

Next day it snowed, but we brought a pack-pony to where the three great bulls lay, and took their heads to camp; the flesh was far too strong to be worth taking, for it was just the height of the rut.

This was the end of my hunt; and a day later Hofer and I, with two pack-ponies, made a rapid push for the Upper Geyser Basin. We travelled fast. The first day was gray and overcast, a cold wind blowing strong in our faces.

Toward evening we came on a bull elk in a willow thicket; he was on his knees in a hollow, thrashing and beating the willows with his antlers. At dusk we halted and went into camp, by some small pools on the summit of the pass north of Red Mountain. The elk were calling all around us. We pitched our cozy tent, dragged great stumps for the fire, cut evergreen boughs for our beds, watered the horses, tethered them to im-provised picketpins in a grassy glade, and then set about getting supper ready. The wind had gone down, and snow was falling thick in large, soft flakes; we were evidently at the beginning of a heavy snowstorm. All night we slept soundly in our snug tent. When we arose at dawn there was a foot and a half of snow on the ground, and the flakes were falling as fast as ever. There is no more tedious work than striking camp in bad weather; and it was over two hours from the time we rose to the time we started. It is sheer misery to untangle picket-lines and to pack animals when the ropes are frozen; and by the time we had loaded the two shivering, wincing pack-ponies, and had bridled and sad-dled our own riding-animals, our hands and feet were numb and stiff with cold, though we were really hampered by our warm clothing. My horse was a wild, nervous roan, and as I swung carelessly into the saddle, he suddenly began to buck before I got my right leg over, and threw me off. My thumb was put out of joint. I pulled it in again, and speed-ily caught my horse in the dead tim-ber. Then I treated him as what the cow-boys call a "mean horse," and mounted him carefully, so as not to let him ei-ther buck or go over backward. Howev-er, his preliminary success had inspirit-ed him, and a dozen times that day he began to buck, usually choosing a down grade, where the snow was deep, and there was much fallen timber.

All day long we pushed steadily through the cold, blinding snowstorm. Neither squirrels nor rabbits were abroad; and a few Clarke's crows, whisky-jacks, and chickadees were the only living things we saw. At nightfall, chilled through, we reached the Upper Geyser Basin. Here I met a party of rail-road surveyors and engineers, coming in from their summer's field-work. One of them lent me a saddle-horse and a pack-pony, and we went on together, breaking our way through the snow-choked roads to the Mammoth Hot Springs, while Hofer took my own hors-es back to Ferguson.

I have described this hunt at length because, though I enjoyed it particularly on account of the comfort in which we travelled and the beauty of the land, yet, in point of success in finding and killing game, in value of trophies procured, and in its alternations of good and bad luck, it may fairly stand as the type of a dozen such hunts I have made. Twice I have been much more successful; the differ-ence being due to sheer luck, as I hunted equally hard in all three instances. Thus on this trip I killed and saw nothing but elk; yet the other members of the party either saw, or saw fresh signs of, not on-ly blacktail deer, but sheep, bear, bison, moose, cougar, and wolf. Now in 1889 I hunted over almost precisely similar country, only farther to the northwest, on the boundary between Idaho and Montana, and, with the exception of sheep, I stumbled on all the animals mentioned, and white goat in addition, so that my bag of twelve head actually included eight species—much the best bag I ever made, and the only one that could really be called out of the com-mon. In 1884, on a trip to the Bighorn Mountains, I killed three bear, six elk and six deer. In laying in the winter stock of meat for my ranch I often far excelled these figures as far as mere numbers went; but on no other regular hunting trip, where the quality and not the quantity of the game was the prime consideration, have I ever equalled them; and on several where I worked hardest I hardly averaged a head a week. The occasional days or weeks of phenomenal luck, are more than earned by the many others where no luck what-ever follows the very hardest work'. Yet, if a man hunts with steady reso-lution he is apt to strike enough lucky days amply to repay him.

On this Shoshone trip I fired fifty-eight shots. In preference to using the knife I generally break the neck of an elk which is still struggling; and I fire at one as long as it can stand, preferring to waste a few extra bullets, rather than see an occasional head of game escape. In consequence of these two traits the nine elk I got (two running at sixty and eighty yards, the others standing, at from thirty to a hundred) cost me twen-tythree bullets; and I missed three shots—all three, it is but fair to say, difficult ones. I also cut off the heads of seventeen grouse, with twenty-two shots; and killed two ducks with ten shots—fifty-eight in all. On the Bighorn trip I used a hundred and two cartridges. On no other trip did I use fifty.

To me still-hunting elk in the moun-tains, when they are calling, is one of the most attractive of sports, not only because of the size and stately beauty of the quarry and the grand nature of the trophy, but because of the magnif-icence of the scenery, and the stirring, manly, exciting nature of the chase it-self. It yields more vigorous enjoyment than does lurking stealthily through the grand but gloomy monotony of the marshy woodland where dwells the moose. The climbing among the steep forest-clad and glade-strewn mountains is just difficult enough thoroughly to test soundness in wind and limb, while without the heart-breaking fatigue of white goat hunting. The actual grapple with an angry grisly is of course far more full of strong, eager pleasure; but bear hunting is the most uncertain, and usually the least productive, of sports.

As regards strenuous, vigorous work, and pleasurable excitement the chase of the bighorn alone stands higher. But the bighorn, grand beast of the chase though he be, is surpassed in size, both of body and of horns, by certain of the giant sheep of Central Asia; whereas the wapiti is not only the most stately and beautiful of American game —far more so than the bison and moose, his only rivals in size—but is also the noblest of the stag kind throughout the world. Whoever kills him has killed the chief of his race; for he stands far above his brethren of Asia and Europe.

THE MOOSE; THE BEAST OF THE WOOD-LAND. THE moose is the giant of all deer; and many hunters esteem it the noblest of American game. Beyond question there are few trophies more prized than the huge shovel horns of this strange dweller in the cold northland forests.

I shot my first moose after making several fruitless hunting trips with this special game in view. The season I finally succeeded it was only after having hunted two or three weeks in vain, among the Bitter Root Mountains, and the ranges lying southeast of them.

I began about the first of September by making a trial with my old hunting friend Willis. We speedily found a country where there were moose, but of the animals themselves we never caught a glimpse. We tried to kill them by hunting in the same manner that we hunted elk; that is, by choosing a place where there was sign, and going carefully through it against or across the wind. However, this plan failed; though at that very time we succeeded in killing elk in this way, devoting one or two days to their pursuit. There were both elk and moose in the country, but they were usually found in different kinds of ground, though often close alongside one another. The former went in herds, the cows, calves, and yearlings by themselves, and they roamed through the higher and more open forests, well up towards timber line. The moose, on the contrary, were found singly or in small parties composed at the outside of a bull, a cow, and her young of two years; for the moose is practically monogamous, in strong contrast to the highly polygamous wapiti and caribou.

The moose did not seem to care much whether they lived among the summits of the mountains or not, so long as they got the right kind of country; for they were much more local in their distribution, and at this season less given to wandering than their kin with round horns. What they wished was a cool, swampy region of very dense growth; in the main chains of the northern Rockies even the valleys are high enough to be cold. Of course many of the moose lived on the wooded summits of the lower ranges; and most of them came down lower in winter than in summer, following about a fortnight after the elk; but if in a large tract of woods the cover was dense and the ground marshy, though it was in a valley no higher than the herds of the ranchmen grazed, or perchance even in the immediate neighborhood of a small frontier hamlet, then it might be chosen by some old bull who wished to lie in seclusion till his horns were grown, or by some cow with a calf to raise. Before settlers came to this high mountain region of Western Montana, a moose would often thus live in an isolated marshy tract surrounded by open country. They grazed throughout the summer on marsh plants, notably lily stems, and nibbled at the tops of the very tall natural hay of the meadows. The legs of the beast are too long and the neck too short to allow it to graze habitually on short grass; yet in the early spring when greedy for the tender blades of young, green marsh grass, the moose will often shuffle down on its knees to get at them, and it will occasionally perform the same feat to get a mouthful or two of snow in winter.

The moose which lived in isolated, exposed localities were speedily killed or driven away after the incoming of settlers; and at the time that we hunted we found no sign of them until we reached the region of continuous forest. Here, in a fortnight's hunting, we found as much sign as we wished, and plenty of it fresh; but the animals themselves we not only never saw but we never so much as heard. Often after hours of careful still-hunting or cautious tracking, we found the footprints deep in the soft earth, showing where our quarry had winded or heard us, and had noiselessly slipped away from the danger. It is astonishing how quietly a moose can steal through the woods if it wishes: and it has what is to the hunter a very provoking habit of making a half or three quarters circle before lying down, and then crouching with its head so turned that it can surely perceive any pursuer who may follow its trail. We tried every method to outwit the beasts. We attempted to track them; we beat through likely spots; sometimes we merely "sat on a log" and awaited events, by a drinking hole, meadow, mud wallow or other such place (a course of procedure which often works well in still-hunting); but all in vain.

Our main difficulty lay in the character of the woods which the moose haunted. They were choked and tangled to the last degree, consisting of a mass of thick-growing conifers, with dead timber strewn in every direction, and young growth filling the spaces between the trunks. We could not see twenty yards ahead of us, and it was almost impossible to walk without making a noise. Elk were occasionally found in these same places; but usually they frequented more open timber, where the hunting was beyond comparison easier. Perhaps more experienced hunters would have killed their game; though in such cover the best tracker and still-hunter alive cannot always reckon on success with really wary animals. But, be this as it may, we, at any rate, were completely baffled, and I began to think that this moose-hunt, like all my former ones, was doomed to end in failure.

However, a few days later I met a crabbed old trapper named Hank Griffin, who was going after beaver in the mountains, and who told me that if I would come with him he would show me moose. I jumped at the chance, and he proved as good as his word; though for the first two trials my ill luck did not change.

At the time that it finally did change we had at last reached a place where the moose were on favorable ground. A high, marshy valley stretched for several miles between two rows of stony mountains, clad with a forest of rather small fir-trees. This valley was covered with reeds, alders, and rank grass, and studded with little willow-bordered ponds and island-like clumps of spruce and graceful tamaracks.

Having surveyed the ground and found moose sign the preceding afternoon, we were up betimes in the cool morning to begin our hunt. Before sunrise we were posted on a rocky spur of the foot-hills, behind a mask of evergreens; ourselves unseen we overlooked all the valley, and we knew we could see any animal which might be either feeding away from cover or on its journey homeward from its feeding ground to its day-bed.

As it grew lighter we scanned the valley with increasing care and eagerness. The sun rose behind us; and almost as soon as it was up we made out some large beast moving among the dwarf willows beside a little lake half a mile in our front. In a few minutes the thing walked out where the bushes were thinner, and we saw that it was a young bull moose browsing on the willow tops. He had evidently nearly finished his breakfast, and he stood idly for some moments, now and then lazily cropping a mouthful of twig tips. Then he walked off with great strides in a straight line across the marsh, splashing among the wet water-plants, and ploughing through boggy spaces with the indifference begotten of vast strength and legs longer than those of any other animal on this continent. At times he entered beds of reeds which hid him from view, though their surging and bending showed the wake of his passage; at other times he walked through meadows of tall grass, the withered yellow stalks rising to his flanks, while his body loomed above them, glistening black and wet in the level sunbeams. Once he stopped for a few moments on a rise of dry ground, seemingly to enjoy the heat of the young sun; he stood motionless, save that his ears were continually pricked, and his head sometimes slightly turned, showing that even in this remote land he was on the alert. Once, with a somewhat awkward motion, he reached his hind leg forward to scratch his neck. Then he walked forward again into the marsh; where the water was quite deep he broke into the long, stretching, springy trot, which forms the characteristic gait of his kind, churning the marsh water into foam. He held his head straight forwards, the antlers resting on his shoulders.

After awhile he reached a spruce is-land, through which he walked to and fro; but evidently could find therein no resting-place quite to his mind, for he soon left and went on to another. Here after a little wandering he chose a point where there was some thick young growth, which hid him from view when he lay down, though not when he stood. After some turning he settled himself in his bed just as a steer would.

He could not have chosen a spot better suited for us. He was nearly at the edge of the morass, the open space between the spruce clump where he was lying and the rocky foot-hills being comparatively dry and not much over a couple of hundred yards broad; while some sixty yards from it, and between it and the hills, was a little hummock, tufted with firs, so as to afford us just the cover we needed. Keeping back from the edge of the morass we were able to walk upright through the forest, until we got the point where he was lying in a line with this little hummock. We then dropped on our hands and knees, and crept over the soft, wet sward, where there was nothing to make a noise. Wherever the ground rose at all we crawled flat on our bellies. The air was still, for it was a very calm morning.

At last we reached the hummock, and I got into position for a shot, taking a final look at my faithful 45-90 Winchester to see that all was in order. Peering cautiously through the shielding evergreens, I at first could not make out where the moose was lying, until my eye was caught by the motion of his big ears, as he occasionally flapped them lazily forward. Even then I could not see his outline; but I knew where he was, and having pushed my rifle forward on the moss, I snapped a dry twig to make him rise. My veins were thrilling and my heart beating with that eager, fierce excitement, known only to the hunter of big game, and forming one of the keenest and strongest of the many pleasures which with him go to make up "the wild joy of living."

As the sound of the snapping twig smote his ears the moose rose nimbly to his feet, with a lightness on which one would not have reckoned in a beast so heavy of body. He stood broadside to me for a moment, his ungainly head slightly turned, while his ears twitched and his nostrils snuffed the air. Drawing a fine bead against his black hide, behind his shoulder and two thirds of his body's depth below his shaggy withers, I pressed the trigger. He neither flinched nor reeled, but started with his regular ground-covering trot through the spruces; yet I knew he was mine, for the light blood sprang from both of his nostrils, and he fell dying on his side before he had gone thirty rods.

Later in the fall I was again hunting among the lofty ranges which continue towards the southeast the chain of the Bitter Root, between Idaho and Montana. There were but two of us, and we were travelling very light, each having but one pack-pony and the saddle animal he bestrode. We were high among the mountains, and followed no regular trail. Hence our course was often one of extreme difficulty. Occasionally, we took our animals through the forest near timber line, where the slopes were not too steep; again we threaded our way through a line of glades, or skirted the foot-hills, in an open, park country; and now and then we had to cross stretches of tangled mountain forest, making but a few miles a day, at the cost of incredible toil, and accomplishing even this solely by virtue of the wonderful docility and sure-footedness of the ponies, and of my companion's skill with the axe and thorough knowledge of woodcraft.

Late one cold afternoon we came out in a high alpine valley in which there was no sign of any man's having ever been before us. Down its middle ran a clear brook. On each side was a belt of thick spruce forest, covering the lower flanks of the mountains. The trees came down in points and isolated clumps to the brook, the banks of which were thus bordered with open glades, rendering the travelling easy and rapid.

Soon after starting up this valley we entered a beaver meadow of considerable size. It was covered with lush, rank grass, and the stream wound through it rather sluggishly in long curves, which were fringed by a thick growth of dwarfed willows. In one or two places it broadened into small ponds, bearing a few lily-pads. This meadow had been all tramped up by moose. Trails led hither and thither through the grass, the willow twigs were cropped off, and the muddy banks of the little black ponds were indented by hoof-marks. Evidently most of the lilies had been plucked. The footprints were unmistakable; a moose's foot is longer and slimmer than a caribou's, while on the other hand it is much larger than an elk's, and a longer oval in shape.

Most of the sign was old, this high alpine meadow, surrounded by snow mountains, having clearly been a favorite resort for moose in the summer; but some enormous, fresh tracks told that one or more old bulls were still frequenting the place.

The light was already fading, and, of course, we did not wish to camp where we were, because we would then certainly scare the moose. Accordingly we pushed up the valley for another mile, through an open forest, the ground being quite free from underbrush and dead timber, and covered with a carpet of thick moss, in which the feet sank noiselessly. Then we came to another beaver-meadow, which offered fine feed for the ponies. On its edge we hastily pitched camp, just at dusk. We tossed down the packs in a dry grove, close to the brook, and turned the tired ponies loose in the meadow, hobbling the little mare that carried the bell. The ground was smooth. We threw a cross-pole from one to the other of two young spruces, which happened to stand handily, and from it stretched and pegged out a piece of canvas, which we were using as a shelter tent. Beneath this we spread our bedding, laying under it the canvas sheets in which it had been wrapped. There was still bread left over from yesterday's baking, and in a few moments the kettle was boiling and the fryingpan sizzling, while one of us skinned and cut into suitable pieces two grouse we had knocked over on our march. For fear of frightening the moose we built but a small fire, and went to bed soon

after supper, being both tired and cold. Fortunately, what little breeze there was blew up the valley.

At dawn I was awake, and crawled out of my buffalo bag, shivering and yawning. My companion still slumbered heavily. White frost covered whatever had been left outside. The cold was sharp, and I hurriedly slipped a pair of stout moccasins on my feet, drew on my gloves and cap, and started through the ghostly woods for the meadow where we had seen the moose sign. The tufts of grass were stiff with frost; black ice skimmed the edges and quiet places of the little brook.

I walked slowly, it being difficult not to make a noise by cracking sticks or brushing against trees, in the gloom; but the forest was so open that it favored me. When I reached the edge of the beaver-meadow it was light enough to shoot, though the front sight still glimmered indistinctly. Streaks of cold red showed that the sun would soon rise.

Before leaving the shelter of the last spruces I halted to listen; and almost immediately heard a curious splashing sound from the middle of the meadow, where the brook broadened into small willow-bordered pools. I knew at once that a moose was in one of these pools, wading about and pulling up the water-lilies by seizing their slippery stems in his lips, plunging his head deep under water to do so. The moose love to feed in this way in the hot months, when they spend all the time they can in the water, feeding or lying down; nor do they altogether abandon the habit even when the weather is so cold that icicles form in their shaggy coats.

Crouching, I stole noiselessly along the edge of the willow thicket. The stream twisted through it from side to side in zigzags, so that every few rods I got a glimpse down a lane of black water. In a minute I heard a slight splashing near me; and on passing the next point of bushes, I saw the shadowy outline of the moose's hindquarters, standing in a bend of the water. In a moment he walked onwards, disappearing. I ran forward a couple of rods, and then turned in among the willows, to reach

the brook where it again bent back towards me. The splashing in the water, and the rustling of the moose's body against the frozen twigs, drowned the little noise made by my moccasined feet.

I strode out on the bank at the lower end of a long narrow pool of water, dark and half frozen. In this pool, half way down and facing me, but a score of yards off, stood the mighty marsh beast, strange and uncouth in look as some monster surviving over from the Pliocene. His vast bulk loomed black and vague in the dim gray dawn; his huge antlers stood out sharply; columns of steam rose from his nostrils. For several seconds he fronted me motionless; then he began to turn, slowly, and as if he had a stiff neck. When quarter way round I fired into his shoulder; whereat he reared and bounded on the bank with a great leap, vanishing in the willows. Through these I heard him crash like a whirlwind for a dozen rods; then down he fell, and when I reached the spot he had ceased to struggle. The ball had gone through his heart.

When a moose is thus surprised at close quarters, it will often stand at gaze for a moment or two, and then turn stiffly around until headed in the right direction; once thus headed aright it starts off with extraordinary speed.

The flesh of the moose is very good; though some deem it coarse. Old hunters, who always like rich, greasy food, rank a moose's nose with a beaver's tail, as the chief of backwood delicacies; personally I never liked either. The hide of the moose, like the hide of the elk, is of very poor quality, much inferior to ordinary buckskin; caribou hide is the best of all, especially when used as webbing for snow-shoes.

The moose is very fond of frequenting swampy woods throughout the summer, and indeed late into the fall. These swampy woods are not necessarily in the lower valleys, some being found very high among the mountains. By preference it haunts those containing lakes, where it can find the long lily-roots of which it is so fond, and where it can escape the torment of the mosquitoes and deer-flies by lying completely submerged save for its nostrils. It is a bold and good swimmer, readily crossing lakes of large size; but it is of course easily slain if discovered by canoe-men while in the water. It travels well through bogs, but not as well as the caribou; and it will not venture on ice at all if it can possibly avoid it.

After the rut begins the animals roam everywhere through the woods; and where there are hardwood forests the winter-yard is usually made among them, on high ground, away from the swamps. In the mountains the deep snows drive the moose, like all other game, down to the lower valleys, in hard winters. In the summer it occasionally climbs to the very summits of the wooded ranges, to escape the flies; and it is said that in certain places where wolves are plenty the cows retire to the tops of the mountains to calve. More often, however, they select some patch of very dense cover, in a swamp or by a lake, for this purpose. Their ways of life of course vary with the nature of the country they frequent. In the towering chains of the Rockies, clad in sombre and unbroken evergreen forests, their habits, in regard to winter-and summer-homes, and choice of places of seclusion for cows with young calves and bulls growing their antlers, differ from those of their kind which haunt the comparatively low, hilly, lake-studded country of Maine and Nova Scotia, where the forests are of birch, beech, and maple, mixed with the pine, spruce, and hemlock.

The moose being usually monogamous is never found in great herds like the wapiti and caribou. Occasionally a troop of fifteen or twenty individuals may be seen, but this is rare; more often it is found singly, in pairs, or in family parties, composed of a bull, a cow, and two or more calves and yearlings. In yarding, two or more such families may unite to spend the winter together in an unusually attractive locality; and during the rut many bulls are sometimes found together, perhaps following the trail of a cow in single file.

In the fall, winter, and early spring, and in certain places during summer, the moose feeds principally by browsing, though always willing to vary its diet by mosses, lichens, fungi, and ferns. In the eastern forests, with their abundance of hardwood, the birch, maple, and moose-wood form its favorite food. In the Rocky Mountains, where the forests are almost purely evergreen, it feeds on such willows, alders, and aspens as it can find, and also, when pressed by necessity, on balsam, fir, spruce, and very young pine. It peels the bark between its hard palate and sharp lower teeth, to a height of seven or eight feet; these "peelings" form conspicuous moose signs. It crops the juicy, budding twigs and stem tops to the same height; and if the tree is too tall it "rides" it, that is, straddles the slender trunk with its fore legs, pushing it over and walking up it until the desired branches are within reach. No beast is more destructive to the young growth of a forest than the moose. Where much persecuted it feeds in the late evening, early morning, and by moonlight. Where rarely disturbed it passes the day much as cattle do, alternately resting and feeding for two or three hours at a time.

Young moose, when caught, are easily tamed, and are very playful, delighting to gallop to and fro, kicking, striking, butting, and occasionally making grotesque faces. As they grow old they are apt to become dangerous, and even their play takes the form of a mock fight. Some lumbermen I knew on the Aroostook, in Maine, once captured a young moose, and put it in a pen of logs. A few days later they captured another, somewhat smaller, and put it in the same pen, thinking the first would be grateful at having a companion. But if it was it dissembled its feelings, for it promptly fell on the unfortunate newcomer and killed it before it could be rescued.

During the rut the bulls seek the cows far and wide, uttering continually throughout the night a short, loud roar, which can be heard at a distance of four or five miles; the cows now and then respond with low, plaintive bellows. The bulls also thrash the tree trunks with their horns, and paw big holes in soft ground; and when two rivals, come together at this season they fight with the most desperate fury. It is chiefly in these battles with one another that the huge antlers are used; in contending with other foes they strike terrible blows with their fore hoofs and also sometimes lash out behind like a horse. The bear occasionally makes a prey of the moose; the cougar is a more dangerous enemy in the few districts where both animals are found at all plentifully; but next to man its most dreaded foe is the big timber wolf, that veritable scourge of all animals of the deer kind. Against all of these the moose defends itself valiantly; a cow with a calf and a rutting bull being especially dangerous opponents. In deep snows through which the great deer flounders while its adversary runs lightly on the crust, a single wolf may overcome and slaughter a big bull moose; but with a fair chance no one or two wolves would be a match for it. Desperate combats take place before a small pack of wolves can master the shovel-horned quarry, unless it is taken at a hopeless disadvantage; and in these battles the prowess of the moose is shown by the fact that it is no unusual thing for it to kill one or more of the ravenous throng; generally by a terrific blow of the foreleg, smashing a wolf's skull or breaking its back. I have known of several instances of wolves being found dead, having perished in this manner. Still the battle usually ends the other way, the wolves being careful to make the attack with the odds in their favor; and even a small pack of the ferocious brutes will in a single winter often drive the moose completely out of a given district. Both cougar and bear generally reckon on taking the moose unawares, when they jump on it. In one case that came to my knowledge a black bear was killed by a cow moose whose calf he had attacked.

In the northeast a favorite method of hunting the moose is by "calling" the bulls in the rutting season, at dawn or nightfall; the caller imitating their cries through a birch-bark trumpet. If the animals are at all wary, this kind of sport can only be carried on in still weather, as the approaching bull always tries to get the wind of the caller. It is also sometimes slain by fire-hunting, from a canoe, as the deer are killed in the Adirondacks. This, however, is but an ignoble sport; and to kill the animal while it is swimming in a lake is worse. However, there is sometimes a spice of excitement even in these unworthy methods of the chase; for a truculent moose will do its best, with hoofs and horns, to upset the boat.

The true way to kill the noble beast, however, is by fair still-hunting. There is no grander sport than still-hunting the moose, whether in the vast pine and birch forests of the northeast, or among the stupendous mountain masses of the Rockies. The moose has wonderfully keen nose and ears, though its eyesight is not remarkable. Most hunters assert that he is the wariest of all game, and the most difficult to kill. I have never been quite satisfied that this was so; it seems to me that the nature of the ground wherein it dwells helps it even more than do its own sharp senses. It is true that I made many trips in vain before killing my first moose; but then I had to hunt through tangled timber, where I could hardly move a step without noise, and could never see thirty yards ahead. If moose were found in open park-like forests like those where I first killed elk, on the Bighorn Mountains, or among brushy coulies and bare hills, like the Little Missouri Bad Lands, where I first killed blacktail deer, I doubt whether they would prove especially difficult animals to bag. My own experience is much too limited to allow me to speak with any certainty on the point; but it is borne out by what more skilled hunters have told me. In the Big Hole Basin, in southwest Montana, moose were quite plentiful in the late 'seventies. Two or three of the old settlers, whom I know as veteran hunters and trustworthy men, have told me that in those times the moose were often found in very accessible localities; and that when such was the case they were quite as easily killed as elk. In fact,

when run across by accident they frequently showed a certain clumsy slowness of apprehension which amounted to downright stupidity. One of the most successful moose-hunters I know is Col. Cecil Clay, of the Department of Law, in Washington; he it was who killed the moose composing the fine group mounted by Mr. Hornaday, in the National Museum. Col. Clay lost his right arm in the Civil War; but is an expert rifleshot nevertheless, using a short, light forty-four calibre old style Winchester carbine. With this weapon he has killed over a score of moose, by fair still-hunting; and he tells me that on similar ground he considers it if anything rather less easy to still-hunt and kill a whitetail deer than it is to kill a moose.

My friend Col. James Jones killed two moose in a day in northwestern Wyoming, not far from the Tetons; he was alone when he shot them and did not find them especially wary. Ordinarily, moose are shot at fairly close range; but another friend of mine, Mr. E. P. Rogers, once dropped one with a single bullet, at a distance of nearly three hundred yards. This happened by Bridger's Lake, near Two-Ocean Pass.

The moose has a fast walk, and its ordinary gait when going at any speed is a slashing trot. Its long legs give it a wonderful stride, enabling it to clear down-timber and high obstacles of all sorts without altering its pace. It also leaps well. If much pressed or startled it breaks into an awkward gallop, which is quite fast for a few hundred yards, but which speedily tires it out. After being disturbed by the hunter a moose usually trots along distance before halting.

One thing which renders the chase of the moose particularly interesting is the fact that there is in it on rare occasions a spice of peril. Under certain circumstances it may be called dangerous quarry, being, properly speaking, the only animal of the deer kind which ever fairly deserves the title. In a hand to hand grapple an elk or caribou, or even under exceptional circumstances a blacktail or a whitetail, may show itself an ugly antagonist; and indeed a maddened elk may for a moment take the offensive;

but the moose is the only one of the tribe with which this attitude is at all common. In bodily strength and capacity to do harm it surpasses the elk; and in temper it is far more savage and more apt to show fight when assailed by man; exactly as the elk in these respects surpasses the common deer. Two hunters with whom I was well acquainted once wintered between the Wind River Mountains and the Three Tetons, many years ago, in the days of the buffalo. They lived on game, killing it on snowshoes; for the most part wapiti and deer, but also bison, and one moose, though they saw others. The wapiti bulls kept their antlers two months longer than the moose; nevertheless, when chased they rarely made an effort to use them, while the hornless moose displayed far more pugnacity, and also ran better through the deep snow. The winter was very severe, the snows were heavy and the crusts hard; so that the hunters had little trouble in overtaking their game, although—being old mountain-men, and not hide-hunters—they killed only what was needed. Of course in such hunting they came very close to the harried game, usually after a chase of from twenty minutes to three hours. They found that the ordinary deer would scarcely charge under any circumstances; that among the wapiti it was only now and then that individuals would turn upon their pursuers—though they sometimes charged boldly; but that both the bison and especially the moose when worried and approached too near, would often turn to bay and make charge after charge in the most resolute manner, so that they had to be approached with some caution.

Under ordinary conditions, however, there is very little danger, indeed, of a moose charging. A charge does not take place once in a hundred times when the moose is killed by fair still-hunting; and it is altogether exceptional for those who assail them from boats or canoes to be put in jeopardy. Even a cow moose, with her calf, will run if she has the chance; and a rutting bull will do the same. Such a bull when wounded may walk slowly forward, grunting savagely, stamping with his forefeet, and slashing the bushes with his antlers; but, if his antagonist is any distance off, he rarely actually runs at him. Yet there are now and then found moose prone to attack on slight provocation; for these great deer differ as widely as men in courage and ferocity. Occasionally a hunter is charged in the fall when he has lured the game to him by calling, or when he has wounded it after a stalk. In one well-authenticated instance which was brought to my attention, a settler on the left bank of the St. Johns, in New Brunswick, was tramped to death by a bull moose which he had called to him and wounded. A New Yorker of my acquaintance, Dr. Merrill, was charged under rather peculiar circumstances. He stalked and mortally wounded a bull which promptly ran towards him. Between them was a gully in which it disappeared. Immediately afterwards, as he thought, it reappeared on his side of the gully, and with a second shot he dropped it. Walking forward he found to his astonishment that with his second bullet he had killed a cow moose; the bull lay dying in the gully, out of which he had scared the cow by his last rush.

However, speaking broadly, the danger to the stillhunter engaged in one of the legitimate methods of the chase is so small that it may be disregarded; for he usually kills his game at some little distance, while the moose, as a rule, only attacks if it has been greatly worried and angered, and if its pursuer is close at hand. When a moose is surprised and shot at by a hunter some way off, its one thought is of flight. Hence, the hunters who are charged by moose are generally those who follow them during the late winter and early spring, when the animals have yarded and can be killed on snow-shoes—by "crusting," as it is termed, a very destructive, and often a very unsportsman-like species of chase.

If the snow-fall is very light, moose do not yard at all; but in a hard winter they begin to make their yards in December. A "yard" is not, as some people seem.to suppose, a trampled-down space, with definite boundaries; the term merely denotes the spot which a

moose has chosen for its winter home, choosing it because it contains plenty of browse in the shape of young trees and saplings, and perhaps also because it is sheltered to some extent from the fiercest winds and heaviest snowdrifts. The animal travels to and for across this space in straight lines and irregular circles after food, treading in its own footsteps, where practicable. As the snow steadily deepens, these lines of travel become beaten paths. There results finally a space half a mile square—sometimes more, sometimes very much less, according to the lay of the land, and the number of moose yarding together—where the deep snow is seamed in every direction by a network of narrow paths along which a moose can travel at speed, its back level with the snow round about. Sometimes, when moose are very plenty, many of these yards lie so close together that the beasts can readily make their way from one to another. When such is the case, the most expert snow-shoer, under the most favorable conditions, cannot overtake them, for they can then travel very fast through the paths, keeping their gait all day. In the early decades of the present century, the first settlers in Aroostook County, Maine, while moose-hunting in winter, were frequently baffled in this manner.

When hunters approach an isolated yard the moose immediately leave it and run off through the snow. If there is no crust, and if their long legs can reach the ground, the snow itself impedes them but little, because of their vast strength and endurance. Snowdrifts which render an ordinary deer absolutely helpless, and bring even an elk to a standstill, offer no impediment whatever to a moose. If, as happens very rarely, the loose snow is of such depth that even the stilt-like legs of the moose cannot touch solid earth, it flounders and struggles forward for a little time, and then sinks exhausted; for a caribou is the only large animal which can travel under such conditions. If there be a crust, even though the snow is not remarkably deep, the labor of the moose is vastly increased, as it breaks through at every step, cutting

its legs and exhausting itself. A caribou, on the other hand, will go across a crust as well as a man on snow-shoes, and can never be caught by the latter, save under altogether exceptional conditions of snowfall and thaw.

"Crusting," or following game on snow-shoes, is, as the name implies, almost always practised after the middle of February, when thaws begin, and the snow crusts on top. The conditions for success in crusting moose and deer are very different. A crust through which a moose would break at every stride may carry a running deer without mishap; while the former animal would trot at ease through drifts in which the latter would be caught as if in a quicksand.

Hunting moose on snow, therefore, may be, and very often is, mere butchery; and because of this possibility or probability, and also because of the fact that it is by far the most destructive kind of hunting, and is carried on at a season when the bulls are hornless and the cows heavy with calf, it is rigidly and properly forbidden wherever there are good game-laws. Yet this kind of hunting may also be carried on under circumstances wh1ch render it if not a legitimate, yet a most exciting and manly sport, only to be followed by men of tried courage, hardihood, and skill. This is not because it ever necessitates any skill whatever in the use of the rifle, or any particular knowledge of hunting-craft; but because under the conditions spoken of the hunter must show great endurance and resolution, and must be an adept in the use of snow-shoes.

It all depends upon the depth of the snow and the state of the crust. If when the snow is very deep there comes a thaw, and if it then freezes hard, the moose are overtaken and killed with ease; for the crust cuts their legs, they sink to their bellies at every plunge, and speedily become so worn out that they can no longer keep ahead of any man who is even moderately skilful in the use of show-shoes; though they do not, as deer so often do, sink exhausted after going a few rods from their yard. Under such circumstances a few hardy hunters or settlers, who are perfectly reckless in slaughtering game, may readily kill all the moose in a district. It is a kind of hunting which just suits the ordinary settler, who is hardy and enduring, but knows little of hunting-craft proper.

If the snow is less deep, or the crust not so heavy, the moose may travel for scores of miles before it is overtaken; and this even though the crust be strong enough to bear a man wearing snow-shoes without breaking. The chase then involves the most exhausting fatigue. Moreover, it can be carried on only by those who are very skilful in the use of snow-shoes. These snow-shoes are of two kinds. In the northeast, and in the most tangled forests of the northwest, the webbed snow-shoes are used; on the bare mountain-sides, and in the open forests of the Rockies, the long narrow wooden skees, or Norwegian snow-skates are preferred, as upon then men can travel much faster, though they are less handy in thick timber. Having donned his snow-shoes and struck the trail of a moose, the hunter may have to follow it three days if the snow is of only ordinary depth, with a moderate crust. He shuffles across the snow without halt while daylight lasts, and lies down wherever he happens to be when night strikes him, probably with a little frozen bread as his only food. The hunter thus goes through inordinate labor, and suffers from exposure; not infrequently his feet are terribly cut by the thongs of the snow-shoes, and become sore and swollen, causing great pain. When overtaken after such a severe chase, the moose is usually so exhausted as to be unable to make any resistance; in all likelihood it has run itself to a standstill. Accordingly, the quality of the fire-arms makes but little difference in this kind of hunting. Many of the most famous old moose-hunters of Maine, in the long past days, before the Civil War, when moose were plenty there, used what were known as "three dollar" guns; light, single-barrelled smooth-bores. One whom I knew used a flint-lock musket, a relic of the War of 1812. Another in the course of an exhausting three days' chase lost the lock off his cheap, percussion-cap gun; and

when he overtook the moose he had to explode the cap by hammering it with a stone.

It is in "crusting," when the chase has lasted but a comparatively short time, that moose most frequently show fight; for they are not cast into a state of wild panic by a sudden and unlooked-for attack by a man who is a long distance from them, but on the contrary, after being worried and irritated, are approached very near by foes from whom they have been fleeing for hours. Nevertheless, in the majority of cases even crusted moose make not the slightest attempt at retaliation. If the chase has been very long, or if the depth of the snow and character of the crust are exceptionally disadvantageous to them, they are so utterly done out, when overtaken, that they cannot make a struggle, and may even be killed with an axe. I know of at least five men who have thus killed crusted moose with an axe; one in the Rocky Mountains, one in Minnesota, three in Maine.

But in ordinary snow a man who should thus attempt to kill a moose would merely jeopardize his own life; and it is not an uncommon thing for chased moose, when closely approached by their pursuers, even when the latter carry guns and are expert snow-shoers, to charge them with such ferocity as to put them in much peril. A brother of one of my cow-hands, a man from Maine, was once nearly killed by a cow moose. She had been in a yard with her last year's calf when started. After two or three hours' chase he overtook them. They were travelling in single file, the cow breaking her path through the snow, while the calf followed close behind, and in his nervousness sometimes literally ran up on her. The man trotted close alongside; but, before he could fire, the old cow spun round and charged him, her mane bristling and her green eyes snapping with rage. It happened that just there the snow became shallow, and the moose gained so rapidly that the man, to save his life, sprang up a tree. As he did so the cow reared and struck at him, one forefoot catching in his snow-shoe and

tearing it clear off, giving his ankle a bad wrench. After watching him a minute or two she turned and continued her flight; whereupon he climbed down the tree, patched up his torn snow-shoe and limped after the moose, which he finally killed.

An old hunter named Purvis told me of an adventure of the kind, which terminated fatally. He was hunting near the Cœur d'Alene Mountains with a mining prospector named Pingree; both were originally from New Hampshire. Late in November there came a heavy fall of snow, deep enough to soon bring a deer to a standstill, although not so deep as to hamper a moose's movement. The men bound on their skees and started to the borders of a lake, to kill some blacktail. I n a thicket close to the lake's brink they suddenly came across a bull moose; a lean old fellow, still savage from the rut. Pingree, who was nearest, fired at and wounded him; whereupon he rushed straight at the man, knocked him down before he could turn round on his skees, and began to pound him with his terrible forefeet. Summoned by his comrade's despairing cries, Purvis rushed round the thickets, and shot the squealing, trampling monster through the body, and immediately after had to swing himself up a small tree to avoid its furious rush. The moose did not turn after this charge, but kept straight on, and was not seen again. The wounded man was past all help, for his chest was beaten in, and he died in a couple of hours.

CHAPTER XII. THE BISON OR AMERICAN BUFFALO. WHEN we became a nation, in 1776, the buffaloes, the first animals to vanish when the wilderness is settled, roved to the crests of the mountains which mark the western boundaries of Pennsylvania, Virginia, and the Carolinas. They wereplentiful in what are now the States of Ohio, Kentucky, and Tennessee. But by the beginning of the present century they had been driven beyond the Mississippi; and for the next eighty years they formed one of the most distinctive and characteristic features of existence on the great plains. Their numbers were countless incredible. In vast herds of hundreds of thousands of individuals, they roamed from the Saskatchewan to the Rio Grande and westward to the Rocky Mountains. They furnished all the means of livelihood to the tribes of Horse Indians, and to the curious population of French Metis, or Half-breeds, on the Red River,as well as to those dauntless and archtypical wanderers, the white hunters and trappers. Their numbers slowly diminished, but the decrease was very gradual until after the Civil War. They were not destroyed by the settlers, but by the railways and the skin hunters. After the ending of the Civil War, the work of constructing trans-continental railway lines was pushed foward with the utmost vigor. These supplied cheap and indispensable, but hitherto wholly lacking, means of transportation to the hunters; and at the same time the demand for buffalo robes and hides became very great, while the enormous numbers of the beasts, and the comparative ease with which they were slaughtered, attracted throngs of adventurers. The result was such a slaughter of big game as the world had never before seen; never before were so many large animals of one species destroyed in so short a time. Several million buffaloes were slain. In fifteen years from the time the destruction fairly began the great herds were exterminated. In all probability there are not now, all told, five hundred head of wild buffaloes on the American continent; and no herd of a hundred individuals has been in existence since 1884.

The first great break followed the building of the Union Pacific Railway. All the buffaloes of the middle region were then destroyed, and the others were split into two vast sets of herds, the northern and the southern. The latter were destroyed first, about 1878; the former not until 1883. My own chief experience with buffaloes was obtained in the latter year, among small bands and scattered individuals, near my ranch on the Little Missouri; I have related it elsewhere. But two of my kinsmen were more fortunate, and took part in the chase of these lordly beasts when

the herds still darkened the prairie as far as the eye could see.

During the first two months of 1877, my brother Elliott, then a lad not seventeen years old, made a buffalohunt toward the edge of the Staked Plains in northern Texas. He was thus in at the death of the southern herds; for all, save a few scattering bands, were destroyed within two years of this time. He was with my cousin, John Roosevelt, and they went out on the range with six other adventurers. It was a party of just such young men as frequently drift to the frontier. All were short of cash, and all were hardy, vigorous fellows, eager for excitement and adventure. My brother was much the youngest of the party, and the least experienced; but he was wellgrown, strong and healthy, and very fond of boxing, wrestling, running, riding, and shooting; moreover, he had served an apprenticeship in hunting deer and turkeys. Their mess-kit, ammunition, bedding, and provisions were carried in two prairie-wagons, each drawn by four horses. In addition to the teams they had six saddle-animals—all of them shaggy, unkempt mustangs. Three or four dogs, setters and half-bred greyhounds, trotted along behind the wagons. Each man took his turn for two days as teamster and cook; and there were always two with the wagons, or camp, as the case might be, while the other six were off hunting, usually in couples. The expedition was undertaken partly for sport and partly with the hope of profit; for, after purchasing the horses and wagons, none of the party had any money left, and they were forced to rely upon selling skins and hides, and, when near the forts, meat.

They started on January 2d, and shaped their course for the head-waters of the Salt Fork of the Brazos, the centre of abundance for the great buffalo herds. During the first few days they were in the outskirts of the settled country, and shot only small game—quail and prairie fowl; then they began to kill turkey, deer, and antelope. These they swapped for flour and feed at the ranches or squalid, straggling frontier towns. On several occasions the hunters were

lost, spending the night out in the open, or sleeping at a ranch, if one was found. Both towns and ranches were filled with rough customers; all of my brother's companions were muscular, hot-headed fellows; and as a consequence they were involved in several savage free fights, in which, fortunately, nobody was seriously hurt. My brother kept a very brief diary, the entries being fairly startling from their conciseness. A number of times, the mention of their arrival, either at a halting-place, a little village, or a rival buffalo-camp is followed by the laconic remark, "big fight," or "big row"; but once they evidently concluded discretion to be the better part of valor, the entry for January 20th being, " On the road—passed through Belknap—too lively, so kept on to the Brazos—very late." The buffalo-camps in particular were very jealous of one another, each party regarding itself as having exclusive right to the range it was the first to find; and on several occasions this feeling came near involving my brother and his companions in serious trouble.

While slowly driving the heavy wagons to the hunting grounds they suffered the usual hardships of plains travel. The weather, as in most Texas winters, alternated between the extremes of heat and cold. There had been little rain; in consequence water was scarce. Twice they were forced to cross wild, barren wastes, where the pools had dried up, and they suffered terribly from thirst. On the first occasion the horses were in good condition, and they travelled steadily, with only occasional short halts, for over thirty-six hours, by which time they were across the waterless country. The journal reads: "January 27th. — Big hunt—no water, and we left Quinn's blockhouse this morning 3 A.M.—on the go all night— hot. January 28th.—No water—hot—at seven we struck water, and by eight Stinking Creek—grand 'hurrah.'" On the second occasion, the horses were weak and travelled slowly, so the party went forty-eight hours without drinking. "February 19th.—Pulled on twenty-one miles—trail bad—freezing night, no water, and wolves after our fresh meat.

20th.—Made nineteen miles over prairie; again only mud, no water, freezing hard—frightful thirst. 21 st.—Thirty miles to Clear Fork, fresh water." These entries were hurriedly jotted down at the time, by a boy who deemed it unmanly to make any especial note of hardship or suffering; but every plainsman will understand the real agony implied in working hard for two nights, one day, and portions of two others, without water, even in cool weather. During the last few miles the staggering horses were only just able to drag the lightly loaded wagon,—for they hadbut one with them at the time,—while the men plodded along in sullen silence, their mouths so parched that they could hardly utter a word. My own hunting and ranching were done in the north where there is more water; so I have never had a similar experience. Once I took a team in thirty-six hours across a country where there was no water; but by good luck it rained heavily in the night, so that the horses had plenty of wet grass, and I caught the rain in my slicker, and so had enough water for myself. Personally, I have but once been as long as twenty-six hours without water.

The party pitched their permanent camp in a canyon of the Brazos known as Canyon Blanco. The last few days of their journey they travelled beside the river through a veritable hunter's paradise. The drought had forced all the animals to come to the larger watercourses, and the country was literally swarming with game. Every day, and all day long, the wagons travelled through the herds of antelopes that grazed on every side, while, whenever they approached the canyon brink, bands of deer started from the timber that fringed the river's course; often, even the deer wandered out on the prairie with the antelope. Nor was the game shy; for the hunters, both red and white, followed only the buffaloes, until the huge, shaggy herds were destroyed, and the smaller beasts were in consequence but little molested.

Once my brother shot five antelopes from a single stand, when the party were short of fresh venison; he was out of sight and to leeward, and the an-telopes seemed confused rather than alarmed at the rifle-reports and the fall of their companions. As was to be expected where game was so plenty, wolves and coyotes also abounded. At night they surrounded the camp, wailing and howling in a kind of shrieking chorus throughout the hours of darkness; one night they came up so close that the frightened horses had to be hobbled and guarded. On another occasion a large wolf actually crept into camp, where he was seized by the dogs, and the yelling, writhing knot of combatants rolled over one of the sleepers; finally, the long-toothed prowler managed to shake himself loose, and vanished in the gloom. One evening they were almost as much startled by a visit of a different kind. They were just finishing supper when an Indian stalked suddenly and silently out of the surrounding darkness, squatted down in the circle of firelight, remarked gravely, "Me Tonk," and began helping himself from the stew. He belonged to the friendly tribe of Tonkaways, so his hosts speedily recovered their equanimity; as for him, he had never lost his, and he sat eating by the fire until there was literally nothing left to eat. The panic caused by his appearance was natural; for at that time the Comanches were a scourge to the buffalo-hunters, ambushing them and raiding their camps; and several bloody fights had taken place.

Their camp had been pitched near a deep pool or water-hole. On both sides the bluffs rose like walls, and where they had crumbled and lost their sheerness, the vast buffalo herds, passing and repassing for countless generations, had worn furrowed trails so deep that the backs of the beasts were but little above the surrounding soil. In the bottom, and in places along the crests of the cliffs that hemmed in the canyon-like valley, there were groves of tangled trees, tenanted by great flocks of wild turkeys. Once my brother made two really remarkable shots at a pair of these great birds. It was at dusk, and they were flying directly overhead from one cliff to the other. He had in his hand a thirty-eight calibre Ballard rifle, and, as the gobblers winged their way heavily by, he brought both down with two successive bullets. This was of course mainly a piece of mere luck; but it meant good shooting, too. The Ballard was a very accurate, handy little weapon; it belonged to me, and was the first rifle I ever owned or used. With it I had once killed a deer, the only specimen of large game I had then shot; and I presented the rifle to my brother when he went to Texas. In our happy ignorance we deemed it quite good enough for buffalo or anything else; but out on the plains my brother soon found himself forced to procure a heavier and more deadly weapon.

When camp was pitched the horses were turned loose to graze and refresh themselves after their trying journey, during which they had lost flesh wofully. They were watched and tended by the two men who were always left in camp, and, save on rare occasions, were only used to haul in the buffalo hides. The camp-guards for the time being acted as cooks; and, though coffee and flour both ran short and finally gave out, fresh meat of every kind was abundant. The camp was never without buffalo-beef, deer and antelope venison, wild turkeys, prairie-chickens, quails, ducks, and rabbits. The birds were simply " potted," as occasion required; when the quarry was deer or antelope, the hunters took the dogs with them to run down the wounded animals. But almost the entire attention of the hunters was given to the buffalo. After an evening spent in lounging round the camp-fire and a sound night's sleep, wrapped in robes and blankets, they would get up before daybreak, snatch a hurried breakfast, and start off in couples through the chilly dawn. The great beasts were very plentiful; in the first day's hunt twenty were slain; but the herds were restless and ever on the move. Sometimes they would be seen right by the camp, and again it would need an all-day's tramp to find them. There was no difficulty in spying them—the chief trouble with forest game; for on the prairie a buffalo makes no effort to hide and its black, shaggy bulk looms up as far as the eye can see. Sometimes they were found in small parties of three or four individuals, sometimes in bands of about two hundred, and again in great herds of many thousands; and solitary old bulls, expelled from the herds, were common. If on broken land, among hills and ravines, there was not much difficulty in approaching from the leeward; for, though the sense of smell in the buffalo is very acute, they do not see well at a distance through their overhanging frontlets of coarse and matted hair. If, as was generally the case, they were out on the open, rolling prairie, the stalking was far more difficult. Every hollow, every earth hummock and sagebush had to be used as cover. The hunter wriggled through the grass flat on his face, pushing himself along for perhaps a quarter of a mile by his toes and fingers, heedless of the spiny cactus. When near enough to the huge, unconscious quarry the hunter began firing, still keeping himself carefully concealed. If the smoke was blown away by the wind, and if the buffaloes caught no glimpse of the assailant, they would often stand motionless and stupid until many of their number had been slain, the hunter being careful not to fire too high, aiming just behind the shoulder, about a third of the way up the body, that his bullet might go through the lungs. Sometimes, even after they saw the man, they would act as if confused and panic-struck, huddling together and staring at the smoke puffs; but generally they were off at a lumbering gallop as soon as they had an idea of the point of danger. When once started, they ran for many miles before halting, and their pursuit on foot was extremely laborious.

One morning my cousin and brother had been left in camp as guards. They were sitting idly warming themselves in the first sunbeams, when their attention was sharply drawn to four buffaloes that were coming to the pool to drink. The beasts came down a game trail, a deep rut in he bluff, fronting where they were sitting, and they did not dare to stir for fear of being discovered. The buffaloes walked into the pool, and, after drink-

ing their fill, stood for some time with the water running out of their mouths, idly lashing their sides with their short tails, enjoying the bright warmth of the early sunshine; then, with much splashing and the gurgling of soft mud, they left the pool and clambered up the bluff with unwieldy agility. As soon as they turned, my brother and cousin ran for their rifles, but before they got back the buffaloes had crossed the bluff crest. Climbing after them, the two hunters found, when they reached the summit, that their game, instead of halting, had struck straight off across the prairie at a slow lope, doubtless intending to rejoin the herd they had left. After a moment's consultation the men went in pursuit, excitement overcoming their knowledge that they ought not, by rights, to leave camp. They struck a steady trot, following the animals by sight until they passed over a knoll, and then trailing them. Where the grass was long, as it was for the first four or five miles, this was a work of no difficulty, and they did not break their gait, only glancing now and then at the trail. As the sun rose and the day became warm, their breathing grew quicker; and the sweat rolled off their faces as they ran across the rough prairie sward, up and down the long inclines, now and then shifting their heavy rifles from one shoulder to the other. But they were in good training, and they did not have to halt. At last they reached stretches of bare ground, sun-baked and grassless, where the trail grew dim; and here they had to go very slowly, carefully examining the faint dents and marks made in the soil by the heavy hoofs, and unravelling the trail from the mass of old footmarks. It was tedious work, but it enabled them to completely recover their breath by the time that they again struck the grassland; and but a few hundred yards from its edge, in a slight hollow, they saw the four buffaloes just entering a herd of fifty or sixty that were scattered out grazing. The herd paid no attention to the new-comers, and these immediately began to feed greedily. After a whispered consultation, the two hunters crept back, and made a long circle that

brought them well to leeward of the herd, in line with a slight rise in the ground. They then crawled up to this rise and, peering through the tufts of tall, rank grass, saw the unconscious beasts a hundred and twenty five or fifty yards away. They fired together, each mortally wounding his animal, and then, rushing in as the herd halted in confusion, and following them as they ran, impeded by numbers, hurry, and panic, they eventually got three more.

On another occasion the same two hunters nearly met with a frightful death, being overtaken by a vast herd of stampeded buffaloes. All animals that go in herds are subject to these instantaneous attacks of uncontrollable terror, under the influence of which they become perfectly mad, and rush headlong in dense masses on any form of death. Horses, and more especially cattle, often suffer from stampedes; it is a danger against which the cowboys are compelled to be perpetually on guard. A band of stampeded horses, sweeping in mad terror up a valley, will dash against a rock or tree with such violence as to leave several dead animals at its base, while the survivors race on without halting; they will overturn and destroy tents and wagons, and a man on foot caught in the rush has but a small chance for his life. A buffalo stampede is much worse—or rather was much worse, in the old days

—because of the great weight and immense numbers of the beasts, which, in a fury of heedless terror, plunged over cliffs and into rivers, and bore down whatever was in their path. On the occasion in question, my brother and cousin were on their way homeward. They were just mounting one of the long, low swells, into which the prairie was broken, when they heard a low, muttering, rumbling noise, like far-off thunder. It grew steadily louder, and, not knowing what it meant, they hurried forward to the top of the rise. As they reached it, they stopped short in terror and amazement, for before them the whole prairie was black with madly rushing buffaloes.

Afterward they learned that another

couple of hunters, four or five miles off, had fired into and stampeded a large herd. This herd, in its rush, gathered others, all thundering along together in uncontrollable and increasing panic.

The surprised hunters were far away from any broken ground or other place of refuge, while the vast herd of huge, plunging, maddened beasts was charging straight down on them not a quarter of a mile distant. Down they came!— thousands upon thousands, their front extending a mile in breadth, while the earth shook beneath their thunderous gallop, and, as they came closer, their shaggy frontlets loomed dimly through the columns of dust thrown up from the dry soil. The two hunters knew that their only hope for life was to split the herd, which, though it had so broad a front, was not very deep. If they failed they would inevitably be trampled to death.

Waiting until the beasts were in close range, they opened a rapid fire from their heavy breech-loading rifles, yelling at the top of their voices. For a moment the result seemed doubtful. The line thundered steadily down on them; then it swayed violently, as two or three of the brutes immediately in their front fell beneath the bullets, while their neighbors made violent efforts to press off sideways. Then a narrow wedge-shaped rift appeared in the line, and widened as it came closer, and the buffaloes, shrinking from their foes in front, strove desperately to edge away from the dangerous neighborhood; the shouts and shots were redoubled; the hunters were almost choked by the cloud of dust, through which they could see the stream of dark huge bodies passing within rifle-length on either side; and in a moment the peril was over, and the two men were left alone on the plain, unharmed, though with their nerves terribly shaken. The herd careered on toward the horizon, save five individuals which had been killed or disabled by the shots.

On another occasion, when my brother was out with one of his friends, they fired at a small herd containing an old bull; the bull charged the smoke, and

the whole herd followed him. Probably they were simply stampeded, and had no hostile intention; at any rate, after the death of their leader, they rushed by without doing any damage.

But buffaloes sometimes charged with the utmost determination, and were then dangerous antagonists. My cousin, a very hardy and resolute hunter, had a narrow escape from a wounded cow which he followed up a steep bluff or sand cliff. Just as he reached the summit, he was charged, and was only saved by the sudden appearance of his dog, which distracted the cow's attention. He thus escaped with only a tumble and a few bruises.

My brother also came in for a charge, while killing the biggest bull that was slain by any of the party. He was out alone, and saw a small herd of cows and calves at some distance, with a huge bull among them, towering above them like a giant. There was no break in the ground, nor any tree nor bush near them, but, by making a halfcircle, my brother managed to creep up against the wind behind a slight roll in the prairie surface, until he was within seventy-five yards of the grazing and unconscious beasts. There were some cows and calves between him and the bull, and he had to wait some moments before they shifted position, as the herd grazed onward and gave him a fair shot; in the interval they had moved so far forward that he was in plain view. His first bullet struck just behind the shoulder; the herd started and looked around, but the bull merely lifted his head and took a step forward, his tail curled up over his back. The next bullet likewise struck fair, nearly in the same place, telling with a loud " pack!" against the thick hide, and making the dust fly up from the matted hair. Instantly the great bull wheeled and charged in headlong anger, while the herd fled in the opposite direction. On the bare prairie, with no spot of refuge, it was useless to try to escape, and the hunter, with reloaded rifle, waited until the bull was not far off, then drew up his weapon and fired. Either he was nervous, or the bull at the moment bounded over some obsta-

cle, for the ball went a little wild; nevertheless, by good luck, it broke a foreleg, and the great beast came crashing to the earth, and was slain before it could struggle to its feet.

Two days after this event, a war party of Comanches swept down along the river. They "jumped" a neighboring camp, killing one man and wounding two more, and at the same time ran off all but three of the horses belonging to our eight adventurers. With the remaining three horses and one wagon they set out homeward. The march was hard and tedious; they lost their way and were in jeopardy from quicksands and cloud-bursts; they suffered from thirst and cold, their shoes gave out, and their feet were lamed by cactus spines. At last they reached Fort Griffen in safety, and great was their ravenous rejoicing when they procured some bread—for during the final fortnight of the hunt they had been without flour or vegetables of any kind, or even coffee, and had subsisted on fresh meat "straight." Nevertheless, it was a very healthy, as well as a very pleasant and exciting experience; and I doubt if any of those who took part in it will ever forget their great buffalo-hunt on the Brazos.

My friend, Gen. W. H. Walker, of Virginia, had an experience in the early '50's with buffaloes on the upper Arkansas River, which gives some idea of their enormous numbers at that time. He was camped with a scouting party on the banks of the river, and had gone out to try to shoot some meat. There were many buffaloes in sight, scattered, according to their custom, in large bands. When he was a mile or two away from the river a dull roaring sound in the distance attracted his attention, and he saw that a herd of buffalo far to the south, away from the river, had been stampeded and was running his way. He knew that if he was caught in the open by the stampeded herd his chance for life would be small, and at once ran for the river. By desperate efforts he reached the breaks in the sheer banks just as the buffaloes reached them, and got into a position of safety on the pinnacle of a little bluff. From this point of vantage he could see the entire plain. To the very verge of the horizon the brown masses of the buffalo bands showed through the dust clouds, coming on with a thunderous roar like that of surf. Camp was a mile away, and the stampede luckily passed to one side of it. Watching his chance he finally dodged back to the tent, and all that afternoon watched the immense masses of buffalo, as band after band tore to the brink of the bluffs on one side, raced down them, rushed through the water, up the bluffs on the other side, and again off over the plain, churning the sandy, shallow stream into a ceaseless tumult. When darkness fell there was no apparent decrease in the numbers that were passing, and all through that night the continuous roar showed that the herds were still threshing across the river. Towards dawn the sound at last ceased, and General Walker arose somewhat irritated, as he had reckoned on killing an ample supply of meat, and he supposed that there would be now no bison left south of the river. To his astonishment, when he strolled up on the bluffs and looked over the plain, it was still covered far and wide with groups of buffalo, grazing quietly. Apparently there were as many on that side as ever, in spite of the many scores of thousands that must have crossed over the river during the stampede of the afternoon and night. The barrenground caribou is the only American animal which is now ever seen in such enormous herds.

In 1862 Mr. Clarence King, while riding along the overland trail through western Kansas, passed through a great buffalo herd, and was himself injured in an encounter with a bull. The great herd was then passing north, and Mr. King reckoned that it must have covered an area nearly seventy miles by thirty in extent; the figures representing his rough guess, made after travelling through the herd crosswise, and upon knowing how long it took to pass a given point going northward. This great herd of course was not a solid mass of buffaloes; it consisted of innumerable bands of every size, dotting the prairie within the limits given. Mr. King was mounted on a somewhat unmanageable horse. On one occasion in following a band he wounded a large bull, and became so wedged in by the maddened animals that he was unable to avoid the charge of the bull, which was at its last gasp. Coming straight toward him it leaped into the air and struck the afterpart of the saddle full with its massive forehead. The horse was hurled to the ground with a broken back, and King's leg was likewise broken, while the bull turned a complete somerset over them and never rose again.

In the recesses of the Rocky Mountains, from Colorado northward through Alberta, and in the depths of the subarctic forest beyond the Saskatchewan, there have always been found small numbers of the bison, locally called the mountain buffalo and wood buffalo; often indeed the old hunters term these animals "bison," although they never speak of the plains animals save as buffalo. They form a slight variety of what was formerly the ordinary plains bison, intergrading with it; on the whole they are darker in color, with longer, thicker hair, and in consequence with the appearance of being heavier-bodied and shorterlegged. They have been sometimes spoken of as forming a separate species; but, judging from my own limited experience, and from a comparison of the many hides I have seen, I think they are really the same animal, many individuals-of the two so-called varieties being quite indistinguishable. In fact the only moderate-sized herd of wild bison in existence to-day, the protected herd in the Yellowstone Park, is composed of animals intermediate in habits and coat between the mountain and plains varieties —as were all the herds of the Bighorn, Big Hole, Upper Madison, and Upper Yellowstone valleys.

However, the habitat of these wood and mountain bison yielded them shelter from hunters in a way that the plains never could, and hence they have always been harder to kill in the one place than in the other; for precisely the same reasons that have held good with the elk, which have been completely exterminated from the plains, while still abundant in many of the forest fastnesses of the Rockies. Moreover, the bison's dull eyesight is no especial harm in the woods, while it is peculiarly hurtful to the safety of any beast on the plains, where eyesight avails more than any other sense, the true game of the plains being the prong-buck, the most keensighted of American animals. On the other hand the bison's hearing, of little avail on the plains, is of much assistance in the woods; and its excellent nose helps equally in both places.

Though it was always more difficult to kill the bison of the forests and mountains than the bison of the prairie, yet now that the species is, in its wild state, hovering on the brink of extinction, the difficulty is immeasurably increased. A merciless and terrible process of natural selection, in which the agents were rifle-bearing hunters, has left as the last survivors in a hopeless struggle for existence only the wariest of the bison and those gifted with the sharpest senses. That this was true of the last lingering individuals that survived the great slaughter on the plains is well shown by Mr. Hornaday in his graphic account of his campaign against the few scattered buffalo which still lived in 1886 between the Missouri and the Yellowstone, along the Big Dry. The bison of the plains and the prairies have now vanished; and so few of their brethren of the mountains and the northern forests are left, that they can just barely be reckoned among American game; but whoever is so fortunate as to find any of these animals must work his hardest, and show all his skill as a hunter if he wishes to get one.

In the fall of 1889 I heard that a very few bison were still left around the head of Wisdom River. Thither I went and hunted faithfully; there was plenty of game of other kind, but of bison not at race did we see. Nevertheless a few days later that same year I came across these great wild cattle at a time when I had no idea of seeing them.

It was, as nearly as we could tell, in Idaho, just south of the Montana boundary line, and some twenty-five miles west of the line of Wyoming. We were camped high among the mountains, with a small pack-train. On the day in question we had gone out to find moose, but had seen no sign of them, and had then begun to climb over the higher peaks with an idea of getting sheep. The old hunter who was with me was, very fortunately, suffering from rheumatism, and he therefore carried a long staff instead of his rifle; I say fortunately, for if he had carried his rifle it would have been impossible to stop his firing at such game as bison, nor would he have spared the cows and calves.

About the middle of the afternoon we crossed a low, rocky ridge, above timber line, and saw at our feet a basin or round valley of singular beauty. Its walls were formed by steep mountains. At its upper end lay a small lake, bordered on one side by a meadow of emerald green. The lake's other side marked the edge of the frowning pine forest which filled the rest of the valley, and hung high on the sides of the gorge which formed its outlet. Beyond the lake the ground rose in a pass evidently much frequented by game in bygone days, their trails lying along it in thick zigzags, each gradually fading out after a few hundred yards, and then starting again in a little different place, as game trails so often seem to do.

We bent our steps towards these trails, and no sooner had we reached the first than the old hunter bent over it with a sharp exclamation of wonder. There in the dust were the unmistakable hoof-marks of a small band of bison, apparently but a few hours old. They were headed towards the lake. There had been a half a dozen animals in the party; one a big bull, and two calves.

We immediately turned and followed the trail. It led down to the little lake, where the beasts had spread and grazed on the tender, green blades, and had drunk their fill. The footprints then came together again, showing where the animals had gathered and walked off in single file to the forest. Evidently they had come to the pool in the early morning, walking, over the game pass from some neighboring valley, and after

drinking and feeding had moved into the pine forest to find some spot for their noontide rest.

It was a very still day, and there were nearly three hours of daylight left. Without a word my silent companion, who had been scanning the whole country with hawk-eyed eagerness, besides scrutinizing the sign on his hands and knees, took the trail, motioning me to follow. In a moment we entered the woods, breathing a sigh of relief as we did so; for while in the meadow we could never tell that the buffalo might not see us, if they happened to be lying in some place with a commanding look-out.

The old hunter was thoroughly roused, and he showed himself a very skilful tracker. We were much favored by the character of the forest, which was rather open, and in most places free from undergrowth and down timber. As in most Rocky Mountain forests the timber was small, not only as compared to the giant trees of the groves of the Pacific coast, but as compared to the forests of the northeast. The ground was covered with pine needles and soft moss, so that it was not difficult to walk noiselessly. Once or twice when I trod on a small dry twig, or let the nails in my shoes clink slightly against a stone, the hunter turned to me with a frown of angry impatience; but as he walked slowly, continually halting to look ahead, as well as stooping over to examine the trail, I did not find it very difficult to move silently. I kept a little behind him, and to one side, save when he crouched to take advantage of some piece of cover, and I crept in his footsteps. I did not look at the trail at all, but kept watching ahead, hoping at any moment to see the game.

It was not very long before we struck their day beds, which were made on a knoll, where the forest was open and where there was much down timber. After leaving the day beds the animals had at first fed separately around the grassy base and sides of the knoll, and had then made off in their usual single file, going straight to a small pool in the forest. After drinking they had left

this pool, and travelled down towards the gorge at the mouth of the basin, the trail leading along the sides of the steep hill, which were dotted by open glades; while the roar of the cataracts by which the stream was broken ascended from below. Here we moved with redoubled caution, for the sign had grown very fresh and the animals had once more scattered and begun feeding. When the trail led across the glades we usually skirted them so as to keep in the timber.

At last, on nearing the edge of one of these glades we saw a movement among the young trees on the other side, not fifty yards away. Peering through the safe shelter yielded by some thick evergreen bushes, we speedily made out three bison, a cow, a calf, and a yearling, grazing greedily on the other side of the glade, under the fringing timber; all with their heads up hill. Soon another cow and calf stepped out after them. I did not wish to shoot, waiting for the appearance of the big bull which I knew was accompanying them.

So for several minutes I watched the great, clumsy, shaggy beasts, as all unconscious they grazed in the open glade. Behind them rose the dark pines. At the left of the glade the ground fell away to form the side of a chasm; down in its depths the cataracts foamed and thundered; beyond, the huge mountains towered, their crests crimsoned by the sinking sun. Mixed with the eager excitement of the hunter was a certain half melancholy feeling as I gazed on these bison, themselves part of the last remnant of a doomed and nearly vanished race. Few, indeed, are the men who now have, or evermore shall have, the chance of seeing the mightiest of American beasts, in all his wild vigor, surrounded by the tremendous desolation of his far-off mountain home.

At last, when I had begun to grow very anxious lest the others should take alarm, the bull likewise appeared on the edge of the glade, and stood with outstretched head, scratching his throat against a young tree, which shook violently. I aimed low, behind his shoulder, and pulled trigger. At the crack of the rifle all the bison, without the momentary halt of terror-struck surprise so common among game, turned and raced off at headlong speed. The fringe of young pines beyond and below the glade cracked and swayed as if a whirlwind were passing, and in another moment they reached the top of a very steep incline, thickly strewn with boulders and dead timber. Down this they plunged with reckless speed; their surefootedness was a marvel in such seemingly unwieldy beasts. A column of dust obscured their passage, and under its cover they disappeared in the forest; but the trail of the bull was marked by splashes of frothy blood, and we followed it at a trot. Fifty yards beyond the border of the forest we found the stark black body stretched motionless. He was a splendid old bull, still in his full vigor, with large, sharp horns, and heavy mane and glossy coat; and I felt the most exulting pride as I handled and examined him; for I had procured a trophy such as can fall henceforth to few hunters indeed.

It was too late to dress the beast that evening; so, after taking out the tongue and cutting off enough meat for supper and breakfast, we scrambled down to near the torrent, and after some search found a good spot for camping. Hot and dusty from the day's hard tramp, I undressed and took a plunge in the stream, the icy water making me gasp. Then, having built a slight lean-to of brush, and dragged together enough dead timber to burn all night, we cut long alder twigs, sat down before some embers raked apart, and grilled and ate our buffalo meat with the utmost relish. Night had fallen; a cold wind blew up the valley; the torrent roared as it leaped past us, and drowned our words as we strove to talk over our adventures and success; while the flame of the fire flickered and danced, lighting up with continual vivid flashes the gloom of the forest round about.

CHAPTER XIII. THE BLACK BEAR. NEXT to the vvhitetail deer the black bear is the commonest and most widely distributed of American big game. It is still found quite plentifully in northern New England, in the Adirondack, Catskills, and along the entire length of the Al-leghanies, as well as in the swamps and canebrakes of the southern States. It is also common in the great forests of northern Michigan, Wisconsin, and Minnesota, and throughout the Rocky Mountains and the timbered ranges of the Pacific coast. In the East it has always ranked second only to the deer among the beasts of chase. The bear and the buck were the staple objects of pursuit of all the old hunters. They were more plentiful than the bison and elk even in the long vanished days when these two great monarchs of the forest still ranged eastward to Virginia and Pennsylvania. The wolf and the cougar were always too scarce and too shy to yield much profit to the hunter. The black bear is a timid, cowardly animal, and usually a vegetarian, though it sometimes preys on the sheep, hogs, and even cattle of the settler, and is very fond of raiding his corn and melons. Its meat is good and its fur often valuable; and in its chase there is much excitement, and occasionally a slight spice of danger, just enough to render it attractive; so it has always been eagerly followed. Yet it still holds its own, though in greatly diminished numbers, in the more thinly settled portions of the country. One of the standing riddles of American zoology is the fact that the black bear, which is easier killed and less prolific than the wolf, should hold its own in the land better than the latter, this being directly the reverse of what occurs in Europe, where the brown bear is generally exterminated before the wolf.

In a few wild spots in the East, in northern Maine for instance, here and there in the neighborhood of the upper Great Lakes, in the east Tennessee and Kentucky mountains and the swamps of Florida and Mississippi, there still lingers an occasional representative of the old wilderness hunters. These men live in log-cabins in the wilderness. They do their hunting on foot, occasionally with the help of a single trailing dog. In Maine they are as apt to kill moose and caribou as bear and deer; but elsewhere the two last, with an occasional cougar or wolf, are the beasts of chase which they follow. Nowadays as these old hunters die there is no one to take their places, though there are still plenty of backwoods settlers in all of the regions named who do a great deal of hunting and trapping. Such an old hunter rarely makes his appearance at the settlements except to dispose of his peltry and hides in exchange for cartridges and provisions, and he leads a life of such lonely isolation as to insure his individual characteristics developing into peculiarities. Most of the wilder districts in the eastern States still preserve memories of some such old hunter who lived his long life alone, waging ceaseless warfare on the vanishing game, whose oddities, as well as his courage, hardihood, and woodcraft, are laughingly remembered by the older settlers, and who is usually best known as having killed the last wolf or bear or cougar ever seen in the locality.

Generally the weapon mainly relied on by these old hunters is the rifle; and occasionally some old hunter will be found even to this day who uses a muzzle loader, such as Kit Carson carried in the middle of the century. There are exceptions to this rule of the rifle however. In the years after the Civil War one of the many noted hunters of southwest Virginia and east Tennessee was Wilbur Waters, sometimes called The Hunter of White Top. He often killed black bear with a knife and dogs. He spent all his life in hunting and was very successful, killing the last gang of wolves to be found in his neighborhood; and he slew innumerable bears, with no worse results to himself than an occasional bite or scratch.

In the southern States the planters living in the wilder regions have always been in the habit of following the black bear with horse and hound, many of them keeping regular packs of bear hounds. Such a pack includes not only pure-bred hounds, but also cross-bred animals, and some sharp, agile, hard-biting fierce dogs and terriers. They follow the bear and bring him to bay but do not try to kill him, although there are dogs of the big fighting breeds which can readily master a black bear if loosed at him three or four at a time; but the dogs of these southern bear-hound packs are not fitted for such work, and if they try to close with the bear he is certain to play havoc with them, disembowelling them with blows of his paws or seizing them in his arms and biting through their spines or legs. The riders follow the hounds through the cane-brakes, and also try to make cutoffs and station themselves at open points where they think the bear will pass, so that they may get a shot at him. The weapons used are rifles, shotguns, and occasionally revolvers.

Sometimes, however, the hunter uses the knife. General Wade Hampton, who has probably killed more black bears than any other man living in the United States, frequently used the knife, slaying thirty or forty with his weapon. His plan was, when he found that the dogs had the bear at bay, to walk up close and cheer them on. They would instantly seize the bear in a body, and he would then rush in and stab it behind the shoulder, reaching over so as to inflict the wound on the opposite side from that where he stood. He escaped scathless from all these encounters save one, in which he was rather severely torn in the forearm. Many other hunters have used the knife, but perhaps none so frequently as he; for he was always fond of steel, as witness his feats with the "white arm" during the Civil War.

General Hampton always hunted with large packs of hounds, managed sometimes by himself and sometimes by his negro hunters. He occasionally took out forty dogs at a time. He found that all his dogs together could not kill a big fat bear, but they occasionally killed three-yearolds, or lean and poor bears. During the course of his life he has himself killed, or been in at the death of, five hundred bears, at least two thirds of them falling by his own hand. In the years just before the war he had on one occasion, in Mississippi, killed sixty-eight bears in five months. Once he killed four bears in a day; at another time three, and frequently two. The two largest bears he himself killed weighed, respectively, 408 and 410 pounds. They

were both shot in Mississippi. But he saw at least one bear killed which was much larger than either of these. These figures were taken down at the time, when the animals were actually weighed on the scales. Most of his hunting for bear was done in northern Mississippi, where one of his plantations was situated, near Greenville. During the half century that he hunted, on and off, in this neighborhood, he knew of two instances where hunters were fatally wounded in the chase of the black bear. Both of the men were inexperienced, one being a raftsman who came down the river, and the other a man from Vicksburg. He was not able to learn the particulars in the last case, but the raftsman came too close to a bear that was at bay, and it broke through the dogs, rushed at and overthrew him, then lying on him, it bit him deeply in the thigh, through the femoral artery, so that he speedily bled to death.

But a black bear is not usually a formidable opponent, and though he will sometimes charge home he is much more apt to bluster and bully than actually to come to close quarters. I myself have but once seen a man who had been hurt by one of these bears. This was an Indian. He had come on the beast close up in a thick wood, and had mortally wounded it with his gun; it had then closed with him, knocking the gun out of his hand, so that he was forced to use his knife. It charged him on all fours, but in the grapple, when it had failed to throw him down, it raised itself on its hind legs, clasping him across the shoulders with its fore-paws. Apparently it had no intention of hugging, but merely sought to draw him within reach of his jaws. He fought desperately against this, using the knife freely, and striving to keep its head back; and the flow of blood weakened the animal, so that it finally fell exhausted, before being able dangerously to injure him. But it had bitten his left arm very severely, and its claws had made long gashes on his shoulders.

Black bears, like grislies, vary greatly in their modes of attack. Sometimes they rush in and bite; and again they

strike with their fore-paws. Two of my cowboys were originally from Maine, where I knew them well. There they were fond of trapping bears, and caught a good many. The huge steel gms, attached by chains to heavy clogs, prevented the trapped beasts from going far; and when found they were always tied tight round some tree or bush, and usually nearly exhausted. The men killed them either with a little 32-calibre pistol or a hatchet. But once did they meet with any difficulty. On this occasion one of them incautiously approached a captured bear to knock it on the head with his hatchet, but the animal managed to partially untwist itself, and with its free fore-arm made a rapid sweep at him; he jumped back just in time, the bear's claws tearing his clothes—after which he shot it. Bears are shy and have very keen noses; they are therefore hard to kill by fair hunting, living, as they generally do, in dense forests or thick brush. They are easy enough to trap, however. Thus, these two men, though they trapped so many, never but once killed them in any other way. On this occasion one of them, in the winter, found in a great hollow log a den where a she and two well-grown cubs had taken up their abode, and shot all three with his rifle as they burst out.

Where they are much hunted, bear become purely nocturnal; but in the wilder forests I have seen them abroad at all hours, though they do not much relish the intense heat of noon. They are rather comical animals to watch feeding and going about the ordinary business of their lives. Once I spent half an hour lying at the edge of a wood and looking at a black bear some three hundred yards off across an open glade. It was in good stalking country, but the wind was unfavorable and I waited for it to shift—waited too long as it proved, for something frightened the beast and he made off before I could get a shot at him. When I first saw him he was shuffling along and rooting in the ground, so that he looked like a great pig. Then he began to turn over the stones and logs to hunt for insects, small reptiles, and the like. A moderate-sized stone he would turn over with a single clap of his paw, and then plunge his nose down into the hollow to gobble up the small creatures beneath while still dazed by the light. The big logs and rocks he would tug and worry at with both paws; once, over-exerting his clumsy strength, he lost his grip and rolled clean on his back. Under some of the logs he evidently found mice and chipmunks; then, as soon as the log was overturned, he would be seen jumping about with grotesque agility, and making quick dabs here and there, as the little, scurrying rodent turned and twisted, until at last he put his paw on it and scooped it up into his mouth. Sometimes, probably when he smelt the mice underneath, he would cautiously turn the log over with one paw, holding the other lifted and ready to strike. Now and then he would halt and sniff the air in every direction, and it was after one of these halts that he suddenly shuffled off into the woods.

Black bear generally feed on berries, nuts, insects, carrion, and the like; but at times they take to killing very large animals. In fact, they are curiously irregular in their food. They will kill deer if they can get at them; but generally the deer are too quick. Sheep and hogs are their favorite prey, especially the latter, for bears seem to have a special relish for pork. Twice I have known a black bear kill cattle. Once the victim was a bull which had got mired, and which the bear deliberately proceeded to eat alive, heedless of the bellows of the unfortunate beast. On the other occasion, a cow was surprised and slain among some bushes at the edge of a remote pasture. In the spring, soon after the long winter sleep, they are very hungry, and are especially apt to attack large beasts at this time; although during the very first days of their appearance, when they are just breaking their fast, they eat rather sparingly, and by preference the tender shoots of green grass and other herbs, or frogs and crayfish; it is not for a week or two that they seem to be overcome by lean, ravenous hunger. They will even attack and master that formidable fighter the moose, springing at it from an ambush as it passes—for a bull moose would surely be an overmatch for one of them if fronted fairly in the open. An old hunter, whom I could trust, told me that he had seen in the snow in early spring the place where a bear had sprung at two moose, which were trotting together; he missed his spring, and the moose got off, their strides after they settled down into their pace being tremendous, and showing how thoroughly they were frightened. Another time he saw a bear chase a moose into a lake, where it waded out a little distance, and then turned to bay, bidding defiance to his pursuer, the latter not daring to approach in the water. I have been told—but cannot vouch for it—that instances have been known where the bear, maddened by hunger, has gone in on a moose thus standing at bay, only to be beaten down under the water by the terrible forehoofs of the quarry, and to yield its life in the contest. A lumberman told me that he once saw a moose, evidently much startled, trot through a swamp, and immediately afterwards a bear came up following the tracks. He almost ran into the man, and was evidently not in a good temper, for he growled and blustered, and two or three times made feints of charging, before he finally concluded to go off.

Bears will occasionally visit hunters' or lumbermen's camps, in the absence of the owners, and play sad havoc with all that therein is, devouring everything eatable, especially if sweet, and trampling into a dirty mess whatever they do not eat. The black bear does not average more than a third the size of the grisly; but, like all its kind, it varies greatly in weight. The largest I myself ever saw weighed was in Maine, and tipped the scale at 346 pounds; but I have a perfectly authentic record of one in Maine that weighed 397, and my friend, Dr. Hart Merriam, tells me that he has seen several in the Adirondacks that when killed weighed about 350.

I have myself shot but one or two black bears, and these were obtained under circumstances of no special interest, as I merely stumbled on them while after other game, and killed them before they had a chance either to run or show fight.

CHAPTER XIV. OLD EPHRAIM, THE GRISLY BEAR. THE king of the game beasts of temperate North America, because the most dangerous to the hunter, is the grisly bear; known to the few remaining old-time trappers of the Rockies and the Great Plains, sometimes as " Old Ephraim " and sometimes as "Moccasin Joe "—the last in allusion to his queer, half-human footprints, which look as if made by some misshapen giant, walking in moccasins.

Bear vary greatly in size and color, no less than in temper and habits. Old hunters speak much of them in their endless talks over the camp fires and in the snow-bound winter huts. They insist on many species; not merely the black and the grisly, but the brown, the cinnamon, the gray, the silver-tip, and others with names known only in certain localities, such as the range bear, the roach-back, and the smut-face. But, in spite of popular opinion to the contrary, most old hunters are very untrustworthy in dealing with points of natural history. They usually know only so much about any given game animal as will enable them to kill it. They study its habits solely with this end in view; and once slain they only examine it to see about its condition and fur. With rare exceptions they are quite incapable of passing judgment upon questions of specific identity or difference. When questioned, they not only advance perfectly impossible theories and facts in support of their views, but they rarely even agree as to the views themselves. One hunter will assert that the true grisly is only found in California, heedless of the fact that the name was first used by Lewis and Clarke as one of the titles they applied to the large bears of the plains country round the Upper Missouri, a quarter of a century before the California grisly was known to fame. Another hunter will call any big brindled bear a grisly no matter where it is found; and he and his companions will dispute by the hour as to whether a bear of large, but not extreme, size is a grisly or a silver-tip. In Oregon the cinnamon bear is a phase of the small black bear; in Montana it is the plains variety of the large mountain silver-tip. I have myself seen the skins of two bears killed on the upper waters of Tongue River; one was that of a male, one of a female, and they had evidently just mated; yet one was distinctly a " silvertip " and the other a " cinnamon." The skin of one very big bear which I killed in the Bighorn has proved a standing puzzle to almost all the old hunters to whom I have showed it; rarely do any two of them agree as to whether it is a grisly, a silver-tip, a cinnamon, or a " smut-face." Any bear with unusually long hair on the spine and shoulders, especially if killed in the spring, when the fur is shaggy, is forthwith dubbed a " roach-back." The average sporting writer moreover joins with the more imaginative members of the "old hunter" variety in ascribing wildly various traits to these different bears. One comments on the superior prowess of the roachback; the explanation being that a bear in early spring is apt to be ravenous from hunger. The next insists that the California grisly is the only really dangerous bear; while another stoutly maintains that it does not compare in ferocity with what he calls the "smaller" silver-tip or cinnamon. And so on, and so on, without end. All of which is mere nonsense.

Nevertheless, it is no easy task to determine how many species or varieties of bear actually do exist in the United States, and I cannot even say without doubt that a very large set of skins and skulls would not show a nearly complete intergradation between the most widely separated individuals. However, there are certainly two very distinct types, which differ almost as widely from each other as a wapiti does from a mule deer, and which exist in the same localities in most heavily timbered portions of the Rockies. One is the small black bear, a bear which will average about two hundred pounds weight, with fine, glossy, black fur, and the foreclaws but little longer than the hinder ones; in fact the hairs of the fore-paw often reach to their tips. This bear is a

tree climber. It is the only kind found east of the great plains, and it is also plentiful in the forest-clad portions of the Rockies, being common in most heavily timbered tracts throughout the United States. The other is the grisly, which weighs three or four times as much as the black, and has a pelt of coarse hair, which is in color gray, grissled, or brown of various shades. It is not a tree climber, and the fore-claws are very long, much longer than the hinder ones. It is found from the great plains west of the Mississippi to the Pacific coast. This bear inhabits indifferently lowland and mountain; the deep woods, and the barren plains where the only cover is the stunted growth fringing the streams. These two types are very distinct in every way, and their differences are not at all dependent upon mere geographical considerations; for they are often found in the same district. Thus I found them both in the Bighorn Mountains, each type being in extreme form, while the specimens I shot showed no trace of intergradation. The huge grissled, long-clawed beast, and its little glossy-coated, short-clawed, tree-climbing brother roamed over exactly the same country in those mountains; but they were as distinct in habits, and mixed as little together as moose and caribou.

On the other hand, when a sufficient number of bears, from widely separated regions are examined, the various distinguishing marks are found to be inconstant and to show a tendency—exactly how strong I cannot say—to fade into one another. The differentiation of the two species seems to be as yet scarcely completed; there are more or less imperfect connecting links, and as regards the grisly it almost seems as if the specific characters were still unstable. In the far northwest, in the basin of the Columbia, the "black" bear is as often brown as any other color; and I have seen the skins of two cubs, one black and one brown, which were shot when following the same dam. When these brown bears have coarser hair than usual their skins are with difficulty to be distinguished from those of certain va-

rieties of the grisly. Moreover, all bears vary greatly in size; and I have seen the bodies of very large black or brown bears with short fore-claws which were fully as heavy as, or perhaps heavier than, some small but full-grown grislies with long fore-claws. These very large bears with short claws are very reluctant to climb a tree; and are almost as clumsy about it as is a young grisly. Among the grislies the fur varies much in color and texture even among bears of the same locality; it is of course richest in the deep forest, while the bears of the dry plains and mountains are of a lighter, more washed-out hue.

A full grown grisly will usually weigh from five to seven hundred pounds; but exceptional individuals undoubtedly reach more than twelve hundredweight. The California bears are said to be much the largest. This I think is so, but I cannot say it with certainty— at any rate I have examined several skins of full-grown Californian bears which were no larger than those of many I have seen from the northern Rockies. The Alaskan bears, particularly those of the peninsula, are even bigger beasts; the skin of one which I saw in the possession of Mr. Webster, the taxidermist, was a good deal larger than the average polar bear skin; and the animal when alive, if in good condition, could hardly have weighed less than 1,400 pounds. Bears vary wonderfully in weight, even to the extent of becoming half as heavy again, according as they are fat or lean; in this respect they are more like hogs than like any other animals.

Both this huge Alaskan bear and the entirely distinct bear of the barren grounds differ widely from the true grisly, at least in their extreme forms.

The grisly is now chiefly a beast of the high hills and heavy timber; but this is merely because he has learned that he must rely on cover to guard him from man, and has forsaken the open ground accordingly. In old days, and in one or two very out-of-the-way places almost to the present time, he wandered at will over the plains. It is only the wariness born of fear which nowadays causes him to cling to the thick brush of the large river-bottoms throughout the plains country. When there were no rifle-bearing hunters in the land, to harass him and make him afraid, he roved hither and thither at will, in burly self-confidence. Then he cared little for cover, unless as a weather-break, or because it happened to contain food he liked. If the humor seized him he would roam for days over the rolling or broken prairie, searching for roots, digging up gophers, or perhaps following the great buffalo herds either to prey on some unwary straggler which he was able to catch at a disadvantage in a washout, or else to feast on the carcasses of those which died by accident. Old hunters, survivors of the long-vanished ages when the vast herds thronged the high plains and were followed by the wild red tribes, and by bands of whites who were scarcely less savage, have told me that they often met bears under such circumstances; and these bears were accustomed to sleep in a patch of rank sage bush, in the niche of awashout, or under the lea of a boulder, seeking their food abroad even in full daylight. The bears of the Upper Missouri basin—which were so light in color that the early explorers often alluded to them as gray or even as "white "—were particularly given to this life in the open. To this day that close kinsman of the grisly known as the bear of the barren grounds continues to lead this same kind of life, in the far north. My friend Mr. Rockhill, of Maryland, who was the first white man to explore eastern Tibet, describes the large, grisly-like bear of those desolate uplands as having similar habits.

However, the grisly is a shrewd beast and shows the usual bear-like capacity for adapting himself to changed conditions. He has in most places become a cover-haunting animal, sly in his ways, wary to a degree, and clinging to the shelter of the deepest forests in the mountains and of the most tangled thickets in the plains. Hence he has held his own far better than such game as the bison and elk. He is much less common than formerly, but he is still to be found throughout most of his former range; save of course in the immediate neighborhood of the large towns.

In most places the grisly hibernates, or as old hunters say " holes up, " during the cold season, precisely as does the black bear; but as with the latter species, those animals which live farthest south spend the whole year abroad in mild seasons. The grisly rarely chooses that favorite den of his little black brother, a hollow tree or log, for his winter sleep, seeking or making some cavernous hole in the ground instead. The hole is sometimes in a slight hillock in a river bottom, but more often on a hill-side, and may be either shallow or deep. In the mountains it is generally a natural cave in the rock, but among the foot-hills and on the plains the bear usually has to take some hollow or opening, and then fashion it into a burrow to his liking with his big digging claws.

Before the cold weather sets in the bear begins to grow restless, and to roam about seeking for a good place in which to hole up. One will often try and abandon several caves or partially dug-out burrows in succession before finding a place to its taste. It always endeavors to choose a spot where there is little chance of discovery or molestation, taking great care to avoid leaving too evident trace of its work. Hence it is not often that the dens are found.

Once in its den the bear passes the cold months in lethargic sleep; yet, in all but the coldest weather, and sometimes even then, its slumber is but light, and if disturbed it will promptly leave its den, prepared for fight or flight as the occasion may require. Many times when a hunter has stumbled on the winter resting-place of a bear and has left it, as he thought, without his presence being discovered, he has returned only to find that the crafty old fellow was aware of the danger all the time, and sneaked off as soon as the coast was clear. But in very cold weather hibernating bears can hardly be wakened from their torpid lethargy.

The length of time a bear stays in its den depends of course upon the severity of the season and the latitude and altitude of the country. In the northernmost and coldest regions all the bears hole up, and spend half the year in a state of lethargy; whereas in the south only the she's with young and the fat he-bears retire for the sleep, and these but for a few weeks, and only if the season is severe.

When the bear first leaves its den the fur is in very fine order, but it speedily becomes thin and poor, and does not recover its condition until the fall. Sometimes the bear does not betray any great hunger for a few days after its appearance; but in a short while it becomes ravenous. During the early spring, when the woods are still entirely barren and lifeless, while the snow yet lies in deep drifts, the lean, hungry brute, both maddened and weakened by long fasting, is more of a flesh eater than at any other time. It is at this period that it is most apt to turn true beast of prey, and show its prowess either at the expense of the wild game, or of the flocks of the settler and the herds of the ranchman. Bears are very capricious in this respect, however. Some are confirmed game, and cattlekillers; others are not; while yet others either are or are not accordingly as the freak seizes them, and their ravages vary almost unaccountably, both with the season and the locality.

Throughout 1889, for instance, no cattle, so far as I heard, were killed by bears anywhere near my range on the Little Missouri in western Dakota; yet I happened to know that during that same season the ravages of the bears among the herds of the cowmen in the Big Hole Basin, in western Montana, were very destructive.

In the spring and early summer of 1888, the bears killed no cattle near my ranch; but in the late summer and early fall of that year a big bear, which we well knew by its tracks, suddenly took to cattle-killing. This was a brute which had its headquarters on some very large brush bottoms a dozen miles below my ranch house, and which ranged to and fro across the broken country flanking the river on each side. It began just before berry time, but continued its career of destruction long after the wild plums and even buffalo berries had ripened. I think that what started it was a feast on a cow which had mired and died in the bed of the creek; at least it was not until after we found that it had been feeding at the carcass and had eaten every scrap, that we discovered traces of its ravages among the livestock. It seemed to attack the animals wholly regardless of their size and strength; its victims including a large bull and a beef steer, as well as cows, yearlings, and gaunt, weak trail "doughgies," which had been brought in very late by a Texas cow-outfit—for that year several herds were driven up from the overstocked, eaten-out, and drought-stricken ranges of the far south. Judging from the signs, the crafty old grisly, as cunning as he was ferocious, usually lay in wait for the cattle when they came down to water, choosing some thicket of dense underbrush and twisted cottonwoods through which they had to pass before reaching the sand banks on the river's brink. Sometimes he pounced on them as they fed through the thick, low cover of the bottoms, where an assailant could either lie in ambush by one of the numerous cattle trails, or else creep unobserved towards some browsing beast. When within a few feet a quick rush carried him fairly on the terrified quarry; and though but a clumsy animal compared to the great cats, the grisly is far quicker than one would imagine from viewing his ordinary lumbering gait. In one or two instances the bear had apparently grappled with his victim by seizing it near the loins and striking a disabling blow over the small of the back; in at least one instance he had jumped on the animal's head, grasping it with his forepaws, while with his fangs he tore open the throat or craunched the neck bone. Some of his victims were slain far from the river, in winding, brushy coulies of the Bad Lands, where the broken nature of the ground rendered stalking easy. Several of the ranchmen, angered at their losses, hunted their foe eagerly, but always with ill success; until one of them put poison in a carcass, and thus at last, in ignoble fashion, slew the cattle-killer.

Mr. Clarence King informs me that he was once eyewitness to a bear's killing a steer, in California. The steer was in a small pasture, and the bear climbed over, partly breaking down, the rails which barred the gateway. The steer started to run, but the grisly overtook it in four or five bounds, and struck it a tremendous blow on the flank with one paw, knocking several ribs clear away from the spine, and killing the animal outright by the shock.

Horses no less than horned cattle at times fall victims to this great bear, which usually spring on them from the edge of a clearing as they graze in some mountain pasture, or among the foothills; and there is no other animal of which horses seem so much afraid. Generally the bear, whether successful or unsuccessful in its raids on cattle and horses, comes off unscathed from the struggle; but this is not always the case, and it has much respect for the hoofs or horns of its should-be prey. Some horses do not seem to know how to fight at all; but others are both quick and vicious, and prove themselves very formidable foes, lashing out behind, and striking with their fore-hoofs. I have elsewhere given an instance of a stallion which beat off a bear, breaking its jaw.

Quite near my ranch, once, a cowboy in my employ found unmistakable evidence of the discomfiture of a bear by a long-horned range cow. It was in the early spring, and the cow with her newborn calf was in a brushbordered valley. The footprints in the damp soil were very plain, and showed all that had happened. The bear had evidently come out of the bushes with a rush, probably bent merely on seizing the calf; and had slowed up when the cow instead of flying faced him. He had then begun to walk round his expected dinner in a circle, the cow fronting him and moving nervously back and forth, so that her sharp hoofs cut and trampled the ground. Finally she had charged savagely; whereupon the bear had bolted; and, whether frightened at the charge, or at the approach of some one, he had not returned.

The grisly is even fonder of sheep and pigs than is its smaller black broth-er. Lurking round the settler's house until after nightfall, it will vault into the fold or sty, grasp a helpless, bleating fleece-bearer, or a shrieking, struggling member of the bristly brotherhood, and bundle it out over the fence to its death. In carrying its prey a bear sometimes holds the body in its teeth, walking along on all-fours and dragging it as a wolf does. Sometimes, however, it seizes an animal in its forearms or in one of them, and walks awkwardly on three legs or two, adopting this method in lifting and pushing the body over rocks and down timber.

When a grisly can get at domestic animals it rarely seeks to molest game, the former being far less wary and more helpless. Its heaviness and clumsiness do not fit it well for a life of rapine against shy woodland creatures. Its vast strength and determined temper, however, more than make amends for lack of agility in the actual struggle with the stricken prey; its difficulty lies in seizing, not in killing, the game. Hence, when a grisly does take to game-killing, it is likely to attack bison, moose, and elk; it is rarely able to catch deer, still less sheep or antelope. In fact these smaller game animals often show but little dread of its neighborhood, and, though careful not to let it come too near, go on grazing when a bear is in full sight. Whitetail deer are frequently found at home in the same thicket in which a bear has its den, while they immediately desert the temporary abiding place of a wolf or cougar. Nevertheless, they sometimes presume too much on this confidence. A couple of years before the occurrence of the feats of cattle-killing mentioned above as happening near my ranch, either the same bear that figured in them, or another of similar tastes, took to gamehunting. The beast lived in the same succession of huge thickets which cover for two or three miles the river bottoms and the mouths of the inflowing creeks; and he suddenly made a raid on the whitetail deer which were plentiful in the dense cover. The shaggy, clumsy monster was cunning enough to kill several of these knowing creatures. The exact course of procedure I never could find out; but apparently the bear laid in wait beside the game trails, along which the deer wandered.

In the old days when the innumerable bison grazed free on the prairie, the grisly sometimes harassed their bands as it now does the herds of the ranchman. The bison was the most easily approached of all game, and the great bear could often get near some outlying straggler, in its quest after stray cows, yearlings, or calves. In default of a favorable chance to make a prey of one of these weaker members of the herds, it did not hesitate to attack the mighty bulls themselves; and perhaps the grandest sight which it was ever the good fortune of the early hunters to witness, was one of these rare battles between a hungry grisly and a powerful buffalo bull. Nowadays, however, the few last survivors of the bison are vanishing even from the inaccessible mountain fastnesses in which they sought a final refuge from their destroyers.

At present the wapiti is of all wild game that which is most likely to fall a victim to the grisly, when the big bear is in the mood to turn hunter. Wapiti are found in the same places as the grisly, and in some spots they are yet very plentiful; they are less shy and active than deer, while not powerful enough to beat off so ponderous a foe; and they live in cover where there is always a good chance either to stalk or to stumble on them. At almost any season bear will come and feast on an elk carcass; and if the food supply runs short, in early spring, or in a fall when the berry crop fails, they sometimes have to do their own killing. Twice I have come across the remains of elk, which had seemingly been slain and devoured by bears. I have never heard of elk making a fight against a bear; yet, at close quarters and at bay, a bull elk in the rutting season is an ugly foe.

A bull moose is even more formidable, being able to strike the most lightning-like blows with his terrible forefeet, his true weapons of defence. I doubt if any beast of prey would rush in on one of these woodland giants, when his horns were grown, and if he was on his guard and bent on fight. Nevertheless, the moose sometimes fall victims to the uncouth prowess of the grisly, in the thick wet forests of the high northern Rockies, where both beasts dwell. An old hunter who a dozen years ago wintered at Jackson Lake, in northwestern Wyoming, told me that when the snows got deep on the mountains the moose came down and took up their abode near the lake, on its western side. Nothing molested them during the winter. Early in the spring a grisly came out of its den, and he found its tracks in many places, as it roamed restlessly about, evidently very hungry. Finding little to eat in the bleak, snow-drifted woods, it soon began to depredate on the moose, and killed two or three, generally by lying in wait and dashing out on them as they passed near its lurking-place. Even the bulls were at that season weak, and of course hornless, with small desire to fight; and in each case the rush of the great bear—doubtless made with the ferocity and speed which so often belie the seeming awkwardness of the animal—bore down the startled victim, taken utterly unawares before it had a chance to defend itself. In one case the bear had missed its spring; the moose going off, for a few rods, with huge jumps, and then settling down into its characteristic trot. The old hunter who followed the tracks said he would never have deemed it possible for any animal to make such strides while in a trot.

Nevertheless, the grisly is only occasionally, not normally, a formidable predatory beast, a killer of cattle and of large game. Although capable of far swifter movement than is promised by his frame of seemingly clumsy strength, and in spite of his power of charging with astonishing suddenness and speed, he yet lacks altogether the supple agility of such finished destroyers as the cougar and the wolf; and for the absence of this agility no amount of mere huge muscle can atone. He is more apt to feast on animals which have met their death by accident, or which have been killed by other beasts or by man, than to do his own killing. He is a very foul feeder, with a strong relish for carrion, and possesses a grewsome and cannibal fondness for the flesh of his own kind; a bear carcass will toll a brother bear to the ambushed hunter better than almost any other bait, unless it is the carcass of a horse.

Nor do these big bears always content themselves merely with the carcasses of their brethren. A black bear would have a poor chance if in the clutches of a large, hungry grisly; and an old male will kill and eat a cub, especially if he finds it at a disadvantage. A rather remarkable instance of this occurred in the Yellowstone National Park, in the spring of 1891. The incident is related in the following letter written to Mr. William Hallett Phillips, of Washington, by another friend, Mr. Elvvood Hofer. Hofer is an old mountain-man; I have hunted with him myself, and know his statements to be trustworthy. He was, at the time, at work in the Park getting animals for the National Museum at Washington, and was staying at Yancey's "hotel" near Tower Falls. His letter which was dated June 21st, 1891, runs in part as follows:

"I had a splendid Grizzly or Roach-back cub and was going to send him into the Springs next morning the team was here, I heard a racket out side went out and found him dead an old bear that made an 9 1-2 inch track had killed and partly eaten him. Last night another one came, one that made an 8 1-2 inch track, and broke Yancy up in the milk business. You know how the cabins stand here. There is a hitching post between the saloon and old house, the little bear was killed there. In a creek close by was a milk house, last night another bear came there and smashed the whole thing up, leaving nothing but a few flattened buckets and pans and boards. I was sleeping in the old cabin, I heard the tin ware rattle but thought it was all right supposed it was cows or horses about. I don't care about the milk but the damn cuss dug up the remains of the cub I had buried in the old ditch, he visited the old meat house but found nothing. Bear are very thick in this part of the Park, and are getting very fresh. I sent in the game to Capt. Anderson, hear its doing well."

Grislies are fond of fish; and on the Pacific slope, where the salmon run, they, like so many other beasts, travel many scores of miles and crowd down to the rivers to gorge themselves upon the fish which are thrown up on the banks. Wading into the water a bear will knock out the salmon right and left when they are running thick.

Flesh and fish do not constitute the grisly's ordinary diet. At most times the big bear is a grubber in the ground, an eater of insects, roots, nuts, and berries. Its dangerous fore-claws are normally used to overturn stones and knock rotten logs to pieces, that it may lap up the small tribes of darkness which swarm under the one and in the other. It digs up the camas roots, wild onions, and an occasional luckless woodchuck or gopher. If food is very plenty bears are lazy, but commonly they are obliged to be very industrious, it being no light task to gather enough ants, beetles, crickets, tumble-bugs, roots, and nuts to satisfy the cravings of so huge a bulk. The sign of a bear's work is, of course, evident to the most unpractised eye; and in no way can one get a better idea of the brute's power than by watching it busily working for its breakfast, shattering big logs and upsetting boulders by sheer strength. There is always a touch of the comic, as well as a touch of the strong and terrible, in a bear's look and actions. It will tug and pull, now with one paw, now with two, now on all fours, now on its hind legs, in the effort to turn over a large log or stone; and when it succeeds it jumps round to thrust its muzzle into the damp hollow and lap up the affrighted mice or beetles while they are still paralyzed by the sudden exposure.

The true time of plenty for bears is the berry season. Then they feast ravenously on huckleberries, blueberries, kinnikinic berries, buffalo berries, wild plums, elderberries, and scores of other fruits. They often smash all the bushes in a berry patch, gathering the fruit with halfluxurious, half-laborious greed, sit-

ting on their haunches, and sweeping the berries into their mouths with dexterous paws. So absorbed do they become in their feasts on the luscious fruit that they grow reckless of their safety, and feed in broad daylight, almost at midday; while in some of the thickets, especially those of the mountain haws, they make so much noise in smashing the branches that it is a comparatively easy matter to approach them unheard. That still-hunter is in luck who in the fall finds an accessible berry-covered hill-side which is haunted by bears; but, as a rule, the berry bushes do not grow close enough together to give the hunter much chance.

Like most other wild animals, bears which have known the neighborhood of man are beasts of the darkness, or at least of the dusk and the gloaming. But they are by no means such true night-lovers as the big cats and the wolves. In regions where they know little of hunters they roam about freely in the daylight, and in cool weather are even apt to take their noontide slumbers basking in the sun. Where they are much hunted they finally almost reverse their natural habits and sleep throughout the hours of light, only venturing abroad after nightfall and before sunrise; but even yet this is not the habit of those bears which exist in the wilder localities where they are still plentiful. In these places they sleep, or at least rest, during the hours of greatest heat, and again in the middle part of the night, unless there is a full moon. They start on their rambles for food about midafternoon, and end their morning roaming soon after the sun is above the horizon. If the moon is full, however, they may feed all night long, and then wander but little in the daytime.

Aside from man, the full-grown grisly has hardly any foe to fear. Nevertheless, in the early spring, when weakened by the hunger that succeeds the winter sleep, it behooves even the grisly, if he dwells in the mountain fastnesses of the far northwest, to beware of a famished troop of great timber wolves. These northern Rocky Mountain wolves are most formidable beasts, and when

many of them band together in time of famine they do not hesitate to pounce on the black bear and cougar; and even a full-grown grisly is not safe from their attacks, unless he can back up against some rock which will prevent them from assailing him from behind. A small ranchman whom I knew well, who lived near Flathead Lake, once in April found where a troop of these wolves had killed a good-sized yearling grisly. Either cougar or wolf will make a prey of a grisly which is but a few months old; while any fox, lynx, wolverine, or fisher will seize the very young cubs. The old story about wolves fearing to feast on game killed by a grisly is all nonsense. Wolves are canny beasts, and they will not approach a carcass if they think a bear is hidden nearby and likely to rush out at them; but under ordinary circumstances they will feast not only on the carcasses of the grisly's victims, but on the carcass of the grisly himself after he has been slain and left by the hunter. Of course wolves would only attack a grisly if in the most desperate straits for food, as even a victory over such an antagonist must be purchased with heavy loss of life; and a hungry grisly would devour either a wolf or a cougar, or any one of the smaller carnivora off-hand if it happened to corner it where it could not get away.

The grisly occasionally makes its den in a cave and spends therein the midday hours. But this is rare. Usually it lies in the dense shelter of the most tangled piece of woods in the neighborhood, choosing by preference some bit where the young growth is thick and the ground strewn with boulders and fallen logs. Often, especially if in a restless mood and roaming much over the country, it merely makes a temporary bed, in which it lies but once or twice; and again it may make a more permanent lair or series of lairs, spending many consecutive nights in each. Usually the lair or bed is made some distance from the feeding ground; but bold bears, in very wild localities, may lie close by a carcass, or in the middle of a berry ground. The deer-killing bear above mentioned had evidently dragged two or three of his victims to his den, which was under an impenetrable mat of bull-berries and dwarf box-alders, hemmed in by a cut bank on one side and a wall of gnarled cottonwoods on the other. Round this den, and rendering it noisome, were scattered the bones of several deer and a young steer or heifer. When we found it we thought we could easily kill the bear, but the fierce, cunning beast must have seen or smelt us, for though we laid in wait for it long and patiently, it did not come back to its place; nor, on our subsequent visits, did we ever find traces of its having done so.

Bear are fond of wallowing in the water, whether in the sand, on the edge of a rapid plains river, on the muddy margin of a pond, or in the oozy moss of a clear, cold mountain spring. One hot August afternoon, as I was clambering down a steep mountain-side near Pend'Oreille lake, I heard a crash some distance below, which showed that a large beast was afoot. On making my way towards the spot, I found I had disturbed a big bear as it was lolling at ease in its bath; the discolored water showed where it had scrambled hastily out and galloped off as I approached. The spring welled out at the base of a high granite rock, forming a small pool of shimmering broken crystal. The soaked moss lay in a deep wet cushion round about, and jutted over the edges of the pool like a floating shelf. Graceful, water-loving ferns swayed to and fro. Above, the great conifers spread their murmuring branches, dimming the light, and keeping out the heat; their brown boles sprang from the ground like buttressed columns. On the barren mountain-side beyond the heat was oppressive. It was small wonder that Bruin should have sought the spot to cool his gross carcass in the fresh spring water.

The bear is a solitary beast, and although many may assemble together, in what looks like a drove, on some favorite feeding-ground—usually where the berries are thick, or by the banks of a salmon-thronged river—the association is never more than momentary, each go-ing its own way as soon as its hunger is satisfied. The males always live alone by choice, save in the rutting season, when they seek the females. Then two or three may come together in the course of their pursuit and rough courtship of the female; and if the rivals are well matched, savage battles follow, so that many of the old males have their heads seamed with scars made by their fellows' teeth. At such times they are evil tempered and prone to attack man or beast on slight provocation.

The she brings forth her cubs, one, two, or three in number, in her winter den. They are very small and helpless things, and it is some time after she leaves her winter home before they can follow her for any distance. They stay with her throughout the summer and the fall, leaving her when the cold weather sets in. By this time they are well grown; and hence, especially if an old male has joined the she, the family may number three or four individuals, so as to make what seems like quite a little troop of bears. A small ranchman who lived a dozen miles from me on the Little Missouri once found a shebear and three half-grown cubs feeding at a berry-patch in a ravine. He shot the old she in the small of the back, whereat she made a loud roaring and squealing. One of the cubs rushed towards her; but its sympathy proved misplaced, for she knocked it over with a hearty cuff, either out of mere temper, or because she thought her pain must be due to an unprovoked assault from one of her offspring. The hunter then killed one of the cubs, and the other two escaped. When bears are together and one is wounded by a bullet, but does not see the real assailant, it often falls tooth and nail upon its comrade, apparently attributing its injury to the latter.

Bears are hunted in many ways. Some are killed by poison; but this plan is only practised by the owners of cattle or sheep who have suffered from their ravages. Moreover, they are harder to poison than wolves. Most often they are killed in traps, which are sometimes deadfalls, on the principle of the little figure-4 trap familiar to every American country boy, sometimes log-pens in which the animal is taken alive, but generally huge steel gins. In some states there is a bounty for the destruction of grislies; and in many places their skins have a market price, although much less valuable than those of the black bear. The men who pursue them for the bounty, or for their fur, as well as the ranchmen who regard them as foes to stock, ordinarily use steel traps. The trap is very massive, needing no small strength to set, and it is usually chained to a bar or log of wood, which does not stop the bear's progress outright, but hampers and interferes with it, continually catching in tree stumps and the like. The animal when trapped makes off at once, biting at the trap and the bar; but it leaves a broad wake and sooner or later is found tangled up by the chain and bar. A bear is by no means so difficult to trap as a wolf or fox although more so than a cougar or a lynx. In wild regions a skilful trapper can often catch a great many with comparative ease. A cunning old grisly however, soon learns the danger, and is then almost impossible to trap, as it either avoids the neighborhood altogether or finds out some way by which to get at the bait without springing the trap, or else deliberately springs it first. I have been told of bears which spring traps by rolling across them, the iron jaws slipping harmlessly off the big round body. An old horse is the most common bait.

It is, of course, all right to trap bears when they are followed merely as vermin or for the sake of the fur. Occasionally, however, hunters who are out merely for sport adopt this method; but this should never be done. To shoot a trapped bear for sport is a thoroughly unsportsmanlike proceeding. A funny plea sometimes advanced in its favor is that it is "dangerous." No doubt in exceptional instances this is true; exactly as it is true that in exceptional instances it is "dangerous" for a butcher to knock over a steer in the slaughter-house. A bear caught only by the toes may wrench itself free as the hunter comes near, and attack him with pain-maddened fury; or if followed at once, and if the trap and bar are light, it may be found in some thicket, still free, and in a frenzy of rage. But even in such cases the beast has been crippled, and though crazy with pain and anger is easily dealt with by a good shot; while ordinarily the poor brute is found in the last stages of exhaustion, tied tight to a tree where the log or bar has caught, its teeth broken to splintered stumps by rabid snaps at the cruel trap and chain. Some trappers kill the trapped grislies with a revolver; so that it may easily be seen that the sport is not normally dangerous. Two of my own cowboys, Seawell and Dow, were originally from Maine, where they had trapped a number of black bears; and they always killed them either with a hatchet or a small 32-calibre revolver. One of them, Seawell, once came near being mauled by a trapped bear, seemingly at the last gasp, which he approached incautiously with his hatchet.

There is, however, one very real danger to which the solitary bear-trapper is exposed, the danger of being caught in his own trap. The huge jaws of the gin are easy to spring and most hard to open. If an unwary passer-by should tread between them and be caught by the leg, his fate would be doubtful, though he would probable die under the steadily growing torment of the merciless iron jaws, as they pressed ever deeper into the sore flesh and broken bones. But if caught by the arms, while setting or fixing the trap, his fate would be in no doubt at all, for it would be impossible for the stoutest man to free himself by any means. Terrible stories are told of solitary mountain hunters who disappeared, and were found years later in the lonely wilderness, as mouldering skeletons, the shattered bones of the forearms still held in the rusty jaws of the gin.

Doubtless the grisly could be successfully hunted with dogs, if the latter were carefully bred and trained to the purpose, but as yet this has not been done, and though dogs are sometimes used as adjuncts in grisly hunting they are rarely of much service. It is sometimes said that very small dogs are the best for this end. But this is only so with grislies that have never been hunted. In such a case the big bear sometimes becomes so irritated with the bouncing, yapping little terriers or fice-dogs that he may try to catch them and thus permit the hunter to creep upon him. But the minute he realizes, as he speedily does, that the man is his real foe, he pays no further heed whatever to the little dogs, who can then neither bring him to bay nor hinder his flight. Ordinary hounds, of the kinds used in the South for fox, deer, wildcat, and black bear, are but little better. I have known one or two men who at different times tried to hunt the grisly with a pack of hounds and fice-dogs wonted to the chase of the black bear, but they never met with success, This was probably largely owing to the nature of the country in which they hunted, a vast tangled mass of forest and craggy mountain; but it was also due to the utter inability of the dogs to stop the quarry from breaking bay when it wished. Several times a grisly was bayed, but always in some inaccessible spot which it took hard climbing to reach, and the dogs were never able to hold the beast until the hunters came up.

Still a well-trained pack of large hounds which were both bold and cunning could doubtless bay even a grisly. Such dogs are the big half-breed hounds sometimes used in the Alleghanies of West Virginia, which are trained not merely to nip a bear, but to grip him by the hock as he runs and either throw him or twirl him round. A grisly could not disregard a wary and powerful hound capable of performing this trick, even though he paid small heed to mere barking and occasional nipping. Nor do I doubt that it would be possible to get together a pack of many large, fierce dogs, trained to dash straight at the head and hold on like a vice, which could fairly master a grisly and, though unable, of course, to kill him, would worry him breathless and hold him down so that he could be slain with ease. There have been instances in which five or six of the big so-called blood-hounds of the southern States—not pure blood-hounds at all, but huge, fierce, ban-

dogs, with a cross of the ferocious Cuban bloodhound, to give them good scenting powers—have by themselves mastered the couq-ar and the black bear. Such instances occurred in the hunting history of my own forefathers on my mother's side, who during the last half of the eighteenth, and the first half of the present, century lived in Georgia and over the border in what are now Alabama and Florida. These big dogs can only overcome such foes by rushing in in a body and grappling all together; if they hang back, lunging and snapping, a cougar or bear will destroy them one by one. With a quarry so huge and redoubtable as the grisly, no number of dogs, however large and fierce, could overcome him unless they all rushed on him in a mass, the first in the charge seizing by the head or throat. If the dogs hung back, or if there were only a few of them, or if they did not seize around the head, they would be destroyed without an effort. It is murder to slip merely one or two closequarter dogs at a grisly. Twice I have known a man take a large bull dog with his pack when after one of these big bears, and in each case the result was the same. In one instance the bear was trotting when the bulldog seized it by the cheek, and without so much as altering its gait, it brushed off the hanging dog with a blow from the forepaw that broke the latter's back. In the other instance the bear had come to bay, and when seized by the ear it got the dog's body up to its jaws, and tore out the life with one crunch.

A small number of dogs must rely on their activity, and must hamper the bear's escape by inflicting a severe bite and avoiding the counter-stroke. The only dog I ever heard of which, single-handed, was really of service in stopping a grisly, was a big Mexican sheep-dog, once owned by the hunter Tazewell Woody. It was an agile beast with powerful jaws, and possessed both intelligence and a fierce, resolute temper. Woody killed three grislies with its aid. It attacked with equal caution and ferocity, rushing at the bear as the latter ran, and seizing the outstretched hock with a grip of iron, stopping the bear short, but letting go before the angry beast could whirl round and seize it. It was so active and wary that it always escaped damage; and it was so strong and bit so severely that the bear could not possibly run from it at any speed. In consequence, if it once came to close quarters with its quarry, Woody could always get near enough for a shot.

Hitherto, however, the mountain hunters—as distinguished from the trappers—who have followed the grisly have relied almost solely on their rifles. In my own case about half the bears I have killed I stumbled across almost by accident; and probably this proportion holds good generally. The hunter may be after bear at the time, or he may be after blacktail deer or elk, the common game in most of the haunts of the grisly; or he may merely be travelling through the country or prospecting for gold. Suddenly he comes over the edge of a cut bank, or round the sharp spur of a mountain or the shoulder of a cliff which walls in a ravine, or else the indistinct game trail he has been following through the great trees twists sharply to one side to avoid a rock or a mass of down timber, and behold he surprises old Elphraim digging for roots, or munching berries, or slouching along the path, or perhaps rising suddenly from the lush, rank plants amid which he has been lying. Or it may be that the bear will be spied afar rooting in an open glade or on a bare hill-side.

In the still-hunt proper it is necessary to find some favorite feeding-ground, where there are many roots or berry-bearing bushes, or else to lure the grisly to a carcass. This last method of "baiting" for bear is under ordinary circumstances the only way which affords even a moderately fair chance of killing them. They are very cunning, with the sharpest of noses, and where they have had experience of hunters they dwell only in cover where it is almost impossible for the best of still-hunters to approach them.

Nevertheless, in favorable ground a man can often find and kill them by fair stalking, in berry time, or more especially in the early spring, before the snow has gone from the mountains, and while the bears are driven by hunger to roam much abroad and sometimes to seek their food in the open. In such cases the still-hunter is stirring by the earliest dawn, and walks with stealthy speed to some high point of observation from which he can overlook the feeding-grounds where he has previously discovered sign. From the coign of vantage he scans the country far and near, either with his own keen eyes or with powerful glasses; and he must combine patience and good sight with the ability to traverse long distances noiselessly and yet at speed. He may spend two or three hours sitting still and looking over a vast tract of country before he will suddenly spy a bear; or he may see nothing after the most careful search in a given place, and must then go on half a dozen miles to another, watching warily as he walks, and continuing this possibly for several days before getting a glimpse of his game. If the bear are digging roots, or otherwise procuring their food on the bare hillsides and table-lands, it is of course comparatively easy to see them; and it is under such circumstances that this kind of hunting is most successful. Once seen, the actual stalk may take two or three hours, the nature of the ground and the direction of the wind often necessitating a long circuit; perhaps a gully, a rock, or a fallen log offers a chance for an approach to within two hundred yards, and although the hunter will, if possible, get much closer than this, yet even at such a distance a bear is a large enough mark to warrant risking a shot.

Usually the berry grounds do not offer such favorable opportunities, as they often lie in thick timber, or are covered so densely with bushes as to obstruct the view; and they are rarely commanded by a favorable spot from which to spy. On the other hand, as already said, bears occasionally forget all their watchfulness while devouring fruit, and make such a noise rending and tearing the bushes that, if once found, a man can creep upon them unobserved.

HUNTING THE GRISLY. IF out in the late fall or early spring, it is often possible to follow a bear's trail in the snow; having come upon it either by chance or hard hunting, or else having found where it leads from some carcass on which the beast has been feeding. In the pursuit one must exercise great caution, as at such times the hunter is easily seen a long way off, and game is always especially watchful for any foe that may follow its trail.

Once I killed a grisly in this manner. It was early in the fall, but snow lay on the ground, while the gray weather boded a storm. My camp was in a bleak, wind-swept valley, high among the mountains which form the divide between the head-waters of the Salmon and Clarke's Fork of the Columbia. All night I had lain in my buffalo-bag, under the lea of a windbreak of branches, in the clump of fir-trees, where I had halted the preceding evening. At my feet ran a rapid mountain torrent, its bed choked with ice-covered rocks; I had been lulled to sleep by the stream's splashing murmur, and the loud moaning of the wind along the naked cliffs. At dawn I rose and shook myself free of the buffalo robe, coated with hoar-frost. The ashes of the fire were lifeless; in the dim morning the air was bitter cold. I did not linger a moment, but snatched up my rifle, pulled on my fur cap and gloves, and strode off up a side ravine; as I walked I ate some mouthfuls of venison, left over from supper.

Two hours of toil up the steep mountain brought me to the top of a spur. The sun had risen, but was hidden behind a bank of sullen clouds. On the divide I halted, and gazed out over a vast landscape, inconceivably wild and dismal. Around me towered the stupendous mountain masses which make up the backbone of the Rockies. From my feet, as far as I could see, stretched a rugged and barren chaos of ridges and detached rock masses. Behind me, far below, the stream wound like a silver ribbon, fringed with dark conifers and the changing, dying foliage of poplar and quaking aspen. In front the bottoms of the valley were filled with the sombre evergreen forest, dotted here and there with black, ice-skimmed tarns; and the dark spruces clustered also in the higher gorges, and were scattered thinly along the mountain sides. The snow which had fallen lay in drifts and streaks, while, where the wind had scope it was blown off, and the ground left bare.

For two hours I walked onwards across the ridges and valleys. Then among some scattered spruces, where the snow lay to the depth of half a foot, I suddenly came on the fresh, broad trail of a grisly. The brute was evidently roaming restlessly about in search of a winter den, but willing, in passing, to pick up any food that lay handy. At once I took the trail, travelling above and to one side, and keeping a sharp look-out 'ahead. The bear was going across wind, and this made my task easy. I walked rapidly, though cautiously; and it was only in crossing the large patches of bare ground that I had to fear making a noise. Elsewhere the snow muffled my footsteps, and made the trail so plain that I scarcely had to waste a glance upon it, bending my eyes always to the front.

At last, peering cautiously over a ridge crowned with broken rocks, I saw my quarry, a big, burly bear, with silvered fur. He had halted on an open hill-side, and was busily digging up the caches of some rock gophers or squirrels. He seemed absorbed in his work, and the stalk was easy. Slipping quietly back, I ran towards the end of the spur, and in ten minutes struck a ravine, of which one branch ran past within seventy yards of where the bear was working. In this ravine was a rather close growth of stunted evergreens, affording good cover, although in one or two places I had to lie down and crawl through the snow. When I reached the point for which I was aiming, the bear had just finished rooting, and was starting off. A slight whistle brought him to a standstill, and I drew a bead behind his shoulder, and low down, resting the rifle across the crooked branch of a dwarf spruce. At the crack he ran off at speed, making no sound, but the thick spatter of blood splashes, showing clear on the white snow, betrayed the mortal nature of the wound. For some minutes I followed the trail; and then, topping a ridge, I saw the dark bulk lying motionless in a snow drift at the foot of a low rock-wall, down which he had tumbled.

The usual practice of the still-hunter who is after grisly is to toll it to baits. The hunter either lies in ambush near the carcass, or approaches it stealthily when he thinks the bear is at its meal.

One day while camped near the Bitter Root Mountains in Montana I found that a bear had been feeding on the carcass of a moose which lay some five miles from the little open glade in which my tent was pitched, and I made up my mind to try to get a shot at it that afternoon. I stayed in camp till about three o'clock, lying lazily back on the bed of sweet-smelling evergreen boughs, watching the pack ponies as they stood under the pines on the edge of the open, stamping now and then, and switching their tails. The air was still, the sky a glorious blue; at that hour in the afternoon even the September sun was hot. The smoke from the smouldering logs of the camp fire curled thinly upwards. Little chipmunks scuttled out from their holes to the packs, which lay in a heap on the ground, and then scuttled madly back again. A couple of drab-colored whiskey-jacks, with bold mien and fearless bright eyes, hopped and fluttered round, picking up the scraps, and uttering an extraordinary variety of notes, mostly discordant; so tame were they that one of them lit on my outstretched arm as I half dozed, basking in the sunshine.

When the shadows began to lengthen, I shouldered my rifle and plunged into the woods. At first my route lay along a mountain side; then for half a mile over a windfall, the dead timber piled about in crazy confusion. After that I went up the bottom of a valley by a little brook, the ground being carpeted with a sponge of soaked moss. At the head of this brook was a pond covered with water-lilies; and a scramble through a rocky pass took me into a high, wet valley, where the thick growth of spruce was broken by occasional strips of meadow. In this valley the moose carcass lay, well at the upper end.

In moccasined feet I trod softly through the soundless woods. Under the dark branches it was already dusk, and the air had the cool chill of evening. As I neared the clump where the body lay, I walked with redoubled caution, watching and listening with strained alertness. Then I heard a twig snap; and my blood leaped, for I knew the bear was at his supper. In another moment I saw his shaggy, brown form. He was working with all his awkward giant strength, trying to bury the carcass, twisting it to one side and the other with wonderful ease. Once he got angry and suddenly gave it a tremendous cuff with his paw; in his bearing he had something half humorous, half devilish. I crept up within forty yards; but for several minutes he would not keep his head still. Then something attracted his attention in the forest, and he stood motionless looking towards it, broadside to me, with his fore-paws planted on the carcass. This gave me my chance. I drew a very fine bead between his eye and ear, and pulled trigger. He dropped like a steer when struck with a pole-axe.

If there is a good hiding-place handy it is better to lie in wait at the carcass. One day on the head-waters of the Madison, I found that a bear was coming to an elk I had shot some days before; and I at once determined to ambush the beast when he came back that evening. The carcass lay in the middle of a valley a quarter of a mile broad. The bottom of this valley was covered by an open forest of tall pines; a thick jungle of smaller evergreens marked where the mountains rose on either hand. There were a number of large rocks scattered here and there, one, of very convenient shape, being only some seventy or eighty yards from the carcass. Up this I clambered. It hid me perfectly, and on its top was a carpet of soft pine needles, on which I could lie at my ease.

Hour after hour passed by. A little black woodpecker with a yellow crest ran nimbly up and down the tree trunks for some time and then flitted away with a party of chickadees and nut-hatches. Occasionally a Clarke's crow soared about overhead or clung in any position to the swaying end of a pine branch, chattering and screaming. Flocks of cross-bills, with wavy flight and plaintive calls, flew to a small mineral lick near by, where they scraped the clay with their queer little beaks.

As the westering sun sank out of sight beyond the mountains these sounds of bird-life gradually died away. Under the great pines the evening was still with the silence of primeval desolation. The sense of sadness and loneliness, the melancholy of the wilderness, came over me like a spell. Every slight noise made my pulses throb as I lay motionless on the rock gazing intently into the gathering gloom. I began to fear that it would grow too dark to shoot before the grisly came.

Suddenly and without warning, the great bear stepped out of the bushes and trod across the pine needles with such swift and silent footsteps that its bulk seemed unreal. It was very cautious, continually halting to peer around; and once it stood up on its hind legs and looked long down the valley towards the red west. As it reached the carcass I put a bullet between its shoulders. It rolled over, while the woods resounded with its savage roaring. Immediately it struggled to its feet and staggered off; and fell again to the next shot, squalling and yelling. Twice this was repeated; the brute being one of those bears which greet every wound with a great outer)', and sometimes seem to lose their feet when hit—although they will occasionally fight as savagely as their more silent brethren. In this case the wounds were mortal, and the bear died before reaching the edge of the thicket.

I spent much of the fall of 1889 hunting on the headwaters of the Salmon and Snake in Idaho, and along the Montana boundary line from the Big Hole Basin and the head of the Wisdom River to the neighborhood of Red Rock Pass and to the north and west of Henry's Lake. During the last fortnight my companion was the old mountain man, already mentioned, named Griffeth or Griffin— I cannot tell which, as he was always called either ' Hank" or " Griff.

" He was a crabbedly honest old fellow, and a very skilful hunter; but he was worn out with age and rheumatism, and his temper had failed even faster than his bodily strength. He showed me a greater variety of game than I had ever seen before in so short a time; nor did I ever before or after make so successful a hunt. But he was an exceedingly disagreeable companion on account of his surly, moody ways. I generally had to get up first, to kindle the fire and make ready breakfast, and he was very quarrelsome. Finally, during my absence from camp one day, while not very far from Red Rock pass, he found my whiskey flask, which I kept purely for emergencies, and drank all the contents. When I came back he was quite drunk. This was unbearable, and after some high words I left him, and struck off homeward through the woods on my own account. We had with us four pack and saddle horses; and of these I took a very intelligent and gentle little bronco mare, which possessed the invaluable trait of always staying near camp, even when not hobbled. I was not hampered with much of an outfit, having only my buffalo sleeping-bag, a fur coat, and my washing kit, with a couple of spare pairs of socks and some handkerchiefs. A frying-pan, some salt, flour, baking-powder, a small chunk of salt pork, and a hatchet, made up a light pack, which, with the bedding, I fastened across the stock saddle by means of a rope and a spare packing cinch. My cartridges and knife were in my belt; my compass and matches, as always, in my pocket. I walked, while the little mare followed almost like a dog, often without my having to hold the lariat which served as halter.

The country was for the most part fairly open, as I kept near the foot-hills where glades and little prairies broke the pine forest. The trees were of small size. There was no regular trail, but the course was easy to keep, and I had no trouble of any kind save on the second day. That afternoon I was following a stream which at last "canyoned up," that is, sank to the bottom of a canyonlike ravine impassable for a horse. I started

up a side valley, intending to cross from its head coulies to those of another valley which would lead in below the canyon.

However, I got enmeshed in the tangle of winding valleys at the foot of the steep mountains, and as dusk was coming on I halted and camped in a little open spot by the side of a small, noisy brook, with crystal water, The place was carpeted with soft, wet, green moss, dotted red with the kinnikinnic berries, and at its edge, under the trees where the ground was dry, I threw down the buffalo bed on the mat of sweet-smelling pine needles. Making camp took but a moment. I opened the pack, tossed the bedding on a smooth spot, knee-haltered the little mare, dragged up a few dry logs, and then strolled off, rifle on shoulder, through the frosty gloaming, to see if I could pick up a grouse for supper.

For half a mile I walked quickly and silently over the pine needles, across a succession of slight ridges separated by narrow, shallow valleys. The forest here was composed of lodge-pole pines, which on the ridges grew close together, with tall slender trunks, while in the valleys the growth was more open. Though the sun was behind the mountains there was yet plenty of light by which to shoot, but it was fading rapidly.

At last, as I was thinking of turning towards camp, I stole up to the crest of one of the ridges, and looked over into the valley some sixty yards off. Immediately I caught the loom of some large, dark object; and another glance showed me a big grisly walking slowly off with his head down. He was quartering to me, and I fired into his flank, the bullet, as I afterwards found, ranging forward and piercing one lung. At the shot he uttered a loud, moaning grunt and plunged forward at a heavy gallop, while I raced obliquely down the hill to cut him off. After going a few hundred feet he reached a laurel thicket, some thirty yards broad, and two or three times as long which he did not leave. I ran up to the edge and there halted, not liking to venture into the mass of twisted, closegrowing stems and glossy foliage. Moreover, as I halted, I heard him utter a peculiar, savage kind of whine from the heart of the brush. Accordingly, I began to skirt the edge, standing on tiptoe and gating earnestly to see if I could not catch a glimpse of his hide. When I was at the narrowest part of the thicket, he suddenly left it directly opposite, and then wheeled and stood broadside to me on the hill-side, a little above. He turned his head stiffly towards me; scarlet strings of froth hung from his lips; his eyes burned like embers in the gloom.

I held true, aiming behind the shoulder, and my bullet shattered the point or lower end of his heart, taking out a big nick. Instantly the great bear turned with a harsh roar of fury and challenge, blowing the bloody foam from his mouth, so that I saw the gleam of his white fangs; and then he charged straight at me, crashing and bounding through the laurel bushes, so that it was hard to aim. I waited until he came to a fallen tree, raking him as he topped it with a ball, which entered his chest and went through the cavity of his body, but he neither swerved nor flinched, and at the moment I did not know that I had struck him. He came steadily on, and in another second was almost upon me. I fired for his forehead, but my bullet went low, entering his open mouth, smashing his lower jaw and going into the neck. I leaped to one side almost as I pulled trigger; and through the hanging smoke the first thing I saw was his paw as he made a vicious side blow at me. The rush of his charge carried him past. As he struck he lurched forward, leaving a pool of bright blood where his muzzle hit the ground; but he recovered himself and made two or three jumps onwards, while I hurriedly jammed a couple of cartridges into the magazine, my rifle holding only four, all of which I had fired. Then he tried to pull up, but as he did so his muscles seemed suddenly to give way, his head drooped, and he rolled over and over like a shot rabbit. Each of my first three bullets had inflicted a mortal wound.

It was already twilight, and I merely opened the carcass, and then trotted back to camp. Next morning I returned and with much labor took off the skin. The fur was very fine, the animal being in excellent trim, and unusually bright-colored. Unfortunately, in packing it out I lost the skull, and had to supply its place with one of plaster. The beauty of the trophy, and the memory of the circumstances under which I procured it, make me value it perhaps more highly than any other in my house.

This is the only instance in which I have been regularly charged by a grisly. On the whole, the danger of hunting these great bears has been much exaggerated. At the beginning of the present century, when white hunters first encountered the grisly, he was doubtless an exceedingly savage beast, prone to attack without provocation, and a redoubtable foe to persons armed with the clumsy, small-bore, muzzle-loading rifles of the day. But at present bitter experience has taught him caution. He has been hunted for sport, and hunted for his pelt, and hunted for the bounty, and hunted as a dangerous enemy to stock, until, save in the very wildest districts, he has learned to be more wary than a deer, and to avoid man's presence almost as carefully as the most timid kind of game. Except in rare cases he will not attack of his own accord, and, as a rule, even when wounded his object is escape rather than battle.

Still, when fairly brought to bay, or when moved by a sudden fit of ungovernable anger, the grisly is beyond peradventure a very dangerous antagonist. The first shot, if taken at a bear a good distance off and previously unwounded and unharried; is not usually fraught with much danger, the startled animal being at the outset bent merely on flight. It is always hazardous, however, to track a wounded and worried grisly into thick cover, and the man who habitually follows and kills this chief of American game in dense timber, never abandoning the bloody trail whithersoever it leads, must show no small degree of skill and hardihood, and must not too closely count the risk to life or limb. Bears differ widely in temper, and occasionally one may be found who will

not show fight, no matter how much he is bullied; but, as a rule, a hunter must be cautious in meddling with a wounded animal which has retreated into a dense thicket, and has been once or twice roused; and such a beast, when it does turn, will usually charge again and again, and fight to the last with unconquerable ferocity. The short distance at which the bear can be seen through the underbrush, the fury of his charge, and his tenacity of life make it necessary for the hunter on such occasions to have steady nerves and a fairly quick and accurate aim. It is always well to have two men in following a wounded bear under such conditions. This is not necessary, however, and a good hunter, rather than lose his quarry, will, under ordinary circumstances, follow and attack it no matter how tangled the fastness in which it has sought refuge; but he must act warily and with the utmost caution and resolution, if he wishes to escape a terrible and probably fatal mauling. An experienced hunter is rarely rash, and never heedless; he will not, when alone, follow a wounded bear into a thicket, if by the exercise of patience, skill, and knowledge of the game's habits he can avoid the necessity; but it is idle to talk of the feat as something which ought in no case to be attempted. While danger ought never to be needlessly incurred, it is yet true that the keenest zest in sport comes from its presence, and from the consequent exercise of the qualities necessary to overcome it. The most thrilling moments of an Amerian hunter's life are those in which, with every sense on the alert, and with nerves strung to the highest point, he is following alone into the heart of its forest fastness the fresh and bloody footprints of an angered grisly; and no other triumph of American hunting can compare with the victory to be thus gained.

These big bears will not ordinarily charge from a distance of over a hundred yards; but there are exceptions to this rule. In the fall of 1890 my friend Archibald Rogers was hunting in Wyoming, south of the Yellowstone Park, and killed seven bears. One, an old he, was out on a bare table-land, grubbing for roots, when he was spied. It was early in the afternoon, and the hunters, who were on a high mountain slope, examined him for some time through their powerful glasses before making him out to be a bear. They then stalked up to the edge of the wood which fringed the table-land on one side, but could get no nearer than about three hundred yards, the plains being barren of all cover. After waiting for a couple of hours Rogers risked fche shot, in despair of getting nearer, and wounded the bear, though not very seriously. The animal made off, almost broadside to, and Rogers ran forward to intercept it. As soon as it saw him it turned and rushed straight for him, not heeding his second shot, and evidently bent on charging home. Rogers then waited until it was within twenty yards, and brained it with his third bullet.

In fact bears differ individually in courage and ferocity precisely as men do, or as the Spanish bulls, of which it is said that not more than one in twenty is fit to stand the combat of the arena. One grisly can scarcely be bullied into resistance; the next may fight to the end, against any odds, without flinching, or even attack unprovoked. Hence men of limited experience in this sport, generalizing from the actions of the two or three bears each has happened to see or kill, often reach diametrically opposite conclusions as to the fighting temper and capacity of the quarry. Even old hunters—who indeed, as a class, are very narrow-minded and opinionated—often generalize just as rashly as beginners. One will portray all bears as very dangerous; another will speak and act as if he deemed them of no more consequence than so many rabbits. I knew one old hunter who had killed a score without ever seeing one show fight. On the other hand, Dr. James C. Merrill, U. S. A., who has had about as much experience with bears as I have had, informs me that he has been charged with the utmost determination three times. In each case the attack was delivered before the bear was wounded or even shot at, the animal being roused by the approach of the hunters from his day bed, and charg-

ing headlong at them from a distance of twenty or thirty paces. All three bears were killed before they could do any damage. There was a very remarkable incident connected with the killing of one of them. It occurred in the northern spurs of the Bighorn range. Dr. Merrill, in company with an old hunter, had climbed down into a deep, narrow canyon. The bottom was threaded with well-beaten elk trails. While following one of these the two men turned a corner of the canyon and were instantly charged by an old she-grisly, so close that it was only by good luck that one of the hurried shots disabled her and caused her to tumble over a cut bank where she was easily finished. They found that she had been lying directly across the game trail, on a smooth well beaten patch of bare earth, which looked as if it had been dug up, refilled, and trampled down. Looking curiously at this patch they saw a bit of hide only partially covered at one end; digging down they found the body of a well grown grisly cub. Its skull had been crushed, and the brains licked out. and there were signs of other injuries. The hunters pondered long over this strange discovery, and hazarded many guesses as to its meaning. At last they decided that probably the cub had been killed, and its brains eaten out, either by some old male-grisly or by a cougar, that the mother had returned and driven away the murderer, and that she had then buried the body and lain above it, waiting to wreak her vengeance on the first passer-by.

Old Tazewell Wood)', during his thirty years' life as a hunter in the Rockies and on the great plains, killed very many grislies. He always exercised much caution in dealing with them; and, as it happened, he was by some suitable tree in almost every case when he was charged. He would accordingly climb the tree (a practice of which I do not approve however); and the bear would look up at him and pass on without stopping. Once, when he was hunting in the mountains with a companion, the latter, who was down in a valley, while Woody was on the hill-side, shot at a

bear. The first thing Woody knew the wounded grisly, running up-hill, was almost on him from behind. As he turned it seized his rifle in its jaws. He wrenched the rifle round, while the bear still gripped it, and pulled trigger, sending a bullet into its shoulder; whereupon it struck him with its paw, and knocked him over the rocks. By good luck he fell in a snow bank and was not hurt in the least. Meanwhile the bear went on and they never got it.

Once he had an experience with a bear which showed a very curious mixture of rashness and cowardice. He and a companion were camped in a little tepee or wigwam, with a bright fire in front of it, lighting up the night. There was an inch of snow on the ground. Just after they went to bed a grisly came close to camp. Their dog rushed out and they could hear it bark round in the darkness for nearly an hour; then the bear drove it off and came right into camp. It went close to the fire, picking up the scraps of meat and bread, pulled a haunch of venison down from a tree, and passed and repassed in front of the tepee, paying no heed whatever to the two men, who crouched in the doorway talking to one another. Once it passed so close that Woody could almost have touched it. Finally his companion fired into it, and off it ran, badly wounded, without an attempt at retaliation. Next morning they followed its tracks in the snow, and found it a quarter of a mile away. It was near a pine and had buried itself under the loose earth, pine needles, and snow; Woody's companion almost walked over it, and putting his rifle to its ear blew out its brains.

In all his experience Woody had personally seen but four men who were badly mauled by bears. Three of these were merely wounded. One was bitten terribly in the back. Another had an arm partially chewed off. The third was a man named George Dow, and the accident happened to him on the Yellowstone, about the year 1878. He was with a pack animal at the time, leading it on a trail through a wood. Seeing a big she-bear with cubs he yelled at her; whereat she ran away, but only to cache her cubs, and in a minute, having hidden them, came racing back at him. His pack animal being slow he started to climb a tree; but before he could get far enough up she caught him, almost biting a piece out of the calf of his leg, pulled him down, bit and cuffed him two or three times, and then went on her way.

The only time Woody ever saw a man killed by a bear was once when he had given a touch of variety to his life by shipping on a New Bedford whaler which had touched at one of the Puget Sound ports. The whaler went up to a part of Alaska where bears were very plentiful and bold. One day a couple of boats' crews landed; and the men, who were armed only with an occasional harpoon or lance, scattered over the beach, one of them, a Frenchman, wading into the water after shell-fish. Suddenly a bear emerged from some bushes and charged among the astonished sailors, who scattered in every direction; but the bear, said Woody, "just had it in for that Frenchman," and went straight at him. Shrieking with terror he retreated up to his neck in the water; but the bear plunged in after him, caught him, and disembowelled him. One of the Yankee mates then fired a bomb lance into the bear's hips, and the savage beast hobbled off into the dense cover of the low scrub, where the enraged sailor folk were unable to get at it.

The truth is that while the grisly generally avoids a battle if possible, and often acts with great cowardice, it is never safe to take liberties with him; he usually fights desperately and dies hard when wounded and cornered, and exceptional individuals take the aggressive on small provocation.

During the years I lived on the frontier I came in contact with many persons who had been severely mauled or even crippled for life by grislies; and a number of cases where they killed men outright were also brought under my ken. Generally these accidents, as was natural, occurred to hunters who had roused or wounded the game.

A fighting bear sometimes uses his claws and sometimes his teeth. I have never known one to attempt to kill an antagonist by hugging, in spite of the popular belief to this effect; though he will sometimes draw an enemy towards him with his paws the better to reach him with his teeth, and to hold him so that he cannot escape from the bitting. Nor does the bear often advance on his hind legs to the attack; though, if the man has come close to him in thick underbrush, or has stumbled on him in his lair unawares, he will often rise up in this fashion and strike a single blow. He will also rise in clinching with a man on horseback. In 1882 a mounted Indian was killed in this manner on one of the river bottoms some miles below where my ranch house now stands, not far from the junction of the Beaver and Little Missouri. The bear had been hunted into a thicket by a band of Indians, in whose company my informant, a white squaw-man, with whom I afterward did some trading, was travelling. One of them in the excitement of the pursuit rode across the end of the thicket; as he did so the great beast sprang at him with wonderful quickness, rising on its hind legs, and knocking over the horse and rider with a single sweep of his terrible fore-paws. It then turned on the fallen man and tore him open, and though the other Indians came promptly to his rescue and slew his assailant, they were not in time to save their comrade's life.

A bear is apt to rely mainly on his teeth or claws according to whether his efforts are directed primarily to killing his foe or to making good his own escape. In the latter event he trusts chiefly to his claws. If cornered, he of course makes a rush for freedom, and in that case he downs any man who is in his way with a sweep of his great paw, but passes on without stopping to bite him. If while sleeping or resting in thick brush some one suddenly stumbles on him close up he pursues the same course, less from anger than from fear, being surprised and startled. Moreover, if attacked at close quarters by men and dogs he strikes right and left in defence.

Sometimes what is called a charge is rather an effort to get away. In localities where he has been hunted, a bear, like every other kind of game, is always on the look-out for an attack, and is prepared at any moment for immediate flight. He seems ever to have in his mind, whether feeding, sunning himself, or merely roaming around, the direction—usually towards the thickest cover or most broken ground—in which he intends to run if molested. When shot at he instantly starts towards this place; or he may be so confused that he simply runs he knows not whither; and in either event he may take a line that leads almost directly to or by the hunter, although he had at first no thought of charging. In such a case he usually strikes a single knock-down blow and gallops on without halting, though that one blow may have taken life. If the claws are long and fairly sharp (as in early spring, or even in the fall, if the animal has been working over soft ground) they add immensely to the effect of the blow, for they cut like blunt axes. Often, however, late in the season, and if the ground has been dry and hard, or rocky, the claws are worn down nearly to the quick, and the blow is then given mainly with the under side of the paw; although even under this disadvantage a thump from a big bear will down a horse or smash in a man's breast. The hunter Hofer once lost a horse in this manner. He shot at and wounded a bear which rushed off, as ill luck would have it, past the place where his horse was picketed; probably more in fright than in anger it struck the poor beast a blow which, in the end, proved mortal.

If a bear means mischief and charges not to escape but to do damage, its aim is to grapple with or throw down its foe and bite him to death. The charge is made at a gallop, the animal sometimes coming on silently, with the mouth shut, and sometimes with the jaws open, the lips drawn back and teeth showing, uttering at the same time a succession of roars or of savage rasping snarls. Certain bears charge without any bluster and perfectly straight; while others first threaten and bully, and even when charging stop to growl, shake the head, and bite at a bush or knock holes in the ground with their fore-paws. Again, some of them charge home with a ferocious resolution which their extreme tenacity of life renders especially dangerous; while others can be turned or driven back even by a shot which is not mortal. They show the same variability in their behavior when wounded. Often a big bear, especially if charging, will receive a bullet in perfect silence, without flinching or seeming to pay any heed to it; while another will cry out and tumble about, and if charging, even though it may not abandon the attack, will pause for a moment to whine or bite at the wound.

Sometimes a single bite causes death. One of the most successful bear hunters I ever knew, an old fellow whose real name I never heard as he was always called Old Ike, was killed in this way in the spring or early summer of 1886 on one of the head-waters of the Salmon. He was a very good shot, had killed nearly a hundred bears with the rifle, and, although often charged, had never met with any accident, so that he had grown somewhat careless. On the day in question he had met a couple of mining prospectors and was travelling with them, when a grisly crossed his path. The old hunter immediately ran after it, rapidly gaining, as the bear did not hurry when it saw itself pursued, but slouched slowly forwards, occasionally turning its head to grin and growl. It soon went into a dense grove of young spruce, and as the hunter reached the edge it charged fiercely out. He fired one hasty shot, evidently wounding the animal, but not seriously enough to stop or cripple it; and as his two companions ran forward they saw the bear seize him with its wide-spread jaws, forcing him to the ground. They shouted and fired, and the beast abandoned the fallen man on the instant and sullenly retreated into the spruce thicket, whither they dared not follow it. Their friend was at his last gasp; for the whole side of the chest had been crushed in by the one bite, the lungs showing between the rent ribs.

Very often, however, a bear does not kill a man by one bite, but after throwing him lies on him, biting him to death.

Usually, if no assistance is at hand, such a man is doomed; although if he pretends to be dead, and has the nerve to lie quiet under very rough treatment, it is just possible that the bear may leave him alive, perhaps after half burying what it believes to be the body. In a very few exceptional instances men of extraordinary prowess with the knife have succeeded in beating off a bear, and even in mortally wounding it, but in most cases a singlehanded struggle, at close quarters, with a grisly bent on mischief, means death.

Occasionally the bear, although vicious, is also frightened, and passes on after giving one or two bites; and frequently a man who is knocked down is rescued by his friends before he is killed, the big beast mayhap using his weapons with clumsiness. So a bear may kill a foe with a single blow of its mighty fore-arm, either crushing in the head or chest by sheer force of sinew, or else tearing open the body with its formidable claws; and so on the other hand he may, and often does, merely disfigure or maim the foe by a hurried stroke. Hence it is common to see men who have escaped the clutches of a grisly, but only at the cost of features marred beyond recognition, or a body rendered almost helpless for life. Almost every old resident of western Montana or northern Idaho has known two or three unfortunates who have suffered in this manner. I have myself met one such man in Helena, and another in Missoula; both were living at least as late as 1889, the date at which I last saw them. One had been partially scalped by a bear's teeth; the animal was very old and so the fangs did not enter the skull. The other had been bitten across the face, and the wounds never entirely healed, so that his disfigured visage was hideous to behold.

Most of these accidents occur in following a wounded or worried bear into thick cover; and under such circumstances an animal apparently hopelessly disabled, or in the death throes, may with a last effort kill one or more of its assailants. In 1874 my wife's uncle, Captain Alexander Moore, U. S. A., and

my friend Captain Bates, with some men of the 2d and 3d Cavalry, were scouting in Wyoming, near the Freezeout Mountains. One morning they roused a bear in the open prairie and followed it at full speed as it ran towards a small creek. At one spot in the creek beavers had built a dam, and as usual in such places there was a thick growth of bushes and willow saplings. Just as the bear reached the edge of this little jungle it was struck by several balls, both of its fore-legs being broken. Nevertheless, it managed to shove itself forward on its hind-legs, and partly rolled, partly pushed itself into the thicket, the bushes though low being so dense that its body was at once completely hidden. The thicket was a mere patch of brush, not twenty yards across in any direction. The leading troopers reached the edge almost as the bear tumbled in. One of them, a tall and powerful man named Miller, instantly dismounted and prepared to force his way in among the dwarfed willows, which were but breast-high. Among the men who had ridden up were Moore and Bates, and also the two famous scouts, Buffalo Bill—long a companion of Captain Moore,—and California Joe, Custer's faithful follower. California Joe had spent almost all his life on the plains and in the mountains, as a hunter and Indian fighter; and when he saw the trooper about to rush into the thicket he called out to him not to do so, warning him of the danger. But the man was a very reckless fellow and he answered by jeering at the old hunter for his overcaution in being afraid of a crippled bear. California Joe made no further effort to dissuade him, remarking quietly: "Very well, sonny, go in; it's your own affair." Miller then leaped off the bank on which they stood and strode into the thicket, holding his rifle at the port. Hardly had he taken three steps when the bear rose in front of him, roaring with rage and pain. It was so close that the man had no chance to fire. Its forearms hung useless and as it reared unsteadily on its hind-legs, lunging forward at him, he seized it by the ears and strove to hold it back. His strength was very great, and he actually kept the huge head from his face and braced himself so that he was not overthrown; but the bear twisted its muzzle from side to side, biting and tearing the man's arms and shoulders. Another soldier jumping down slew the beast with a single bullet, and rescued his comrade; but though alive he was too badly hurt to recover and died after reaching the hospital. Buffalo Bill was given the bear-skin, and I believe has it now.

The instances in which hunters who have rashly followed grislies into thick cover have been killed or severely mauled might be multiplied indefinitely. I have myself known of eight cases in which men have met their deaths in this manner.

It occasionally happens that a cunning old grisly will lie so close that the hunter almost steps on him; and he then rises suddenly with a loud, coughing growl and strikes down or seizes the man before the latter can fire off his rifle. More rarely a bear which is both vicious and crafty deliberately permits the hunter to approach fairly near to, or perhaps pass by, its hiding-place, and then suddenly charges him with such rapidity that he has barely time for the most hurried shot. The danger in such a case is of course great.

Ordinarily, however, even in the brush, the bear's object is to slink away, not to fight, and very many are killed even under the most unfavorable circumstances without accident. If an unwounded bear thinks itself unobserved it is not apt to attack; and in thick cover it is really astonishing to see how one of these large animals can hide, and how closely it will lie when there is danger. About twelve miles below my ranch there are some large river bottoms and creek bottoms covered with a matted mass of cottonwood, box-alders, bullberry bushes, rosebushes, ash, wild plums, and other bushes. These bottoms have harbored bears ever since I first saw them; but though, often in company with a large party, I have repeatedly beaten through them, and though we must at times have been very near indeed to the game, we never so much as

heard it run.

When bears are shot, as they usually must be, in open timber or on the bare mountain, the risk is very much less. Hundreds may thus be killed with comparatively little danger; yet even under these circumstances they will often charge, and sometimes make their charge good. The spice of danger, especially to a man armed with a good repeating rifle, is only enough to add zest to the chase, and the chief triumph is in outwitting the war' quarry and getting within range. Ordinarily the only excitement is in the stalk, the bear doing nothing more than keep a keen look-out and manifest the utmost anxiety to get away. As is but natural, accidents occasionally occur; yet they are usually due more to some failure in man or weapon than to the prowess of the bear. A good hunter whom I once knew, at a time when he was living in Butte, received fatal injuries from a bear he attacked in open woodland. The beast charged after the first shot, but slackened its pace on coming almost up to the man. The latter's gun jammed, and as he was endeavoring to work it he kept stepping slowly back, facing the bear which followed a few yards distant, snarling and threatening. Unfortunately while thus walking backwards the man struck a dead log and fell over it, whereupon the beast instantly sprang on him and mortally wounded him before help arrived.

On rare occasions men who are not at the time hunting it fall victims to the grisly. This is usually because they stumble on it unawares and the animal attacks them more in fear than in anger. One such case, resulting fatally, occurred near my own ranch. The man walked almost over a bear while crossing a little point of brush, in a bend of the river, and was brained with a single blow of the paw. In another instance which came to my knowledge the man escaped with a shaking up, and without even a fright. His name was Perkins, and he was out gathering huckleberries in the woods on a mountain side near Pend'Oreille Lake. Suddenly he was sent flying head over heels, by a blow which completely knocked the breath

out of his body; and so instantaneous was the whole affair that all he could ever recollect about it was getting a vague glimpse of the bear just as he was bowled over. When he came to he found himself lying some distance down the hill-side, much shaken, and without his berry pail, which had rolled a hundred yards below him, but not otherwise the worse for his misadventure; while the footprints showed that the bear, after delivering the single hurried stroke at the unwitting disturber of its day-dreams, had run off up-hill as fast as it was able.

A she-bear with cubs is a proverbially dangerous beast; yet even under such conditions different grislies act in directly opposite ways. Some she-grislies, when their cubs are young, but are able to follow them about, seem always worked up to the highest pitch of anxious and jealous rage, so that they are likely to attack unprovoked any intruder or even passer-by. Others when threatened by the hunter leave their cubs to their fate without a visible qualm of any kind, and seem to think only of their own safety.

In 1882 Mr. Caspar W. Whitney, now of New York, met with a very singular adventure with a she-bear and cub. He was in Harvard when I was, but left it and, like a good many other Harvard men of that time, took to cow-punching in the West. He went on a ranch in Rio Arriba County, New Mexico, and was a keen hunter, especially fond of the chase of cougar, bear, and elk. One day while riding a stony mountain trail he saw a little grisly cub watching him from the chaparral above, and he dismounted to try to capture it; his rifle was a 40-90 Sharp's. Just as he neared the cub, he heard a growl and caught a glimpse of the old she, and he at once turned up-hill, and stood under some tall, quaking aspens. From this spot he fired at and wounded the she, then seventy yards off; and she charged furiously. He hit her again, but as she kept coming like a thunderbolt he climbed hastily up the aspen, dragging his gun with him, as it had a strap. When the bear reached the foot of the aspen she reared, and bit and clawed the slender trunk, shaking it for a moment, and he shot her through the eye. Off she sprang for a few yards, and then spun round a dozen times, as if dazed or partially stunned; for the bullet had not touched the brain. Then the vindictive and resolute beast came back to the tree and again reared up against it; this time to receive a bullet that dropped her lifeless. Mr. Whitney then climbed down and walked to where the cub had been sitting as a looker-on. The little animal did not move until he reached out his hand; when it suddenly struck at him like an angry cat, dove into the bushes, and was seen no more.

In the summer of 1888 an old-time trapper, named Charley Norton, while on Loon Creek, of the middle fork of the Salmon, meddled with a she and her cubs. She ran at him and with one blow of her paw almost knocked off his lower jaw; yet he recovered, and was alive when I last heard of him.

Yet the very next spring the cowboys with my own wagon on the Little Missouri round-up killed a mother bear which made but little more fight than a coyote. She had two cubs, and was surprised in the early morning on the prairie far from cover. There were eight or ten cowboys together at the time, just starting off on a long circle, and of course they all got down their ropes in a second, and putting spurs to their fiery little horses started toward the bears at a run, shouting and swinging their loops round their heads. For a moment the old she tried to bluster and made a half-hearted threat of charging; but her courage failed before the rapid onslaught of her yelling, rope-swinging assailants; and she took to her heels and galloped off, leaving the cubs to shift for themselves. The cowboys were close behind, however, and after half a mile's run she bolted into a shallow cave or hole in the side of a butte, where she stayed cowering and growling, until one of the men leaped off his horse, ran up to the edge of the hole, and killed her with a single bullet from his revolver, fired so close that the powder burned her hair. The unfortunate cubs were

roped, and then so dragged about that they were speedily killed instead of being brought alive to camp, as ought to have been done.

In the cases mentioned above the grisly attacked only after having been itself assailed, or because it feared an assault, for itself or for its young. In the old days, however, it may almost be said that a grisly was more apt to attack than to flee. Lewis and Clarke and the early explorers who immediately succeeded them, as well as the first hunters and trappers, the " Rocky Mountain men" of the early decades of the present century, were repeatedly assailed in this manner; and not a few of the bear hunters of that period found that it was unnecessary to take much trouble about approaching their quarry, as the grisly was usually prompt to accept the challenge and to advance of its own accord, as soon as it discovered the foe. All this is changed now. Yet even at the present day an occasional vicious old bear may be found, in some far off and little trod fastness, which still keeps up the former habit of its kind. All old hunters have tales of this sort to relate, the prowess, cunning, strength, and ferocity of the grisly being favorite topics for campfire talk throughout the Rockies; but in most cases it is not safe to accept these stories without careful sifting.

Still, it is just as unsafe to reject them all. One of my own cowboys was once attacked by a grisly, seemingly in pure. wantonness. He was riding up a creek bottom, and had just passed a clump of rose and bullberry bushes when his horse gave such a leap as almost to unseat him, and then darted madly forward. Turning round in the saddle to his utter astonishment he saw a large bear galloping after him, at the horse's heels. For a few jumps the race was close, then the horse drew away and the bear wheeled and went into a thicket of wild plums. The amazed and indignant cowboy, as soon as he could rein in his steed, drew his revolver and rode back to and around the thicket, endeavoring to provoke his late pursuer to come out and try conclusions on more equal terms; but prudent Ephraim had appar-

ently repented of his freak of ferocious bravado, and declined to leave the secure shelter of the jungle.

Other attacks are of a much more explicable nature. Mr. Huffman, the photographer, of Miles City, informed me that once when butchering some slaughtered elk he was charged twice by a she-bear and two well-grown cubs. This was a piece of sheer bullying, undertaken solely with the purpose of driving away the man and feasting on the carcasses; for in each charge the three bears, after advancing with much blustering, roaring, and growling, halted just before coming to close quarters. In another instance a gentleman I once knew, a Mr. S. Carr, was charged by a grisly from mere ill temper at being disturbed at meal-time. The man was riding up a valley; and the bear was at an elk carcass, near a clump of firs. As soon as it became aware of the approach of the horseman, while he was yet over a hundred yards distant, it jumped on the carcass, looked at him a moment, and then ran straight for him. There was no particular reason why it should have charged, for it was fat and in good trim, though when killed its head showed scars made by the teeth of rival grislies. Apparently it had been living so well, principally on flesh, that it had become quarrelsome; and perhaps its not over sweet disposition had been soured by combats with others of its own kind. In yet another case, a grisly charged with even less excuse. An old trapper, from whom I occasionally bought fur, was toiling up a mountain pass when he spied a big bear sitting on his haunches on the hill-side above. The trapper shouted and waved his cap; whereupon, to his amazement, the bear uttered a loud "wough" and charged straight down on him—only to fall a victim to misplaced boldness.

I am even inclined to think that there have been wholly exceptional occasions when a grisly has attacked a man with the deliberate purpdse of making a meal of him; when, in other words, it has started on the career of a man-eater. At least, on any other theory I find it difficult to account for an attack which once came to my knowledge. I was at Sand Point, on Pend'Oreille Lake, and met some French and Mdti trappers, then in town with their bales of beaver, otter, and sable. One of them, who gave his name as Baptiste Lamoche, had his head twisted over to one side, the result of the bite of a bear. When the accident occurred he was out on a trapping trip with two companions. They had pitched camp right on the shore of a cove in a little lake, and his comrades were off fishing in a dugout or pirogue. He himself was sitting near the shore, by a little lean-to, watching some beaver meat which was sizzling over the dying embers. Suddenly, and without warning, a great bear, which had crept silently up beneath the shadows of the tall evergreens, rushed at him, with a guttural roar, and seized him before he could rise to his feet. It grasped him with its jaws at the junction of the neck and shoulder, making the teeth meet through bone, sinew, and muscle; and turning, racked off towards the forest, dragging with it the helpless and paralyzed victim. Luckily the two men in the canoe had just paddled round the point, in sight of, and close to, camp. The man in the bow, seeing the plight of their comrade, seized his rifle and fired at the bear. The bullet went through the beast's lungs, and it forthwith dropped its prey, and running off some two hundred yards, lay down on its side and died. The rescued man recovered full health and strength, but never again carried his head straight.

Old hunters and mountain-men tell many stories, not only of malicious grislies thus attacking men in camp, but also of their even dogging the footsteps of some solitary hunter and killing him when the favorable opportunity occurs. Most of these tales are mere fables; but it is possible that in altogether exceptional instances they rest on a foundation of fact. One old hunter whom I knew told me such a story. He was a truthful old fellow, and there was no doubt that he believed what he said, and that his companion was actually killed by a bear; but it is probable that he was mistaken in reading the signs of his comrade's fate, and that the latter was not dogged by the bear at all, but stumbled on him and was slain in the surprise of the moment.

At any rate, cases of wanton assaults by grislies are altogether out of the common. The ordinary hunter may live out his whole life in the wilderness and never know aught of a bear attacking a man unprovoked; and the great majority of bears are shot under circumstances of no special excitement, as they either make no fight at all, or, if they do fight, are killed before there is any risk of their doing damage. If surprised on the plains, at some distance from timber or from badly broken ground, it is no uncommon feat for a single horseman to kill them with a revolver. Twice of late years it has been performed in the neighborhood of my ranch. In both instances the men were not hunters out after game, but simply cowboys, riding over the range in early morning in pursuance of their ordinary duties among the cattle. I knew both men and have worked with them on the round-up. Like most cowboys they carried 44-calibre Colt revolvers, and were accustomed to and fairly expert in their use, and they were mounted on ordinary cowponies—quick, wiry, plucky little beasts. In one case the bear was seen from quite a distance, lounging across a broad table-land. The cowboy, by taking advantage of a winding and rather shallow coulie, got quite close to him. He then scrambled out of the coulie, put spurs to his pony, and raced up to within fifty yards of the astonished bear ere the latter quite understood what it was that was running at him through the gray dawn. He made no attempt at fight, but ran at top speed towards a clump of brush not far off at the head of a creek. Before he could reach it, however, the galloping horseman was alongside, and fired three shots into his broad back. He did not turn, but ran on into the bushes and then fell over and died.

In the other case the cowboy, a Texan, was mounted on a good cutting pony, a spirited, handy, agile little animal, but excitable, and with a habit of dancing, which rendered it difficult to shoot from its back. The man was with the round-up wagon, and had been sent off by himself to make a circle through some low, barren buttes, where it was not thought more than a few head of stock would be found. On rounding the corner of a small washout he almost ran over a bear which was feeding on the carcass of a steer that had died in an alkali hole. After a moment of stunned surprise the bear hurled himself at the intruder with furious impetuosity; while the cowboy, wheeling his horse on its haunches and dashing in the spurs, carried it just clear of his assailant's headlong rush. After a few springs he reined in and once more wheeled half round, having drawn his revolver, only to find the bear again charging and almost on him. This time he fired into it, near the joining of the neck and shoulder, the bullet going downwards into the chest hollow; and again by a quick dash to one side he just avoided the rush of the beast and the sweep of its mighty forepaw. The bear then halted for a minute, and he rode close by it at a run, firing a couple of shots, which brought on another resolute charge. The ground was somewhat rugged and broken, but his pony was as quick on its feet as a cat, and never stumbled, even when going at full speed to avoid the bear's first mad rushes. It speedily became so excited, however, as to render it almost impossible for the rider to take aim. Sometimes he would come up close to the bear and wait for it to charge, which it would do, first at a trot, or rather rack, and then at a lumbering but swift gallop; and he would fire one or two shots before being forced to run. At other times, if the bear stood still in a good place, he would run by it, firing as he rode. He spent many cartridges, and though most of them were wasted, occasionally a bullet went home. The bear fought with the most savage courage, champing its bloody jaws, roaring with rage, and looking the very incarnation of evil fury. For some minutes it made no effort to flee, either charging or standing at bay. Then it began to move slowly towards a patch of ash and wild plums in the head of a coulie, some distance off.

Its pursuer rode after it, and when close enough would push by it and fire, while the bear would spin quickly round and charge as fiercely as ever, though evidently beginning to grow weak. At last, when still a couple of hundred yards from cover the man found he had used up all his cartridges, and then merely followed at a safe distance. The bear no longer paid heed to him, but walked slowly forwards, swaying its great head from side to side, while the blood streamed from between its half-opened jaws. On reaching the cover he could tell by the waving of the bushes that it walked to the middle and then halted. A few minutes afterwards some of the other cowboys rode up, having been attracted by the incessant firing. They surrounded the thicket, firing and throwing stones into the bushes. Finally, as nothing moved, they ventured in and found the indomitable grisly warrior lying dead.

Cowboys delight in nothing so much as the chance to show their skill as riders and ropers; and they always try to ride down and rope any wild animal they come across in favorable ground and close enough up. If a party of them meets a bear in the open they have great fun; and the struggle between the shouting, galloping rough-riders and their shaggy quarry is full of wild excitement and not unaccompanied by danger. The bear often throws the noose from his head so rapidly that it is a difficult matter to catch him; and his frequent charges scatter his tormentors in every direction while the horses become wild with fright over the roaring, bristling beast—for horses seem to dread a bear more than any other animal. If the bear cannot reach cover, however, his fate is sealed. Sooner or later, the noose tightens over one leg, or perchance over the neck and fore-paw, and as the rope straightens with a "pluck," the horse braces itself desperately and the bear tumbles over. Whether he regains his feet or not the cowboy keeps the rope taut; soon another noose tightens over a leg, and the bear is speedily rendered helpless.

I have known of these feats being performed several times in northern Wyoming, although never in the immediate neighborhood of my ranch. Mr. Archibald Roger's cowhands have in this manner caught several bears, on or near his ranch on the Gray Bull, which flows into the Bighorn; and those of Mr. G. B. Grinnell have also occasionally done so. Any set of moderately good ropers and riders, who are accustomed to back one another up and act together, can accomplish the feat if they have smooth ground and plenty of room. It is, however, indeed a feat of skill and daring for a single man; and yet I have known of more than one instance in which it has been accomplished by some reckless knight of the rope and the saddle. One such occurred in 1887 on the Flathead Reservation, the hero being a halfbreed; and another in 1890 at the mouth of the Bighorn, where a cowboy roped, bound, and killed a large bear single-handed.

My friend General "Red" Jackson, of Bellemeade, in the pleasant mid-county of Tennessee, once did a feat which casts into the shade even the feats of the men of the lariat. General Jackson, who afterwards became one of the ablest and most renowned of the Confederate cavalry leaders, was at the time a young officer in the Mounted Rifle Regiment, now known as the 3d United States Cavalry. It was some years before the Civil War, and the regiment was on duty in the Southwest, then the debatable land of Comanche and Apache. While on a scout after hostile Indians, the troops in their march roused a large grisly which sped off across the plain in front of them. Strict orders had been issued against firing at game, because of the nearness of the Indians. Young Jackson was a man of great strength, a keen swordsman, who always kept the finest edge on his blade, and he was on a swift and mettled Kentucky horse, which luckily had but one eye. Riding at full speed he soon overtook the quarry. As the horse hoofs sounded nearer, the grim bear ceased its flight, and whirling round stood at bay, raising itself on its hind-legs and threatening its pursuer with bared fangs and spread claws.

Carefully riding his horse so that its blind side should be towards the monster, the cavalryman swept by at a run, handling his steed with such daring skill that he just cleared the blow of the dreaded fore-paw, while with one mighty sabre stroke he cleft the bear's skull, slaying the grinning beast as it stood upright.

CHAPTER XVI. THE COUGAR.

O animal of the chase is so difficult to kill by fair in the West as mountain lion, in the Southwest as Mexican lion, and in the southern continent as lion and puma.

Without hounds its pursuit is so uncertain that from the still-hunter's standpoint it hardly deserves to rank as game at all—though, by the way, it is itself a more skilful still-hunter than any human rival. It prefers to move abroad by night or at dusk; and in the daytime usually lies hid in some cave or tangled thicket where it is absolutely impossible even to stumble on it by chance. It is a beast of stealth and rapine; its great, velvet paws, never make a sound, and it is always on the watch whether for prey or for enemies, while it rarely leaves shelter even when it thinks itself safe. Its soft, leisurely movements and uniformity of color make it difficult to discover at best, and its extreme watchfulness helps it; but it is the cougar's reluctance to leave cover at any time, its habit of slinking off through the brush, instead of running still-hunting as the cougar—that beast of many names, known in the East as panther and painter, in the open, when startled, and the way in which it lies motionless in its lair even when a man is within twenty yards, that render it so difficult to still-hunt.

In fact it is next to impossible with any hope of success regularly to hunt the cougar without dogs or bait. Most cougars that are killed by still-hunters are shot by accident while the man is after other game. This has been my own experience. Although not common, cougars are found near my ranch, where the ground is peculiarly favorable for the solitary rifleman; and for ten years I have, off and on, devoted a day or two to their pursuit; but never successfully. One December a large cougar took up his abode on a densely wooded bottom two miles above the ranch house. I did not discover his existence until I went there one evening to kill a deer, and found that he had driven all the deer off the bottom, having killed several, as well as a young heifer. Snow was falling at the time, but the storm was evidently almost over; the leaves were all off the trees and bushes; and I felt that next day there would be such a chance to follow the cougar as fate rarely offered. In the morning by dawn I was at the bottom, and speedily found his trail. Following it I came across his bed, among some cedars in a dark, steep gorge, where the buttes bordered the bottom. He had evidently just left it, and I followed his tracks all day. But I never caught a glimpse of him, and late in the afternoon I trudged wearily homewards. When I went out next morning I found that as soon as I abandoned the chase, my quarry, according to the uncanny habit sometimes displayed by his kind, coolly turned likewise, and deliberately dogged my footsteps to within a mile of the ranch house; his round footprints being as clear as writing in the snow.

This was the best chance of the kind that I ever had; but again and again I have found fresh signs of cougar, such as a lair which they had just left, game they had killed, or one of our venison caches which they had robbed, and have hunted for them all day without success. My failures were doubtless due in part to various shortcomings in hunter's-craft on my own part; but equally without doubt they were mainly due to the quarry's wariness and its sneaking ways.

I have seen a wild cougar alive but twice, and both times by chance. On one occasion one of my men, Merrifield, and I surprised one eating a skunk in a bullberry patch; and by our own bungling frightened it away from its unsavory repast without getting a shot.

On the other occasion luck befriended me. I was with a pack train in the Rockies, and one day, feeling lazy, and as we had no meat in camp, I determined to try for deer by lying in wait beside a recently travelled game trail. The spot I chose was a steep, pine-clad slope leading down to a little mountain lake. I hid behind a breastwork of rotten logs, with a few young evergreens in front—an excellent ambush. A broad game trail slanted down the hill directly past me. I lay perfectly quiet for about an hour, listening to the murmur of the pine forests, and the occasional call of a jay or woodpecker, and gazing eagerly along the trail in the waning light of the late afternoon. Suddenly, without noise or warning of any kind, a cougar stood in the trail before me. The unlooked for and unheralded approach of the beast was fairly ghost-like. With its head lower than its shoulders, and its long tail twitching, it slouched down the path, treading as softly as a kitten. I waited until it had passed and then fired into the short ribs, the bullet ranging forward. Throwing its tail up in the air, and giving a bound, the cougar galloped off over a slight ridge. But it did not go far; within a hundred yards I found it stretched on its side, its jaws still working convulsively.

The true way to hunt the cougar is to follow it with dogs. If the chase is conducted in this fashion, it is very exciting, and resembles on a larger scale the ordinary method of hunting the wildcat or small lynx, as practised by the sport-loving planters of the southern States. With a very little training, hounds readily and eagerly pursue the cougar, showing in this kind of chase none of the fear and disgust they are so prone to exhibit when put on the trail of the certainly no more dangerous wolf. The cougar, when the hounds are on its track, at first runs, but when hard-pressed takes to a tree, or possibly comes to bay in thick cover. Its attention is then so taken up with the hounds that it can usually be approached and shot without much difficulty; though some cougars break bay when the hunters come near, and again make off, when they can only be stopped by many large and fierce hounds. Hounds are often killed in these fights; and if hungry a cougar will pounce on any dog for food; yet, as I have elsewhere related, I know of one instance in which a small pack of big, savage hounds killed a cougar unassisted. General Wade Hampton, who with horse and hound has been the mightiest hunter America has ever seen, informs me that he has killed with his pack some sixteen cougars, during the fifty years he has hunted in South Carolina and Mississippi. I believe they were all killed in the latter State. General Hampton's hunting has been chiefly for bear and deer, though his pack also follows the lynx and the gray fox; and, of course, if good fortune throws either a wolf or a cougar in his way it is followed as the game of all others. All the cougars he killed were either treed or brought to bay in a canebrake by the hounds; and they often handled the pack very roughly in the death struggle. He found them much more dangerous antagonists than the black bear when assailed with the hunting knife, a weapon of which he was very fond. However, if his pack had held a few very large, savage dogs, put in purely for fighting when the quarry was at bay, I think the danger would have been minimized.

General Hampton followed his game on horseback; but in following the cougar with dogs this is by no means always necessary. Thus Col. Cecil Clay, of Washington, killed a cougar in West Virginia, on foot with only three or four hounds. The dogs took the cold trail, and he had to run many miles over the rough, forest-clad mountains after them. Finally they drove the cougar up a tree; where he found it, standing among the branches, in a halferect position, its hind-feet on one limb and its fore-feet on another, while it glared down at the dogs, and switched its tail from side to side. He shot it through both shoulders, and down it came in a heap, whereupon the dogs jumped in and worried it, for its fore-legs were useless, though it managed to catch one dog in its jaws and bite him severely.

A wholly exceptional instance of the kind was related to me by my old hunting friend Willis. In his youth, in southwest Missouri, he knew a half-witted "poor white" who was very fond of hunting coons. He hunted at night, armed with an axe, and accompanied by his dog Penny, a large, savage, half-starved cur. One dark night the dog treed an animal which he could not see; so he cut down the tree, and immediately Penny jumped in and grabbed the beast. The man sung out " Hold on, Penny," seeing that the dog had seized some large, wild animal; the next moment the brute knocked the dog endways, and at the same instant the man split open its head with the axe. Great was his astonishment, and greater still the astonishment of the neighbors next day when it was found that he had actually killed a cougar. These great cats often take to trees in a perfectly foolish manner. My friend, the hunter Woody, in all his thirty years' experience in the wilds never killed but one cougar. He was lying out in camp with two dogs at the time; it was about midnight, the fire was out, and the night was pitch-black. He was roused by the furious barking of his two dogs, who had charged into the gloom, and were apparently baying at something in a tree close by. He kindled the fire, and to his astonishment found the thing in the tree to be a cougar. Coming close underneath he shot it with his revolver; thereupon it leaped down, ran some forty yards, and climbed up another tree, where it died among the branches.

If cowboys come across a cougar in open ground they invariably chase and try to rope it—as indeed they do with any wild animal. I have known several instances of cougars being roped in this way; in one the animal was brought into camp alive by two strapping cowpunchers.

The cougar sometimes stalks its prey, and sometimes lies in wait for it beside a game-trail or drinking pool— very rarely indeed does it crouch on the limb of a tree. When excited by the presence of game it is sometimes very bold. Willis once fired at some bighorn sheep, on a steep mountain-side; he missed, and immediately after his shot, a cougar made a dash into the midst of the flying band, in hopes to secure a victim. The cougar roams over long distances, and

often changes its hunting ground, perhaps remaining in one place two or three months, until the game is exhausted, and then shifting to another. When it does not lie in wait it usually spends most of the night, winter and summer, in prowling restlessly a/ound the places where it thinks it may come across prey, and it will patiently follow an animal's trail. There is no kind of game, save the full-grown grisly and buffalo, which it does not at times assail and master. It readily snaps up grisly cubs or buffalo calves; and in at least one instance, I have known of it springing on, slaying, and eating a fullgrown wolf. I presume the latter was taken by surprise. On the other hand, the cougar itself has to fear the big timber wolves when maddened by the winter hunger and gathered in small parties; while a large grisly would of course be an overmatch for it twice over, though its superior agility puts it beyond the grisly's power to harm it, unless by some unlucky chance taken in a cave. Nor could a cougar overcome a bull moose, or a bull elk either, if the latter's horns were grow n, save by taking it unawares. By choice, with such big game, its victims are the cows and young. The prong-horn rarely comes within reach of its spring; but it is the dreaded enemy of bighorn, white goat, and every kind of deer, while it also preys on all the smaller beasts, such as foxes, coons, rabbits, beavers, and even gophers, rats, and mice. It sometimes makes a thorny meal of the porcupine, and if sufficiently hungry attacks and eats its smaller cousin the lynx. It is not a brave animal; nor does it run its prey down in open chase. It always makes its attacks by stealth, and if possible from behind, and relies on two or three tremendous springs to bring it on the doomed creature's back. It uses its claws as well as its teeth in holding and killing the prey. If possible it always seizes a large,animal by the throat, whereas the wolf's point of attack is more often the haunch or flank. Small deer or sheep it will often knock over and kill, merely using its big paws; sometimes it breaks their necks. It has a small head compared to the jaguar, and

its bite is much less dangerous. Hence, as compared to its larger and bolder relative, it places more trust in its claws and less in its teeth.

Though the cougar prefers woodland, it is not necessarily a beast of the dense forests only; for it is found in all the plains country, living in the scanty timber belts which fringe the streams, or among the patches of brush in the Bad Lands. The persecution of hunters however always tends to drive it into the most thickly wooded and broken fastnesses of the mountains. The she has from one to three kittens, brought forth in a cave or a secluded lair, under a dead log or in very thick brush. It is said that the old he's kill the small male kittens when they get a chance. They certainly at times during the breeding season fight desperately among themselves. Cougars are very solitary beasts; it is rare to see more than one at a time, and then only a mother and young, or a mated male and female. While she has kittens, the mother is doubly destructive to game. The young begin to kill for themselves very early. The first fall, after they are born, they attack large game, and from ignorance are bolder in making their attacks than their parents; but they are clumsy and often let the prey escape. Like all cats, cougars are comparatively easy to trap, much more so than beasts of the dog kind, such as the fox and wolf.

They are silent animals; but old hunters say that at mating time the males call loudly, while the females have a very distinct answer. They are also sometimes noisy at other seasons. I am not sure that I ever heard one; but one night, while camped in a heavily timbered coulie near Kildeer Mountains, where, as their footprints showed, the beasts were plentiful, I twice heard a loud, wailing scream ringing through the impenetrable gloom which shrouded the hills around us. My companion, an old plainsman, said that this was the cry of the cougar prowling for its prey. Certainly no man could well listen to a stranger and wilder sound.

Ordinarily the rifleman is in no danger from a hunted cougar; the beast's one idea seems to be flight, and even if its assailant is very close, it rarely charges if there is any chance for escape. Yet there are occasions when it will show fight. In the spring of 1890, a man with whom I had more than once worked on the round-up—though I never knew his name—was badly mauled by a cougar near my ranch. He was hunting with a companion and they unexpectedly came on the cougar on a shelf of sandstone above their heads, only some ten feet off. It sprang down on the man, mangled him with teeth and claws for a moment, and then ran away. Another man I knew, a hunter named Ed. Smith, who had a small ranch near Helena, was once charged by a wounded cougar; he received a couple of deep scratches, but was not seriously hurt.

Many old frontiersmen tell tales of the cougar's occasionally itself making the attack, and dogging to his death some unfortunate wayfarer. Many others laugh such tales to scorn. It is certain that if such attacks occur they are altogether exceptional, being indeed of such extreme rarity that they may be entirely disregarded in practice. I should have no more hesitation in sleeping out in a wood where there were cougars, or walking through it after nightfall, than I should have if the cougars were tomcats.

Yet it is foolish to deny that in exceptional instances attacks may occur. Cougars vary wonderfully in size, and no less in temper. Indeed I think that by nature they are as ferocious and bloodthirsty as they are cowardly; and that their habit of sometimes dogging wayfarers for miles is due to a desire for bloodshed which they lack the courage to realize. In the old days, when all wild beasts were less shy than at present, there was more danger from the cougar; and this was especially true in the dark canebrakes of some of the southern States, where the man a cougar was most likely to encounter was a nearly naked and unarmed negro. General Hampton tells me that near his Mississippi plantation, many years ago, a negro who was one of a gang engaged in building a railroad through low and wet ground was waylaid and killed by a cougar late one night as he was walking alone through the swamp.

I knew two men in Missoula who were once attacked by cougars in a very curious manner. It was in January, and they were walking home through the snow after a hunt, each carrying on his back the saddle, haunches, and hide of a deer he had slain. Just at dusk, as they were passing through a narrow ravine, the man in front heard his partner utter a sudden loud call for help. Turning, he was dumbfounded to see the man lying on his face in the snow, with a cougar which had evidently just knocked him down standing over him, grasping the deer meat; while another cougar was galloping up to assist. Swinging his rifle round he shot the first one in the brain, and it dropped motionless, whereat the second halted, wheeled, and bounded into the woods. His companion was not in the least hurt or even frightened, though greatly amazed. The cougars were not full grown, but young of the year.

Now in this case I do not believe the beasts had any real intention of attacking the men. They were young animals, bold, stupid, and very hungry. The smell of the raw meat excited them beyond control, and they probably could not make out clearly what the men were, as they walked bent under their burdens, with the deer skins on their backs. Evidently the cougars were only trying to get at the venison.

In 1886 a cougar killed an Indian near Flathead Lake. Two Indians were hunting together on horseback when they came on the cougar. It fell at once to their shots, and they dismounted and ran towards it Just as they reached it it came to, and seized one, killing him instantly with a couple of savage bites in the throat and chest; it then raced after the other, and, as he sprung on his horse, struck him across the buttocks, inflicting a deep but not dangerous scratch. I saw this survivor a year later. He evinced great reluctance to talk of the event, and insisted that the thing which had slain his companion was not really a cougar at all, but a devil.

A she-cougar does not often attempt to avenge the loss of her young, but sometimes she does. A remarkable instance of the kind happened to my friend, Professor John Bache McMaster, in 1875. He was camped near the head of Green River, Wyoming. One afternoon he found a couple of cougar kittens, and took them into camp; they were clumsy, playful, friendly little creatures The next afternoon he remained in camp with the cook. Happening to look up he suddenly spied the mother cougar running noiselessly down on them, her eyes glaring and tail twitching. Snatching up his rifle, he killed her when she was barely twenty yards distant.

A ranchman, named. Trescott, who was at one time my neighbor, told me that while he was living on a sheepfarm in the Argentine, he found pumas very common, and killed many. They were very destructive to sheep and colts, but were singularly cowardly when dealing with men. Not only did they never attack human beings, under any stress of hunger, but they made no effective resistance when brought to bay, merely scratching and cuffing like a big cat; so that if found in a cave, it was safe to creep in and shoot them with a revolver. Jaguars, on the contrary, were very dangerous antagonists.

A PECCARY HUNT ON THE NUECES.

IN the United States the peccary is only found in the southernmost corner of Texas. In April, 1892, I made a flying visit to the ranch country of this region, starting from the town of Uvalde with a Texan friend, Mr. John Moore. My trip being very hurried, I had but a couple of days to devote to hunting.

Our first halting-place was at a ranch on the Frio; a low, wooden building, of many rooms, with open galleries between them, and verandas round about. The country was in some respects like, in others strangely unlike, the northern plains with which I was so well acquainted. It was for the most part covered with a scattered growth of tough, stunted mesquite trees, not dense enough to be called a forest, and yet sufficiently close to cut off the view. It was very dry, even as compared with the northern plains. The bed of the Frio was filled with corase gravel, and for the most part dry as a bone on the surface, the water seeping through underneath, and only appearing in occasional deep holes. These deep holes or ponds never fail, even after a year's drouth; they were filled with fish. One lay quite near the ranch house, under a bold rocky bluff; at its edge grew giant cypress trees. In the hollows and by the watercourses were occasional groves of pecans, live-oaks, and elms. Strange birds hopped among the bushes; the chaparral cock—a big, handsome ground-cuckoo of remarkable habits, much given to preying on small snakes and lizards—ran over the ground with extraordinary rapidity. Beautiful swallow-tailed kingbirds with rosy plumage perched on the tops of the small trees, and soared and flitted in graceful curves above them. Blackbirds of many kinds scuttled in flocks about the corrals and outbuildings around the ranches. Mocking-birds abounded, and were very noisy, singing almost all the daytime, but with their usual irritating inequality of performance, wonderfully musical and powerful snatches of song being interspersed with imitations of other bird notes and disagreeable squalling. Throughout the trip I did not hear one of them utter the beautiful love song in which they sometimes indulge at night.

The country was all under wire fence, unlike the northern regions, the pastures however being sometimes many miles across. When we reached the Frio ranch a herd of a thousand cattle had just been gathered, and two or three hundred beeves and young stock were being cut out to be driven northward over the trail. The cattle were worked in pens much more than in the North, and on all the ranches there were chutes with steering gates, by means of which the individuals of a herd could be dexterously shifted into various corrals. The branding of the calves was done ordinarily in one of these corrals and on foot, the calf being always roped by both forelegs; otherwise the work of the cowpunchers was much like that of their

brothers in the North. As a whole, however, they were distinctly more proficient with the rope, and at least half of them were Mexicans.

There were some bands of wild cattle living only in the densest timber of the river bottoms which were literally as wild as deer, and moreover very fierce and dangerous. The pursuit of these was exciting and hazardous in the extreme. The men who took part in it showed not only the utmost daring but the most consummate horsemanship and wonderful skill in the use of the rope, the coil being hurled with the force and precision of an iron quoit; a single man speedily overtaking, roping, throwing, and binding down the fiercest steer or bull.

There had been many peccaries, or, as the Mexicans and cowpunchers of the border usually call them, javalinas, round this ranch a few years before the date of my visit Until 1886, or thereabouts, these little wild hogs were not much molested, and abounded in the dense chaparral around the lower Rio Grande. In that year, however, it was suddenly discovered that their hides had a market value, being worth four bits— that is, half a dollar—apiece; and many Mexicans and not a few shiftless Texans went into the business of hunting them as a means of livelihood They were more easily killed than deer, and, as a result, they were speedily exterminated in many localities where they had formerly been numerous, and even where they were left were to be found only in greatly diminished numbers. On this particular Frio ranch the last little band had been killed nearly a year before. There were three of them, a boar and two sows, and a couple of the cowboys stumbled on them early one morning while out with a dog. After half a mile's chase the three peccaries ran into a hollow pecan tree, and one of the cowboys, dismounting, improvised a lance by tying his knife to the end of a pole, and killed them all.

Many anecdotes were related to me of what they had done in the old days when they were plentiful on the ranch. They were then usually found in parties of from twenty to thirty, feeding in the

dense chaparral, the sows rejoining the herd with the young very soon after the birth of the latter, each sow usually having but one or two at a litter. At night they sometimes lay in the thickest cover, but always, where possible, preferred to house in a cave or big hollow log, one invariably remaining as a sentinel close to the mouth, looking out. If this sentinel were shot, another would almost certainly take his place. They were subject to freaks of stupidity, and were pugnacious to a degree. Not only would they fight if molested, but they would often attack entirely without provocation.

Once my friend Moore himself, while out with another cowboy on horseback, was attacked in sheer wantonness by a drove of these little wild hogs. The two men were riding by a grove of live-oaks along a wood-cutter's cart track, and were assailed without a moment's warning. The little creatures completely surrounded them, cutting fiercely at the horses' legs and jumping up at the riders' feet. The men, drawing their revolvers, dashed through and were closely followed by their pursuers for three or four hundred yards, although they fired right and left with good effect. Both of the horses were badly cut. On another occasion the bookkeeper of the ranch walked off to a water hole but a quarter of a mile distant, and came face to face with a peccary on a cattle trail, where the brush was thick. Instead of getting out of his way the creature charged him instantly, drove him up a small mesquite tree, and kept him there for nearly two hours, looking up at him and champing its tusks.

I spent two days hunting round this ranch but saw no peccary sign whatever, although deer were quite plentiful. Parties of wild geese and sandhill cranes occasionally flew overhead. At nightfall the poor-wills wailed everywhere through the woods, and coyotes yelped and yelled, while in the early morning the wild turkeys gobbled loudly from their roosts in the tops of the pecan trees.

Having satisfied myself that there were no javalinas left on the Frio ranch, and being nearly at the end of my holiday, I was about to abandon the effort to get any, when a passing cowman happened to mention the fact that some were still to be found on the Nueces River thirty miles or thereabouts to the southward. Thither I determined to go, and next morning Moore and I started in a buggy drawn by a redoubtable horse, named Jim Swinger, which we were allowed to use because he bucked so under the saddle that nobody on the ranch could ride him. We drove six or seven hours across the dry, waterless plains. There had been a heavy frost a few days before, which had blackened the budding mesquite trees, and their twigs still showed no signs of sprouting. Occasionally we came across open spaces where there was nothing but short brown grass. In most places, however, the leafless, sprawling mesquites were scattered rather thinly over the ground, cutting off an extensive view and merely adding to the melancholy barrenness of the landscape. The road was nothing but a couple of dusty wheel-tracks; the ground was parched, and the grass cropped close by the gaunt, starved cattle. As we drove along buzzards and great hawks occasionally soared overhead. Now and then we passed lines of wild-looking, long-horned steers, and once we came on the grazing horses of a cow-outfit, just preparing to start northward over the trail to the fattening pastures. Occasionally we encountered one or two cowpunchers: either Texans, habited exactly like their brethren in the North, with broad-brimmed gray hats, blue shirts, silk neckerchiefs, and leather leggings; or else Mexicans, more gaudily dressed, and wearing peculiarly stiff, very broad-brimmed hats, with conical tops.

Toward the end of our ride we got where the ground was more fertile, and there had recently been a sprinkling of rain. Here we came across wonderful flower prairies. In one spot I kept catching glimpses through the mesquite trees of lilac stretches which I had first thought must be ponds of water. On coming nearer they proved to be acres on acres thickly covered with beautiful lilac-colored flowers. Farther on we came to where broad bands of red flowers covered the ground for many furlongs; then their places were taken by yellow blossoms, elsewhere by white. Generally each band or patch of ground was covered densely by flowers of the same color, making a great vivid streak across the landscape; but in places they were mixed together, red, yellow, and purple, interspersed in patches and curving bands, carpeting the prairie in a strange, bright pattern.

Finally, toward evening we reached the Nueces. Where we struck it first the bed was dry, except in occasional deep, malarial-looking pools, but a short distance below there began to be a running current. Great blue herons were stalking beside these pools, and from one we flushed a white ibis. In the woods were reddish cardinal birds, much less brilliant in plumage than the true cardinals and the scarlet tanagers; and yellow-headed titmice which had already built large domed nests.

In the valley of the Nueces itself, the brush grew thick. There were great groves of pecan trees, and evergreen live-oaks stood in many places, long, wind-shaken tufts of gray moss hanging from their limbs. Many of the trees in the wet spots were of giant size, and the whole landscape was semi-tropical in character. High on a bluff shoulder overlooking the course of the river was perched the ranch house, toward which we were bending our steps; and here we were received with the hearty hospitality characteristic of the ranch country everywhere.

The son of the ranchman, a tall, well-built young fellow, told me at once that there were peccaries in the neighborhood, and that he had himself shot one but two or three days before, and volunteered to lend us horses and pilot us to the game on the morrow, with the help of his two dogs. The last were big black curs with, as we were assured, "considerable hound" in them. One was at the time staying at the ranch house, the other was four or five miles off with a Mexican goat-herder, and it was arranged that early in the morning we should ride down to the latter place, taking the first dog with us and procuring his companion when we reached the goat-herder's house.

We started after breakfast, riding powerful cow-ponies, well trained to gallop at full speed through the dense chaparral. The big black hound slouched at our heels. We rode down the banks of the Nueces, crossing and recrossing the stream. Here and there were long, deep pools in the bed of the river, where rushes and lilies grew and huge mailed garfish swam slowly just beneath the surface of the water. Once my two companions stopped to pull a mired cow out of a slough, hauling with ropes from their saddle horns. In places there were half-dry pools, out of the regular current of the river, the water green and fetid. The trees were very tall and large. The streamers of pale gray moss hung thickly from the branches of the live-oaks, and when many trees thus draped stood close together they bore a strangely mournful and desolate look.

We finally found the queer little hut of the Mexican goat-herder in the midst of a grove of giant pecans. On the walls were nailed the skins of different beasts, raccoons, wild-cats, and the tree-civet, with its ringed tail. The Mexican's brown wife and children were in the hut, but the man himself and the goats were off in the forest, and it took us three or four hours' search before we found him. Then it was nearly noon, and we lunched in his hut, a square building of split logs, with bare earth floor, and roof of clap-boards and bark. Our lunch consisted of goat's meat and *pan de mats*. The Mexican, a broadchested man with a stolid Indian face, was evidently quite a sportsman, and had two or three half-starved hounds, besides the funny, hairless little house dogs, of which Mexicans seem so fond.

Having borrowed the javalina hound of which we were in search, we rode off in quest of our game, the two dogs trotting gayly ahead. The one which had been living at the ranch had evidently fared well, and was very fat; the other was little else but skin and bone, but as alert and knowing as any New York street-boy, with the same air of disreputable capacity. It was this hound which always did most in finding the javalinas and bringing them to bay, his companion's chief use being to make a noise and lend the moral support of his presence.

We rode away from the river on the dry uplands, where the timber, though thick, was small, consisting almost exclusively of the thorny mesquites. Mixed among them were prickly pears, standing as high as our heads on horseback, and Spanish bayonets, looking in the distance like small palms; and there were many other kinds of cactus, all with poisonous thorns. Two or three times the dogs got on an old trail and rushed off giving tongue, whereat we galloped madly after them, ducking and dodging through and among the clusters of spine-bearing trees and cactus, not without getting a considerable number of thorns in our hands and legs. It was very dry and hot. Where the javalinas live in droves in the river bottoms they often drink at the pools; but when some distance from water they seem to live quite comfortably on the prickly pear, slaking their thirst by eating its hard, juicy fibre.

At last, after several false alarms, and gallops which led to nothing, when it lacked but an hour of sundown we struck a band of five of the little wild hogs. They were running off through the mesquites with a peculiar hopping or bounding motion, and we all, dogs and men, tore after them instantly.

Peccaries are very fast for a few hundred yards, but speedily tire, lose their wind, and come to bay. Almost immediately one of these, a sow, as it turned out, wheeled and charged at Moore as he passed, Moore never seeing her but keeping on after another. The sow then stopped and stood still, chattering her teeth savagely, and I jumped off my horse and dropped her dead with a shot in the spine, over the shoulders. Moore meanwhile had dashed off after his pig in one direction, and killed the little beast with a shot from the saddle when it had come to bay, turning and going straight at him. Two of the peccaries got

off; the remaining one, a rather large boar, was followed by the two dogs, and as soon as I had killed the sow I leaped again on my horse and made after them, guided by the yelping and baying. In less than a quarter of a mile they were on his haunches, and he wheeled and stood under a bush, charging at them when they came near him, and once catching one, inflicting an ugly cut. All the while his teeth kept going like castanets, with a rapid champing sound. I ran up close and killed him by a shot through the backbone where it joined the neck. His tusks were fine.

The few minutes' chase on horseback was great fun, and there was a certain excitement in seeing the fierce little creatures come to bay; but the true way to kill these peccaries would be with the spear. They could often be speared on horseback, and where this was impossible, by using dogs to bring them to bay they could readily be killed on foot; though, as they are very active absolutely fearless, and inflict a most formidable bite, it would usually be safest to have two men go at one together. Peccaries are not difficult beasts to kill, because their short wind and their pugnacity make them come to bay before hounds so quickly. Two or three good dogs can bring to a halt a herd of considerable size. They then all stand in a bunch, or else with their sterns against a bank, chattering their teeth at their antagonists. When angry and at bay, they get their legs close together, their shoulders high, and their bristles all ruffled, and look the very incarnation of anger, and they fight with reckless indifference to the very last. Hunters usually treat them with a certain amount of caution; but, as a matter of fact, I know of but one case where a man was hurt by them. He had shot at and wounded one, was charged both by it and by its two companions, and started to climb a tree; but as he drew himself from the ground, one sprang at him and bit him through the calf, inflicting a very severe wound. I have known of several cases of horses being cut, however, and dogs are very commonly killed. Indeed, a dog new to the business is almost certain to get very

badly scarred, and no dog that hunts steadily can escape without some injury. If it runs in right at the heads of the animals, the probabilities are that it will get killed; and, as a rule, even two good-sized hounds cannot kill a peccary, though it is no larger than either of them. However, a wary, resolute, hard-biting dog of good size speedily gets accustomed to the chase, and can kill a peccary single-handed, seizing it from behind and worrying it to death, or watching its chance and grabbing it by the back of the neck where it joins the head.

Peccaries have delicately moulded short legs, and their feet are small, the tracks looking peculiarly dainty in consequence. Hence, they do not swim well, though they take to the water if necessary. They feed on roots, prickly pears, nuts, insects, lizards, etc. They usually keep entirely separate from the droves of half-wild swine that are so often found in the same neighborhoods; but in one case, on this very ranch where I was staying, a peccary deliberately joined a party of nine pigs and associated with them. When the owner of the pigs came up to them one day the peccary manifested great suspicion at his presence, and finally sidled close up and threatened to attack him, so that he had to shoot it. The ranchman's son told me that he had never but once had a peccary assail him unprovoked, and even in this case it was his dog that was the object of attack, the peccary rushing out at it as it followed him home one evening through the chaparral. Even around this ranch the peccaries had very greatly decreased in numbers, and the survivors were learning some caution. In the old days it had been no uncommon thing for a big band to attack entirely of their own accord, and keep a hunter up a tree for hours at a time.

HUNTING WITH HOUNDS. IN hunting American big game with hounds, several entirely distinct methods are pursued. The true wilderness hunters, the men who in the early days lived alone in, or moved in parties through, the Indianhaunted solitudes, like their successors of to-day, rarely made use of a pack of hounds, and, as a rule, did not use dogs at all. In the eastern forests occasionally an oldtime hunter would own one or two track-hounds, slow, with a good nose, intelligent and obedient, of use mainly in following wounded game. Some Rocky Mountain hunters nowadays employ the same kind of dog, but the old-time trappers of the great plains and the Rockies led such wandering lives of peril and hardship that they could not readily take dogs with them. The hunters of the Alleghanies and the Adirondacks have, however, always used hounds to drive deer, killing the animal in the water or at a runaway.

As soon, however, as the old wilderness hunter type passes away, hounds come into use among his successors, the rough border settlers of the backwoods and the plains. Every such settler is apt to have four or five large mongrel dogs with hound blood in them, which serve to drive off beasts of prey from the sheepfold and cattle-shed, and are also used, when the occasion suits, in regular hunting, whether after bear or deer.

Many of the southern planters have always kept packs of fox-hounds, which are used in the chase, not only of the gray and the red fox, but also of the deer, the black bear, and the wildcat. The fox the dogs themselves run down and kill, but as a rule in this kind of hunting, when after deer, bear, or even wildcat, the hunters carry guns with them on their horses, and endeavor either to get a shot at the fleeing animal by hard and dexterous riding, or else to kill the cat when treed, or the bear when it comes to bay. Such hunting is great sport.

Killing driven game by lying in wait for it to pass is the very poorest kind of sport that can be called legitimate. This is the way the deer is usually killed with hounds in the East. In the North the red fox is often killed in somewhat the same manner, being followed by a slow hound and shot at as he circles before the dog. Although this kind of fox-hunting is inferior to hunting on horseback, it nevertheless has its merits, as the man must walk and run well, shoot with some accuracy, and show considerable knowledge both of the country and of the habits of the game.

During the last score of years an entirely different type of dog from the fox-hound has firmly established itself in the field of American sport. This is the greyhound, whether the smooth-haired, or the rough-coated Scotch deer-hound. For half a century the army officers posted in the far West have occasionally had greyhounds with them, using the dogs to course jack-rabbit, coyote, and sometimes deer, antelope, and gray wolf. Many of them were devoted to this sport,—General Custer, for instance. I have myself hunted with many of the descendants of Custer's hounds. In the early 70's the ranchmen of the great plains themselves began to keep greyhounds for coursing (as indeed they had already been used for a considerable time in California, after the Pacific coast jackrabbit), and the sport speedily assumed large proportions and a permanent form. Nowadays the ranchmen of the cattle country not only use their greyhounds after the jack-rabbit, but also after every other kind of game animal to be found there, the antelope and coyote being especial favorites. Many ranchmen soon grew to own fine packs, coursing being the sport of all sports for the plains. In Texas the wild turkey was frequently an object of the chase, and wherever the locality enabled deer to be followed in the open, as for instance in the Indian territory, and in many places in the neighborhood of the large plains rivers, the whitetail was a favorite quarry, the hunters striving to surprise it in the early morning when feeding on the prairie.

I have myself generally coursed with scratch packs, including perhaps a couple of greyhounds, a wire-haired deer-hound, and two or three long-legged mongrels. However, we generally had at least one very fast and savage dog—a strike dog—in each pack, and the others were of assistance in turning the game, sometimes in tiring it, and usually in helping to finish it at the worry. With such packs I have had many a wildly exciting ride over the great grassy plains lying near the Little Missouri and the Knife and Heart rivers. Usually our proceedings on such a hunt were perfectly simple. We started on horseback and when reaching favorable ground beat across it in a long scattered line of men and dogs. Anything that we put up, from a fox to a coyote or a prong-buck, was fair game, and was instantly followed at full speed. The animals we most frequently killed were jack-rabbits. They always gave good runs, though like other game they differed much individually in speed. The foxes did not run so well, and whether they were the little swift, or the big red prairie fox, they were speedily snapped up if the dogs had a fair showing. Once our dogs roused a black-tail buck close up out of a brush coulie where the ground was moderately smooth, and after a headlong chase of a mile they ran into him, threw him, and killed him before he could rise. (His stiff-legged bounds sent him along at a tremendous pace at first, but he seemed to tire rather easily.) On two or three occasions we killed whitetail deer, and several times antelope. Usually, however, the antelopes escaped. The bucks sometimes made a good fight, but generally they were seized while running, some dogs catching by the throat, others by the shoulders, and others again by the flank just in front of the hind-leg. Wherever the hold was obtained, if the dog made his spring cleverly, the buck was sure to come down with a crash, and if the other dogs were anywhere near he was probably killed before he could rise, although not infrequently the dogs themselves were more or less scratched in the contests. Some greyhounds, even of high breeding, proved absolutely useless from timidity, being afraid to take hold; but if they got accustomed to the chase, being worked with old dogs, and had any pluck at all, they proved singularly fearless. A big ninety-pound greyhound or Scotch deer-hound is a very formidable fighting dog; I saw one whip a big mastiff in short order, his wonderful agility being of more account than his adversary's superior weight.

The proper way to course, however, is to take the dogs out in a wagon and drive them thus until the game is seen.

This prevents their being tired out. In my own hunting, most of the antelope aroused got away, the dogs being jaded when the chase began. But really fine greyhounds, accustomed to work together and to hunt this species of game, will usually render a good account of a prong-buck if two or three are slipped at once, fresh, and within a moderate distance.

Although most Westerners take more kindly to the rifle, now and then one is found who is a devotee of the hound. Such a one was an old Missourian, who may be called Mr. Cowley, whom I knew when he was living on a ranch in North Dakota, west of the Missouri. Mr. Cowley was a primitive person, of much nerve, which he showed not only in the hunting field but in the startling political conventions of the place and period. He was quite well off, but he was above the niceties of personal vanity. His hunting garb was that in which he also paid his rare formal calls—calls throughout which he always preserved the gravity of an Indian, though having a disconcerting way of suddenly tip-toeing across the room to some unfamiliar object, such as a peacock screen or a vase, feeling it gently with one forefinger, and returning with noiseless gait to his chair, unmoved, and making no comment. On the morning of a hunt he would always appear on a stout horse, clad in a long linen duster, a huge club in his hand, and his trousers working half-way up his legs. He hunted everything on all possible occasions; and he never under any circumstances shot an animal that the dogs could kill. Once when a skunk got into his house, with the direful stupidity of its perverse kind, he turned the hounds on it; a manifestation of sporting spirit which aroused the ire of even his longsuffering wife. As for his dogs, provided they could run and fight, he cared no more for their looks than for his own; he preferred the animal to be half greyhound, but the other half could be fox-hound, colley, or setter, it mattered nothing to him. They were a wicked, hardbiting crew for all that, and Mr. Cowley, in his flapping linen duster, was a first-class hunter and

a good rider. He went almost mad with excitement in every chase. His pack usually hunted coyote, fox, jack-rabbit, and deer; and I have had more than one good run with it.

My own experience is too limited to allow me to pass judgment with certainty as to the relative speed of the different beasts of the chase, especially as there is so much individual variation. I consider the antelope the fleetest of all however; and in this opinion I am sustained by Col. Roger D. Williams, of Lexington. Kentucky, who, more than any other American, is entitled to speak upon coursing, and especially upon coursing large game. Col. Williams, like a true son of Kentucky, has bred his own thoroughbred horses and thoroughbred hounds for many years; and during a series of long hunting trips extending over nearly a quarter of a century he has tried his pack on almost every game animal to be found among the foot-hills of the Rockies and on the great plains. His dogs, both smooth-haired greyhounds and rough-coated deer-hounds, have been bred by him for generations with a special view to the chase of big game— not merely of hares; they are large animals, excelling not only in speed but in strength, endurance, and ferocious courage. The survivors of his old pack are literally seamed all over with the scars of innumerable battles. When several dogs were together they would stop a bull-elk, and fearlessly assail a bear or cougar. This pack scored many a triumph over blacktail, whitetail, and prong-buck. For a few hundred yards the deer were very fast; but in a run of any duration the antelope showed much greater speed, and gave the dogs far more trouble, although always overtaken in the end, if a good start had been obtained. Col. Williams is a firm believer in the power of the thoroughbred horse to outrun any animal that breathes, in a long chase; he has not infrequently run down deer, when they were jumped some miles from cover; and on two or three occasions he ran down uninjured antelope, but in each case only after a desperate ride of miles, which in one instance resulted in the

death of his gallant horse.

This coursing on the prairie, especially after big game, is an exceedingly manly and attractive sport; the furious galloping, often over rough ground with an occasional deep washout or gully, the sight of the gallant hounds running and tackling, and the exhilaration of the pure air and wild surroundings, all combine to give it a peculiar zest. But there is really less need of bold and skilful horsemanship than in the otherwise less attractive and more artificial sport of fox-hunting, or riding to hounds, in a closed and long-settled country.

Those of us who are in part of southern blood have a hereditary right to be fond of cross-country riding; for our forefathers in Virginia, Georgia, or the Carolinas, have for six generations followed the fox with horse, horn, and hound. In the long-settled Northern States the sport has been less popular, though much more so now than formerly; yet it has always existed, here and there, and in certain places has been followed quite steadily.

In no place in the Northeast is hunting the wild red fox put on a more genuine and healthy basis than in the Genesee Valley, in central New York. There has always been fox-hunting in this valley, the farmers having good horses and being fond of sport; but it was conducted in a very irregular, primitive manner, until some twenty years ago Mr. Austin Wadsworth turned his attention to it. He has been master of fox-hounds ever since, and no pack in the country has yielded better sport than his, or has brought out harder riders among the men and stronger jumpers among the horses. Mr. Wadsworth began his hunting by picking up some of the various trencher-fed hounds of the neighborhood, the hunting of that period being managed on the principle of each farmer bringing to the meet the hound or hounds he happened to possess, and appearing on foot or horseback as his fancy dictated. Having gotten together some of these native hounds and started fox-hunting in localities where the ground was so open as to necessitate following the chase on horseback, Mr.

Wadsworth imported a number of dogs from the best English kennels. He found these to be much faster than the American dogs and more accustomed to work together, but less enduring, and without such good noses. The American hounds were very obstinate and self-willed. Each wished to work out the trail for himself. But once found, they would puzzle it out, no matter how cold, and would follow it if necessary for a day and night. By a judicious crossing of the two Mr. Wadsworth finally got his present fine pack, which for its own particular work on its own ground would be hard to beat. The country ridden over is well wooded, and there are many foxes. The abundance of cover, however, naturally decreases the number of kills. It is a very fertile land, and there are few farming regions more beautiful, for it is prevented from being too tame in aspect by the number of bold hills and deep ravines. Most of the fences are high posts-and-rails or "snake" fences, although there is an occasional stone wall, haha, or water-jump. The steepness of the ravines and the density of the timber make it necessary for a horse to be sure-footed and able to scramble anywhere, and the fences are so high that none but very good jumpers can possibly follow the pack. Most of the horses used are bred by the farmers in the neighborhood, or are from Canada, and they usually have thoroughbred or trotting-stock blood in them.

One of the pleasantest days I ever passed in the saddle was after Mr. Wadsworth's hounds. I was staying with him at the time, in company with my friend Senator Cabot Lodge, of Boston. The meet was about twelve miles distant from the house. It was only a small field of some twentyfive riders, but there was not one who did not mean going. I was mounted on a young horse, a powerful, big-boned black, a great jumper, though perhaps a trifle hot-headed. Lodge was on a fine bay, which could both run and jump. There were two or three other New Yorkers and Bostonians present, several men who had come up from Buffalo for the run, a couple of retired army officers, a num

ber of farmers from the neighborhood; and finally several members of a noted local family of hard riders, who formed a class by themselves, all having taken naturally to every variety of horsemanship from earliest infancy.

It was a thoroughly democratic assemblage; every one was there for sport, and nobody cared an ounce how he or anybody else was dressed. Slouch hats, brown coats, corduroy breeches, and leggings, or boots, were the order of the day. We cast off in a thick wood. The dogs struck a trail almost immediately and were off with clamorous yelping, while the hunt thundered after them like a herd of buffaloes. We went headlong down the hill-side into and across a brook. Here the trail led straight up a sheer bank. Most of the riders struck off to the left for an easier place, which was unfortunate for them, for the eight of us who went straight up the side (one man's horse falling back with him) were the only ones who kept on terms with the hounds. Almost as soon as we got to the top of the bank we came out of the woods over a low but awkward rail fence, where one of our number, who was riding a very excitable sorrel colt, got a fall. This left but six, including the whip. There were two or three large fields with low fences; then we came to two high, stiff doubles, the first real jumping of the day, the fences being over four feet six, and so close together that the horses barely had a chance to gather themselves. We got over, however, crossed two or three stump-strewn fields, galloped through an open wood, picked our way across a marshy spot, jumped a small brook and two or three stiff fences, and then came a check. Soon the hounds recovered the line and swung off to the right, back across four or five fields, so as to enable the rest of the hunt, by making an angle, to come up. Then we jumped over a very high board fence into the main road, out of it again, and on over ploughed fields and grass land, separated by stiff snake fences. The run had been fast and the horses were beginning to tail. By the time we suddenly rattled down into a deep ravine and scrambled up the other

side through thick timber there were but four of us left, Lodge and myself being two of the lucky ones. Beyond this ravine we came to one of the worst jumps of the day, a fence out of the wood, which was practicable only at one spot, where a kind of cattle trail led up to a panel. It was within an inch or two of five feet high. However, the horses, thoroughly trained to timber jumping and to rough and hard scrambling in awkward places, and by this time well quieted, took the bars without mistake, each one in turn trotting or cantering up to within a few yards, then making a couple of springs and bucking over with a great twist of the powerful haunches. I may explain that there was not a horse of the four that had not a record of five feet six inches in the ring. We now got into a perfect tangle of ravines, and the fox went to earth; and though we started one or two more in the course of the afternoon, we did not get another really first-class run.

At Geneseo the conditions for the enjoyment of this sport are exceptionally favorable. In the Northeast generally, although there are now a number of well-established hunts, at least nine out of ten runs are after a drag. Most of the hunts are in the neighborhood of great cities, and are mainly kept up by young men who come from them. A few of these are men of leisure, who can afford to devote their whole time to pleasure; but much the larger number are men in business, who work hard and are obliged to make their sports accommodate themselves to their more serious occupations. Once or twice a week they can get off for an afternoon's ride across country, and they then wish to be absolutely certain of having their run, and of having it at the appointed time; and the only way to insure this is to have a drag-hunt. It is not the lack of foxes that has made the sport so commonly take the form of riding to drag-hounds, but rather the fact that the majority of those who keep it up are hardworking business men who wish to make the most out of every moment of the little time they can spare from their regular occupations. A single ride across country, or an afternoon at polo, will yield more exercise, fun, and excitement than can be got out of a week's decorous and dull riding in the park, and many young fellows have waked up to this fact.

At one time I did a good deal of hunting with the Meadowbrook hounds, in the northern part of Long Island. There were plenty of foxes around us, both red and gray, but partly for the reasons given above, and partly because the covers were so large and so nearly continuous, they were not often hunted, although an effort was always made to have one run every week or so after a wild fox, in order to give a chance for the hounds to be properly worked and to prevent the runs from becoming a mere succession of steeple-chases. The sport was mainly drag-hunting, and was most exciting, as the fences were high and the pace fast. The Long Island country needs a peculiar style of horse, the first requisite being that he shall be a very good and high timber jumper. Quite a number of crack English and Irish hunters have at different times been imported, and some of them have turned out pretty well; but when they first come over they are utterly unable to cross our country, blundering badly at the high timber. Few of them have done as well as the American horses. I have hunted half a dozen times in England, with the Pytchely, Essex, and North Warwickshire, and it seems to me probable that English thoroughbreds, in a grass country, and over the peculiar kinds of obstacles they have on the other side of the water, would gallop away from a field of our Long Island horses; for they have speed and bottom, and are great weight carriers. But on our own ground, where the cross-country riding is more like leaping a succession of five-and six-bar gates than anything else, they do not as a rule, in spite of the enormous prices paid for them, show themselves equal to the native stock. The highest recorded jump, seven feet two inches, was made by the American horse Filemaker, which I saw ridden in the very front by Mr. H. L. Herbert, in the hunt at Sagamore Hill, about to be described.

When I was a member of the Meadowbrook hunt, most of the meets were held within a dozen miles or so of the kennels: at Farmingdale, Woodbury, Wheatly, Locust Valley, Syosset, or near any one of twenty other queer, quaint old Long Island hamlets. They were almost always held in the afternoon, the business men who had come down from the city jogging over behind the hounds to the appointed place, where they were met by the men who had ridden over direct from their country-houses. If the meet was an important one, there might be a crowd of onlookers in every kind of trap, from a four-in-hand drag to a spider-wheeled buggy drawn by a pair of long-tailed trotters, the money value of which many times surpassed that of the two best hunters in the whole field. Now and then a breakfast would be given the hunt at some country-house, when the whole day was devoted to the sport; perhaps after wild foxes in the morning, with a drag in the afternoon.

After one meet, at Sagamore Hill, I had the curiosity to go on foot over the course we had taken, measuring the jumps; for it is very difficult to form a good estimate of a fence's height when in the field, and five feet of timber seems a much easier thing to take when sitting around the fire after dinner than it does when actually faced while the hounds are running. On the particular hunt in question we ran about ten miles, at a rattling pace, with only two checks, crossing somewhat more than sixty fences, most of them post-and-rails, stiff as steel, the others being of the kind called "Virginia" or snake, and not more than ten or a dozen in the whole lot under four feet in height. The highest measured five feet and half an inch, two others were four feet eleven, and nearly a third of the number averaged about four and a half. There were also several rather awkward doubles. When the hounds were cast off some forty riders were present, but the first fence was a savage one, and stopped all who did not mean genuine hard going. Twenty-six horses crossed it, one of them ridden by a lady. A mile or so farther on, before there had been a chance for much

tailing, we came to a five-bar gate, out of a road—a jump of just four feet five inches from the take-off. Up to this, of course, we went one at a time, at a trot or hand-gallop, and twenty-five horses cleared it in succession without a single refusal and with but one mistake. Owing to the severity of the pace, combined with the average height of the timber (although no one fence was of phenomenally noteworthy proportions), a good many falls took place, resulting in an unusually large percentage of accidents. The master partly dislocated one knee, another man broke two ribs, and another—the present writer—broke his arm. However, almost all of us managed to struggle through to the end in time to see the death.

On this occasion I owed my broken arm to the fact that my horse, a solemn animal originally taken out of a buggy, though a very clever fencer, was too coarse to gallop alongside the blooded beasts against which he was pitted. But he was so easy in his gaits, and so quiet, being ridden with only a snaffle, that there was no difficulty in following to the end of the run. I had divers adventures on this horse. Once I tried a pair of so-called "safety" stirrups, which speedily fell out, and I had to ride through the run without any, at the cost of several tumbles. Much the best hunter I ever owned was a sorrel horse named Sagamore. He was from Geneseo, was fast, a remarkably good jumper, of great endurance, as quick on his feet as a cat, and with a dauntless heart He never gave me a fall, and generally enabled me to see all the run.

It would be very unfair to think the sport especially dangerous on account of the occasional accidents that happen. A man who is fond of riding, but who sets a good deal of value, either for the sake of himself, his family, or his business, upon his neck and limbs, can hunt with much safety if he gets a quiet horse, a safe fencer, and does not try to stay in the front rank. Most accidents occur to men on green or wild horses, or else to those who keep in front only at the expense of pumping their mounts; and a fall with a done-out beast is always peculiarly disagreeable. Most falls, however, do no harm whatever to either horse or rider, and after they have picked themselves up and shaken themselves, the couple ought to be able to go on just as well as ever. Of course a man who wishes to keep in the first flight must expect to face a certain number of tumbles; but even he will probably not be hurt at all, and he can avoid many a mishap by easing up his horse whenever he can—that is, by always taking a gap when possible, going at the lowest panel of every fence, and not calling on his animal for all there is in him unless it cannot possibly be avoided. It must be remembered that hard riding is a very different thing from good riding; though a good rider to hounds must also at times ride hard.

Cross-country riding in the rough is not a difficult thing to learn; always provided the would-be learner is gifted with or has acquired a fairly stout heart, for a constitutionally timid person is out of place in the hunting field. A really finished cross-country rider, a man who combines hand and seat, heart and head, is of course rare; the standard is too high for most of us to hope to reach. But it is comparatively easy to acquire a light hand and a capacity to sit fairly well down in the saddle; and when a man has once got these, he will find no especial difficulty in following the hounds on a trained hunter.

Fox-hunting is a great sport, but it is as foolish to make a fetish of it as it is to decry it. The fox is hunted merely because there is no larger game to follow. As long as wolves, deer, or antelope remain in the land, and in a country where hounds and horsemen can work, no one would think of following the fox. It is pursued because the bigger beasts of the chase have been killed out. In England it has reached its present prominence only within two centuries; nobody followed the fox while the stag and boar were common. At the present day, on Exmoor, where the wild stag is still found, its chase ranks ahead of that of the fox. It is not really the hunting proper which is the point in fox-hunting. It is the horsemanship, the galloping and

jumping, and the being out in the open air. Very naturally, however, men who have passed their lives as foxhunters grow to regard the chase and the object of it alike with superstitious veneration. They attribute almost mythical characters to the animal. I know some of my good Virginian friends, for instance, who seriously believe that the Virginia red fox is a beast quite unparalleled for speed and endurance no less than for cunning. This is of course a mistake. Compared with a wolf, an antelope, or even a deer, the fox's speed and endurance do not stand very high. A good pack of hounds starting him close would speedily run into him in the open. The reason that the hunts last so long in some cases is because of the nature of the ground which favors the fox at the expense of the dogs, because of his having the advantage in the start, and because of his cunning in turning to account everything which will tell in his favor and against his pursuers. In the same way I know plenty of English friends who speak with bated breath of fox-hunting but look down upon riding to drag-hounds. Of course there is a difference in the two sports, and the fun of actually hunting the wild beast in the one case more than compensates for the fact that in the other the riding is apt to be harder and the jumping higher; but both sports are really artificial, and in their essentials alike. To any man who has hunted big game in a wild country the stress laid on the differences between them seems a little absurd, in fact cockney. It is of course nothing against either that it is artificial; so are all sports in long-civilized countries, from lacrosse to ice yachting.

It is amusing to see how natural it is for each man to glorify the sport to which he has been accustomed at the expense of any other. The old-school French sportsman, for instance, who followed the boar, stag, and hare with his hounds, always looked down upon the chase of the fox; whereas the average Englishman not only asserts but seriously believes that no other kind of chase can compare with it, although in actual fact the very points in which the

Englishman is superior to the continental sportsman—that is, in hard and straight riding and jumping—are those which drag-hunting tends to develop rather more than fox-hunting proper. In the mere hunting itself the continental sportsman is often unsurpassed.

Once, beyond the Missouri, I met an expatriated German baron, an unfortunate who had failed utterly in the rough life of the frontier. He was living in a squalid little hut, almost unfurnished, but studded around with the diminutive horns of the European roebuck. These were the only treasures he had taken with him to remind him of his former life, and he was never tired of describing what fun it was to shoot roebucks when driven by the little crookedlegged *dachshunds*. There were plenty of deer and antelope roundabout, yielding good sport to any rifleman, but this exile cared nothing for them; they were not roebucks, and they could not be chased with his beloved *dachshunds*. So, among my neighbors in the cattle country, is a gentleman from France, a very successful ranchman, and a thoroughly good fellow; he cares nothing for hunting big game, and will not go after it, but is devoted to shooting cotton-tails in the snow, this being a pastime having much resemblance to one of the recognized sports of his own land.

However, our own people afford precisely similar instances. I have met plenty of men accustomed to killing wild tu1 keys and deer with small-bore rifles in the southern forests who, when they got on the plains and in the Rockies, were absolutely helpless. They not only failed to become proficient in the art of killing big game at long ranges with the large-bore rifle, at the cost of fatiguing tramps, but they had a positive distaste for the sport and would never allow that it equalled their own stealthy hunts in eastern forests. So I know plenty of men, experts with the shotgun, who honestly prefer shooting quail in the East over well-trained setters or pointers, to the hardier, manlier sports of the wilderness.

As it is with hunting, so it is with riding. The cowboy's scorn of every method of riding save his own is as profound and as ignorant as is that of the school rider, jockey, or fox-hunter. The truth is that each of these is best in his own sphere and is at a disadvantage when made to do the work of any of the others. For all-around riding and horsemanship, I think the West Point graduate is somewhat ahead of any of them. Taken as a class, however, and compared with other classes as numerous, and not with a few exceptional individuals, the cowboy, like the Rocky Mountain stage-driver, has no superiors anywhere for his own work; and they are fine fellows, these ironnerved reinsmen and rough-riders.

When Buffalo Bill took his cowboys to Europe they made a practice in England, France, Germany, and Italy of offering to break and ride, in their own fashion, any horse given them. They were frequently given spoiled animals from the cavalry services in the different countries through which they passed, animals with which the trained horse-breakers of the European armies could do nothing; and yet in almost all cases the cowpunchers and broncobusters with Buffalo Bill mastered these beasts as readily as they did their own western horses. At their own work of mastering and riding rough horses they could not be matched by their more civilized rivals; but I have great doubts whether they in turn would not have been beaten if they had essayed kinds of horsemanship utterly alien to their past experience, such as riding mettled thoroughbreds in a steeple-chase, or the like. Other things being equal (which, however, they generally are not), a bad, big horse fed on oats offers a rather more difficult problem than a bad little horse fed on grass. After Buffalo Bill's men had returned, I occasionally heard it said that they had tried cross-country riding in England, and had shown themselves pre-eminently skilful thereat, doing better than the English fox-hunters, but this I take the liberty to disbelieve. I was in England at the time, hunted occasionally myself, and was with many of the men who were all the time riding in the most famous hunts; men, too,

who were greatly impressed with the exhibitions of rough riding then being given by Buffalo Bill and his men, and who talked of them much; and yet I never, at the time, heard of an instance in which one of the cowboys rode to hounds with any marked success. In the same way I have sometimes in New York or London heard of men who, it was alleged, had been out West and proved better riders than the broncobusters themselves, just as I have heard of similar men who were able to go out hunting in the Rockies or on the plains and get more game than the western hunters; but in the course of a long experience in the West I have yet to see any of these men, whether from the eastern States or from Europe, actually show such superiority or perform such feats.

It would be interesting to compare the performances of the Australian stockriders with those of our own cowpunchers, both in cow-work and in riding. The Australians have an entirely different kind of saddle, and the use of the rope is unknown among them. A couple of years ago the famous western rifle-shot, Carver, took some cowboys out to Australia, and I am informed that many of the Australians began themselves to practise with the rope after seeing the way it was used by the Americans. An Australian gentleman, Mr. A. J. Sage, of Melbourne, to whom I had written asking how the saddles and styles of riding compared, answered me as follows: It is, however, quite possible, now that Buffalo Bill's company has crossed the water several times, that a number of the cowboys have by practice become proficient in riding to hounds, and in steeple-chasing.

"With regard to saddles, here it is a moot question which is the better, yours or ours, for buck-jumpers. Carver's boys rode in their own saddles against our Victorians in theirs, all on Australian buckers, and honors seemed easy. Each was good in his own style, but the horses were not what I should call really good buckers, such as you might get on a back station, and so there was nothing in the show that could un-

seat the cowboys. It is only back in the bush that you can get a really good bucker. I have often seen one of them put both man and saddle off."

This last is a feat I have myself seen performed in the West. I suppose the amount of it is that both the American and the Australian rough riders are, for their own work, just as good as men possibly can be.

One spring I had to leave the East in the midst of the hunting season, to join a round-up in the cattle country of western Dakota, and it was curious to compare the totally different styles of riding of the cowboys and the crosscountry men. A stock-saddle weighs thirty or forty pounds instead of ten or fifteen, and needs an utterly different seat from that adopted in the East. A cowboy rides with very long stirrups, sitting forked well down between his high pommel and cantle, and depends upon balance as well as on the grip of his thighs. In cutting out a steer from a herd, in breaking a vicious wild horse, in sitting a bucking bronco, in stopping a night stampede of many hundred maddened animals, or in the performance of a hundred other feats of reckless and daring horsemanship, the cowboy is absolutely unequalled; and when he has his own horse gear he sits his animal with the ease of a centaur. Yet he is quite helpless the first time he gets astride one of the small eastern saddles. One summer, while purchasing cattle in Iowa, one of my ranch foremen had to get on an ordinary saddle to ride out of town and see a bunch of steers. He is perhaps the best rider on the ranch, and will without hesitation mount and master beasts that I doubt if the boldest rider in one of our eastern hunts would care to tackle; yet his uneasiness on the new saddle was fairly comical. At first he did not dare to trot, and the least plunge of the horse bid fair to unseat him, nor did he begin to get accustomed to the situation until the very end of the journey. In fact, the two kinds of riding are so very different that a man only accustomed to one, feels almost as ill at ease when he first tries the other as if he had never sat on a horse's back before. It is rather funny to see a man who only knows one kind, and is conceited enough to think that that is really the only kind worth knowing, when first he is brought into contact with the other. Two or three times I have known men try to follow hounds on stock-saddles, which are about as ill-suited for the purpose as they well can be; while it is even more laughable to see some young fellow from the East or from England who thinks he knows entirely too much about horses to be taught by barbarians, attempt in his turn to do cow-work with his ordinary riding or hunting rig. It must be said, however, that in all probability cowboys would learn to ride well across country much sooner than the average cross-country rider would master the dashing and peculiar style of horsemanship shown by those whose life business is to guard the wandering herds of the great western plains.

Of course, riding to hounds, like all sports in long settled, thickly peopled countries, fails to develop in its followers some of the hardy qualities necessarily incident to the wilder pursuits of the mountain and the forest. While I was on the frontier I was struck by the fact that of the men from the eastern States or from England who had shown themselves at home to be good riders to hounds or had made their records as college athletes, a larger proportion failed in the life of the wilderness than was the case among those who had gained their experience in such rough pastimes as mountaineering in the high Alps, winter caribou-hunting in Canada, or deer-stalking—not deer-driving—in Scotland.

Nevertheless, of all sports possible in civilized countries, riding to hounds is perhaps the best if followed as it should be, for the sake of the strong excitement, with as much simplicity as possible, and not merely as a fashionable amusement. It tends to develop moral no less than physical qualities; the rider needs nerve and head; he must possess daring and resolution, as well as a good deal of bodily skill and a certain amount of wiry toughness and endurance.

CHAPTER XIX. WOLVES AND WOLF-HOUNDS. THE wolf is the arch type of ravin, the beast of waste and desolation. It is still found scattered thinly throughout all the wilder portions of the United States, but has everywhere retreated from the advance of civilization.

Wolves show an infinite variety in color, size, physical formation, and temper. Almost all the varieties intergrade with one another, however, so that it is very difficult to draw a hard and fast line between any two of them. Nevertheless, west of the Mississippi there are found two distinct types. One is the wolf proper, or big wolf, specifically akin to the wolves of the eastern States. The other is the little coyote, or prairie wolf. The coyote and the big wolf are found together in almost all the wilder districts from the Rio Grande to the valleys of the upper Missouri and the upper Columbia. Throughout this region there is always a sharp line of demarkation, especially in size, between the coyotes and the big wolves of any given district; but in certain districts the big wolves are very much larger than their brethren in other districts. In the upper Columbia country, for instance, they are very large; along the Rio Grande they are small. Dr. Hart Merriam informs me that, according to his experience, the coyote is largest in southern California. In many respects the coyote differs altogether in habits from its big relative. For one thing it is far more tolerant of man. In some localities coyotes are more numerous around settlements, and even in the close vicinity of large towns, than they are in the frowning and desolate fastnesses haunted by their grim elder brother.

Big wolves vary far more in color than the coyotes do. I have seen white, black, red, yellow, brown, gray, and grisled skins, and others representing every shade between, although usually each locality has its prevailing tint. The grisled, gray, and brown often have precisely the coat of the coyote. The difference in size among wolves of different localities, and even of the same locality, is quite remarkable, and so, curiously enough, is the difference in the size of the teeth, in some cases even when the body of one wolf is as big as that of another. I have seen wolves from Texas and New Mexico which were under-sized, slim animals with rather small tusks, in no way to be compared to the long-toothed giants of their race that dwell in the heavily timbered mountains of the Northwest and in the far North. As a rule, the teeth of the coyote are relatively smaller than those of the gray wolf.

Formerly wolves were incredibly abundant in certain parts of the country, notably on the great plains, where they were known as buffalo wolves, and were regular attendants on the great herds of the bison. Every traveller and hunter of the old days knew them as among the most common sights of the plains, and they followed the hunting parties and emigrant trains for the sake of the scraps left in camp. Now, however, there is no district in which they are really abundant. The wolfers, or professional wolf-hunters, who killed them by poisoning for the sake of their fur, and the cattle-men, who likewise killed them by poisoning because of their raids on the herds, have doubtless been the chief instruments in working their decimation on the plains. In the '70's, and even in the early '80'sj many tens of thousands of wolves were killed by the wolfers in Montana and northern Wyoming and western Dakota. Nowadays the surviving wolves of the plains have learned caution; they no longer move abroad at midday, and still less do they dream of hanging on the footsteps of hunter and traveller. Instead of being one of the most common they have become one of the rarest sights of the plains. A hunter may wander far and wide through the plains for months nowadays and never see a wolf, though he will probably see many coyotes. However, the diminution goes on, not steadily but by fits and starts, and, moreover, the beasts now and then change their abodes, and appear in numbers in places where they have been scarce for a long period. In the present winter of 1892-93 big wolves are more plentiful in the neighborhood of my ranch than they have been for ten years, and have worked some havoc among the cattle and young horses. The cowboys have been carrying on the usual vindictive campaign against them; a number have been poisoned, and a number of others have fallen victims to their greediness, the cowboys surprising them when gorged to repletion on the carcass of a colt or calf, and, in consequence, unable to run, so that they are easily ridden down, roped, and then dragged to death.

Yet even the slaughter wrought by man in certain localities does not seem adequate to explain the scarcity or extinction of wolves, throughout the country at large. In most places they are not followed any more eagerly than are the other large beasts of prey, and they are usually followed with less success. Of all animals the wolf is the shyest and hardest to slay. It is almost or quite as difficult to still-hunt as the cougar, and is far more difficult to kill with hounds, traps, or poison; yet it scarcely holds its own as well as the great cat, and it does not begin to hold its own as well as the bear, a beast certainly more readily killed, and one which produces fewer young at a birth. Throughout the East the black bear is common m many localities from which the wolf has vanished completely. It at present exists in very scanty numbers in northern Maine and the Adirondacks; is almost or quite extinct in Pennsylvania; lingers here and there in the mountains from West Virginia to east Tennessee, and is found in Florida; but is everywhere less abundant than the bear. It is possible that this destruction of the wolves is due to some disease among them, perhaps to hydrophobia, a terrible malady from which it is known that they suffer greatly at times. Perhaps the bear is helped by its habit of hibernating, which frees it from most dangers during winter; but this cannot be the complete explanation, for in the South it does not hibernate, and yet holds its own as well as in the North. What makes it all the more curious that the American wolf should disappear sooner than the bear is that the reverse is the case with the allied species of Europe, where the bear is much sboner killed out of the land.

Indeed the differences of this sort between nearly related animals are literally inexplicable. Much of the difference in temperament between such closely allied species as the American and European bears and wolves is doubtless due to their surroundings and to the instincts they have inherited through many generations; but for much of the variation it is not possible to offer any explanation. In the same way there are certain physical differences for which it is very hard to account, as the same conditions seem to operate in directly reverse ways with different animals. No one can explain the process of natural selection which has resulted in the otter of America being larger than the otter of Europe, while the badger is smaller; in the mink being with us a much stouter animal than its Scandinavian and Russian kinsman, while the reverse is true of our sable or pine marten. No one can say why the European red deer should be a pigmy compared to its giant brother, the American wapiti; why the Old World elk should average smaller in size than the almost indistinguishable New World moose; and yet the bison of Lithuania and the Caucasus be on the whole larger and more formidable than its American cousin. In the same way no one can tell why under like conditions some game, such as the white goat and the spruce grouse, should be tamer than other closely allied species, like the mountain sheep and ruffed grouse. No one can say why on the whole the wolf of Scandinavia and northern Russia should be larger and more dangerous than the average wolf of the Rocky Mountains, while between the bears of the same regions the comparison must be exactly reversed.

The difference even among the wolves of different sections of our own country is very notable. It may be true that the species as a whole is rather weaker and less ferocious than the European wolf; but it is certainly not true of the wolves of certain localities. The great timber wolf of the central and northern chains of the Rockies and coast ranges is in every way a more formidable creature than the buffalo wolf of the plains, although they intergrade. The skins and skulls of the wolves of northwestern Montana and Washington which I have seen were quite as large and showed quite as stout claws and teeth as the skins and skulls of Russian and Scandinavian wolves, and I believe that these great timber wolves are in every way as formidable as their Old World kinsfolk. However, they live where they come in contact with a population of rifle-bearing frontier hunters, who are very different from European peasants or Asiatic tribesmen; and they have, even when most hungry, a wholesome dread of human beings. Yet I doubt if an unarmed man would be entirely safe should he, while alone in the forest in midwinter, encounter a fair-sized pack of ravenously hungry timber wolves.

A full-grown dog-wolf of the northern Rockies, in exceptional instances, reaches a height of thirty-two inches and a weight of 130 pounds; a big buffalo-wolf of the upper Missouri stands thirty or thirty-one inches at the shoulder and weighs about 110 pounds; a Texan wolf may not reach over eighty pounds. The bitch-wolves are smaller; and moreover there is often great variation even in the wolves of closely neighboring localities.

The wolves of the southern plains were not often formidable to large animals, even in the days when they most abounded. They rarely attacked the horses of the hunter, and indeed were but little regarded by these experienced animals. They were much more likely to gnaw off the lariat with which the horse was tied, than to try to molest the steed himself. They preferred to prey on young animals, or on the weak and disabled. They rarely molested a full-grown cow or steer, still less a full-grown buffalo, and, if they did attack such an animal, it was only when emboldened by numbers. In the plains of the upper Missouri and Saskatchewan the wolf was, and is, more dangerous, while in the northern Rockies his courage and ferocity attain their highest pitch. Near my own ranch the wolves have sometimes committed great depredations on cattle, but they seem to have queer freaks of slaughter. Usually they prey only upon calves and sickly animals; but in midwinter I have known one single-handed to attack and kill a well-grown steer or cow, disabling its quarry by rapid snaps at the hams or flanks. Only rarely have I known it to seize by the throat. Colts are likewise a favorite prey, but with us wolves rarely attack full-grown horses. They are sometimes very bold in their assaults, falling on the stock while immediately around the ranch houses. They even venture into the hamlet of Medora itself at night—as the coyotes sometimes do by day. In the spring of '92 we put on some eastern two-year-old steers; they arrived, and were turned loose from the stockyards, in a snowstorm, though it was in early May. Next morning we found that one had been seized, slain, and partially devoured by a big wolf at the very gate of the stockyard; probably the beast had seen it standing near the yard after nightfall, feeling miserable after its journey, in the storm and its unaccustomed surroundings, and had been emboldened to make the assault so near town by the evident helplessness of the prey.

The big timber wolves of the northern Rocky Mountains attack every four-footed beast to be found where they live. They are far from contenting themselves with hunting deer and snapping up the pigs and sheep of the farm. When the weather gets cold and food scarce they band together in small parties, perhaps of four or five individuals, and then assail anything, even a bear or a panther. A bull elk or bull moose, when on its guard, makes a most dangerous fight; but a single wolf will frequently master the cow of either animal, as well as domestic cattle and horses. In attacking such large game, however, the wolves like to act in concert, one springing at the animal's head, and attracting its attention, while the other hamstrings it. Nevertheless, one such big wolf will kill an ordinary horse. A man I knew, who was engaged in packing into the Cœur d'Alenes, once witnessed such a feat on the part of a wolf. He was taking his pack train down into a valley when he saw a horse grazing therein; it had been turned loose by another packing outfit, because it became exhausted. He lost sight of it as the trail went down a zigzag, and while it was thus out of sight he suddenly heard it utter the appalling scream, unlike and more dreadful than any other sound, which a horse only utters in extreme fright or agony. The scream was repeated, and as he came in sight again he saw that a great wolf had attacked the horse. The poor animal had been bitten terribly in its haunches and was cowering upon them, while the wolf stood and looked at it a few paces off. In a moment or two the horse partially recovered and made a desperate bound forward, starting at full gallop. Immediately the wolf was after it, overhauled it in three or four jumps, and then seized it by the hock, while its legs were extended, with such violence as to bring it completely back on its haunches. It again screamed piteously; and this time with a few savage snaps the wolf hamstrung and partially disembowelled it, and it fell over, having made no attempt to defend itself. I have heard of more than one incident of this kind. If a horse is a good fighter, however, as occasionally, though not often, happens, it is a most difficult prey for any wild beast, and some veteran horses have no fear of wolves whatsoever, well knowing that they can either strike them down with their fore-feet or repulse them by lashing out behind.

Wolves are cunning beasts and will often try to lull their prey into unsuspicion by playing round and cutting capers. I once saw a young deer and a wolf-cub together near the hut of the settler who had captured both. The wolf was just old enough to begin to feel vicious and bloodthirsty, and to show symptoms of attacking the deer. On the occasion in question he got loose and ran towards it, but it turned, and began to hit him with its fore-feet, seemingly in sport; whereat he rolled over on his back before it, and acted like a puppy at play. Soon it turned and walked off; immediately the wolf, with bristling hair, crawled after, and with a pounce seized it by the haunch, and would doubtless have murdered the bleating, struggling creature, had not the bystanders interfered.

Where there are no domestic animals, wolves feed on almost anything from a mouse to an elk. They are redoubted enemies of foxes. They are easily able to overtake them in fair chase, and kill numbers. If the fox can get into the underbrush, however, he can dodge around much faster than the wolf, and so escape pursuit. Sometimes one wolf will try to put a fox out of a cover while another waits outside to snap him up. Moreover, the wolf kills even closer kinsfolk than the fox. When pressed by hunger it will undoubtedly sometimes seize a coyote, tear it in pieces and devour it, although during most of the year the two animals live in perfect harmony. I once myself, while out in the deep snow, came across the remains of a coyote that had been killed in this manner. Wolves are also very fond of the flesh of dogs, and if they get a chance promptly kill and eat any dog they can master—and there are but few that they cannot. Nevertheless, I have been told of one instance in which a wolf struck up an extraordinary friendship with a strayed dog, and the two lived and hunted together for many months, being frequently seen by the settlers of the locality. This occurred near Thompson's Falls, Montana.

Usually wolves are found singly, in pairs, or in family parties, each having a large beat over which it regularly hunts, and also at times shifting its grounds and travelling immense distances in order to take up a temporary abode in some new locality—for they are great wanderers. It is only under stress of severe weather that they band together in packs. They prefer to creep on their prey and seize it by a sudden pounce, but, unlike the cougar, they also run it down in fair chase. Their slouching, tireless gallop enables them often to overtake deer, antelope, or other quarry; though under favorable circumstances, especially if near a lake, the latter frequently escape Whether wolves run cunning I do not know; but I think they must, for coyotes certainly do. A coyote cannot run down a jack-rabbit; but two or three working together will often catch one. Once I saw three start a jack, which ran right away from them; but they spread out, and followed. Pretty soon the jack turned slightly, and ran near one of the outside ones, saw it, became much frightened, and turned at right angles, so as soon to nearly run into the other outside one, which had kept straight on. This happened several times, and then the confused jack lay down under a sage-bush and was seized. So I have seen two coyotes attempting to get at a newly dropped antelopekid. One would make a feint of attack, and lure the dam into a rush at him, while the other stole round to get at the kid. The dam, as always with these spirited little prong-bucks, made a good fight, and kept the assailants at bay; yet I think they would have succeeded in the end, had I not interfered. Coyotes are bold and cunning in raiding the settlers' barn-yards for lambs and hens; and they have an especial liking for tame cats. If there are coyotes in the neighborhood a cat which gets into the habit of wandering from home is surely lost.

Though, I have never known wolves to attack a man, yet in the wilder portion of the far Northwest I have heard them come around camp very close, growling so savagely as to make one almost reluctant to leave the camp fire and go out into the darkness unarmed. Once I was camped in the fall near a lonely little lake in the mountains, by the edge of quite a broad stream. Soon after night-fall three or four wolves came around camp and kept me awake by their sinister and dismal howling. Two or three times they came so close to the fire that I could hear them snap their jaws and growl, and at one time I positively thought that they intended to try to get into camp, so excited were they by the smell of the fresh meat. After a while they stopped howling; and then all was silent for an hour or so. I let the fire go out and was turning into bed when I suddenly heard some animal of con-

siderable size come down to the stream nearly opposite me and begin to splash across, first wading, then swimming. It was pitch dark and I could not possibly see, but I felt sure it was a wolf. However after coming half-way over it changed its mind and swam back to the opposite bank; nor did I see or hear anything more of the night marauders.

Five or six times on the plains or on my ranch I have had shots at wolves, always obtained by accident and always, I regret to say, missed. Often the wolf when seen was running at full speed for cover, or else was so far off that though motionless my shots went wide of it. But once have I with my own rifle killed a wolf, and this was while travelling with a pack train in the mountains. We had been making considerable noise, and I never understood how an animal so wary permitted our near approach. He did, nevertheless, and just as we came to a little stream which we were to ford I saw him get on a dead log some thirty yards distant and walk slowly off with his eyes turned toward us. The first shot smashed his shoulders and brought him down.

The wolf is one of the animals which can only be hunted successfully with dogs. Most dogs however do not take at all kindly to the pursuit. A wolf is a terrible fighter. He will decimate a pack of hounds by rabid snaps with his giant jaws while suffering little damage himself; nor are the ordinary big dogs, supposed to be fighting dogs, able to tackle him without special training. I have known one wolf to kill a bulldog which had rushed at it with a single snap, while another which had entered the yard of a Montana ranch house slew in quick succession both of the large mastiffs by which it was assailed.' The immense agility and ferocity of the wild beast, the terrible snap of his long-toothed jaws, and the admirable training in which he always is, give him a great advantage over fat, small-toothed, smooth-skinned dogs, even though they are nominally supposed to belong to the fighting classes. In the way that bench competitions are arranged nowadays this is but natural, as there is no temptation to produce

a worthy class of fighting dog when the rewards are given upon technical points wholly unconnected with the dog's usefulness. A prize-winning mastiff or bulldog may be almost useless for the only purposes for which his kind is ever useful at all. A mastiff, if properly trained and of sufficient size, might possibly be able to meet a young or undersized Texan wolf; but I have never seen a dog of this variety which I would esteem a match single-handed for one of the huge timber wolves of western Montana. Even if the dog was the heavier of the two, his teeth and claws would be very much smaller and weaker and his hide less tough. Indeed I have known of but one dog which single-handed encountered and slew a wolf; this was the large vicious mongrel whose feats are recorded in my *Hunting Trips of a Ranchman.*

General Marcy of the United States Army informed me that he once chased a huge wolf which had gotten away with a small trap on its foot. It was, I believe, in Wisconsin, and he had twenty or thirty hounds with him, but they were entirely untrained to wolf-hunting, and proved unable to stop the crippled beast. Few of them would attack it at all, and those that did went at it singly and with a certain hesitation, and so each in turn was disabled by a single terrible snap, and left bleeding on the snow. General Wade Hampton tells me that in the course of his fifty years' hunting with horse and hound in Mississippi, he has on several occasions tried his pack of fox-hounds (southern deer-hounds) after a wolf. He found that it was with the greatest difficulty, however, that he could persuade them to so much as follow the trail. Usually, as soon they came across it, they would growl, bristle up, and then retreat with their tails between their legs. But one of his dogs ever really tried to master a wolf by itself, and this one paid for its temerity with its life; for while running a wolf in a cane-brake the beast turned and tore it to pieces. Finally General Hampton succeeded in getting a number of his hounds so they would at any rate follow the trail in full cry, and thus drive the wolf out of the thicket, and give a chance to the hunter to get a shot. In this way he killed two or three.

The true way to kill wolves, however, is to hunt them with greyhounds on the great plains. Nothing more exciting than this sport can possibly be imagined. It is not always necessary that the greyhounds should be of absolutely pure blood. Prize-winning dogs of high pedigree often prove useless for the purposes. If by careful choice, however, a ranchman can get together a pack composed both of the smooth-haired greyhound and the rough-haired Scotch deer-hound, he can have excellent sport. The greyhounds sometimes do best if they have a slight cross of bulldog in their veins; but this is not necessary. If once a greyhound can be fairly entered to the sport and acquires confidence, then its wonderful agility, its sinewy strength and speed, and the terrible snap with which its jaws come together, render it a most formidable assailant. Nothing can possibly exceed the gallantry with which good greyhounds, when their blood is up, fling themselves on a wolf or any other foe. There does not exist, and there never has existed on the wide earth, a more perfect type of dauntless courage than such a hound. Not Cushing when he steered his little launch through the black night against the great ram Albemarle, not Custer dashing into the valley of the Rosebud to die with all his men, not Farragut himself lashed in the rigging of the Hartford as she forged past the forts to encounter her iron-clad foe, can stand as a more perfect type of dauntless valor.

Once I had the good fortune to witness a very exciting hunt of this character among the foot-hills of the northern Rockies. I was staying at the house of a friendly cowman, whom I will call Judge Yancy Stump. Judge Yancy Stump was a Democrat who, as he phrased it, had fought for his Democracy; that is, he had been in the Confederate Army. He was at daggers drawn with his nearest neighbor, a cross-grained mountain farmer, who may be known as old man Prindle. Old man Prindle had been in the Union Army,

and his Republicanism was of the blackest and most uncompromising type. There was one point, however, on which the two came together. They were exceedingly fond of hunting with hounds. The Judge had three or four track-hounds, and four of what he called swift-hounds, the latter including one pure-bred greyhound bitch of wonderful speed and temper, a duncolored yelping animal which was a cross between a greyhound and a fox-hound, and two others that were crosses between a greyhound and a wire-haired Scotch deer-hound. Old man Prindle's contribution to the pack consisted of two immense brindled mongrels of great strength and ferocious temper. They were unlike any dogs I have ever seen in this country. Their mother herself was a cross between a bull mastiff and a Newfoundland, while the father was described as being a big dog that belonged to a " Dutch Count." The "Dutch Count" was an outcast German noble, who had drifted to the West, and, after failing in the mines and failing in the cattle country, had died in a squalid log shanty while striving to eke out an existence as a hunter among the foot-hills. His dog, I presume, from the description given me, must have been a boar-hound or Ulm dog.

As I was very anxious to see a wolf-hunt the Judge volunteered to get one up, and asked old man Prindle to assist, for the sake of his two big fighting dogs; though the very names of the latter, General Grant and Old Abe, were gall and wormwood to the unreconstructed soul of the Judge. Still they were the only dogs anywhere around capable of tackling a savage timber wolf, and without their aid the Judge's own high-spirited animals ran a serious risk of injury, for they were altogether too game to let any beast escape without a struggle.

Luck favored us. Two wolves had killed a calf and dragged it into a long patch of dense brush where there was a little spring, the whole furnishing admirable cover for any wild beast. Early in the morning we started on horseback for this bit of cover, which was some three miles off. The party consisted of

the Judge, old man Prindle, a cowboy, myself, and the dogs. The Judge and I carried our rifles and the cowboy his revolver, but old man Prindle had nothing but a heavy whip, for he swore, with many oaths, that no one should interfere with his big dogs, for by themselves they would surely '' make the wolf feel sicker than a stuck hog." Our shaggy ponies racked along at a five-mile gait ov»r the dewy prairie grass. The two big dogs trotted behind their master, grim and ferocious. The track-hounds were tied in couples, and the beautiful greyhounds loped lightly and gracefully alongside the horses. The country was fine. A mile to our right a small plains river wound in long curves between banks fringed with cottonwoods. Two or three miles to our left the foot-hills rose sheer and bare, with clumps of black pine and cedar in their gorges. We rode over gently rolling prairie, with here and there patches of brush at the bottoms of the slopes around the dry watercourses.

At last we reached a somewhat deeper valley, in which the wolves were harbored. Wolves lie close in the daytime and will not leave cover if they can help it; and as they had both food and waterwithin we knew it was most unlikely that this couple would be gone. The valley was a couple of hundred yards broad and three or four times as long, filled with a growth of ash and dwarf elm and cedar, thorny underbrush choking the spaces between. Posting the cowboy, to whom he gave his rifle, with two greyhounds on one side of the upper end, and old man Prindle with two others on the opposite side, while I was left at the lower end to guard against the possibility of the wolves breaking back, the Judge himself rode into the thicket near me and loosened the track-hounds to let them find the wolves' trail. The big dogs also were uncoupled and allowed to go in with the hounds. Their power of scent was very poor, but they were sure to be guided aright by the baying of the hounds, and their presence would give confidence to the latter and make them ready to rout the wolves out of the thicket, which they would probably have shrunk from doing alone. There was a moment's pause of expectation after the Judge entered the thicket with his hounds. We sat motionless on our horses, eagerly looking through the keen fresh morning air. Then a clamorous baying from the thicket in which both the horseman and dogs had disappeared showed that the hounds had struck the trail of their quarry and were running on a hot scent. For a couple of minutes we could not be quite certain which way the game was going to break. The hounds ran zigzag through the brush, as we could tell by their baying, and once some yelping and a great row showed that they had come rather closer than they had expected upon at least one of the wolves.

In another minute, however, the latter found it too hot for them and bolted from the thicket. My first notice of this was seeing the cowboy, who was standing by the side of his horse, suddenly throw up his rifle and fire, while the greyhounds who had been springing high in the air, half maddened by the clamor in the thicket below, for a moment dashed off the wrong way, confused by the report of the gun. I rode for all I was worth to where the cowboy stood, and instantly caught a glimpse of two wolves, grisly-gray and brown, which having been turned by his shot had started straight over the hill across the plain toward the mountains three miles away. As soon as I saw them I saw also that the rearmost of the couple had been hit somewhere in the body and was lagging behind, the blood running from its flanks, while the two greyhounds were racing after it; and at the same moment the track-hounds and the big dogs burst out of the thicket, yelling savagely as they struck the bloody trail. The wolf was hard hit, and staggered as he ran. He did not have a hundred yards' start of the dogs, and in less than a minute one of the greyhounds ranged up and passed him with a savage snap that brought him too; and before he could recover the whole pack rushed at him. Weaken ed as he was he could make no effective fight against so many foes, and indeed had a chance for but

one or two rapid snaps before he was thrown down and completely covered by the bodies of his enemies. Yet with one of these snaps he did damage, as a shrill yell told, and in a second an over-rash track-hound came out of the struggle with a deep gash across his shoulders. The worrying, growling, and snarling were terrific, but in a minute the heaving mass grew motionless and the dogs drew off, save one or two that still continued to worry the dead wolf as it lay stark and stiff with glazed eyes and rumpled fur.

No sooner were we satisfied that it was dead than the Judge, with cheers and oaths and crackings of his whip, urged the dogs after the other wolf. The two greyhounds that had been with old man Prindle had fortunately not been able to see the wolves when they first broke from the cover, and never saw the wounded wolf at all, starting off at full speed after the unwounded one the instant he topped the crest of the hill. He had taken advantage of a slight hollow and turned, and now the chase was crossing us half a mile away. With whip and spur we flew towards them, our two greyhounds stretching out in front and leaving us as if we were standing still, the track-hounds and big dogs running after them just ahead of the horses. Fortunately the wolf plunged for a moment into a little brushy hollow and again doubled back, and this gave us a chance to see the end of the chase from nearby. The two greyhounds which had first taken up the pursuit were then but a short distance behind. Nearer they crept until they were within ten yards, and then with a tremendous race the little bitch ran past him and inflicted a vicious bite in the big beast's ham. He whirled around like a top and his jaws clashed like those of a sprung bear-trap, but quick though he was she was quicker and just cleared his savage rush. In another moment he resumed his flight at full speed, a speed which only that of the greyhounds exceeded; but almost immediately the second greyhound ranged alongside, and though he was not able to bite, because the wolf kept running with its head turned around

threatening him, yet by his feints he delayed the beast's flight so that in a moment or two the remaining couple of swift hounds arrived on the scene. For a moment the wolf and all four dogs galloped along in a bunch; then one of the greyhounds, watching his chance, pinned the beast cleverly by the hock and threw him completely over. The others jumped on it in an instant; but rising by main strength the wolf shook himself free, catching one dog by the ear and tearing it half off. Then he sat down on his haunches and the greyhounds ranged themselves around him some twenty yards off, forming a ring which forbade his retreat, though they themselves did not dare touch him. However the end was at hand. In another moment Old Abe and General Grant came running up at headlong speed and smashed into the wolf like a couple of battering-rams. He rose on his hind-legs like a wrestler as they came at him, the greyhounds also rising and bouncing up and down like rubber balls. I could just see the wolf and the first big dog locked together, as the second one made good his throat-hold. In another moment overall three tumbled, while the greyhounds and one or two of the track-hounds jumped in to take part in the killing. The big dogs more than occupied the wolf's attention and took all the punishing, while in a trice one of the greyhounds, having seized him by the hind-leg, stretched him out, and the others were biting his undefended belly. The snarling and yelling of the worry made a noise so fiendish that it was fairly bloodcurdling; then it gradually died down, and the second wolf lay limp on the plain, killed by the dogs unassisted. This wolf was rather heavier and decidedly taller than either of the big dogs, with more sinewy feet and longer fangs.

I have several times seen wolves run down and stopped by greyhounds after a break-neck gallop and a wildly exciting finish, but this was the only occasion on which I ever saw the dogs kill a big, full-grown he-wolf unaided. Nevertheless various friends of mine own packs that have performed the feat again and again. One pack, formerly kept at Fort

Benton, until wolves in that neighborhood became scarce, had nearly seventy-five to its credit, most of them killed without any assistance from the hunter; killed moreover by the greyhounds alone, there being no other dogs with the pack. These greyhounds were trained to the throat-hold, and did their own killing in fine style; usually six or eight were slipped together. General Miles informs me that he once had great fun in the Indian Territory hunting wolves with a pack of greyhounds. They had with the pack a large stub-tailed mongrel, of doubtful ancestry but most undoubted fighting capacity. When the wolf was started the greyhounds were sure to overtake it in a mile or two; they would then bring it to a halt and stand around it in a ring until the fighting dog came up. The latter promptly tumbled on the wolf, grabbing him anywhere, and often getting a terrific wound himself at the same time. As soon as he had seized the wolf and was rolling over with him in the grapple the other dogs joined in the fray and dispatched the quarry without much danger to themselves.

During the last decade many ranchmen in Colorado, Wyoming, and Montana, have developed packs of greyhounds able to kill a wolf unassisted. Greyhounds trained for this purpose always seize by the throat; and the light dogs used for coursing jack-rabbits are not of much service, smooth or rough-haired greyhounds and deer-hounds standing over thirty inches at the shoulder and weighing over ninety pounds being the only ones that, together with speed, courage, and endurance, possess the requisite power.

One of the most famous packs in the West was that of the Sun River Hound Club, in Montana, started by the stockmen of Sun River to get rid of the curse of wolves which infested the neighborhood and worked very serious damage to the herds and flocks. The pack was composed of both greyhounds and deerhounds, the best being from the kennels of Colonel Williams and of Mr. Van Hummel, of Denver; they were handled by an old plainsman and veteran wolf-

hunter named Porter. In the season of '86 the astonishing number of 146 wolves were killed with these dogs. Ordinarily, as soon as the dogs seized a wolf, and threw or held it, Porter rushed in and stabbed it with his hunting-knife; one day, when out with six hounds, he thus killed no less than twelve out of the fifteen wolves started, though one of the greyhounds was killed, and all the others were cut and exhausted. But often the wolves were killed without his aid. The first time the two biggest hounds— deer-hounds or wire-haired greyhounds—were tried, when they had been at the ranch only three days, they performed such a feat. A large wolf had killed and partially eaten a sheep in a corral close to the ranch house, and Porter started on the trail, and followed him at a jogtrot nearly ten miles before the hounds sighted him. Running but a few rods, he turned viciously to bay, and the two great greyhounds struck him like stones hurled from a catapult, throwing him as they fastened on his throat; they held him down and strangled him before he could rise, two other hounds getting up just in time to help at the end of the worry.

Ordinarily, however, no two greyhounds or deer-hounds are a match for a gray wolf, but I have known of several instances in Colorado, Wyoming, and Montana, in which three strong veterans have killed one. The feat can only be performed by big dogs of the highest courage, who all act together, rush in at top speed, and seize by the throat; for the strength of the quarry is such that otherwise he will shake off the dogs, and then speedily kill them by rabid snaps with his terribly armed jaws. Where possible, half a dozen dogs should be slipped at once, to minimize the risk of injury to the pack; unless this is done, and unless the hunter helps the dogs in the worn', accidents will be frequent, and an occasional wolf will be found able to beat off, maiming or killing, a lesser number of assailants. Some hunters prefer the smooth greyhound, because of its great speed, and others the wire-coated animal, the rough deer-hound, because of its superior

strength; both, if of the right kind, are dauntless fighters.

Colonel Williams' greyhounds have performed many notable feats in wolf-hunting. He spent the winter of 1875 in the Black Hills, which at that time did not contain a single settler, and fairly swarmed with game. Wolves were especially numerous and very bold and fierce, so that the dogs of the party were continually in jeopardy of their lives. On the other hand they took an ample vengeance, for many wolves were caught by the pack. Whenever possible, the horsemen kept close enough to take an immediate hand in the fight, if the quarry was a full-grown wolf, and thus save the dogs from the terrible punishment they were otherwise certain to receive. The dogs invariably throttled, rushing straight at the throat, but the wounds they themselves received were generally in the flank or belly; in several instances these wounds resulted fatally. Once or twice a wolf was caught, and held by two greyhounds until the horsemen came up; but it took at least five dogs to overcome and slay unaided a big timber wolf. Several times the feat was performed by a party of five, consisting of two greyhounds, one rough-coated deer-hound, and two cross-bloods; and once by a litter of seven young greyhounds, not yet come to their full strength.

Once or twice the so-called Russian wolf-hounds or silky coated greyhounds, the " borzois," have been imported and tried in wolf-hunting on the western plains; but hitherto they have not shown themselves equal, at either running or fighting, to the big American-bred greyhounds of the type produced by Colonel Williams and certain others of our best western breeders. Indeed I have never known any foreign greyhounds, whether Scotch, English, or from continental Europe, to perform such feats of courage, endurance, and strength, in chasing and killing dangerous game, as the homebred greyhounds of Colonel Williams.

IN COWBOY LAND. OUT on the frontier, and generally among those who spend their lives in, or on the borders of, the wilderness, life is reduced to its elemental conditions. The passions and emotions of these grim hunters of the mountains, and wild rough-riders of the plains, are simpler and stronger than those of people dwelling in more complicated states of society. As soon as the communities become settled and begin to grow with any rapidity, the American instinct for law asserts itself; but in the earlier stages each individual is obliged to be a law to himself and to guard his rights with a strong hand. Of course the transition periods are full of incongruities. Men have not yet adjusted their relations to morality and law with any niceness. They hold strongly by certain rude virtues, and on the other hand they quite fail to recognize even as shortcomings not a few traits that obtain scant mercy in older communities. Many of the desperadoes, the man-killers, and road-agents have good sides to their characters. Often they are people who, in certain stages of civilization, do, or have done, good work, but who, when these stages have passed, find themselves surrounded by conditions which accentuate their worst qualities, and make their best qualities useless. The average desperado, for instance, has, after all, much the same standard of morals that the Norman nobles had in the days of the battle of Hastings, and, ethically and morally, he is decidedly in advance of the vikings, who were the ancestors of these same nobles—and to whom, by the way, he himself could doubtless trace a portion of his blood. If the transition from the wild lawlessness of life in the wilderness or on the border to a higher civilization were stretched out over a term of centuries, he and his descendants would doubtless accommodate themselves by degrees to the changing circumstances. But unfortunately in the far West the transition takes place with marvellous abruptness, and at an altogether unheard-of speed, and many a man's nature is unable to change with sufficient rapidity to allow him to harmonize with his environment. In consequence, unless he leaves for still wilder lands, he ends by getting hung instead of founding a family

which would revere his name as that of a very capable, although not in all respects a conventionally moral, ancestor. Most of the men with whom I was intimately thrown during my life on the frontier and in the wilderness were good fellows, hard-working, brave, resolute, and truthful. At times, of course, they were forced of necessity to do deeds which would seem startling to dwellers in cities and in old settled places; and though they waged a very stern and relentless warfare upon evil-doers whose misdeeds had immediate and tangible bad results, they showed a wide toleration of all save the most extreme classes of wrong, and were not given to inquiring too curiously into a strong man's past, or to criticising him over-harshly for a failure to discriminate in finer ethical questions. Moreover, not a few of the men with whom I came in contact—with some of whom my relations were very close and friendly—had at different times led rather tough careers. This fact was accepted by them and by their companions as a fact, and nothing more. There were certain offences, such as rape, the robbery of a friend, or murder under circumstances of cowardice and treachery, which were never forgiven; but the fact that when the country was wild a young fellow had gone on the road—that is, become a highwayman, or had been chief of a gang of desperadoes, horse-thieves, and cattle-killers, was scarcely held to weigh against him, being treated as a regrettable, but certainly not shameful, trait of youth. He was regarded by his neighbors with the same kindly tolerance which respectable mediatval Scotch borderers doubtless extended to their wilder young men who would persist in raiding English cattle even in time of peace.

Of course if these men were asked outright as to their stories they would have refused to tell them or else would have lied about them; but when they had grown to regard a man as a friend and companion they would often recount various incidents of their past lives with perfect frankness, and as they combined in a very curious degree both a decided sense of humor, and a failure to appre-

ciate that there was anything especially remarkable in what they related, their tales were always entertaining.

Early one spring, now nearly ten years ago, I was out hunting some lost horses. They had strayed from the range three months before, and we had in a roundabout way heard that they were ranging near some broken country, where a man named Brophy had a ranch, nearly fifty miles from my own. When I started thither the weather was warm, but the second day out it grew colder and a heavy snowstorm came on. Fortunately I was able to reach the ranch all right, finding there one of the sons of a Little Beaver ranchman, and a young cowpuncher belonging to a Texas outfit, whom I knew very well. After putting my horse into the corral and throwing him down some hay I strode into the low hut, made partly of turf and partly of cottonwood logs, and speedily warmed myself before the fire. We had a good warm supper, of bread, potatoes, fried venison, and tea. My two companions grew very sociable and began to talk freely over their pipes. There were two bunks one above the other. I climbed into the upper, leaving my friends, who occupied the lower, sitting together on a bench recounting different incidents in the careers of themselves and their cronies during the winter that had just passed. Soon one of them asked the other what had become of a certain horse, a noted cutting pony, which I had myself noticed the preceding fall. The question aroused the other to the memory of a wrong which still rankled, and he began (I alter one or two of the proper names):

"Why, that was the pony that got stole. I had been workin' him on rough ground when I was out with the Three Bar outfit and he went tender forward, so I turned him loose by the Lazy B ranch, and when I come back to git him there wasn't anybody at the ranch and I couldn't find him. The sheep-man who lives about two miles west, under Red Clay butte, told me he seen a fellow in a wolfskin coat, ridin' a pinto bronco, with white eyes, leadin' that pony of mine just two days before; and I hunted round till I hit his trail and then I followed to where I'd reckoned he was headin' for—the Short Pine Hills. When I got there a rancher told me he had seen the man pass on towards Cedartown, and sure enough when I struck Cedartown I found he lived there in a dobe house, just outside the town. There was a boom on the town and it looked pretty slick. There was two hotels and I went into the first, and I says, ' Where's the justice of the peace?' says I to the bartender.

"' There ain't no justice of the peace,' says he, 'the justice of the peace got shot.'

"' Well, where's the constable?' says I.

"' Why, it was him that shot the justice of the peace!' says he; 'he's skipped the country with a bunch of horses.'

"'Well, ain't there no officer of the law left in this town?' says I.

"' Why, of course,' says he, 'there's a probate judge; he is overtendin' bar at the Last Chance Hotel.'

"So I went over to the Last Chance Hotel and I walked in there. 'Mornin',' says I.

"' Mornin',' says he.

"' You 're the probate judge?' says I.

"' That's what I am,' says he. 'What do you want?' says he.

'" I want justice,' says I. "' What kind of justice do you want?' says he. 'What's it for?'

"' It's for stealin' a horse,' says I.

"' Then by God you 'll git it,' says he. 'Who stole the horse?' says he.

"' It is a man that lives in a 'dobe house, just outside the town there,' says I.

"' Well, where do you come from yourself?' said he.

"' From Medory,' said I.

"With that he lost interest and settled kind o' back, and says he, 'There wont no Cedartown jury hang a Cedartown man for stealin' a Medory man's horse,' said he.

"' Well, what am I to do about my horse?' says I.

"' Do?' says he; 'well, you know where the man lives, don't you?' says he; 'then sit up outside his house tonight and shoot him when he comes in,' says he, 'and skip out with the horse.'

"'All right,' says I, 'that is what I 'll do,' and I walked off.

"So I went off to his house and I laid down behind some sage-brushes to wait for him. He was not at home, but I could see his wife movin' about inside now and then, and I waited and waited, and it growed darker, and I begun to say to myself, ' Now here you are lyin' out to shoot this man when he comes home; and it's gettin' dark, and you don't know him, and if you do shoot the next man that comes into that house, like as not it won't be the fellow you 're after at all, but some perfectly innocent man a-comin' there after the other man's wife!'

"So I up and saddled the bronc' and lit out for home," concluded the narrator with the air of one justly proud of his own self-abnegating virtue.

The "town" where the judge abovementioned dwelt was one of those squalid, pretentiously named little clusters of makeshift dwellings which on the edge of the wild country spring up with the rapid growth of mushrooms, and are often no longer lived. In their earlier stages these towns are frequently built entirely of canvas, and are subject to grotesque calamities. When the territory purchased from the Sioux, in the Dakotas, a couple of years ago, was thrown open to settlement, there was a furious inrush of men on horseback and in wagons, and various ambitious cities sprang up overnight. The new settlers were all under the influence of that curious craze which causes every true westerner to put unlimited faith in the unknown and untried; many had left all they had in a far better farming country, because they were true to their immemorial belief that, wherever they were, their luck would be better if they went somewhere else. They were always on the move, and headed for the vague beyond. As miners see visions of all the famous mines of history in each new camp, so these would-be city founders saw future St. Pauls and Omahas in every forlorn group of tents pitched by some muddy stream in a desert of gumbo and sage-brush; and they named both the towns and the canvas buildings in accordance with their bright hopes for the morrow, rather than with reference to the mean facts of the day. One of these towns, which when twentyfour hours old boasted of six saloons, a "court-house," and an "opera house," was overwhelmed by early disaster. The third day of its life a whirlwind came along and took off the opera house and half the saloons; and the following evening lawless men nearly finished the work of the elements. The riders of a huge trail-outfit from Texas, to their glad surprise discovered the town and abandoned themselves to a night of roaring and lethal carousal. Next morning the city authorities were lamenting, with oaths of bitter rage, that "them hell-and-twenty Flying A cowpunchers had cut the court-house up into pants." It was true. The cowboys were in need of shaps, and with an admirable mixture of adventurousness, frugality, and ready adaptability to circumstances, had made substitutes therefor in the shape of canvas overalls, cut from the roof and walls of the shaky temple of justice.

One of my valued friends in the mountains, and one of the best hunters with whom I ever travelled, was a man who had a peculiarly light-hearted way of looking at conventional social obligations. Though in some ways a true backwoods Donatello, he was a man of much shrewdness and of great courage and resolution. Moreover, he possessed what only a few men do possess, the capacity to tell the truth. He saw facts as they were, and could tell them as they were, and he never told an untruth unless for very weighty reasons. He was pre-eminently a philosopher, of a happy, sceptical turn of mind. He had no prejudices. He never looked down, as so many hard characters do, upon a person possessing a different code of ethics. His attitude was one of broad, genial tolerance. He saw nothing out of the way in the fact that he had himself been a road-agent, a professional gambler, and a desperado at different stages of his career. On the other hand, he did not in the least hold it against any one that he had always acted within the law. At the time that I knew him he had become a man of some substance, and naturally a staunch upholder of the existing order of things. But while he never boasted of his past deeds, he never apologized for them, and evidently would have been quite as incapable of understanding that they needed an apology as he would have been incapable of being guilty of mere vulgar boastfulness. He did not often allude to his past career at all. When he did, he recited its incidents perfectly naturally and simply, as events, without any reference to or regard for their ethical significance. It was this quality which made him at times a specially pleasant companion, and always an agreeable narrator. The point of his story, or what seemed to him the point, was rarely that which struck me. It was the incidental sidelights the story threw upon his own nature and the somewhat lurid surroundings amid which he had moved.

On one occasion when we were out together we killed a bear, and after skinning it, took a bath in a lake. I noticed he had a scar on the side of his foot and asked him how he got it, to which he responded, with indifference:

"Oh, that? Why, a man shootin' at me to make me dance, that was all."

I expressed some curiosity in the matter, and he went on:

"Well, the way of it was this: It was when I was keeping a saloon in New Mexico, and there was a man there by the name of Fowler, and there was a reward on him of three thousand dollars"

"Put on him by the State?"

"No, put on by his wife," said my friend; "and there was this"

"Hold on," I interrupted; "put on by his wife did you say?"

"Yes, by his wife. Him and her had been keepin' a faro bank, you see, and they quarrelled about it, so she just put a reward on him, and so"

"Excuse me," I said "but do you mean to say that this reward was put on publicly?" to which my friend answered, with an air of gentlemanly boredom at being interrupted to gratify my thirst for irrelevant detail:

"Oh, no, not publicly. She just mentioned it to six or eight intimate personal friends."

"Go on," I responded, somewhat overcome by this instance of the primitive simplicity with which New Mexican matrimonial disputes were managed, and he continued:

"Well, two men come ridin' in to see me to borrow my guns. My guns was Colt's self-cockers. It was a new thing then, and they was the only ones in town. These come to me, and 'Simpson,' says they, 'we want to borrow your guns; we are goin' to kill Fowler.'

"' Hold on for a moment,' said I, 'I am willin' to lend you them guns, but I ain't goin' to know what you Y goin' to do with them, no sir; but of course you can have the guns.'" Here my friend's face lightened pleasantly, and he continued: "Well, you may easily believe I felt surprised next day when Fowler come ridin' in, and, says he, 'Simpson, here's your guns!' He had shot them two men!' Well, Fowler,' says I, ' if I had known them men was after you, I 'd never have let them have them guns nohow,' says I. That was n't true, for I did know it, but there was no cause to tell him that." I murmured my approval of such prudence, and Simpson continued, his eyes gradually brightening with the light of agreeable reminiscence:

"Well, they up and they took Fowler before the justice of the peace. The justice of the peace was a Turk."

"Now, Simpson, what do you mean by that?" I interrupted:

"Well, he come from Turkey," said Simpson, and I again sank back, wondering briefly what particular variety of Mediterranean outcast had drifted down to New Mexico to be made a justice of the peace. Simpson laughed and continued.

"That Fowler was a funny fellow. The Turk, he committed Fowler, and Fowler, he riz up and knocked him down and tromped all over him and made him let him go!"

"That was an appeal to a higher law," I observed. Simpson assented cheerily, and continued:

"Well, that Turk, he got nervous for fear Fowler he was goin' to kill him, and so he comes to me and offers me twenty-five dollars a day to protect him from Fowler; and I went to Fowler, and ' Fowler,' says I, 'that Turk's offered me twenty-five dollars a day to protect him from you. Now, I ain't goin' to get shot for no twenty-five dollars a day, and if you are goin' to kill the Turk, just say so and go and do it; but if you ain't goin' to kill the Turk, there 's no reason why I should n't earn that twenty-five dollars a day!' and Fowler, says he, 'I ain't goin' to touch the Turk; you just go right ahead and protect him.'"

So Simpson "protected" the Turk from the imaginary danger of Fowler, for about a week, at twenty-five dollars a day. Then one evening he happened to go out and met Fowler, "and," said he, " the moment I saw him I knowed he felt mean, for he begun to shoot at my feet," which certainly did seem to offer presumptive evidence of meanness. Simpson continued:

"I did n't have no gun, so I just had to stand there and take it until something distracted his attention, and I went off home to get my gun and kill him, but I wanted to do it perfectly lawful; so I went up to the mayor (he was playin' poker with one of the judges), and says I to him, 'Mr. Mayor,' says l, 'I am goin' to shoot Fowler. And the mayor he riz out of his chair and he took me by the hand, and says he, 'Mr. Simpson, if you do I will stand by you '; and the judge, he says, 'I 'll go on your bond.'"

Fortified by this cordial approval of the executive and judicial branches of the government, Mr. Simpson started on his quest. Meanwhile, however, Fowler had cut up another prominent citizen, and they already had him in jail. The friends of law and order feeling some little distrust as to the permanency of their own zeal for righteousness, thought it best to settle the matter before there was time for cooling, and accordingly, headed by Simpson, the mayor, the judge, the Turk, and other prominent citizens of the town, they broke into the jail and hanged Fowler. The point in the hanging which especially tickled my friend's fancy, as he lingered over the reminiscence, was one that was rather too ghastly to appeal to our own sense of humor. In the Turk's mind there still rankled the memory of Fowler's very unprofessional conduct while figuring before him as a criminal. Said Simpson, with a merry twinkle of the eye: " Do you know that Turk, he was a right funny fellow too after all. Just as the boys were going to string up Fowler, says he, 'Boys, stop; one moment, gentlemen,— Mr. Fowler, good-by,' and he blew a kiss to him!"

In the cow-country, and elsewhere on the wild borderland between savagery and civilization, men go quite as often by nicknames as by those to which they are lawfully entitled. Half the cowboys and hunters of my acquaintance are known by names entirely unconnected with those they inherited or received when they were christened. Occasionally some would-be desperado or make-believe mighty hunter tries to adopt what he deems a title suitable to his prowess; but such an effort is never attempted in really wild places, where it would be greeted with huge derision; for all of these names that are genuine are bestowed by outsiders, with small regard to the wishes of the person named. Ordinarily the name refers to some easily recognizable accident of origin, occupation, or aspect; as witness the innumerable Dutcheys, Frencheys, Kentucks, Texas Jacks, Bronco Bills, Bear Joes, Buckskins, Red Jims, and the like. Sometimes it is apparently meaningless; one of my cowpuncher friends is always called " Sliver" or " Splinter"—why, I have no idea. At other times some particular incident may give rise to the title: a clean-looking cowboy formerly in my employ was always known as " Muddy Bill," because he had once been bucked off his horse into a mud hole.

The grewsome genesis of one such name is given in the following letter which I have just received from an old hunting-friend in the Rockies, who took a kindly interest in a frontier cabin which the Boone and Crockett Club was putting up at the Chicago World's Fair.

"Feb 16th 1893; Der Sir: I see in the newspapers that your club the Daniel Boon and Davey Crockit you Intend to erect a fruntier Cabin at the world's Far at Chicago to represent the erley Pianears of our country I would like to see you maik a success I have all my life been a fruntiersman and feel interested in your undertaking and I hoap you wile get a good assortment of relicks I want to maik one suggestion to you that is in regard to geting a good man and a genuine Mauntanner to take charg of your haus at Chicago I want to recommend a man for you to get it is Liver-eating Johnson that is the naim he is generally called he is an olde mauntneer and large and fine looking and one of the Best Story Tellers in the country and Very Polight genteel to every one he meets I wil tel you how he-got that naim Livereating in a hard Fight with the Black Feet Indians thay Faught all day Johnson and a few Whites Faught a large Body of Indians all day after the fight Johnson cam in contact with a wounded Indian and Johnson was aut of ammunition and thay faught it out with thar Knives and Johnson got away with the Indian and in the fight cut the livver out of the Indian and said to the Boys did thay want any Liver to eat that is the way he got the naim of Liver-eating Johnson

"Yours truly" etc., etc.

Frontiersmen are often as original in their theories of life as in their names; and the originality may take the form of wild savagery, of mere uncouthness, or of an odd combination of genuine humor with simple acceptance of facts as they are. On one occasion I expressed some surprise at learning that a certain Mrs. P. had suddenly married, though her husband was alive and in jail in a neighboring town; and received for answer: "Well, you see, old man Pete he skipped the country, and left his widow behind him, and so Bob Evans he up and married her!"—which was evidently felt to be a proceeding requiring no explanation whatever.

In the cow-country there is nothing more refreshing than the light-hearted belief entertained by the average man to the effect that any animal which by main force has been saddled and ridden, or harnessed and driven a couple of times, is a " broke horse." My present foreman is firmly wedded to this idea, as well as to its complement, the belief that any animals with hoofs, before any vehicle with wheels, can be driven across any country. One summer on reaching the ranch I was entertained with the usual accounts of the adventures and misadventures which had befallen my own men and my neighbors since I had been out last. In the course of the conversation my foreman remarked: "We had a great time out here about six weeks ago. There was a professor from Ann Arbor came out with his wife to see the Bad Lands, and they asked if we could rig them up a team, and we said we guessed we could, and Foley's boy and I did; but it ran away with him and broke his leg! He was here for a month. I guess he did n't mind it though." Of this I was less certain, forlorn little Medora being a "busted" cow-town, concerning which I once heard another of my men remark, in reply to an inquisitive commercial traveller: "How many people lives here? Eleven—counting the chickens—when they 're all in town!"

My foreman continued: "By George, there was something that professor said afterwards that made me feel hot. I sent word up to him by Foley's boy that seein' as how it had come out we would n't charge him nothin' for the rig; and that professor he answered that he was glad we were showing him some sign of consideration, for he'd begun to believe he'd fallen into a den of sharks, and that we gave him a runaway team a purpose. That made me hot, calling that a runaway team. Why, there was one of them horses never *could* have run away before; it had n't never been druv but twice! and the other horse maybe had run away a few times, but there was lots of times he *had rit* run away. I esteemed that team full as liable not to run away as it was to run away," concluded my foreman, evidently deeming this as good a warranty of gentleness as the most exacting could require.

The definition of good behavior on

the frontier is even more elastic for a saddle-horse than for a team. Last spring one of the Three-Seven riders, a magnificent horseman, was killed on the round-up near Belfield, his horse bucking and falling on him. "It was accounted a plumb gentle horse too," said my informant, "only it sometimes sulked and acted a little mean when it was cinched up behind." The unfortunate rider did not know of this failing of the "plumb gentle horse," and as soon as he was in the saddle it threw itself over sideways with a great bound, and he fell on his head, and never spoke again.

Such accidents are too common in the wild country to attract very much attention; the men accept them with grim quiet, as inevitable in such lives as theirs—lives that are harsh and narrow in their toil and their pleasure alike, and that are ever-bounded by an iron horizon of hazard and hardship. During the last year and a half three other men from the ranches in my immediate neighborhood have met their deaths in the course of their work. One, a trail boss of the O X, was drowned while swimming his herd across a swollen river. Another, one of the fancy ropers of the W Bar, was killed while roping cattle in a corral; his saddle turned, the rope twisted round him, he was pulled off, and was trampled to death by his own horse.

The fourth man, a cowpuncher named Hamilton, lost his life during the last week of October, 1891, in the first heavy snowstorm of the season. Yet he was a skilled plainsman, on ground he knew well, and just before straying himself, he successfully instructed two men who did not know the country how to get to camp. They were all three with the round-up, and were making a circle through the Bad Lands; the wagons had camped on the eastern edge of these Bad Lands, where they merge into the prairie, at the head of an old disused road, which led about due east from the Little Missouri. It was a gray, lowering day, and as darkness came on Hamilton's horse played out, and he told his two companions not to wait, as it had begun to snow, but to keep on towards the north, skirting some particularly

rough buttes, and as soon as they struck the road to turn to the right and follow it out to the prairie, where they would find camp; he particularly warned them to keep a sharp look-out, so as not to pass over the dim trail unawares in the dusk and the storm. They followed his advice, and reached camp safely; and after they had left him nobody ever again saw him alive. Evidently he himself, plodding northwards, passed over the road without seeing it in the gathering gloom; probably he struck it at some point where the ground was bad, and the dim trail in consequence disappeared entirely, as is the way with these prairie roads—making them landmarks to be used with caution. He must then have walked on and on, over rugged hills and across deep ravines, until his horse came to a standstill; he took off its saddle and picketed it to a dwarfed ash. Its frozen carcass was found, with the saddle near by, two months later. He now evidently recognized some landmark, and realized that he had passed the road, and was far to the north of the round-up wagons; but he was a resolute, self-confident man, and he determined to strike out for a line camp, which he knew lay about due east of him, two or three miles out on the prairie, on one of the head branches of Knife River. Night must have fallen by this time, and he missed the camp, probably passing it within less than a mile; but he did pass it, and with it all hopes of life, and walked wearily on to his doom, through the thick darkness and the driving snow. At last his strength failed, and he lay down in the tall grass of a little hollow. Five months later, in the early spring, the riders from the line camp found his body, resting face downwards, with the forehead on the folded arms.

Accidents of less degree are common. Men break their collar-bones, arms, or legs by falling when riding at speed over dangerous ground, when cutting cattle or trying to control a stampeded herd, or by being thrown or rolled on by bucking or rearing horses; or their horses, and on rare occasions even they themselves, are gored by fighting steers. Death by storm or in flood, death in

striving to master a wild and vicious horse, or in handling maddened cattle, and too often death in brutal conflict with one of his own fellows—any one of these is the not unnatural end of the life of the dweller on the plains or in the mountains.

But a few years ago other risks had to be run from savage beasts, and from the Indians. Since I have been ranching on the Little Missouri, two men have been killed by bears in the neighborhood of my range; and in the early years of my residence there, several men living or travelling in the country were slain by small war-parties of young braves. All the old-time trappers and hunters could tell stirring tales of their encounters with Indians.

My friend, Tazewell Woody, was among the chief actors in one of the most noteworthy adventures of this kind. He was a very quiet man, and it was exceedingly difficult to get him to talk over any of his past experiences; but one day, when he was in high good-humor with me for having made three consecutive straight shots at elk, he became quite communicative, and I was able to get him to tell me one story which I had long wished to hear from his lips, having already heard of it through one of the other survivors of the incident. When he found that I already knew a good deal old Woody told me the rest.

It was in the spring of 1875, and Woody and two friends were trapping on the Yellowstone. The Sioux were very bad at the time and had killed many prospectors, hunters, cowboys, and settlers; the whites retaliated whenever they got a chance, but, as always in Indian warfare, the sly, lurking, bloodthirsty savages inflicted much more loss than they suffered.

The three men, having a dozen horses with them, were camped by the riverside in a triangular patch of brush, shaped a good deal like a common flatiron. On reaching camp they started to put out their traps; and when he came back in the evening Woody informed his companions that he had seen a great deal of Indian sign, and that he believed there were Sioux in the neighborhood. His companions both laughed at him, assuring him that they were not Sioux at all but friendly Crows, and that they would be in camp next morning; "and sure enough," said Woody, meditatively, "they *were* in camp next morning. " By dawn one of the men went down the river to look at some of the traps, while Woody started out to where the horses were, the third man remaining in camp to get breakfast. Suddenly two shots were heard down the river, and in another moment a mounted Indian swept towards the horses. Woody fired, but missed him, and he drove off five while Woody, running forward, succeeded in herding the other seven into camp. Hardly had this been accomplished before the man who had gone down the river appeared, out of breath with his desperate run, having been surprised by several Indians, and just succeeding in making his escape by dodging from bush to bush, threatening his pursuers with his rifle.

These proved to be but the forerunners of a great war party, for when the sun rose the hills around seemed black with Sioux. Had they chosen to dash right in on the camp, running the risk of losing several of their men in the charge, they could of course have eaten up the three hunters in a minute; but such a charge is rarely practised by Indians, who, although they are admirable in defensive warfare, and even in certain kinds of offensive movements, and although from their skill in hiding they usually inflict much more loss than they suffer when matched against white troops, are yet very reluctant to make any movement where the advantage gained must be offset by considerable loss of life. The three men thought they were surely doomed, but being veteran frontiersmen and long inured to every kind of hardship and danger, they set to work with cool resolution to make as effective a defence as possible, to beat off their antagonists if they might, and if this proved impracticable, to sell their lives as dearly as they could. Having tethered the horses in a slight hollow, the only one which offered any protec-

tion, each man crept out to a point of the triangular brush patch and lay down to await events.

In a very short while the Indians began closing in on them, taking every advantage of cover, and then, both from their side of the river and from the opposite bank. opened a perfect fusillade, wasting their cartridges with a recklessness which Indians are apt to show when excited. The hunters could hear the hoarse commands of the chiefs, the war-whoops, and the taunts in broken English which some of the warriors hurled at them. Very soon all of their horses were killed, and the brush was fairly riddled by the incessant volleys; but the three men themselves, lying flat on the ground and well concealed, were not harmed. The more daring young warriors then began to creep toward the hunters, going stealthily from one piece of cover to the next; and now the whites in turn opened fire. They did not shoot recklessly, as did their foes, but coolly and quietly, endeavoring to make each shot tell. Said Woody: " I only fired seven times all day; I reckoned on getting meat every time I pulled trigger." They had an immense advantage over their enemies, in that whereas they lay still and entirely concealed, the Indians of course had to move from cover to cover in order to approach, and so had at times to expose themselves. When the whites fired at all they fired at a man, whether moving or motionless, whom they could clearly see, while the Indians could only shoot at the smoke, which imperfectly marked the position of their unseen foes. In consequence the assailants speedily found that it was a task of hopeless danger to try in such a manner to close in on three plains veterans, men of iron nerve and skilled in the use of the rifle. Yet some of the more daring crept up very close to the patch of brush, and one actually got inside it, and was killed among the bedding that lay by the smouldering camp-fire. The wounded and such of the dead as did not lie in too exposed positions were promptly taken away by their comrades; but seven bodies fell into the hands of the three hunters. I asked Woody how many he

himself had killed. He said he could only be sure of two that he got; one he shot in the head as he peeped over a bush, and the other he shot through the smoke as he attempted to rush in. "My, how that Indian did yell," said Woody, retrospectively; "*he* was no great of a Stoic. " After two or three hours of this deadly skirmishing, which resulted in nothing more serious to the whites than in two of them being slightly wounded, the Sioux became disheartened by the loss they were suffering and withdrew, confining themselves thereafter to a long range and harmless fusillade. When it was dark the three men crept out to the river bed, and taking advantage of the pitchy night broke through the circle of their foes; they managed to reach the settlements without further molestation, having lost everything except their rifles.

For many years one of the most important of the wilderness dwellers was the West Point officer, and no man has played a greater part than he in the wild warfare which opened the regions beyond the Mississippi to white settlement. Since 1879, there has been but little regular Indian fighting in the North, though there have been one or two very tedious and wearisome campaigns waged against the Apaches in the South. Even in the North, however, there have been occasional uprisings which had to be quelled by the regular troops.

After my elk hunt in September, 1891, I came out through the Yellowstone Park, as I have elsewhere related, riding in company with a surveyor of the Burlington and Quincy railroad, who was just coming in from his summer's work. It was the first of October. There had been a heavy snow-storm and the snow was still falling. Riding a stout pony each, and leading another packed with our bedding, etc., we broke our way from the upper to the middle geyser basin. Here we found a troop of the 1st Cavalry camped, under the command of old friends of mine, Captain Frank Edwards and Lieutenant (now Captain) John Pitcher. They gave us hay for our horses and insisted upon our stopping to lunch, with the ready hospitality always shown by army officers. After lunch we began exchanging stories. My travelling companion, the surveyor, had that spring performed a feat of note, going through one of the canyons of the Big Horn for the first time. He went with an old mining inspector, the two of them dragging a cottonwood sledge over the ice. The walls of the canyon are so sheer and the water so rough that it can be descended only when the stream is frozen. However, after six days' labor and hardship the descent was accomplished; and the surveyor, in concluding, described his experience in going through the Crow Reservation.

This turned the conversation upon Indians, and it appeared that both of our hosts had been actors in Indian scrapes which had attracted my attention at the time they occurred, as they took place among tribes that I knew and in a country which I had sometime visited, either when hunting or when purchasing horses for the ranch. The first, which occurred to Captain Edwards, happened late in 1886, at the time when the Crow Medicine Chief, Sword-Bearer, announced himself as the Messiah of the Indian race, during one of the usual epidemics of ghost dancing. Sword-Bearer derived his name from always wearing a medicine sword—that is, a sabre painted red He claimed to possess magic power, and, thanks to the performance of many dextrous feats of juggling, and the lucky outcome of certain prophecies, he deeply stirred the Indians, arousing the young warriors in particular to the highest pitch of excitement. They became sullen, began to paint, and armed themselves; and the agent and the settlers nearby grew so apprehensive that the troops were ordered to go to the reservation. A body of cavalry, including Captain Edwards' troop, was accordingly marched thither, and found the Crow warriors, mounted on their war ponies and dressed in their striking battlegarb, waiting on a hill.

The position of troops at the beginning of such an affair is always peculiarly difficult. The settlers roundabout are sure to clamor bitterly against them, no matter what they do, on the ground that they are not thorough enough and are showing favor to the savages, while on the other hand, even if they fight purely in self-defence, a large number of worthy but weak-minded sentimentalists in the East are sure to shriek about their having brutally attacked the Indians. The war authorities always insist that they must not fire the first shot under any circumstances, and such were the orders at this time. The Crows on the hill-top showed a sullen and threatening front, and the troops advanced slowly towards them and then halted for a parley. Meanwhile a mass of black thunder-clouds gathering on the horizon threatened one of those cloudbursts of extreme severity and suddenness so characteristic of the plains country. While still trying to make arrangements for a parley, a horseman started out of the Crow ranks and galloped headlong down towards the troops. It was the medicine chief, SwordBearer. He was painted and in his battle-dress, wearing his war-bonnet of floating, trailing eagle feathers, while the plumes of the same bird were braided in the mane and tail of his fiery little horse. On he came at a gallop almost up to the troops and then began to circle around them, calling and singing and throwing his crimson sword into the air, catching it by the hilt as it fell. Twice he rode completely around the soldiers, who stood in uncertainty, not knowing what to make of his performance, and expressly forbidden to shoot at him. Then paying no further heed to them he rode back towards the Crows. It appears that he had told them that he would ride twice around the hostile force, and by his incantations would call down rain from heaven, which would make the hearts of the white men like water, so that they should go back to their homes. Sure enough, while the arrangements for the parley were still going forward, down came the cloudburst, drenching the command and making the ground on the hills in front nearly impassable; and before it dried a courier arrived with orders to the troops to go back to camp.

This fulfilment of Sword-Bearer's prophecy of course raised his reputation to the zenith and the young men of the tribe prepared for war, while the older chiefs, who more fully realized the power of the whites, still hung back. When the troops next appeared they came upon the entire Crow force, the women and children with their tepees being off to one side beyond a little stream while almost all the warriors of the tribe were gathered in front. Sword-Bearer started to repeat his former ride, to the intense irritation of the soldiers. Luckily, however, this time some of his young men could not be restrained. They too began to ride near the troops, and one of them was unable to refrain from firing on Captain Edwards' troop, which was in the van. This gave the soldiers their chance. They instantly responded with a volley, and Captain Edwards' troop charged. The fight lasted but a minute or two, for Sword-Bearer was struck by a bullet and fell, and as he had boasted himself invulnerable, and promised that his warriors should be invulnerable also if they would follow him, the hearts of the latter became as water and they broke in every direction. One of the amusing, though irritating, incidents of the affair was to see the plumed and painted warriors race headlong for the camp, plunge into the stream, wash off their war paint, and remove their feathers; in another moment they would be stolidly sitting on the ground, with their blankets over their shoulders, rising to greet the pursuing cavalry with unmoved composure and calm assurances that they had always been friendly and had much disapproved the conduct of the young bucks who had just been scattered on the field outside. It was much to the credit of the discipline of the army that no bloodshed followed the fight proper. The loss to the whites was small.

The other incident, related by Lieutenant Pitcher, took place in 1890, near Tongue River, in northern Wyoming. The command with which he was serving was camped near the Cheyenne Reservation. One day two young Cheyenne bucks, met one of the government herders, and promptly killed him—in a sudden fit, half of ungovernable blood lust, half of mere ferocious lightheartedness. They then dragged his body into the brush and left it. The disappearance of the herder of course attracted attention, and a search was organized by the cavalry. At first the Indians stoutly denied all knowledge of the missing man; but when it became evident that the search party would shortly find him, two or three of the chiefs joined them, and piloted them to where the body lay; and acknowledged that he had been murdered by two of their band, though at first they refused to give their names. The commander of the post demanded that the murderers be given up. The chiefs said that they were very sorry, that this could not be done, but that they were willing to pay over any reasonable number of ponies to make amends for the death. This offer was of course promptly refused, and the commander notified them that if they did not surrender the murderers by a certain time he would hold the whole tribe responsible and would promptly move out and attack them. Upon this the chiefs, after holding full counsel with the tribe, told the commander that they had no power to surrender the murderers, but that the latter had said that sooner than see their tribe involved in a hopeless struggle they would of their own accord come in and meet the troops anywhere the latter chose to appoint, and die fighting. To this the commander responded: "All right; let them come into the agency in half an hour." The chiefs acquiesced, and withdrew.

Immediately the Indians sent mounted messengers at speed from camp to camp, summoning all their people to witness the act of fierce self-doom; and soon the entire tribe of Cheyennes, many of them having their faces blackened in token of mourning, moved down and took up a position on the hillside close to the agency. At the appointed hour both young men appeared in their handsome war dress, galloped to the top of the hill near the encampment, and deliberately opened fire on the troops. The latter merely fired a few shots to keep the young desperadoes off, while Lieutenant Pitcher and a score of cavalrymen left camp to make a circle and drive them in; they did not wish to hurt them, but to capture and give them over to the Indians, so that the latter might be forced themselves to inflict the punishment. However, they were unable to accomplish their purpose; one of the young braves went straight at them, firing his rifle and wounding the horse of one of the cavalrymen, so that, simply in self-defence, the latter had to fire a volley, which laid low the assailant; the other, his horse having been shot, was killed in the brush, fighting to the last. All the while, from the moment the two doomed braves appeared until they fell, the Cheyennes on the hill-side had been steadily singing the death chant. When the young men had both died, and had thus averted the fate which their misdeeds would else have brought upon the tribe, the warriors took their bodies and bore them away for burial honors, the soldiers looking on in silence. Where the slain men were buried the whites never knew; but all that night they listened to the dismal wailing of the dirges with which the tribesmen celebrated their gloomy funeral rites.

Frontiersmen are not, as a rule, apt to be very superstitious. They lead lives too hard and practical, and have too little imagination in things spiritual and supernatural. I have heard but few ghost stories while living on the frontier, and these few were of a perfectly commonplace and conventional type.

But I once listened to a goblin story which rather impressed me. It was told by a grisled, weather-beaten old mountain hunter, named Bauman, who was born and had passed all his life on the frontier. He must have believed what he said, for he could hardly repress a shudder at certain points of the tale; but he was of German ancestry, and in childhood had doubtless been saturated with all kinds of ghost and goblin lore, so that many fearsome superstitions were latent in his mind; besides, he knew well the stories told by the Indian medicine men in their winter camps, of the snow-walkers, and the spectres, and the formless evil beings that haunt the forest depths, and dog and waylay the lonely wanderer who after nightfall passes through the regions where they lurk; and it may be that when overcome by the horror of the fate that befell his friend, and when oppressed by the awful dread of the unknown, he grew to attribute, both at the time and still more in remembrance, weird and elfin traits to what was merely some abnormally wicked and cunning wild beast; but whether this was so or not, no man can say.

When the event occurred Bauman was still a young man, and was trapping with a partner among the mountains dividing the forks of the Salmon from the head of Wisdom River. Not having had much luck, he and his partner determined to go up into a particularly wild and lonely pass through which ran a small stream said to contain many beaver. The pass had an evil reputation because the year before a solitary hunter who had wandered into it was there slain, seemingly by a wild beast, the halfeaten remains being afterwards found by some mining prospectors who had passed his camp only the night before.

The memory of this event, however, weighed very lightly with the two trappers, who were as adventurous and hardy as others of their kind. They took their two lean mountain ponies to the foot of the pass, where they left them in an open beaver meadow, the rocky timberclad ground being from thence onwards impracticable for horses. They then struck out on foot through the vast, gloomy forest, and in about four hours reached a little open glade where they concluded to camp, as signs of game were plenty.

There was still an hour or two of daylight left, and after building a brush lean-to and throwing down and opening their packs, they started up stream. The country was very dense and hard to travel through, as there was much down timber, although here and there the sombre woodland was broken by small glades of mountain grass.

At dusk they again reached camp. The glade in which it was pitched was not many yards wide, the tall, close-set pines and firs rising round it like a wall. On one side was a little stream, beyond which rose the steep mountainslopes, covered with the unbroken growth of the evergreen forest.

They were surprised to find that during their short absence something, apparently a bear, had visited camp, and had rummaged about among their things, scattering the contents of their packs, and in sheer wantonness destroying their lean-to. The footprints of the beast were quite plain, but at first they paid no particular heed to them, busying themselves with rebuilding the lean-to, laying out their beds and stores, and lighting the fire.

While Bauman was making ready supper, it being already dark, his companion began to examine the tracks more closely, and soon took a brand from the fire to follow them up, where the intruder had walked along a game trail after leaving the camp. When the brand flickered out, he returned and took another, repeating his inspection of the footprints very closely. Coming back to the fire, he stood by it a minute or two, peering out into the darkness, and suddenly remarked: "Bauman, that bear has been walking on two legs." Bauman laughed at this, but his partner insisted that he was right, and upon again examining the tracks with a torch, they certainly did seem to be made by but two paws, or feet. However, it was too dark to make sure. After discussing whether the footprints could possibly be those of a human being, and coming to the conclusion that they could not be, the two men rolled up in their blankets, and went to sleep under the lean-to.

At midnight Bauman was awakened by some noise, and sat up in his blankets. As he did so his nostrils were struck by a strong, wild-beast odor, and he caught the loom of a great body in the darkness at the mouth of the lean-to. Grasping his rifle, he fired at the vague, threatening shadow, but must have missed, for immediately afterwards he heard the smashing of the underwood as the thing, whatever it was, rushed off into the impenetrable blackness of the forest and the night.

After this the two men slept but little, sitting up by the rekindled fire, but they heard nothing more. In the morning they started out to look at the few traps they had set the previous evening and to put out new ones. By an unspoken agreement they kept together all day, and returned to camp towards evening.

On nearing it they saw, hardly to their astonishment, that the lean-to had been again torn down. The visitor of the preceding day had returned, and in wanton malice had tossed about their camp kit and bedding, and destroyed the shanty. The ground was marked up by its tracks, and on leaving the camp it had gone along the soft earth by the brook, where the footprints were as plain as if on snow, and, after a careful scrutiny of the trail, it certainly did seem as if, whatever the thing was, it had walked off on but two legs.

The men, thoroughly uneasy, gathered a great heap of dead logs, and kept up a roaring fire throughout the night, one or the other sitting on guard most of the time. About midnight the thing came down through the forest opposite, across the brook, and stayed there on the hill-side for nearly an hour. They could hear the branches crackle as it moved about, and several times it uttered a harsh, grating, long-drawn moan, a peculiarly sinister sound. Yet it did not venture near the fire.

In the morning the two trappers, after discussing the strange events of the last thirty-six hours, decided that they would shoulde1 their packs and leave the valley that afternoon. They were the more ready to do this because in spite of seeing a good deal of game sign they had caught very little fur. However, it was necessary first to go along the line of their traps and gather them, and this they started out to do.

All the morning they kept together, picking up trap after trap, each one empty. On first leaving camp they had the disagreeable sensation of being followed. In the dense spruce thickets they occasionally heard a branch snap after they had passed; and now and then there were slight rustling noises among the small pines to one side of them.

At noon they were back within a couple of miles of camp. In the high, bright sunlight their fears seemed absurd to the two armed men, accustomed as they were, through long years of lonely wandering in the wilderness to face every kind of danger from man, brute, or element. There were still three beaver traps to collect from a little pond in a wide ravine nearby. Bauman volunteered to gather these and bring them in, while his companion went ahead to camp and made ready the packs.

On reaching the pond Bauman found three beaver in the traps, one of which had been pulled loose and carried into a beaver house. He took several hours in securing and preparing the beaver, and when he started homewards he marked with some uneasiness how low the sun was getting. As he hurried towards camp, under the tall trees, the silence and desolation of the forest weighed on him. His feet made no sound on the pine needles, and the slanting sun rays, striking through among the straight trunks, made a gray twilight in which objects at a distance glimmered indistinctly. There was nothing to break the ghostly stillness which, when there is no breeze, always broods over these sombre primeval forests.

At last he came to the edge of the little glade where the camp lay, and shouted as he approached it, but got no answer. The camp fire had gone out, though the thin blue smoke was still curling upwards. Near it lay the packs, wrapped and arranged. At first Bauman could see nobody; nor did he receive an answer to his call. Stepping forward he again shouted, and as he did so his eye fell on the body of his friend, stretched beside the trunk of a great fallen spruce. Rushing towards it the horrified trapper found that the body was still warm, but that the neck was broken, while there were four great fang marks in the throat.

The footprints of the unknown beast-creature, printed deep in the soft soil, told the whole story.

The unfortunate man, having finished his packing, had sat down on the spruce log with his face to the fire, and his back to the dense woods, to wait for his companion. While thus waiting, his monstrous assailant, which must have been lurking nearby in the woods, waiting for a chance to catch one of the adventurers unprepared, came silently up from behind, walking with long, noiseless steps, and seemingly still on two legs. Evidently unheard, it reached the man, and broke his neck by wrenching his head back with its forepaws, while it buried its teeth in his throat. It had not eaten the body, but apparently had romped and gambolled round it in uncouth, ferocious glee, occasionally rolling over and over it; and had then fled back into the soundless depths of the woods.

Bauman, utterly unnerved, and believing that the creature with which he had to deal was something either half human or half devil, some great goblin-beast, abandoned everything but his rifle and struck off at speed down the pass, not halting until he reached the beaver meadows where the hobbled ponies were still grazing. Mounting, he rode onwards through the night, until far beyond the reach of pursuit.

HUNTING LORE. IT has been my good-luck to kill every kind of game properly belonging to the United States: though one beast which I never had a chance to slay, the jaguar, from the torrid South, sometimes comes just across the Rio Grande; nor have I ever hunted the musk-ox and polar bear in the boreal wastes where they dwell, surrounded by the frozen desolation of the uttermost North.

I have never sought to make large bags, for a hunter should not be a game butcher. It is always lawful to kill dangerous or noxious animals, like the bear, cougar, and wolf; but other game should only be shot when there is need of the meat, or for the sake of an unusually fine trophy. Killing a reasonable number of bulls, bucks, or rams does no harm whatever to the species; to slay half the males of any kind of game would not stop the natural increase, and they yield the best sport, and are the legitimate objects of the chase. Cows, does, and ewes, on the contrary, should only be killed (unless barren) in case

of necessity; during my last five years' hunting I have killed but five—one by a mischance, and the other four for the table.

From its very nature, the life of the hunter is in most places evanescent; and when it has vanished there can be no real substitute in old settled countries. Shooting in a private game preserve is but a dismal parody; the manliest and healthiest features of the sport are lost with the change of conditions. We need, in the interest of the community at large, a rigid system of game laws rigidly enforced, and it is not only admissible, but one may almost say necessary, to establish, under the control of the State, great national forest reserves, which shall also be breeding grounds and nurseries for wild game; but I should much regret to see grow up in this country a system of large private game preserves, kept for the enjoyment of the very rich. One of the chief attractions of the life of the wilderness is its rugged and stalwart democracy; there every man stands for what he actually is, and can show himself to be.

There are, in different parts of our country, chances to try so many various kinds of hunting, with rifle or with horse and hound, that it is nearly impossible for one man to have experience of them all. There are many hunts I long hoped to take, but never did and never shall; they must be left for men with more time, or for those whose homes are nearer to the hunting grounds. I have never seen a grisly roped by the riders of the plains, nor a black bear killed with the knife and hounds in the southern canebrakes; though at one time I had for many years a standing invitation to witness this last feat on a plantation in Arkansas. The friend who gave it, an old backwoods planter, at one time lost almost all his hogs by the numerous bears who infested his neighborhood. He took a grimly humorous revenge each fall by doing his winter killing among the bears instead of among the hogs they had slain; for as the cold weather approached he regularly proceeded to lay in a stock of bear-bacon, scouring the canebrakes in a series of

systematic hunts, bringing the quarry to bay with the help of a big pack of hard-fighting mongrels, and then killing it with his long, broad-bladed bowie.

Again, I should like to make a trial at killing peccaries with the spear, whether on foot or on horseback, and with or without dogs. I should like much to repeat the experience of a friend who cruised northward through Bering Sea, shooting walrus and polar bear; and that of two other friends who travelled with dog-sleds to the Barren Grounds, in chase of the caribou, and of that last survivor of the Ice Age, the strange musk-ox. Once in a while it must be good sport to shoot alligators by torchlight in the everglades of Florida or the bayous of Louisiana.

If the big-game hunter, the lover of the rifle, has a taste for kindred field sports with rod and shotgun, many are his chances for pleasure, though perhaps of a less intense kind. The wild turkey really deserves a place beside the deer; to kill a wary old gobbler with the small-bore rifle, by fair still-hunting, is a triumph for the best sportsman. Swans, geese, and sandhill cranes likewise may sometimes be killed with the rifle; but more often all three, save perhaps the swan, must be shot over decoys. Then there is prairie-chicken shooting on the fertile grain prairies of the middle West, from Minnesota to Texas; and killing canvas-backs from behind blinds, with the help of that fearless swimmer, the Chesapeake Bay dog. in Californian mountains and valleys live the beautiful plumed quails, and who does not know their cousin bob-white, the bird of the farm, with his cheery voice and friendly ways? For pure fun, nothing can surpass a night scramble through the woods after coon and possum.

The salmon, whether near Puget Sound or the St. Lawrence, is the royal fish; his only rival is the giant of the warm Gulf waters, the silver-mailed tarpon; while along the Atlantic coast the great striped bass likewise yields fine sport to the men of rod and reel. Every hunter of the mountains and the northern woods knows the many kinds of spotted trout; for the black bass he cares less; and least of all for the sluggish pickerel, and his big brother of the Great Lakes, the muscallonge.

Yet the sport yielded by rod and smooth-bore is really less closely kin to the strong pleasures so beloved by the hunter who trusts in horse and rifle than are certain other outdoor pastimes, of the rougher and hardier kind. Such a pastime is snow-shoeing, whether with webbed rackets, in the vast northern forests, or with skees, on the bare slopes of the Rockies. Such is mountaineering, especially when joined with bold exploration of the unknown. Most of our mountains are of rounded shape, and though climbing them is often hard work, it is rarely difficult or dangerous, save in bad weather, or after a snowfall. But there are many of which this is not true; the Tetons, for instance, and various glacier-bearing peaks in the Northwest; while the lofty, snow-clad ranges of British Columbia and Alaska offer one of the finest fields in the world for the daring cragsman. Mountaineering is among the manliest of sports; and it is to be hoped that some of our young men with a taste for hard work and adventure among the high hills will attempt the conquest of these great untrodden mountains of their own continent. As with all pioneer work, there would be far more discomfort and danger, far more need to display resolution, hardihood, and wisdom in such an attempt than in any expedition on well known and historic ground like the Swiss Alps; but the victory would be a hundred-fold better worth winning.

The dweller or sojourner in the wilderness who most keenly loves and appreciates his wild surroundings, and all their sights and sounds, is the man who also loves and appreciates the books which tell of them.

Foremost of all American writers on outdoor life is John Burroughs; and I can scarcely suppose that any man who cares for existence outside the cities would willingly be without anything that he has ever written. To the naturalist, to the observer and lover of nature, he is of course worth many times

more than any closet systematist; and though he has not been very much in really wild regions, his pages so thrill with the sights and sounds of outdoor life that nothing by any writer who is a mere professional scientist or a mere professional hunter can take their place, or do more than supplement them—for scientist and hunter alike would do well to remember that before a book can take the highest rank in any particular line it must also rank high in literature proper. Of course, for us Americans, Burroughs has a peculiar charm that he cannot have for others, no matter how much they, too, may like him; for what he writes of is our own, and he calls to our minds memories and associations that are very dear. His books make us homesick when we read them in foreign lands; for they spring from our soil as truly as *Snowbound* or *The Biglow Papers?*

As a woodland writer, Thoreau comes second only to Burroughs.

For natural history in the narrower sense there are still no better books than Audubon and Bachman's Mammals and Audubon's Birds. There are also good works by men like Coues and Bendire; and if Hart Merriam, of the Smithsonian, will only do for the mammals of the United States what he has already done for those of the Adirondacks, we shall have the best book of its kind in existence. Nor, among less technical writings, should one overlook such essays as those of Maurice Thompson and Olive Thorne Miller.

There have been many American hunting-books; but too often they have been very worthless, even when the writers possessed the necessary firsthand knowledge, and the rare capacity of seeing the truth. Few of the old

'I am under many obligations to the writings of Mr. Burroughs (though there are one or two of his theories from which I should dissent); and there is a piece of indebtedness in this very volume of which I have only just become aware. In my chapter on the prong-buck there is a paragraph which will at once suggest to any lover of Burroughs some sentences in his essay on " Birds and Poets." I did not notice the resemblance

until happening to reread the essay after my own chapter was written, and at the time I had no idea that I was borrowing from anybody, the more so as I was thinking purely of western wilderness life and western wilderness game, with which I knew Mr. Burroughs had never been familiar. I have concluded to leave the paragraph in with this acknowledgment.

time hunters ever tried to write of what they had seen and done; and of those who made the effort fewer still succeeded. Innate refinement and the literary faculty— that is, the faculty of writing a thoroughly interesting and readable book, full of valuable information— may exist in uneducated people; but if they do not, no amount of experience in the field can supply their lack. However, we have had some good works on the chase and habits of big game, such as Caton's *Deer and Antelope of America*, Van Dyke's *Still-Hunter*, Elliott's *Carolina Sports*, and Dodge's *Hunting Grounds of the Gnat West*, besides the Century Company's *Sport with Rod and Gun*. Then there is Catlin's book, and the journals of the explorers from Lewis and Clarke down; and occasional volumes on outdoor life, such as Theodore Winthrop's *Canoe and Saddle*, and Clarence King's *Mountaineering in the Sierra Nevada*.

Two or three of the great writers of American literature, notably Parkman in his *Oregon Trail* and, with less interest, Irving in his *Trip on the Prairies* have written with power and charm of life in the American wilderness; but no one has arisen to do for the far western plainsmen and Rocky Mountain trappers quite what Hermann Melville did for the South Sea whaling folk in *Omoo* and *Moby Dick*. The best description of these old-time dwellers among the mountains and on the plains is to be found in a couple of good volumes by the Englishman Ruxton. However, the backwoodsmen proper, both in their forest homes and when they first began to venture out on the prairie, have been portrayed by a master hand. In a succession of wonderfully drawn characters, ranging from "Aaron Thousandacres" to

"Ishmael Bush," Fenimore Cooper has preserved for always the likenesses of these stark pioneer settlers and backwoods hunters; uncouth, narrow, hard, suspicious, but with all the virile virtues of a young and masterful race, a race of mighty breeders, mighty fighters, mighty commonwealth builders. As for Leatherstocking, he is one of the undying men of story; grand, simple, kindly, pure-minded, staunchly loyal, the type of the steel-thewed and ironwilled hunter-warrior.

Turning from the men of fiction to the men of real life, it is worth noting how many of the leaders among our statesmen and soldiers have sought strength and pleasure in the chase, or in kindred vigorous pastimes. Of course field sports, or at least the wilder kinds, which entail the exercise of daring, and the endurance of toil and hardship, and which lead men afar into the forests and mountains, stand above athletic exercises; exactly as among the latter, rugged outdoor games, like football and lacrosse, are much superior to mere gymnastics and calisthenics.

With a few exceptions the men among us who have stood foremost in political leadership, like their fellows who have led our armies, have been of stalwart frame and sound bodily health. When they sprang from the frontier folk, as did Lincoln and Andrew Jackson, they usually hunted much in their youth, if only as an incident in the prolonged warfare waged by themselves and their kinsmen against the wild forces of nature. Old Israel Putnam's famous wolf-killing feat comes strictly under this head. Doubtless he greatly enjoyed the excitement of the adventure; but he went into it as a matter of business, not of sport. The wolf, the last of its kind in his neighborhood, had taken heavy toll of the flocks of himself and his friends; when they found the deep cave in which it had made its den it readily beat off the dogs sent in to assail it; and so Putnam crept in himself, with his torch and his flint-lock musket, and shot the beast where it lay.

When such men lived in long settled and thickly peopled regions, they needs

had to accommodate themselves to the conditions and put up with humbler forms of sport. Webster, like his great rival for Whig leadership, Henry Clay, cared much for horses, dogs, and guns; but though an outdoor man he had no chance to develop a love for biggame hunting. He was, however, very fond of the rod and shotgun. Mr. Cabot Lodge recently handed me a letter written to his grandfather by Webster, and describing a day's trout fishing. It may be worth giving for the sake of the writer, and because of the fine heartiness and zest in enjoyment which it shows:

Sandw1ch, June 4,

Saturday mor'g

6 o'clock

Dear S1r:

I send you eight or nine trout, which I took yesterday, in that chief of all brooks, Mashpee. I made a long day of it, and with good success, for me. John was with me, full of good advice, but did not fish—nor carry a rod.

I took 26 trouts, all weighing... 17lb. 12 oz.

The largest (you have him) weighed at Crokers 2" 4"

The s largest 3" 5"

The eight largest r 1" 8"

I got these by following your advice; that is, *by careful & thorough* fishing of the difficult places, which others do not fish. The brook is fished, nearly every day. I entered it, not so high up as we sometimes do, between 7 & 8 o'clock, & at 12 was hardly more than half "way down to the meeting house path. You see I did not hurry. The day did not hold out to fish the whole brook properly. The largest trout I took at 3 P.m. (you see I am precise) below the meeting house, under a bush on the right bank, two or three rods below the large *beeches*. It is singular, that in the whole day, I did not take two trouts out of the same hole. I found both ends, or parts of the Brook about equally productive. Small fish not plenty, in either. So many hooks get everything which is not hid away in the manner large trouts take care of themselves. I hooked one, which I suppose to be larger than any which I took, as he broke my line, by

fair pulling, after I had pulled him out of his den, & was playing him in fair open water.

Of what I send you, I pray you keep what you wish yourself, send three to Mr. Ticknor, & three to Dr. Warren; or two of the larger ones, to each will perhaps be enough—& if there be any left, there is Mr. Callender & Mr. Blake, & Mr. Davis, either of them not "averse to fish." Pray let Mr. Davis *see* them—especially the large one.—As he promised to come, & fell back, I desire to excite his regrets. I hope you will have the large one on your own table.

The day was fine—not another hook in the Brook. John steady as a judge—and every thing else exactly right. I never, on the whole, had so agreeable a day's fishing tho the result, in pounds or numbers, is not great;—nor ever expect such another.

Please preserve this letter; but rehearse not these particulars to the uninitiated.

I think the Limerick *not* the best hook. Whether it pricks too soon, or for what other reason, I found, or thought I found, the fish more likely to let go his hold, from this, than from the old fashioned hook.

Yrs.

H. Cabot, Esq. D. Webster.

The greatest of Americans, Washington, was very fond of hunting, both with rifle or fowling-piece, and especially with horse, horn, and hound. Essentially the representative of all that is best in our national life, standing high as a general, high as a statesman, and highest of all as a man, he could never have been what he was had he not taken delight in feats of hardihood, of daring, and of bodily prowess. He was strongly drawn to those field sports which demand in their follower the exercise of the manly virtues—courage, endurance, physical address. As a young man, clad in the distinctive garb of the backwoodsman, the fringed and tasselled hunting-shirt, he led the life of a frontier surveyor; and like his fellow adventurers in wilderness exploration and Indian campaigning, he was often forced to trust to the long rifle for keeping his party in food. When at his home, at Mount Vernon, he hunted from simple delight in the sport.

His manuscript diaries, preserved in the State Department at Washington, are full of entries concerning his feats in the chase; almost all of them naturally falling in the years between the ending of the French war and the opening of the Revolutionary struggle against the British, or else in the period separating his service as Commander-in-chief of the Continental armies from his term of office as President of the Republic. These entries are scattered through others dealing with his daily duties in overseeing his farm and mill, his attendance at the Virginia House of Burgesses, his journeys, the drill of the local militia, and all the various interests of his many-sided life. Fond though he was of hunting, he was wholly incapable of the career of inanity led by those who make sport, not a manly pastime, but the one serious business of their lives

The entries in the diaries are short, and are couched in the homely vigorous English, so familiar to the readers of Washington's journals and private letters. Sometimes they are brief jottings in reference to shooting trips; such as: "Rid out with my gun "; "went pheasant hunting"; "went ducking," and "went a gunning up the Creek." But far more often they are: " Rid out with my hounds," "went a fox hunting," or "went a hunting." In their perfect simplicity and good faith they are strongly characteristic of the man. He enters his blank days and failures as conscientiously as his red-letter days of success; recording with equal care on one day, "Fox hunting with Captain Posey—catch a Fox," and another, "Went a hunting with Lord Fairfax... catched nothing."

Occasionally he began as early as August and continued until April; and while he sometimes made but eight or ten hunts in a season, at others he made as many in a month. Often he hunted from Mt. Vernon, going out once or twice a week, either alone or with a party of his friends and neighbors; and again he would meet with these same neighbors at one of their houses, and de-

vote several days solely to the chase. The country was still very wild, and now and then game was encountered with which the fox-hounds proved unable to cope; as witness entries like: "found both a Bear and a Fox, but got neither"; "went a hunting... started a Deer & then a Fox but got neither"; and "Went a hunting and after trailing a fox a good while the Dogs Raized a Deer & ran out of the Neck with it & did not some of them at least come home till the next day." If it was a small animal, however, it was soon accounted for. "Went a Hunting... catched a Rakoon but never found a Fox."

The woods were so dense and continuous that it was often impossible for the riders to keep close to the hounds throughout the run; though in one or two of the best covers, as the journal records, Washington "directed paths to be cut for Fox Hunting." This thickness of the timber made it difficult to keep the hounds always under control; and there are frequent allusions to their going off on their own account, as "Joined some dogs that were self hunting." Sometimes the hounds got so far away that it was impossible to tell whether they had killed or not, the journal remarking " catched nothing that we know of," or "found a fox at the head of the blind Pocoson which we suppose was killed in an hour but could not find it."

Another result of this density and continuity of cover was the frequent recurrence of days of ill success. There are many such entries as: " Went Fox hunting, but started nothing"; "Went a hunting, but catched nothing''; "found nothing"; "found a Fox and lost it." Often failure followed long and hard runs: "Started a Fox, run him four hours, took the Hounds off at night"; "found a Fox and run it 6 hours and then lost"; "Went a hunting above Darrells. .. found a fox by two Dogs but lost it upon joining the Pack." In the season of 1772-73 Washington hunted eighteen days and killed nine foxes; and though there were seasons when he was out much more often, this proportion of kills to runs was if anything above the

average. At the beginning of 1768 he met with a series of blank days which might well have daunted a less patient and persevering hunter. In January and the early part of February he was out nine times without getting a thing; but his diary does not contain a word of disappointment or surprise, each successive piece of ill-luck being entered without comment, even when one day he met some more fortunate friends "who had just catched 2 foxes." At last, on February 12th, he himself "catched two foxes "; the six or eight gentlemen of the neighborhood who made up the field all went home with him to Mt. Vernon, to dine and pass the night, and in the hunt of the following day they repeated the feat of a double score. In the next seven days' hunting he killed four times.

The runs of course varied greatly in length; on one day he "found a bitch fox at Piney Branch and killed it in an hour"; on another he "killed a Dog fox after having him on foot three hours & hard running an hour and a qr."; and on yet another he "catched a fox with a bobd Tail & cut ears after 7 hours chase in which most of the Dogs were worsted." Sometimes he caught his fox in thirty-five minutes, and again he might run it nearly the whole day in vain; the average run seems to have been from an hour and a half to three hours. Sometimes the entry records merely the barren fact of the run; at others a few particulars are given, with homespun, telling directness, as: "Went a hunting with Jacky Custis and catched a Bitch Fox after three hours chace— founded it on ye. ck. by I. Soals "; or " went a Fox hunting with Lund Washington—took the drag of a fox by Isaac Gates & carrd. it tolerably well to the old Glebe then touched now and then upon a cold scent till we came into Col. Fairfaxes Neck where we found about half after three upon the Hills just above Accotinck Creek—after running till quite Dark took off the Dogs and came home."

The foxes were doubtless mostly of the gray kind, and besides going to holes they treed readily. In January, 1770, he was out seven days, killing four foxes; and two of the entries in the journal relate to foxes which treed; one, on the 10th, being, " I went a hunting in the Neck and visited the plantn. there found and killed a bitch fox after treeing it 3 t. chasg. it abt. 3 hrs.," and the other, on the 23d: "Went a hunting after breakfast & found a Fox at muddy hole & killed her (it being a bitch) after a chase of better than two hours and after treeing her twice the last of which times she fell dead out of the Tree after being therein sevl. minutes apparently." In April, 1769, he hunted four days, and on every occasion the fox treed. April 7th, "Dog fox killed, ran an hour & treed twice." April 11th, " Went a fox hunting and took a fox alive after running him to a Tree—brot him home." April 12th, "Chased the above fox an hour & 45 minutes when he treed again after which we lost him." April 13th, "Killed a dog fox after treeing him in 35 minutes."

Washington continued his fox-hunting until, in the spring of 1775, the guns of the minute-men in Massachusetts called him to the command of the Revolutionary soldiery. When the eight weary years of campaigning were over, he said good-by to the war-worn veterans whom he had led through defeat and disaster to ultimate triumph, and became once more a Virginia country gentleman. Then he took up his fox-hunting with as much zest as ever. The entries in his journal are now rather longer, and go more into detail than formerly. Thus, on December 12th, 1785, he writes that after an early breakfast he went on a hunt and found a fox at half after ten, " being first plagued with the dogs running hogs," followed on his drag for some time, then ran him hard for an hour, when there came a fault; but when four dogs which had been thrown out rejoined the pack they put the fox up afresh, and after fifty minutes' run killed him in an open field, " every Rider & every Dog being present at the Death." With his usual alternations between days like this, and days of illluck, he hunted steadily every season until his term of private life again drew to a close and he was called to the headship of

the nation he had so largely helped to found.

In a certain kind of fox-hunting lore there is much reference to a Warwickshire squire who, when the Parliamentary and Royalist armies were forming for the battle at Edgehill, was discovered between the hostile lines, unmovedly drawing the covers for a fox. Now, this placid sportsman should by rights have been slain offhand by the first trooper who reached him, whether Cavalier or Roundhead. He had mistaken means for ends, he had confounded the healthful play which should fit a man for needful work with the work itself; and mistakes of this kind are sometimes criminal. Hardy sports of the field offer the best possible training for war; but they become contemptible when indulged in while the nation is at deathgrips with her enemies.

It was not in Washington's strong nature to make such an error. Nor yet, on the other hand, was he likely to undervalue either the pleasure, or the real worth of outdoor sports. The qualities of heart, mind, and body, which made him delight in the hunting-field, and which he there exercised and developed, stood him in good stead in many a long campaign and on many a stricken field; they helped to build that stern capacity for leadership in war which he showed alike through the bitter woe of the winter at Valley Forge, on the night when he ferried his men across the half-frozen Delaware to the overthrow of the German mercenaries at Trenton, and in the brilliant feat of arms whereof the outcome was the decisive victory of Yorktown.

IN this volume I have avoided repeating what was contained in either of my former books, the *Hunting Trips of a Ranchman* and *Ranch Life and the Hunting Trail*. For many details of life and work in the cattle country I must refer the reader to these two volumes; and also for more full accounts of the habits and methods of hunting such game as deer and antelope. As far as I know, the description in my *Ranch Life* of the habits and the chase of the mountain sheep is the only moderately complete

account thereof that has ever been published. The five game-heads figured in this volume are copied exactly from the originals, now in my home; the animals were, of course, shot by myself.

There have been many changes, both in my old huntinggrounds and my old hunting-friends, since I first followed the chase in the far western country. Where the buffalo and the Indian ranged, along the Little Missouri, the branded herds of the ranchmen now graze; the scene of my elk-hunt at Two Ocean Pass is now part of the National Forest Reserve; settlers and miners have invaded the ground where I killed bear and moose; and steamers ply on the lonely waters of Kootenai Lake. Of my hunting companions some are alive; others—among them my staunch and valued friend, Will Dow, and crabbed, surly old Hank Griffen—are dead; while yet others have drifted away, and I know not what has become of them.

I have made no effort to indicate the best kind of camp kit for hunting, for the excellent reason that it depends so much upon the kind of trip taken, and upon the circumstances of the person taking it. The hunting trip may be made with a packtrain, or with a wagon, or with a canoe, or on foot; and the hunter may have half a dozen attendants, or he may go absolutely alone. I have myself made trips under all of these circumstances. At times I have gone with two or three men, several tents, and an elaborate apparatus for cooking, cases of canned goods, and the like. On the other hand, I have made trips on horseback, with nothing whatsoever beyond what I had on, save my oil-skin slicker, a metal cup, and some hardtack, tea, and salt in the saddle pockets; and I have gone for a week or two's journey on foot, carrying on my shoulders my blanket, a fryingpan, some salt, a little flour, a small chunk of bacon, and a hatchet. So it is with dress. The clothes should be stout, of a neutral tint; the hat should be soft, without too large a brim; the shoes heavy, and the soles studded with small nails, save when moccasins or rubber-soled shoes are worn; but within these limits there is room for plenty of variation. Avoid, however, the socalled deer-stalker's cap, which is an abomination; its peaked brim giving no protection whatsoever to the eyes when facing the sun quartering, a position in which many shots must be taken. In very cold regions, fur coats, caps, and mittens, and all-wool underclothing are necessary. I dislike rubber boots when they can possibly be avoided. In hunting in snow in the winter I use the so-called German socks and felt overshoes where possible. One winter I had an ermine cap made. It was very good for peeping over the snowy ridge crests when game was on the other side; but, except when the entire landscape was snow-covered, it was an unmitigated nuisance. In winter, webbed snow-shoes are used in the thick woods, and skees in the open country.

There is an endless variety of opinion about rifles, and all that can be said with certainty is that any good modern rifle will do. It is the man behind the rifle that counts, after the weapon has reached a certain stage of perfection. One of my friends invariably uses an old Government Springfield, a 45-calibre, with an ounce bullet. Another cares for nothing but the 40-90 Sharps', a weapon for which I myself have much partiality. Another uses always the old 45-calibre Sharps', and yet another the 45calibre Remington. Two of the best bear and eik hunters I know prefer the 32-and 38-calibre Marlin's, with long cartridges, weapons with which I myself would not undertake to produce any good results. Yet others prefer pieces of very large calibre. The amount of it is that each one of these guns possesses some excellence which the others lack, but which is in most cases atoned for by some corresponding defect. Simplicity of mechanism is very important, but so is rapidity of fire; and it is hard to get both of them developed to the highest degree in the same piece. In the same way, flatness of trajectory, penetration, range, shock, and accuracy are all qualities which must be attained; but to get one in perfection usually means the sacrifice of some of the rest. For instance, other things being equal, the smallest calibre has the greatest penetration, but gives the least shock; while a very flat trajectory, if acquired by heavy charges of powder, means the sacrifice of accuracy. Similarly, solid and hollow pointed bullets have, respectively, their merits and demerits. There is no use of dogmatizing about weapons. Some which prove excellent for particular countries and kinds of hunting are useless in others.

There seems to be no doubt, judging from the testimony of sportsmen in South Africa and in India, that very heavy calibre double-barrelled rifles are best for use in the dense jungles and against the thick-hided game of those regions; but they are of very little value with us. In 1882 one of the buffalo hunters on the Little Missouri obtained from some Englishman a doublebarrelled ten-bore rifle of the kind used against rhinoceros, buffalo, and elephant in the Old World; but it proved very inferior to the 40-and 45-calibre Sharps' buffalo guns when used under the conditions of American buffalo hunting, the tremendous shock given by the bullet not compensating for the gun's great relative deficiency in range and accuracy, while even the penetration was inferior at ordinary distances. It is largely also a matter of individual taste. At one time I possessed a very expensive doublebarrelled 500 Express, by one of the crack English makers; but I never liked the gun, and could not do as well with it as with my repeater, which cost barely a sixth as much. So one day I handed it to a Scotch friend, who was manifestly ill at ease with a Winchester exactly like my own. He took to the double-barrel as naturally as I did to the repeater, and did excellent work with it. Personally, I have always preferred the Winchester. I now use a 45-90, with my old buffalo gun, a 40-90 Sharps', as spare rifle. Both, of course, have specially tested barrels, and are stocked and sighted to suit myself.

Accidents to the ranch wagon, 46; to cowboys, 427

Americans in the wilderness, 44

American, the, wilderness, 1; hunting-books, 454

Lightning Source UK Ltd.
Milton Keynes UK
UKOW07f1940270315

248680UK00008B/206/P